THE UNIVERSITY OF MISSISSIPPI

THE UNIVERSITY OF MISSISSIPPI

A SESQUICENTENNIAL HISTORY

DAVID G. SANSING

UNIVERSITY PRESS OF MISSISSIPPI • JACKSON

http://www.upress.state.ms.us

Book and cover design by John Costa, New Orleans

Manufactured in the United States of America

02 01 00 99 4 3 2 1

The paper in this book meets the guidelines for permanence and durability of the Committee on Production Guidelines for Book Longevity of the Council on Library Resources.

Library of Congress Cataloging-in-Publication Data

Sansing, David G.
The University of Mississippi : a sesquicentennial history / David G. Sansing.
p. cm.
Includes bibliographical references and index.
ISBN 1-57806-091-5 (cloth : alk. paper). — ISBN 1-57806-107-5 (ltd. ed. : alk. paper)
1. University of Mississippi—History. I. Title.
LD3413.S26 1999
378.762'83—dc21
98-37388
CIP

British Library Cataloging-in-Publication Data available

It is a small university,
but there are those who love it.

This book is dedicated to them.

CONTENTS

PREFACE

Across the contours of time the University of Mississippi has become a special place, to some it is like a sacred space. Some have called it holy ground, others hallowed ground. During a recent Black Alumni Reunion Danny Covington called Ole Miss addictive. The student newspaper said the words Ole Miss are magic and cast a spell on those who hear them. There is a mystique about Ole Miss and the love its graduates have for it goes far beyond the filial affection alumni have for their alma mater. In a world of ravishing change, when Ole Miss alumni come back to Oxford, they do not just stroll across the campus and through the Grove, they retrace the steps of their forebears, not just over place and space, but back through time as well. For many alumni, Ole Miss is more than their alma mater, it is a link, a nexus to who they were and are, and where they came from. This sesquicentennial history is written for them, the students, faculty, friends, patrons and alumni of the university.

L. Stacy Davidson is the quintessential Ole Miss alumnus and I want to recognize Stacy and Fay Davidson, and their family, for their support of the university. A graduate of the University of Mississippi Medical Center, Dr. Davidson and his family recently endowed the L. Stacy Davidson Chair in the college of liberal arts, a one million dollar gift that will enrich the university for time to come. Stacy is like thousands of alumni who love Ole Miss for what it gave to them in their youth and who give back to it in their maturity. By acknowledging Stacy Davidson I recognize the thousands of others like him.

At the end of the long process of producing a book it is always a pleasure to thank the people who helped make it possible. Chancellor Robert Khayat commissioned this study in June 1995 as part of the university's celebration of the one hundred and fiftieth anniversary of its founding. I want to express my deep appreciation to him for underwriting the project and for his encouragement over the last three years. Chancellor Khayat took great interest in this project. He inquired of its progress, read parts of it, made suggestions, but in the end gave me complete freedom to write the history of the university. My admiration for him as chancellor and as a person was enhanced by this experience.

I also want to thank Provost Gerald Walton for his continuing support throughout the process. To Gloria Kellum, executive director of the sesquicentennial, Brian Reithel, co-chair of the sesquicentennial, and Donna Patton, coordinator of the Commitment to Excellence Campaign, I express my special thanks. Seetha Srinivasan, executive director of the University Press, worked closely with me from the beginning of this project and I express my appreciation to her, and to Carol Cox who copy edited the manuscript. I would also like to express my appreciation to Anne Stascavage, John Langston, and John Costa who guided this book through the publication process.

Many others provided information and assistance and I want to thank them. Unfortunately, there are so many that I can only list their names: Frank Anderson, Barbara Austin, Ron Bartlett, Martha Bigelow, Neal B. Biggers, Jr., Ronald F. and Bonnie Borne, Martha Bowles, Brenda Brannon, Billy Ross and Lynn Brown, Maralyn Howell Bullion, Charlie Capps, Jr., William Chadwick, Rick Cleveland, Nadine Cohodas, A. Wallace Conerly, John Crews, Julius Cruse, James Davis, Herbert E. Dewees, Jr., Read and Barbara Dunn, Jr., Mrs. H. G. Duvall, Billy Ellis, Bill and Marcia Ferris, Shirley Fisher, Mrs. Porter L. Fortune, Jr., Kees Gispen, Sandra Guest, Tina Hahn, John Hall, J. J. and Lillian Hayden, Charles and Cornelia Henry, Verner and Mary Holmes, Richard and Lisa Howorth, Burl and Clara Hunt, Masaru Inoue, professor of American literature at Ferris University, Yokohama, Japan, Winthrop Jordan, Donald E. Kessinger, Leone King, Bonnie Krause, Barbara Lago, Michael Landon, Will and Patty Lewis, Robert E. Lewis, Jr., Bonita Terry-Malone, Bill Martin, Brent McLarty, Jack and Betty Love McLarty, Stark Miller, Andrew P. Mullins, James F. Payne, Langston Rogers, Mary Sexton, Marion and Carolyn Vance Smith, John Sobotka, Linda Spargo, Jane Stanley, Richard Stanley, Carolyn Ellis Staton, Mr. and Mrs. Ralph J. Stoudt, Steve Stubbs, Nell Thomas, Gene and Peggy Threadgill, Jody Varner, Joe Walker, Thomas Wallace, Clara Wallace, Bill and Carroll Waller, Joyce Jones Watson, Brenda West, John Owen Williams, and Charles Reagan Wilson.

To John M. Meador, Jr., dean of university libraries, and his excellent staff in the John Davis Williams Memorial Library, I express my sincerest gratitude. Throughout my nearly thirty years at the University of Mississippi, the library staff has been cordial, cheerful, competent and indulgent to me and has never wearied of my requests for bits and pieces of information. Only the limitation of space prevents me from listing every one of them by name. I must single out, however, Dr. Thomas Verich and his staff in the archives and special collections. To Dr. Verich, Lisa Kay Speer, Sharron Sarthou, Naomi Leavell, and Leigh McWhite I owe much more than I can express in these few words. They were of consistent good cheer, tolerated my intrusions into their well-ordered world, and never failed to find anything I asked for. I also want to thank Elbert Hilliard, director of the Mississippi Department of Archives and History in Jackson, and his fine staff for their assistance not only on this project but for their assistance and cooperation over many years.

To Dale Abadie, dean of the college of liberal arts, and Robert Haws, chairman of the department of history, and to my colleagues in the department I express my appreciation for their support and encouragement during this undertaking. I also want to personally thank Joanna Williams McClure, Fara Shook and Betty Harness, the departmental secretaries, for their constant good cheer and for never saying they could not do something "today."

I am under special obligation to Charles E. Noyes, former associate vice chancellor for academic affairs. This learned and erudite professor of English read the entire manuscript with great care, and, plainly put, the book is better because he read it, and I sincerely thank him. Lisa Kay Speer also read the manuscript with care and skill, and her extensive knowledge of the university archives and institutional history significantly improved the manuscript. I am also indebted to Professor Emeritus Franklin E. Moak, who read a large portion of the manuscript and made available to me his unpublished history of the university. Ann J. Abadie, associate director of the Center for the Study of Southern Culture, also read the entire manuscript, made many helpful suggestions, and worked closely with me from the beginning of this project. I want to acknowledge my debt to her and thank her for her counsel. Thomas Sparky Reardon read parts of the manuscript in various editions and contributed significantly to my understanding of student life at Ole Miss. I deeply appreciate his assistance. The late Evans Harrington, Betty Harrington, Gerald Walton, Don L. Fruge, Dennis Watts, and Charles Eagles also read all or parts of the manuscript and made many useful suggestions.

I cannot in this space and with these few words fairly acknowledge my debt to Willie Morris. He and I have spent many hours talking about the university, about history, about this book, and about writing. Willie Morris is an inspiring person and has one of the best minds I have ever known. I thank him for his friendship.

Parts of this book, perhaps the best parts, were written in Natchez at Mount Repose, the ancestral home of the Bislands. While I was working on the manuscript, and when it seemed that I most needed peace and quiet, Butch and Shields Brown would invite Elizabeth and me to spend a few days at Mount Repose, to slow the pace of time, to rest in the shade of the Henry Clay oaks and swap tall tales with J. W. and Marti Seibert. Sometimes Willie Morris and Joanne Prichard would also be at Mount Repose. Now that John Leslie has retired as Mayor of Oxford, Willie and I agree that Mayor Butch Brown of Natchez is the finest mayor in small town America. On January 19, 1998, Mount Repose was draped in mourning and the Ole Miss family paused to mourn the death of Caroline Shields Brown, class of 1998, who was killed in an automobile accident.

Finally, I want thank my family Elizabeth, David Jr., Cindy, Cherish, Beth, John, Mary Love, Michael, Jeannie, Kimberly, Elizabeth Grace, and Perry for filling my house with happiness.

THE UNIVERSITY OF MISSISSIPPI

CHAPTER 1
FOUNDING THE UNIVERSITY, 1802–1844

The day that witnesses the completion of this magnificent temple of learning will be the dawning of a new day in the history of letters.
GOVERNOR ALBERT GALLATIN BROWN, 1848

He was not even old enough to vote when he built his log cabin in the land of the Longtown. Thomas Dudley Isom, perhaps the first white settler in Lafayette County and one of the founders of Oxford, was only nineteen years old when he came to work in his uncle's trading post among the Chickasaws who lived in a hundred villages scattered across northeast Mississippi called the Longtown. Isom had not come to trade with the Chickasaws, who were being removed to Oklahoma, but with the white settlers who would soon appear by the thousands to clear the land, grow cotton, build towns and cities and found a university.

When the Chickasaw nation ceded its tribal lands to the United States in 1832 and moved to Oklahoma, Mississippi entered a long period of unprecedented prosperity. At a banquet in Natchez celebrating the Chickasaw Cession, Robert J. Walker, the future secretary of the treasury under President Andrew Jackson, proclaimed, "Already the feet of thousands press upon the borders of this new purchase to pitch their tents in the wilderness. Kentucky's coming, Tennessee's coming, Alabama's coming, and they're coming to join the joyous crowds of Mississippians." Walker's words "echoed the wild enthusiasm of a citizenry" on the brink of a land boom "the likes of which the Mississippi valley had not seen since the 'Mississippi Bubble' of John Law" a hundred years earlier.

During the "flush times" of the 1830s, a small army of speculators besieged the federal land office in the town of Pontotoc, where millions of acres of public domain were sold in forty-acre plots, for fifty dollars a plot, on credit. Land prices skyrocketed from $1.25 to $40 an acre, Mississippi's population soared from 136,000 in 1830 to 400,000 in 1840, and twenty-six new counties were created in north Mississippi. In his recollection of those heady days, Joseph Baldwin wrote, an "unexampled prosperity seemed to cover the land with a golden canopy [and] where yesterday the wilderness darkened the earth with her wild forests, today the cotton plantation whitened the earth.... Money is scarce, but credit is plenty, and he who has no money can do as much as he who has."

One of the twenty-six counties created from the Indian Cessions was Lafayette, named in honor of Marquis de Lafayette who fought alongside George Washington in the American Revolution. Like Isom, Lafayette was only nineteen when he landed on America's golden shores. When the board of supervisors was considering a name for the county seat in 1836, young Thomas Isom suggested Oxford, hoping the name might give the town an edge in persuading the legislature to locate the state university there, something the lawmakers had been talking about for the last thirty years or so. One of the arguments against founding a state university was that there were already several colleges in Mississippi.

In those early days of the American republic, academicians, like entrepreneurs, were infected with the ethic of growth and greatness. The idea of one national university in the country's capital where "the youth of all the states" would be molded into a composite American was just that, an idea, doomed from the beginning. In this broad land, devotion to place and the doctrine of local control would make America a "culture with many capitals" and a country with many colleges. From the founding of Harvard in 1636 to the founding of the Republic in 1776, only nine colleges were established in America. From the end of the Revolution to the beginning of the Civil War, more than seven hundred colleges were founded, one about every forty-five days. Most of them eventually failed.

Mississippi's first venture in college building came in 1802 on the recommendation of its twenty-six-year-old governor, William Charles Cole Claiborne. Governor Claiborne was a member of Congress from Tennessee when the 1800 presidential election between Thomas Jefferson and Aaron Burr was thrown into the House of Representatives. Jefferson and Burr tied in the electoral college. After several weeks of acrimonious debate, often amidst the talk of civil war, Jefferson was elected on the thirty-fifth ballot. Two weeks later he succeeded President John Adams. The peaceful transfer of power imbued the young Claiborne with a profound belief in republican government. Shortly after taking office,

President Jefferson, who believed Claiborne's support was crucial in his election, appointed him governor of the Mississippi Territory.

When Claiborne arrived at Natchez in 1801, Mississippi was a wild frontier on the outer rim of the young republic, and he was determined to make it a safe haven for self-rule. Like Jefferson, who was one of the new nation's earliest advocates of free schools, Claiborne believed the preservation of republican government "in its genuine purity and energy depends upon the diffusion of knowledge among the body of society." To Governor Claiborne, the village green must have a schoolhouse as well as a courthouse and a church house.

On May 4, 1802, Governor Claiborne sent to Mississippi's nine-member territorial assembly a message recommending the establishment of a system of free schools and a "seminary of learning." In the nineteenth century the terms *seminary of learning, college, institute, academy,* and *university* designated institutions of higher learning. Governor Claiborne clearly intended for the school system and the collegiate institution to be supported by public funds. "I am sure," he wrote, "in point of pecuniary resources the Territory is well enabled to defray the expenses of Literary Institutions."

The assembly established a collegiate institution but rejected Governor Claiborne's recommendation for a free school system. The notion of free schools was so new in the early 1800s that few legislatures anywhere in America had shown an inclination to tax the rich to teach the poor. Besides, the national government had already established a generous policy of setting aside every sixteenth section of the public domain for free schools and providing land grants to each state for the support of seminaries of learning. The assemblymen saw no reason to burden the citizens with school taxes.

Although the assembly rejected Claiborne's request for a free school system, the lawmakers did establish a college in 1802 and named it in honor of Thomas Jefferson. Jefferson College was located in Washington, six miles east of Natchez, in the remote southwestern corner of the state. The assembly did not, however, appropriate any public funds for the support of Mississippi's first institution of higher learning. Disappointed with the assembly's refusal to allocate public funds for Jefferson College, Governor Claiborne sent a second message to the lawmakers in December 1802 asking them to place a tax on marriage licenses and endow the college with the revenue from that source. He also asked the assembly to petition the Congress for a land grant to support Jefferson College.

On March 3, 1803, Congress responded to the general assembly's request and granted Jefferson College a township of land (23,400 acres). Unfortunately, the township was in the area along the lower Tombigbee River in the uninhabited southeastern part of the territory, and the land grant brought little revenue to Jefferson College. In a futile effort to keep it afloat, the Mississippi lawmakers allocated the proceeds from all escheats to Jefferson College and lent the institution six thousand dollars in 1816 and another four thousand in 1820. Many of the state's taxpayers, including several prominent public officials, considered Jefferson College a private enterprise that was beyond the "fostering hand" of state government.

In 1825 the Jefferson College board of trustees informed the legislature that the institution could not repay its loans and did not have sufficient funds to continue operation. The board temporarily suspended the collegiate department. While lawmakers were discussing this report, Representative William Haile of Wilkinson County introduced a resolution to clarify and enhance the status of Jefferson College by designating it a state institution and appropriating public funds for its support. During the debate over Haile's resolution, several legislators expressed support for designating Jefferson College the state university, but only if it were relocated to a more "central situation." After extensive debate, the legislature chose not to relocate Jefferson College or provide any additional financial support.

Four years later, in an 1829 message to the legislature, Governor Gerard Brandon reviewed the "troubled history" of Jefferson College and again raised the issue of a state university. Governor Brandon asserted that Mississippi was not providing its young men and women with the means of instruction that he, like Claiborne, considered essential to the success of self-government. As an immediate remedy Governor Brandon suggested that Jefferson College surrender its charter to the state. The legislature could then provide financial support for "a college at a [location] more likely to meet with public patronage," but Governor Brandon did not recommend the founding of a new institution. Instead, he recommended that the legislature designate Mississippi Academy, a preparatory school at Clinton, the state university.

Mississippi Academy (established in 1826 as Hampstead Academy) was already receiving part of the proceeds from a second township of land granted to Mississippi in 1819. Governor Brandon's argument was not persuasive, and the legislature did not make Mississippi Academy the state university. The lawmakers did, however, provide a five-thousand-dollar loan to the academy. At the 1830 legislative session, several of the academy's trustees appeared before the legislature to express their appreciation for the loan and to make another appeal for the school's designation as the state university. Although their appeal, like Brandon's the year before, was unsuccessful, the legislature did elevate the academy to collegiate status and authorized its board of trustees to grant degrees; with this elevation of status, the trustees changed the academy's name to Mississippi College. After the legislature authorized Mississippi College to grant degrees, and especially after the establishment of Oakland College, public support for a state university waned, at least temporarily.

Founded in 1830 by the Mississippi Presbytery at Rodney in Jefferson County, Oakland College was a successful residential liberal arts college. Also known as the "old-time college," the liberal arts college was the predominant collegiate institution in antebellum America. There were no universities in the modern sense, and even state universities were hardly more than liberal arts colleges, though some did have medical schools and law departments. Many antebellum colleges, including some state universities, operated preparatory departments, and some of the smaller ones, out of financial necessity, maintained primary departments. The traditional liberal arts college was like "a large family, sleeping, eating, studying and worshiping together under one roof" where the development of character was more important than the development of intellect. In pre-Civil War America, most collegiate officials agreed with President Robert Finley of the University of Georgia, who said the primary purpose of a college education was "to militate the condition of man and to direct his heart to heaven."

The method of instruction in antebellum colleges, including state universities, was predicated on the theory of "faculty psychology," which held that the mind was divided into faculties such as will, emotion, imagination, memory, reason, and judgment. "Patient investigation and close observation," wrote one college president, "will prove that the attributes or faculties of the mind are as distinctly marked, as are the different parts or systems which constitute the science of anatomy." In most American colleges professors did not encourage their students to read widely or to think for themselves. They were given assignments in required textbooks and recited for their professors what they had memorized each day. A thorough grounding in the classics was the best means of managing, training, and disciplining the mind, and most collegiate officials believed "with the study of Greek and Latin languages, sound learning flourishes or declines." Consequently, antebellum students took a prescribed course of study in Latin and Greek, ancient history and literature, philosophy, logic, rhetoric, and the "evidences of Christianity." The classical curriculum and its corollary, the "genteel tradition," were based on the assumption that a classical education produced Christian gentlemen and that Greek and Latin were necessary for an understanding of that grand body of knowledge that was "the substance of western civilization."

In this tradition, Oakland College educated by the mid-1850s more than a thousand young men and graduated more than a hundred. Oakland's 250-acre campus with nineteen buildings, including a library with more than four thousand volumes, made it one of the premier liberal arts colleges in the Deep South. Much of its success rested with Oakland's longtime president, Jeremiah Chamberlain. The best testament to his leadership was that Oakland College survived his sudden and violent death during the secession controversy of 1851. President Chamberlain, a unionist, was accused of punishing a student for making a secessionist speech at the college. Chamberlain denied the charge, but one of his accusers, a student secessionist, fatally stabbed him.

Oakland, like Jefferson College, was in the extreme southwest corner of Mississippi, which made it virtually inaccessible to the burgeoning population in the northern part of the state. Oakland's impressive achievements notwithstanding, public support for a state university at a more "central situation" regained momentum. In his inaugural address on January 8, 1833, Governor Abram Scott repeated, perhaps even more eloquently, the pleadings of his predecessors and urged Mississippi's lawmakers to establish a "general system of Schools and Academies, so organized that the means of instruction may be placed within the reach of the poorest of our citizens." The "first great duty of a republic," he said, is "to provide for all its members the means of instruction."

Governor Scott's message was followed a few days later by a report from T. B. J. Hadley, the state auditor. Hadley offered the legislature a painless plan for providing the means of instruction. Hadley reported that a second township granted to Mississippi in 1819 for a seminary of learning had produced only $8,378.50 in lease income, most of which had been allocated to Mississippi College. Rather than continue leasing the land, Hadley suggested the state sell the township outright and invest the proceeds in bank stock. According to his estimate, the lands would bring about two hundred thousand dollars. Hadley then waxed eloquent about the benefits of such a windfall: "From the interest alone arising from the sale of these lands a seminary of learning might be supported, which could annually receive from the lap of penury 200 children, and as often return a like number to the bosom of society, prepared for the useful occupations of life." He continued, "Thus would a pathway be opened from the door of the humblest cottage [and] the genius of the child of misfortune would be placed in honorable competition with that of the most opulent."

In response to Governor Scott's plea and Hadley's plan, Senator Jacob B. Morgan of Hinds County introduced a bill on January 19, 1833, to establish a state university. For reasons that are not clear, he withdrew his bill on February 11. Morgan probably withdrew his bill, which would have created the state university before any funds were available, in favor of another bill authorizing the sale of the seminary lands. That statute, enacted on March 2, 1833, directed the auditor to invest the proceeds from the sale of the 1819 township in the Planters' Bank. By the end of the year, the state had sold the seminary lands at auction on three-year notes at 10 percent interest for a total of $277,332.52.

The sale of the seminary lands produced a bounty far greater than anyone expected, exceeding by almost a hundred thousand dollars Hadley's projected sale price. After receiving this encouraging report, Governor Hiram G. Runnels informed the legislature on January 21, 1835, that sufficient funds were now available "to justify the State to go into the establishment of a University." Anticipating a controversy over its geographic location, Governor Runnels recommended the "appointment of commissioners from the four extremes of the State, and one from the center, whose duty it shall be to select the spot for its location, having due regard for the healthfulness of its situation."

Governor Runnels's recommendation was rejected for several complicated reasons. His successor, Governor John Anthony Quitman, and many others among the state's power structure preferred the establishment of free common schools to the founding of a public university. Although he did not favor the "utopian idea, of conferring a complete scientific education upon every member of the community," Governor Quitman did believe that "the means of plain practical education should be extended to every free child in the country, cost what it may." Sounding a popular theme in antebellum Mississippi, Governor Quitman said the state should first establish "an effective Common School System" before it establishes a public university. Founding a public university when there were no common or preparatory schools was "vain ostentation," he said. Besides, Quitman added, there were already "several respectable colleges" in Mississippi.

Quitman's successor, Governor Charles Lynch, was as ardent in his support for a state university as Quitman was reluctant. Governor Lynch informed the legislature in January 1837 that the revenue from the sale of the 1819 township, known as the seminary fund, was approximately $310,000. At 10 per cent interest the fund would provide an annual revenue of more than $30,000. "With such ample endowment," he said, "your immediate attention should be directed to the establishment of a seminary of learning upon a large and liberal scale, in which both sexes may secure a finished education." Lynch's recommendation for a coeducational state university was a highly innovative exception to the prevailing practice of educating the sexes at separate colleges.

What a difference a year can make. In his final message to the legislature on January 4, 1838, Governor Lynch spoke of a "season of unusual pressure and prostration of commercial operations [when] so many of our fellow citizens are about to be stripped of their last pittance." The Panic of 1837 wrecked the state's economy and would eventually cause every bank in Mississippi to fail, including the Planters' Bank in which the seminary fund was invested.

The hard times caused by the Panic of 1837 prompted, as hard times always do in a democracy, recriminations between the contending political parties. The economic dislocation caused by the Panic of 1837 opened a period of bitter partisanship between the downtrodden Andrew Jackson Democrats and the wealthy Henry Clay Whigs. The parallel lines of class and party divided the common people from the aristocrats and embittered their dialogue in antebellum Mississippi. One of the differences between Democrats and Whigs was their position on free schools. With a few notable exceptions, Whigs considered education a luxury rather than a right, and believed that, like other luxuries, education should be enjoyed by those who could afford it.

In the 1837 fall election, as the economic crisis was deepening and the political rift was widening, Alexander G. McNutt, a Jacksonian Democrat, was elected governor. In spite of the economic dislocation and the severity of the times, Governor McNutt recommended in January 1838 an ambitious and expensive plan for "free schools in every township" and "universities of learning at eligible points." The *Woodville Republican,* a Whig newspaper in Wilkinson County, castigated McNutt's inaugural: "It is about such a production as might be supposed to emanate from a brain, composed of Whiskey, Irish potatoes and Bonnyclabber, put in a green gourd, stirred up and fastened to the decapitated neck of an Automaton Chess-Player." The Whigs often ridiculed the governor as "Alexander, The Great McNutt, Commander-in-Chief of the Army and Navy of Mississippi."

On the day Governor McNutt delivered his inaugural address, a number of prominent citizens from across the state met in Jackson to organize the Mississippi Association for the Promotion of Education. An outgrowth of an informal meeting of citizens in Clinton the previous July, the association praised Governor McNutt for his strong support of free schools and public universities. The association appointed a committee to study the educational systems of other states and directed the committee to recommend at its January 2, 1839, meeting a comprehensive plan of education for Mississippi that would include a system of common schools and a state university. The report would also include an estimate of the appropriations necessary to finance the entire educational package.

The *Piney Woods Planter,* published at Liberty in Amite County, carried a lengthy report on the association's activities, including the minutes and resolutions of the Jackson meeting. The editor's commentary speaks as well to our time as his own. "Reports on systems and appropriations," he wrote, "can not educate youths. If appropriations could educate us, we would all be educated. Instruct the parents first, convince them of the necessity and importance of educating their children and more is done for the cause of education in Mississippi than would be by an appropriation of half the annual revenue of the state."

Governor McNutt's inaugural message and the resolution supporting the establishment of a state university by the Mississippi Association for the Promotion of Education were two indications that public support for a state university had regained some of its earlier momentum. Additional evidence of that support surfaced in the 1838 legislative session. On January 11, Representative H. Phillips presented a petition from the citizens of Sharon, a small community in Madison County, "praying the Legislature to locate the University in that town." The citizens of Sharon would convey to the state university an endowment of twenty thousand dollars, which they had accumulated for a local college, if the legislature located the institution in their town. The twenty-page petition also informed the legislature that a female college with seventy-two students was located at Sharon and that "no ardent spirits are sold in their village."

A week after Phillips presented the Sharon petition, Representative Kemp S. Holland of Marshall County introduced a bill "to establish a state university and define the powers of the board of regents." Adams County Representative T. Armat moved to table Holland's bill. After the motion to table lost, S. M. Puckett of Rankin County moved to reject the bill. After Puckett's motion failed, the bill to establish a state university was sent to the recently established joint select committee on the seminary fund. Holland's bill never got out of this committee, and the legislature again postponed the establishment of a state university.

This latest postponement was disappointing to an increasing number of supporters of a state university, especially to citizens in the towns that had a chance of being selected as the site of the institution. On February 15, 1838, Charles A. Bradford, editor of the Pontotoc *Chickasaw Union,* informed his readers that he had received "the unpleasant intelligence that the location of this institution will probably not be made at the present session." He reassured his readers, however, that "the prospect of Pontotoc is highly flattering should the question be put to a vote." Bradford was confident that "if our claims were fully known by those who are governed by no other than the selection of a judicious and appropriate site, there would not be a dissenting vote."

When the legislature met in special session in January 1839 to address the state's economic problems, Governor McNutt sent a message to the legislature in which he sounded the first alarm that the seminary fund might be in danger. By his estimate the seminary fund amounted to $314,146.24, plus interest. Many of the promissory notes deposited in the Planters' Bank were being contested, Governor McNutt reported, and he doubted if all of them could ever be collected. McNutt also reported that the state auditor had embezzled about eight thousand dollars of the seminary fund. "Unless the university is speedily established, and the funds placed under the management of the regents of the university," he warned, "a large portion of it may be lost." There had been some support for dividing the funds among the existing colleges in the state, but Governor McNutt rejected that suggestion because the terms of the federal land grant prohibited "a division of the fund." The governor said "the best interests of the state require the immediate establishment of the seminary."

In addition to safeguarding the seminary fund, Governor McNutt offered two additional reasons for acting expeditiously. First, there was a critical need for qualified teachers in the state's schools and academies and for tutors of the children of the gentry. A state university, Governor McNutt said, could "furnish an ample supply of good teachers." More important, he argued, Mississippi had been sending "our youth" and "immense sums" out of the state for many years. McNutt estimated that Mississippians were spending one million dollars a year educating their children outside the state.

There was more to it than just money. "Patriotism, no less than economy," he said, "urges upon us the duty of educating our children at home. Those opposed to us in principle can not safely be entrusted with the education of our sons and daughters." Governor McNutt concluded his message with a plea to the lawmakers to shield the state university from "sectarian and party influence" and to locate it at a place beneficial "to every portion of the state." McNutt's counsel was given in good faith, but it would be impossible for the legislature to place the university beyond the reach of rival factions or to shield it from the sense of place in a frontier state where distance was not measured in miles but in days.

McNutt's arguments were sound but not persuasive. The legislature did not establish a state university. Instead, the lawmakers yielded to local interests and chartered six new colleges: Grenada College, Chulahoma College in Marshall County, Mississippi Female College in Columbus, North Mississippi College at College Hill in Lafayette County, Centenary College at Brandon, and Holly Springs University. The establishment of these six institutions increased the number of chartered colleges to twelve. The others were Jefferson College, Mississippi College, Oakland College, Elizabeth Female Academy at Natchez, Sharon College in Madison County, and Judson Institute at Middleton in Carroll County.

By the time the legislature chartered the university in 1844, the number of colleges in Mississippi was reduced from twelve to ten. The Methodists moved Centenary College to Louisiana, and Holly Springs University closed. At the end of its first session the trustees announced: "Holly Springs University not having succeeded last session has been disposed of to the Methodist Church. They aim to establish a medical and law department." Ironically, the institution fared no better under the Wesleyans than it had under the original proprietors but survived just long enough to eliminate Holly Springs from consideration as the site of the state university.

The legislature elected in the fall of 1839, when the Methodists took control of Holly Springs University, would select the site for the state university. In that same election Alexander McNutt, the incumbent Jacksonian Democrat, won reelection over Edward Turner, a wealthy Whig aristocrat from Natchez, by 3,000 votes out of 34,531 votes cast. The 1839 general election had been a long, bitter, and acrimonious campaign. The editor of the *Raymond Times* was glad it was finally over: "For the last five or six months we have been continually beset with the din of electioneering. We have been candidate-ridden, and palavered, and soft-soaped, and bowed at, and smiled at, and cajoled, and humbugged, to such a degree, that really, it seems as if the millennium were approaching to deliver us from at best one half of the follies to which poor humanity is subject."

After the Democratic sweep in the 1839 elections, Governor McNutt addressed a circular letter to the presidents of the state's colleges and academies. In the circular, which appeared in newspapers throughout the state in December 1839, the governor stated: "The next legislature, no doubt, will make a final disposition of our Seminary Fund, and I should be gratified to receive your views in relation to the establishment of our State Seminary, as well as the adoption of a system relative to colleges and Free Schools." The governor also requested in his letter to the presidents specific information about endowments, bylaws, library holdings, the cost of tuition, room and board, faculty salaries, and the number of graduates of their institutions. In its embryonic form, this was the first of many studies of higher education in Mississippi.

The twenty-six new counties carved out of the Choctaw and Chickasaw land cessions of 1830 and 1832 controlled the legislature that convened in January 1840. During the 1830s political power in Mississippi shifted from the aristocratic Whig counties of the Old Natchez District to the Jacksonian Democrats in the new northern counties. Democrats were more sectional than Whigs on such issues as the tariff, slavery, and states' rights. Democrats were also more sectional and solid in their support for locating the state university in the northern part of the state.

Governor McNutt did not deliver a second inaugural in January 1840, but he did send several written messages to the legislature shortly after it convened. In the first of those messages he wrote, "I again invoke your speedy action on the seminary fund. The law providing for the collection and custody of this fund is very defective and a large portion of it will certainly be lost, unless it is taken from the possession of those [Planters' Bank] who now control it." McNutt acknowledged that the "discordant views of the members of the legislature, in relation to the location of our State Seminary, has heretofore prevented" its establishment, and he reiterated his earlier admonition to locate the institution "at a healthy place, of convenient access to the people of the state, where the expenses of living would be cheap."

Governor McNutt, a writer of folk tales and a man of literary attainments, understood that a university without common schools and preparatory academies would be of doubtful benefit to Mississippi. He asked the legislature to study the chapter on education in *Pray's Code,* which the legislature commissioned but had not yet adopted. P. Rutilius R. Pray, the chairman of Mississippi's Constitutional Convention in 1832 and a judge of the High Court of Errors and Appeals, drafted the code in 1836. Chapter fourteen of *Pray's Code* provided for a state system of education that included free common schools, regional liberal arts colleges, and a state university that would be the capstone of the unified system. Under this enlightened and ambitious plan, the state university would be sustained by the seminary fund. Some of the existing private colleges would be designated public institutions and would receive state aid. The regional colleges and the common school system would be financed by an annual property tax.

Governor McNutt considered this tax absolutely essential to the establishment and continued success of the unified system. "Objections, no doubt, will be made by those who have either no children to educate, or are blessed with ample means to school them abroad," he conceded, "but when it is considered that the right of suffrage with us is extended to all, and that the perpetuity of our free institutions depend upon the knowledge of all our citizens, this objection will be found unworthy of consideration." The "legislature that establishes a system of free schools, where every child, rich or poor, can obtain knowledge at the same fountain, free of charge," McNutt predicted, "will be immortalized in the annals of the state." The legislature was not moved by McNutt's rhetoric and did not establish a common school system.

Several days after sending his message to the legislature, Governor McNutt submitted copies of the eleven reports he had received in response to his December circular. For the most part, the presidents' responses were requests for a portion, large or small, of the seminary fund. Trustees of the still struggling Jefferson College assured the governor that "a liberal sum" allocated each year from the seminary fund would "place the institution in the most prosperous circumstances." The president of the Female Collegiate Institute, a preparatory academy at Holly Springs, wrote, "Whatever disposition may be made of our seminary fund, it is not, I trust, the intention of the executive or legislature to confer its favors exclusively on our male population." That was precisely their intent, at least for the time being.

Perhaps the most interesting response to Governor McNutt's circular came from Alexander Campbell, president of Sharon College. One of the most unusual colleges in Mississippi, and perhaps in the nation, Sharon College was an interdenominational institution in the town of Sharon in Madison County. According to its bylaws, four of its five professors would be ministers chosen from the four major evangelical denominations. The fifth professor would be a layman who would not be disqualified for a "want of religious profession." Few colleges anywhere in antebellum America would have appointed an acknowledged atheist or agnostic to its faculty.

In a lengthy and thoughtful response, President Campbell recommended that the University of Mississippi not be modeled after European universities. The state university, Campbell predicted, would have to accept students at much lower levels of preparation than European institutions, because Mississippi had no common school system and few preparatory academies. President Campbell also suggested a set of priorities for the new institution. "The great mistake of American colleges," he cautioned the governor, "is too great expedition at the commencement, in erecting buildings, just as if bricks and mortar constitute a college, and thus reducing their funds as to be unable to pay professors or collect libraries." The learned president of Sharon College then made his pitch: "I would respectfully suggest, that there would be great propriety in basing the university on some college already in operation. This is the plan, as your Excellency is aware, pursued by the State of Virginia, in locating her great university."

Of the eleven collegiate officials who responded to Governor McNutt's letter, only President Jeremiah Chamberlain of Oakland College opposed the establishment of common schools and a state university. In a broadside against the few existing public schools, Chamberlain complained that they were squandering the funds they were currently receiving and saw no reason to allocate more money to a failing system. His opposition to a state university was both pragmatic and philosophical. Oakland College was the most successful old-time college in Mississippi and had the most to lose from the establishment of a public university. President Chamberlain also maintained that state universities were established for the aristocracy, who "appropriate funds of the public to the education of the rich." A state university "never has been, or ever can be, in this *free country*," he argued, "a real blessing to the community at large." President Chamberlain was an old school Presbyterian who believed that education was "the legitimate business of the church rather than the state."

Most Southern Methodists agreed, at least as far as state universities were concerned. The *Southern Christian Advocate,* the official organ of

Southern Methodists, characterized a state university as "so inadequate to the wants of the population [and] so aristocratic and exclusive, that the unlettered feel no interest in its operation or results." Southern theologians of all denominations considered the emerging state universities a "threat to traditional religious views." The evangelical clergy was wary of secular professors like George Frederick Holmes (the first president of the University of Mississippi) who held "an optimistic . . . belief in human progress [and] a liberalism in religion which bordered on . . . infidelity." State universities were public institutions that owed their allegiance to the state rather than the church. They were financed by taxes and land grants, not tithes and offerings, and their rise foretold the beginning of the end of higher education "as a sectarian responsibility."

Eventually, the objections to a state university in Mississippi and the obstructions that had delayed its founding for so long were overcome by a combination of two circumstances. First, the rapid depletion of the seminary fund following the Panic of 1837 demanded a remedy. The only way to save the fund from complete loss was to establish a public university and place the fund under the control of its board of trustees. Second, the deepening sense of urgency about educating their children at home finally convinced Mississippi's leadership to establish the University of Mississippi.

In a time of increasing sectional strife, many Mississippians traveling in the North had encounters like the one a Vicksburg gentleman experienced during a visit to Philadelphia in 1837. The *Vicksburg Sentinel & Expositor* reported that the gentleman, who was traveling to Philadelphia to enroll his daughters in school, was accosted in a railroad car by a "female abolitionist [who] presented him with one of those Tracts, with which the whole north is now literally shingled." When the gentleman "flung it out of the car," the lady abolitionist "became furious, and continued to pour out an eloquent torrent of the foul and monstrous slanders which the demons of abolition have concocted." As she lectured the Southern gentleman, other "passengers and bystanders crowded around, and the gentleman and his family were for some minutes compelled to a tirade of abuse." In disbelief, the *Sentinel* added, "Yet we have seen our planters yearly seeking an education for their children among a people . . . who encourage a system of the most flagitious falsehood—this ought not to be." The *Sentinel* concluded its report of this encounter with a pronouncement: "It is immaterial where and by whom the luxuries which surround us are produced, but it is of the deepest importance that the minds of our youth of both sexes should be trained up under our own glorious institutions."

As the sectional crisis deepened and the agitation over slavery intensified, Mississippians developed a siege mentality, formed a closed society, and concluded, "Those opposed to us in principle can not be entrusted with the education of our sons and daughters." The founders of the state university understood that education is "the process by which a culture transmits itself across the generations." They claimed a society's right, if not its obligation, to defend itself against change. They would make the University of Mississippi a bastion in the defense of the Southern Way of Life.

Chapter 2

OXFORD AND THE UNIVERSITY, 1844–1848

Oxford is one of the most pleasant towns in all that region.
Besancon's Annual Register, 1838

In early February 1840, Representative James Alexander Ventress, chairman of the house committee on the seminary fund, introduced a bill "to provide for the location of the State University." The house passed the bill on February 10 and sent it to the senate. The upper house quickly passed it and Governor Alexander G. McNutt signed the bill into law on February 20. Ventress's bill did two things. First, it provided that "all sums of money belonging, or hereafter accruing to the seminary fund, be appropriated for the use and benefit of the University of the State of Mississippi." Second, the bill authorized a joint session of the legislature to nominate seven prospective sites for the university. According to the statute, all sites nominated must be "designated by a distinctive name" rather than a geographic location, and only one site in each county would be eligible for consideration.

The house and senate convened in joint session on February 21 and nominated forty-eight prospective sites for the university. Supporters of Lexington, Natchez, Jackson, Cud-de-hunk (Lowndes County), and Mount Pleasant (Marshall County) withdrew their nominations in favor of other sites in their counties. After all nominations were made, the joint session proceeded through a series of ballots to narrow the list to seven sites. In early balloting the lawmakers eliminated Redbone, Bare-foot, Brandywine, Sweet Water, and Good Springs. The seven finalists were Louisville, Kosciusko, Mississippi City, Brandon, Oxford, Middleton (in Carroll County), and Monroe Missionary Station (in Pontotoc County). Holly Springs was eighth and thus eliminated.

After determining the seven sites, the joint session appointed three commissioners, one from each of the state's three judicial districts. William L. Sharkey was commissioner for the first district, William L.

Brandon for the second, and Thomas H. Williams for the third. After Sharkey and Brandon declined to serve, Governor McNutt appointed Joshua Russell and J. A. Van Hoesen to the commission. The three commissioners, along with the state architect, William Nichols, conducted an on-site inspection of each community and reported their findings to the legislature at its next meeting. The statute directed the commission to consider the following conditions and circumstances of each site: geographic centrality and accessibility, quality and availability of water and building materials, general health conditions in the area and the months in which local diseases were most prevalent, cost of living, and the general character of the people. Under normal circumstances the commission would have had two years to conduct its study, because the legislature met biennially. A special session was called for January 1841, however, and the commissioners filed their report then.

When the Mississippi legislature met in 1841, it was the seventh session in five years and the fourth special session. Governor McNutt convened the legislature to address the banking crisis caused by the failure of the Union Bank and the Planters' Bank. Mississippi had issued approximately seven million dollars in state bonds with which it purchased stock in the two banks. The bank stock was now worthless because both banks had failed, but Mississippi was still obligated to pay the bonds. In 1841 Mississippi had a budget deficit of over four hundred thousand dollars, and Governor McNutt saw no way of paying the installment then due on the bonds except by a general tax on the people. "Such an enormous tax," he told the lawmakers, "can never be collected from the hard earnings of the people of Mississippi. They will not elect representatives who will impose it, or tax gatherers who will collect it." Governor McNutt then made a stunning declaration. Mississippi must repudiate those bonds, many of which were held by European investors, including the Rothschilds. Both houses rejected McNutt's recommendation and by a joint resolution proclaimed that "Mississippi will pay her bonds and preserve her faith inviolate." The governor vetoed the joint resolution with a cryptic comment. The Rothschilds, he said, might hold a mortgage on "the sepulcher of our Savior," but they will never hold a "mortgage on our cotton fields and make serfs of our children."

Repudiation was an issue almost as volatile as slavery and states' rights and became the focus of the 1841 general election. Tilghman Tucker, an antibond Democrat who campaigned for governor on a pledge to repudiate the bonds, defeated David Shattuck, a Methodist minister and bond-paying Whig. Tucker's election was a public endorsement of McNutt's policy, and the state did not honor the bonds, though the issue resurfaced periodically over the next hundred and fifty years.

As the legislature was grappling with repudiation during the 1841 special session, the commission appointed to examine the prospective sites for the university made its report. The commission reported all sites favorably and each location, except Middleton, which was nominated by the former Choctaw chieftain Greenwood LeFlore, lobbied for its selection. "Middleton," the commission reported, "is a flourishing country village, with a Literary Institution, and two academies with male and female departments, containing in all about 200 pupils." Ironically, the community that called itself the "Athens of Mississippi" was originally named Oxford. Realizing that a large well-financed public university would displace their small college, the trustees and supporters of the local college lobbied against the selection of Middleton. The citizens of Middleton fulfilled the ancient prophecy, "where there is no vision, the people perish." The Mississippi Central Railroad bypassed Middleton in the 1850s. The railroad would certainly have been routed through Middleton if the state university had been located there. Time and the railroad bypassed Middleton, and the Athens of Mississippi, like so many other promising villages in the southern forest, gradually "marched back into the wilderness."

On the first ballot, the legislature eliminated Middleton, leaving Mississippi City, Oxford, Brandon, Monroe Missionary Station, Louisville, and Kosciusko. On the next three ballots, Louisville, Kosciusko, and Brandon were eliminated, leaving Mississippi City (forty-nine votes), Oxford (thirty-eight), and Monroe Station (twenty-eight). On January 21, 1841, after eliminating Monroe Station, the lawmakers selected Oxford over Mississippi City by a vote of fifty-eight to fifty-seven. Although the house and senate journals did not record the votes, the vote was clearly sectional. Oxford received all but eight of the twenty-eight votes that had gone to Monroe Mission, a northern site. If the legislature had made its selection on the basis of "geographic centrality," it would have selected Kosciusko, the geographic center of the state, and a great deal of later squabbling could have been avoided. Perhaps that is what Representative Shelman Durham had in mind when he presented a petition from Attala County citizens asking the legislature to reconsider its vote. His motion was tabled, and the selection of Oxford was final.

Oxford, which is "romantically situated" on a ridge between the "Tallahatchie and the Yockony Patawfy Rivers," was established on a parcel of land deeded to three pioneer settlers in 1836 by Hoka, a princess of the Chickasaw nation. Its elevation, slight as it was, gave Oxford an advantage over the other sites because higher elevations were freer of fevers and other contagious diseases. The site commission reported that "there is little or no sickness about Oxford," and the town was a good choice in that regard. The university suspended operation for health reasons only once, in 1853 during an outbreak of smallpox, and delayed its opening only three times, during the yellow fever epidemics in 1878, 1888, and 1897.

A town with two histories, one in fact and one in fiction, Oxford can be found on any standard map of the state of Mississippi. Oxford is also a site in the "postage stamp" world of William Faulkner. Within three years after its founding, a guidebook to Mississippi's towns and cities described Oxford as "one of the most pleasant towns in all that region." Its four hundred good citizens had constructed a twenty-three-thousand-dollar courthouse and a four-thousand-dollar jail, both of brick, had organized two churches, built two hotels and opened six mercantile establishments, one of which was Neilson's Department Store. Also located in this tiny frontier town deep in the southern forest were two seminaries of learning—a male academy and a female academy. As the founders of Faulkner's fictional Yoknapatawpha County were laying off the square of Jefferson, the county seat, one of them said, "And we're going to build a school, too, soon as we get around to it. But today we're going to build the court house." Oxford's founders, in fact and in fiction, linked statecraft with schooling and learning with liberty.

Unlike the village elders of Middleton, Oxford's founding fathers were visionaries who lobbied diligently and successfully for its selection. Their town offered another advantage in addition to its healthy elevation. Oxford was "situated on the great stage road, leading from Jackson . . . to Memphis" and linked by a stage road to Columbus, where several other major stage lines intersected. As remote as the university was, students could reach it from almost any region of the state by stagecoach. The stage from Jackson to Oxford, with nighttime layovers, took three to four days, depending on the weather conditions. Travel by stagecoach was arduous, expensive, and slow — 6½ cents per mile at 6 miles per hour — and that was in the dry season. In the rainy season, it was said, "buzzards flew at their own risk for their shadows were liable to mire in the mud of the roads." Private conveyances, such as buggies, carriages, and wagons, were more reliable and more comfortable than stagecoaches though not usually as fast. Mrs. B. L. C. Wailes, the wife of the university's assistant professor of geology, once boasted that she had traveled in her private carriage forty-nine miles in one day, between sunrise and 4:00 P.M.

Since its founding in 1837, Oxford has remained a small town with a special charm, and the town and gown relationship has been congenial, mutual and enduring. Natives and visitors alike, then and now, speak of Oxford's charm and beauty and of its graceful hospitality. The good citizens of Oxford, according to an early student publication, were "noted for their kindness and hospitality, especially to students." The student publication also noted that Oxford merchants were "generally busy counting students' money." In May 1844, three months after the University of Mississippi was chartered, the Oxford *Observer* described the village where the university would be located: "Our village at this time presents a beautiful and most lively aspect. The splendid four-horse mail coach . . . comes dashing through every day, save Monday. Our beautiful shade trees, so nicely arranged, are in full vigor. Our academies and schools are in flourishing condition and,

> Our folks when dress'd up in their best
> All go to church on Sunday;
> The boys and girls, in smiles and curls,
> All go to school on Monday."

A year after the university graduated its first class in 1851, a visitor who identified herself as "The Cumberland Girl" recorded her impression of Oxford: "This *modern Oxford* we find to be a neat cheerful, social homelike place; just as beautiful as a sonnet, as bright as Eden ever was." Her explanation for Oxford's charm was simple: "Good kind hearts and happy faces, the holiday robes of most villages . . . are worn here as an every day dress."

In the late 1850s when the university was swept up in the sectional crisis and the agitation over slavery, there was talk of moving it to Jackson where it could be under the watchful eye of the legislature. J. D. Stevenson, the radical states' rights and secessionist editor of the Oxford *Mercury,* was extremely critical of the university and endorsed the effort to move it. The Oxford *Intelligencer,* which friends of the university established in June 1860 as an alternative to the *Mercury,* condemned in unsparing language any talk of moving or closing the university. The *Intelligencer* estimated that the University of Mississippi brought at least a hundred thousand dollars in business to Oxford every year, and had transformed it from "an insignificant county seat . . . to a thriving prosperous town." More important, Oxford would reap even greater benefits in the future from the Mississippi Central Railroad, which was routed through Oxford rather than College Hill because the university was in Oxford. In a slam at the *Mercury* and a reminder to the citizens of Oxford, the *Intelligencer* wrote that whatever is good for the university is good for Oxford and enjoined its residents never to do or say anything that would "weaken its hold upon the public favor."

For Howard Falconer, the youthful editor of the *Intelligencer,* there was more to the relationship between Oxford and the university than just money. In the summer of 1860, Falconer complained about how dull Oxford was without the students: "When the University is in session the town presents an aspect of cheerfulness and activity; but now that the students have departed [the] stillness is scarcely broken." In early September, the editor could hardly contain his glee: "Persons who have only known Oxford in the vacation, would hardly recognize it as the same town, now that the University [is] in full operation. The stores are crowded, the merchants are in good humor [and] the streets . . . resound with the merry welcomings and hearty laughter of . . . students." The editor gushed, "We feel as if we were a College boy again, among old friends."

The selection of Oxford, despite its endearing qualities, did not meet with universal accord. The Mississippi press praised some lawmakers for its selection, and castigated others. The *Vicksburg Daily Whig* lauded Thomas H. Hill, "the popular and indefatigable senator from Lafayette and Panola County." To "his zeal and industry combined with his personal popularity and address," wrote the editor, "our friends in the North are indebted for the selection of Oxford as the site of the University more than any other man in the legislature." According to the Vicksburg editor, "Tom was an over match for Mr. Hanson Alsbury, the champion of the sea shore humbug." Senator Alsbury represented the district on the Gulf Coast in which Mississippi City was located. This commentary also included an observation that would loom much larger over the next few years. The editor predicted that the university would be "of immense advantage to *that section of the state,*" an implication that the central and southern parts of Mississippi would enjoy few of its benefits.

While the Vicksburg paper lauded Senator Hill, the Holly Springs press excoriated Richard Graves, a representative from Choctaw County. The Holly Springs *Conservative and Banner,* which identified Graves as an "unflinching unprincipled demagogue" and the "Loco-foco candidate for State Treasurer" in the upcoming general election, accused him of preventing the selection of Holly Springs as the site for the university. The editor reported that Graves "makes it his boast" that he singlehandedly deprived Holly Springs of that honor. The voters of Marshall County, promised the editor, "will have an eye to his aspirations in November next." Graves did not carry Marshall County but was elected state treasurer in 1841, though he did not serve out his full term as treasurer or, subsequently, his time as an inmate. Midway through his term Graves was arrested for embezzling state funds. When his wife visited him during his incarceration, they exchanged clothes, and he escaped wearing her dress. Graves may have voted against or even spoken in opposition to the selection of Holly Springs. Alexander M. Clayton, one of Marshall County's foremost citizens, however, wrote several years later that Holly Springs was not selected because there was already a university there. The editor of the *Ripley Advertiser* in Tippah County agreed with those who thought the legislature should have placed the university at a more central location, but he was confident that the University of Mississippi would flourish in the "beautiful village of Oxford" and would become as famous as its "transatlantic namesake."

With the location of the university settled, at least for the time being, the legislature demanded an accounting of the seminary fund from the state auditor. On January 25, 1841, the auditor informed the legislature that approximately $129,000 was lost when the Planters' Bank failed in 1840. An additional $168,518.92 was payable to the state, but much of that was at least six years in arrears and was probably uncollectible. Some of the debtors were insolvent and many had "gone to Texas." In a brief history of the seminary fund written several years later, Chancellor Edward Mayes concluded, "It is too plain for argument that the [seminary] lands were sold not to put the fund into a permanent and productive shape, but to foster the Planters' Bank."

In decrying the loss of the seminary fund, which he now identified as the university fund, William Delay of the Oxford *Observer* blasted "the thieving banks." He wrote,"We can not characterize this act of the [Planters'] Bank or its officers by any other name than stealing; and we sincerely believe that they would receive justice were they to obtain quarters in the penitentiary for their villainous and thieving act. . . . When will the State and country at large cease to be robbed by these 'incorporated thieves' who steal and commit all kinds of villainy under acts of legislation?" The enduring antipathy for banks virtually guaranteed the election of antibond Democrats at the state and local levels throughout the remainder of the antebellum period.

Albert Gallatin Brown, an antibond Democrat, benefitted from that sentiment during his campaign for governor in 1843, and his election marks a turning point in the educational history of Mississippi. In a well-crafted inaugural address on January 10, 1844, Governor Brown declared that it was time for Mississippi to stop "sending our youth abroad, where they sometimes contract bad habits [and] false prejudices against our home institutions and laws." The establishment of a state university would keep the young men at home and redound to the state's glory abroad. Mississippi would never "be appreciated at home nor sufficiently honored abroad," he said, until it built a great university which "her educated youth shall acknowledge as their *alma mater.*"

A month after Governor Brown's inaugural, Representative John F. Cushman of Lafayette County introduced a bill to charter the University of Mississippi. The house quickly passed the bill and sent it to the senate. Senator Alexander Pegues of Oxford, who had succeeded Thomas Hill, managed the bill in the senate where it passed with little opposition. Governor Brown signed the law chartering the university on February 24, 1844. The charter created a thirteen-member, self-perpetuating board of trustees who "constituted a body politic and corporate by the name and style of the 'University of Mississippi' [with] full power and entire control over . . . the 'Seminary Fund.' " The charter also authorized the board of trustees to "devise and adopt a system of learning" for the university and "to appoint commissioners to contract for the erection of the University buildings so soon as they may think advisable." The University of Mississippi's original board of trustees was a small assembly of remarkable men. The trustees' power to name their successors was an advantage in keeping the university above the political fray, but it was also the basis for the charge that the university was an institution created for the state's landed elite. The selection of trustees, most of whom were wealthy planters or elite members of the Mississippi bar, underscored that notion.

The first trustee listed in the university's charter was James Alexander Ventress, the favored son of a wealthy family in Wilkinson County who took full advantage of his fortunate circumstance. As a young man, he had traveled extensively in Europe, studying at Oxford University, the University of Edinburgh, the Sorbonne in Paris and the University of Berlin. During his nine years abroad (1825 to 1833), he became acquainted with some of Europe's leading intellectuals, published articles in literary and scientific journals, dabbled in fiction, and translated several French and German articles into English.

Ventress was not a member of any religious denomination and was vigilant against the intrusion of sectarianism into the university's curriculum. He was also instrumental in the appointment of George Frederick Holmes and Frederick A. P. Barnard, both of whom were scholars rather than moralists. Ventress was especially close to Barnard. He supported Barnard's emphasis on experimental sciences and was protective of the chancellor when he and the university were swept into the sectional controversy of the 1850s. Ventress's reluctant acceptance of secession was typical of the Southern planter class. His friend B. L. C. Wailes, a unionist and former assistant professor of geology at the university, wrote in July 1860, "Mr. Ventress . . . is for breaking up the union & seems to desire the election of Lincoln to bring about that result. This I fear is the temper and feeling of a great many of our Citizens who [were] formerly Staunch supporters of the Union."

According to family tradition, a raiding party of federal soldiers set fire to LaGrange, Ventress's plantation mansion, in July 1864. When

Ventress addressed the German officer in charge in his native language, the officer was so pleased that he ordered his men to extinguish the fire, sparing LaGrange. Ventress was among the few Mississippi planters who survived the ravages of war. Today, James Alexander Ventress IV lives on the land he inherited from his illustrious forebear and holds a degree from the university his great-great-grandfather was instrumental in founding. James Alexander Ventress was officially designated "Father of the University of Mississippi" by the Mississippi legislature on April 19, 1938.

John Johnston McCaughan's tenure on the board of trustees was short but tumultuous. McCaughan moved to the Mississippi Gulf Coast from his native Kentucky during the early 1830s. As one of the founders of Mississippi City, McCaughan was disappointed that it was not selected as the site for the state university. In 1846 McCaughan was in the state legislature, and a member of the board of trustees, when a bill was introduced to repeal the university's charter and establish several colleges across the state. This bill, which met intense opposition and prompted loose talk of secession by some southern counties, offered McCaughan another opportunity to locate a college at Mississippi City. During this heated controversy, as legend has it, McCaughan, a fiery, 280-pound Scotch-Irish Catholic, struck another member of the legislature with his gold-headed walking cane.

Following his failed effort to locate the university on the Gulf Coast, McCaughan devoted himself to making the University of Mississippi at Oxford a first-class institution. He was active in the early meetings of the board, proposing elaborate but well-conceived campus designs and architectural plans for the buildings. The original design of the campus, with some slight modifications, is basically the plan recommended by McCaughan and executed by William Nichols, the university architect. McCaughan was also active in shaping the academic organization of the university. Along with James Ventress and Edward C. Wilkinson, McCaughan strongly opposed a college course on Christianity and the appointment of ministers to the faculty. When he lost that battle on July 10, 1848, he dashed off a fifteen-page letter of resignation to the board. On the same day McCaughan resigned, the Reverend John Newton Waddel, a Presbyterian minister, also resigned from the board of trustees to accept the chair of ancient languages. McCaughan strenuously objected to Waddel's appointment, which was one reason McCaughan resigned. In his memoirs Waddel recalled the controversy surrounding his appointment and referred to McCaughan as "a pronounced infidel."

One of the most distinguished members of the original board of trustees was William Lewis Sharkey, described as the "ablest jurist" in antebellum Mississippi and the "most anti-secessionist man" in the state. According to one historian, Sharkey's "unionism was the polar star of his political career." Judge Sharkey was not an active board member before the Civil War, his attendance was irregular, and he did not take an active role in committee work. He was, however, a strong supporter of Chancellor Barnard and endorsed virtually all of Barnard's initiatives to enlarge the university. Sharkey's most enduring contribution to the University of Mississippi came after the Civil War. On June 13, 1865, President Andrew Johnson appointed Sharkey provisional governor of Mississippi and instructed him to begin the process of restoring Mississippi to the Union. One of Governor Sharkey's first official acts was to convene the board of trustees of the state university. Just three months after Appomattox, the board met at Oxford and announced that the university would reopen in October.

None of the original board members was more closely identified with the university's early history and development than Alexander M. Clayton, a member of the board of trustees on three separate occasions. Clayton resigned from the board in 1852 to become American consul in Havana. Following his tour in Cuba, he was reelected to the board in 1857 and served until the Reconstruction board was installed in 1870. Clayton was a states' rights, proslavery, secessionist Democrat who made a rousing speech on the floor of the Mississippi secession convention in 1861. Along with L. Q. C. Lamar, he was on the committee that drafted the Ordinance of Secession. During the Civil War, Clayton served in the Congress of the Confederate States until President Jefferson Davis appointed him to the Confederate District Court of Mississippi. After Reconstruction, Governor John Marshall reappointed Clayton to the board of trustees and he served until his death in 1889, at the age of eighty-nine. During his third tenure on the board of trustees, Clayton was influential in the adoption of coeducation at the University of Mississippi in 1882.

The most prominent member of the original board of trustees, at least nationally, was Congressman Jacob Thompson, who moved to Oxford from his native North Carolina during the "flush times" of the 1830s. An 1831 graduate of the University of North Carolina, Thompson married the daughter of a local planter, opened a law office, and soon became one of the most popular politicians in the area. In 1839 he was elected to the United States Congress and was reelected to five consecutive terms. Thompson's first tenure on the board ended with his resignation in 1857, when President James Buchanan appointed him secretary of the interior. When Mississippi seceded on January 9, 1861, Thompson resigned his cabinet post and was reelected to the board of trustees. While serving on General John C. Pemberton's staff at Vicksburg, Thompson was taken prisoner when Vicksburg surrendered but paroled on his pledge not to take up arms until he was properly exchanged. In 1863 President Jefferson Davis appointed Thompson a "confidential agent" of the Confederate government and sent him to Canada with secret orders. Thompson formed an alliance of some sort with Clement L. Vallandingham, the leader of a northern antiwar group known as "Copperheads." The two men "plotted a fantastic variety of activities" including subsidizing antiwar newspapers, counterfeiting American currency, burning northern towns, and liberating Confederate prisoners at Johnson's Island on Lake Erie and Camp Douglas near Chicago. In early 1865 Thompson fled to France with a large but undetermined amount of Confederate funds. After living "in high style in the elegant Grand Hotel in Paris" for four years, Thompson returned for a brief stay in Oxford before settling in Memphis, where he remained until his death in 1885.

James Moorman Howry was a central figure in the founding and early success of the University of Mississippi. Like several other board members, Howry came to Oxford during the "flush times." In 1841 he defeated the incumbent, F. W. Huling, for judge of the eighth judicial district. Huling contested the election and refused to vacate the office. Lawyers were in such a quandary that they refused to take cases before either judge. Eventually the state supreme court ruled in favor of Howry. Judge Howry served in the state senate from 1858 to 1861 and was also editor of the Oxford *Falcon.* Howry was an original member of the executive committee of the board of trustees, secretary of the board and, after the death of Thomas H. Williams in 1851, the board treasurer. In addition to those two positions, he also served as university proctor (bursar, registrar, and superintendent of grounds) from 1848 to 1859. Like other board members from Oxford, Howry served on most of the standing and special committees during the university's early history. When Union troops burned Oxford during the Civil War, Howry's home was badly damaged, and some of the early records of the university he kept there were lost. Howry remained on the board from 1844 until the Reconstruction board was appointed in 1870. His son, C. B. Howry, served on the university's board of trustees from 1882 to 1894.

Alexander Hamilton Pegues moved to Lafayette County in 1836 from Marlborough County, South Carolina. After an extended long-distance courtship, he married his cousin Rebecca in 1844. Pegues was a member of the legislature that chartered the University of Mississippi and his peers named him to its original board of trustees. He was one of its most active trustees, holding membership on the executive committee and on most standing and special committees. He remained on the board until 1860. After his resignation, the board of trustees elected Rebecca's younger brother, Thomas E. B. Pegues, to fill his seat. Alexander Pegues was a Methodist, but he became an Episcopalian at Rebecca's urging and was one of the founders of St. Peter's Episcopal Church in Oxford. Pegues was a personal and political ally of President Augustus B. Longstreet, the university's second president, and especially of Longstreet's son-in-law, L. Q. C. Lamar. Pegues was Lamar's mentor and patron, often lending him money and promoting his political career.

Alexander and Rebecca made their Orange Hill Plantation on Woodson's Ridge a lively gathering place for students and professors. Several sons and nephews of Alexander Pegues attended the university, and they often brought other students out to Orange Hill for weekends. Rebecca's diary mentions the frequent and sometimes lengthy visits of professors, and she often critiques their conversations. She especially enjoyed the visits of Frederick and Margaret Barnard. On one occasion she wrote, "Oh, what a mind Dr. Barnard has." Rebecca Pegues was a remarkably well-read woman with broad intellectual interests. After the completion of the Mississippi Central Railroad in 1860, its board of directors took a grand excursion to Niagara Falls. As a member of the board, Alexander went on the trip, but without his wife. In declining the invitation, Rebecca said, "I wish to remain home to have a little time for reading. My mind [is] famished. I have books and papers innumerable awaiting me."

Alexander Pegues was a strong states' rights Democrat. One of his daughters wrote, "Papa was a red-hot Democrat and swore, figuratively, by John C. Calhoun." One of his closest associates and his personal physician was Dr. Thomas Dudley Isom, who had obtained a medical degree in Philadelphia. On one occasion a political discussion between Isom, an anti-secessionist Henry Clay Whig, and Pegues became so heated that Pegues physically threatened his best friend. Pegues quickly apologized, and they both agreed never to talk politics again.

In January 1861 Pegues accompanied his protege Lamar to Jackson for the Mississippi secession convention. After the state seceded and war became more likely, Pegues raised and equipped a military company known as the Pegues Defenders. Like most other Southern planters, Pegues was ruined by the war, as his wealth was in land and slaves. After the war he moved into Oxford and purchased the house that later became Bramlett Hospital. He died in 1871. In a eulogy of his friend and benefactor, Lamar praised Alexander Pegues for "laying the foundations of [the University of Mississippi], that noble institution."

Although not a member of the original board of trustees, Thomas H. Williams is cited in a biographical directory of the American Congress as the "Father of the University." Williams moved to Pontotoc from his native Tennessee in the early stages of the cotton boom. In 1838 the legislature appointed him to the United States Senate to fill the unexpired term of James F. Trotter, who later became a law professor at the University of Mississippi. Williams was elected to the board at its first meeting on January 1, 1845, when William Y. Gholson resigned. He took his seat on the board at its July 14 meeting at Oxford and was elected treasurer. During his six-year tenure, Williams, who died in 1851, was one of the board's most active members. Four other trustees who were present at the creation of the university and contributed to its early development, though they were not members of the original board, were Isaac Newton Davis, John J. McRae, George Hampton Young and James Brown.

One of the original settlers of Lafayette County and one of its wealthiest landowners, James Brown was elected to the board of trustees in 1846. He was active in the governance of the university and served on the executive committee for several years. During Chancellor Barnard's administration, Brown supervised the construction of the observatory and several other buildings. In April 1852, Colonel Brown was angered by "a malicious mischief" perpetrated on his favorite horse. Some students had cut off the animal's tail. An infuriated board ordered the faculty to identify and punish the guilty students. As of July, the faculty had not identified the perpetrators. At its meeting on July 13, 1852, the board demanded an explanation from President Longstreet as to why no one had been punished. Longstreet explained that "though my best exertions were used to get a clew [*sic*] to the offenders, I entirely failed." Longstreet did, however, "deliver a general lecture to the students . . . in severe terms of reprobation." The day after Longstreet's report to the board of trustees, a student delegation petitioned the board for permission to use the large room in the Lyceum "for the purpose of giving a complimentary party to the Graduating class on the evening of commencement day." The board voted to decline their request until the "indignity" to Colonel Brown was "disclaimed" by the students. In a hastily called meeting, the student body unanimously adopted a resolution disclaiming and disavowing "the indignity offered to Col. Brown of April last." After receiving a written copy of this resolution, the board granted the use of the Lyceum for the commencement ball. In the days leading up to Mississippi's secession, there were several fires in Oxford and Lafayette County, which local officials thought to be the work of "incendiaries." James Brown's house in Oxford was one of those damaged. When General Ulysses S. Grant occupied Oxford in December 1862, he made James Brown's home on Depot Street his headquarters. Brown remained on the board of trustees until 1870, when the Republican legislature reorganized the board.

Isaac Newton Davis, who migrated to Panola County, Mississippi, from Georgia in 1840, was elected to the board of trustees in 1845. Davis was one of the board's most conscientious members during the antebellum period and had perhaps the best attendance record. His legacy to the university was the admission of irregular, or "partial course," students. At the July 15, 1848, meeting, Davis introduced a resolution to allow the admission of students on a part-time basis and permit them to take only the courses they elected or were academically prepared to take.

The board adopted this policy, which James Ventress also supported, by a five-to-four vote. One of Frederick Barnard's first recommendations when he became president in 1856 was to discontinue the admission of "partial course" students. Although Barnard failed to achieve that reform, Davis resented his attempt to abolish the system. Davis also opposed Barnard's reorganization of the university in 1858 and was the spokesman for a small group of dissidents on the board. His son, Isaac Davis, Jr., a law student at the university, persuaded his father to change his mind, however, and Davis eventually supported Barnard's reorganization. In the early 1850s Davis was a strong unionist and several newspapers endorsed him for governor on the union ticket in 1851, though he did not seek the nomination. While serving in the state senate during the late 1850s, Davis changed his views dramatically. He became an ardent secessionist, proslavery Democrat, and Southern nationalist. Davis did not live to see the establishment of the Southern Confederacy or to see his namesake die at Shiloh in its defense. He died on January 21, 1861.

John J. McRae, the founder of the Jackson *Clarion-Ledger,* was known in his youth as "Johnny McRae of Chickasawhay." He sailed his steamer *Triumph* up and down the Chickasawhay River as if it were the Mississippi itself. After graduating from Miami University in Oxford, Ohio, McRae read law under Judge P. Rutilius R. Pray and was admitted to the Mississippi bar. He was a states' rights Democrat who served in the state house of representatives from 1848 to 1850. In 1851, after Jefferson Davis became secretary of war in President Franklin Pierce's cabinet, the state legislature appointed McRae to fill Davis's unexpired term in the United States Senate. He also served as governor of Mississippi from 1854 to 1858.

McRae was elected to the board of trustees in 1850 and served until his death in 1868. While he was a member of the board, and while serving as governor in 1857, he signed into law the statute that made the governor ex officio chairman of the board of trustees. He took an active role in university governance and supported Chancellor Barnard's effort to place the university in the front rank of American institutions. After the board of trustees closed the university in November 1861, and as Chancellor Barnard was preparing to leave Mississippi, McRae said to Barnard, "I shall always have one source of satisfaction in the recollection that I have voted for every measure which you have ever recommended."

George Hampton Young was elected to the board of trustees in 1848, when John Waddel resigned to accept appointment to the university's first faculty. Young was a wealthy planter who built Waverley mansion, which an architectural historian described as "one of the unique houses in America." Built in Lowndes County near Columbus, Waverley was more than a mansion. It was a village built on the banks of the Tombigbee River, with bathhouses atop artesian wells, orchards, kennels, a sawmill, gristmill, warehouses, a merchant house, a ferryboat, and quarters for the plantation's slave population. Waverley was valued in 1860 at $532,000. Young and his wife, with their six sons and four daughters, lived an idyllic life. L. Q. C. Lamar wrote that Young was a "typical Southern gentleman of the Old School [but] without any of the blemishes sometimes found in them." Young attended the University of Georgia and took a law degree from Columbia College in New York. He practiced law in Georgia and served in the Georgia legislature. During the "flush times," Young came to Pontotoc to buy land for his Georgia clients, but found conditions so enticing that he moved to the region. Like many of the Southern gentry, Young was a planter-statesman who felt an obligation to enter public service. He served one term in the Mississippi legislature and twelve years on the board of trustees of the state university. He took a great interest in the university's affairs and, unlike some of his wealthy peers who sent their sons north to school, Young sent four of his six sons to the University of Mississippi.

Young was probably the determining influence on Frederick Barnard's reluctant acceptance of the chair of mathematics in 1854. As Barnard and a friend, who was interviewing for the chair of chemistry, were traveling from Tuscaloosa to Oxford in the summer of 1854, they visited Young at Waverley. Barnard and Young formed an immediate and personal friendship that lasted until Young's death in 1880. Young suggested to Barnard that he apply for the chair of chemistry. After Barnard said he would not compete with his friend for that position, Young encouraged him to apply for the chair of mathematics. Barnard was flattered by the attention he received from Young and other board members, and he accepted the chair of mathematics before discussing the appointment with Mrs. Barnard. After Barnard moved to Oxford, Young lent him money to buy a horse and three slaves, and Barnard often consulted Young about his professional and personal affairs.

This illustrious board of trustees held its first meeting on January 15, 1845, in Jackson. It was the policy of the board to meet twice a year, at Jackson in January when the legislature was in session and at Oxford in July during the university's commencement exercises. Because the board met only twice a year, the trustees empowered the executive committee to act for the full board between its regular meetings. The board's primary concern at its first meeting was the status of the seminary fund and the amount of funds available for the construction of university buildings. State Treasurer William Clark informed the board that there was eighty-nine thousand dollars in notes and warrants in the seminary fund but no cash on hand. Undaunted by that discouraging report, the board authorized its president, Alexander Clayton, to secure architectural plans for university buildings and allotted $250 for that purpose.

At the July meeting in Oxford, Clayton informed the board that the state treasurer would not honor his draft against the seminary fund without a warrant from the state auditor. Clayton did not press the issue but did ask the treasurer for an updated account of the seminary fund. To Clayton's dismay and disbelief, the treasurer reported that the current amount of the fund was seventy-seven thousand dollars, twelve thousand less than it had been six months earlier and a hundred thousand less than a recent estimate made by the commissioner of the seminary fund. The legislature had established a commissioner of the seminary fund in 1843.

In an attempt to reconcile the discrepancies between the two reports and to ascertain once and for all, if possible, the actual amount in the seminary fund, the board appointed a special committee to examine the conflicting reports. The next day, the committee, chaired by James Ventress, who also chaired a legislative committee on the seminary fund, informed the board that a reconciliation between the two reports was impossible. Ventress's committee then asked the board to "clothe it with all the authority this board can confer, to call upon the Governor, Auditor and Treasurer of the State, and the Commissioner of the Seminary Fund, and all other persons, who may be supposed to have any information on this subject, for the purpose of examining all the papers and records relating to this subject, in their several offices." The board clothed the committee with all such authority, but the law of unintended consequences took control of the situation.

When the special board committee demanded to see "all the papers and records" in various public offices, it became apparent that the 1844 law giving the university's board of trustees "entire control" of the seminary fund conflicted with the 1843 law creating the commissioner of the seminary fund, who was directed by the statute to "collect and invest" the fund. With the legislature meeting so often and passing so many laws, it was bound to lose track of some of them. To resolve the conflict between the 1843 law and the 1844 law, the legislature passed another law in 1846 revoking the law giving the trustees control of the seminary fund. The editor of the *Natchez Free Trader,* taking notice that the national congress and the state assembly were both in session at the same time, commented, "There is no nation under heaven where there is half so much legislation as in these United States."

In January 1846, after the legislature removed the seminary fund from the board's control, James Ventress explained to the board that there was no fund for them to control anyway. According to his latest findings, the university fund consisted of $117,172.29 in judgments and notes against the Planters' Bank, which was in liquidation, and $89,900 in Planters' Bank stock, which was worthless, for a total of $207,072.29. There was an additional $150,000 in notes payable to the state. "It appears," Ventress said, "that the grand aggregate of the fund collectible and uncollectible is $357,072.29." Ventress expressed little hope, based on his discussion with the commissioner of the seminary fund, that much of the "grand aggregate" could ever be collected. Ventress also reported that, in addition to the varying amounts embezzled or lost through neglect, several thousand dollars was "wrongly abstracted" from the fund from 1827 to 1833 and appropriated to Mississippi College.

While Ventress was giving his report to the board of trustees, Governor Brown was giving a similar report to the legislature, though he estimated the fund to be about $250,000, more than $100,000 less than Ventress's "grand aggregate." After recounting the "heavy and ruinous losses which [the seminary fund] has sustained in the hands from which it has been slowly wrung," Brown asserted that the state was under "the most solemn obligation" to recoup the funds. He then recommended the establishment of a $200,000 permanent endowment at 8 percent interest and a special appropriation of $50,000 to the university for its initial building program. Of the $16,000 annual interest generated by the permanent endowment, $8,000 would go to the university and the other $8,000 would be equally distributed among ten preparatory academies established geographically throughout the state. Each academy would receive $800 annually from the seminary fund and would be under the same governing board as the university. Governor Brown, who had attended both Jefferson College and Mississippi College, told the lawmakers, "Nothing is clearer to my mind than that the college will not succeed without the aid of auxiliary schools."

Governor Brown's recommendation of a $50,000 special appropriation provoked another bitter sectional debate and a reconsideration of Oxford as the site of the university. The twenty-six counties established in the Choctaw and Chickasaw Cessions gave north Mississippi a small majority in the legislature. "South Mississippi," it was said, "felt that the scepter had departed Judah." When Representative John F. Cushman of Lafayette County introduced a bill to appropriate $50,000 for the construction of buildings at the university, Representative Horatio Fleming Simrall of Wilkinson County (in the southwestern corner of the state) spoke in opposition to Cushman's bill and offered a substitute motion. "This university," Simrall said, "situated as it is, resembles the coruscations of the north pole, which are the most brilliant known, but are not seen or enjoyed by near one-fourth of the globe; so will it be with this great 'northern light' of Mississippi; the greater portion of the State will never derive any benefit from it."

Simrall predicted the University of Mississippi, with its self-perpetuating board of trustees, would soon be governed by men from Oxford and would become just another local collegiate institution. To prevent that and to guarantee that the seminary fund would be used "for the greatest good to the greatest number," Simrall proposed a division of the state into four collegiate districts, the distribution of the seminary fund equally among those districts, and the establishment of colleges and universities at the most accessible locations in each district. Simrall's proposal was a sincere and nearly successful effort to repeal the university's charter and establish several local public colleges in its stead.

Representative Cushman warned the lawmakers if the state university was not established now, at Oxford, it might never be. He was adamantly opposed to dividing the seminary fund, questioned the legality of such a division, and reported that no other state had done so. To fully discuss Simrall's motion and to give all members an opportunity to address this issue, the house of representatives went into a committee of the whole. H. W. Allen of Claiborne County supported Simrall's motion because he favored common schools for the masses rather than one university for the landed elite. S. C. Farrar of Rankin County argued against the motion, saying the university's board of trustees were "men of distinguished talent and extensive information" who would not allow the university to become a local institution. J. M. Maxey of Noxubee County conceded that he had opposed Oxford as the location of the university but said he would not now attack the university or support the squandering of the seminary fund among several colleges.

Representative James L. Alcorn of Coahoma County made perhaps the most interesting argument. Alcorn was one of the wealthiest landowners and slave holders in the state. He had moved to Mississippi from Kentucky and amassed a fortune in cotton and slaves. He later served as a Confederate general and was governor of Mississippi during Reconstruction. In the debate over Simrall's motion, Alcorn expressed his opposition "to any institution which was fostered by the state" because "the tendency of such institutions is to promote the interests of that class of citizens which do not require the fostering hand of the community." If the legislature really wanted "to disseminate knowledge," it should "bring education to the poor who were not able to educate their children." The wealthy slaveholder said "this university [would] never benefit that class of citizens who should be looked to by the legislature." At the conclusion of this protracted debate, the house defeated Simrall's motion by a vote of thirty-nine to thirty-six, with most legislators voting along sectional lines. The legislature took no action on Governor Brown's recommendation for a permanent endowment or the establishment of preparatory schools, but made a special appropriation of fifty thousand dollars to the university's building program. Half of the fifty thousand dollar appropriation was available in 1846 and the other twenty-five thousand was appropriated the following year.

One of the University of Mississippi's early legends tells of Thomas H. Williams's heroic horseback ride from Jackson up the Natchez Trace, the haunt of hoodlums and bushwhackers, to his home in Pontotoc with fifteen thousand dollars in gold sovereigns stuffed into his saddle bags. On that now-famous ride in early June 1846, Williams, the treasurer of the board of trustees, was hurrying the first installment of the fifty-thousand-dollar special appropriation to Oxford to pay the carpenters and craftsmen for their work on the university's original buildings.

At its January 1846 meeting, the board of trustees appointed William Nichols university architect and approved his basic design of the Lyceum. In the following weeks, Nichols submitted plans for two faculty houses, two dormitories, and a steward's hall. Soon after the construction of the buildings began, the board of trustees held a public ceremony laying the cornerstone of the Lyceum. At ten o'clock on Tuesday morning, July 14, 1846, a procession formed at the Oxford square. Captain Davidson's volunteer fire company led the parade, followed by Captain Ragland's Infantry, the local clergymen, the Freemasons and their Grand Master, a local band of musicians, trustees of the state university, and the proud citizens of Oxford and Lafayette County. Bringing up the rear was Captain Cook's cavalry. The ladies had already assembled on the university grounds.

The procession wound slowly through the woods and up a slight incline to the site of the new state university, one mile distant from the square. The trustees of the university and other dignitaries occupied a platform in front of the building site. In an elaborate Masonic ceremony conducted in "a very solemn and imposing manner," the Grand Master "proceeded to lay the corner stone of the principal edifice of the University." According to a contemporary newspaper account, "There was deposited in a leaden box, which fitted in the cavity of the corner stone, a copy of the law creating the University" and eighteen other items including contemporary newspapers, the Declaration of Independence, gold and silver coins, and a Bible.

This cornerstone has been the object of many searches over the years but has never been located. When the cornerstone was laid, construction of the Lyceum had barely begun, and the outer walls were probably not far enough along for the stone to be placed in the structure itself. The

Lyceum was not completed until the early months of 1848, more than a year and a half later. The board of trustees may have intentionally rushed the cornerstone ceremony to ward off any future attempts to relocate the university. The cornerstone was probably placed at ground level at the northeast corner of the Lyceum and workers, unaware of its existence, may have covered over the stone. It is also possible that carpenters or brick layers moved the stone during the construction of the Lyceum and mistakenly carted it off with other rubbish and debris from the building site. On April 28, 1847, the board required "each of the various contractors to remove all out buildings and rubbish from the University grounds . . . before a final settlement is made with them." In a hasty effort to reach a "final settlement," one of the contractors could have inadvertently removed the cornerstone.

After the cornerstone ceremony, local musicians treated the assembly to vocal and instrumental music, and William Forbes Stearns, a twenty-eight-year-old attorney from Holly Springs, presented "a beautiful oration." Stearns began his speech with a somber discussion of the temporal nature of all things. "Our fathers," he asked, "where are they; and the prophets, do they live forever? No. . . . Proud cities [and] Empires whose power once overshadowed the whole earth have arisen, flourished and fallen; the abodes of heroes are unattended, save by the prowling beast that makes his lair among their ruins. The wearied eye searches in vain among the records of hoary antiquity for something of merely human origin which exhibits no symptoms of decline." Those were dreary words for such a happy occasion, and his audience might have wondered at their meaning.

Stearns was warning the friends of the university that a legislative charter and fine buildings gave no assurance that this "infant institution" would endure. "The establishment of numerous collegiate institutions," he recalled, "has been attempted at different periods, in various places of the South-West, but, from some strange and almost unaccountable fatality . . . nearly every one of those attempts has resulted in failure and disappointment." He and his listeners knew of the short history of Holly Springs University. After its founding in 1839, the university "wobbled on for three years," then "went down, unwept and unhonored." Stearns did not have to remind the friends of the university that Horatio Simrall's bill to revoke its charter had failed seven months earlier by only three votes.

The founding of the University of Mississippi had been delayed for so many years, and there was still so much opposition to it, that its future was by no means secure. Stearns was frank with his listeners: "The experiment is now about to be tried in earnest, whether or not an institution of learning can be established in the South-West upon a permanent foundation. There is no good reason why an institution may not here be founded, which shall rank with the first in any portion of our confederacy." Stearns concluded his oration on a note of high optimism: "Let this institution succeed and no man can estimate how many poets, orators, statesmen, divines may here be formed" or measure "the influence that will be exerted for good, through its agency, upon the generations who are to succeed us."

Following Stearns's oration and the benediction, the happy throng had a picnic. But the barbecue was not quite ready, an unfortunate circumstance that called for yet another speech. The Oxford *Observer* reported, "Dinner not being quite ready... Mr. John J. McCaughan, one of the Trustees of the University [addressed] the large audience, in a speech remarkable for its original and well-digested views of government.... He left an impression behind him which will not soon be forgotten by those who think for themselves." After McCaughan's speech, the militia units, decked out no doubt in their most dashing dress, "escorted the ladies to the table, where the whole company partook of a sumptuous republican barbecue." The Oxford newspaper reported the event in the most glowing terms and boasted that the "large crowd behaved exceedingly well—there being no instance of impropriety observed on the occasion." Following the picnic the procession re-formed and returned to the square "where they were dismissed in peace and harmony."

Over the next year and a half the university began to take on "a visible existence." On December 23, 1847, James M. Howry, chairman of the executive committee of the board of trustees, filed a report with Governor Brown detailing "the buildings now in progress" at the university. William Nichols assured Howry, and Howry assured Governor Brown the buildings would be completed and ready for the opening of the university in November. In presenting Howry's report to the legislature, Governor Brown conceded that the university was not in the most "central situation," but noted that Oxford was "a healthy and pleasant [village] in the midst of an intelligent and growing population." The young governor, who had done so much to bring the University of Mississippi into existence, then proudly announced that "this magnificent temple of learning" would open in the fall of 1848.

Chapter 3

THE FORMATIVE YEARS, 1848–1856

In the success of this University, the people of Mississippi have a very deep interest.

Jackson *Mississippian*, August 18, 1849

On January 11, 1848, the board of trustees of the University of Mississippi convened in Jackson to "devise and adopt a system of learning" for the nation's newest state university. When the Reverend John N. Waddel, chairman of the committee to design the "system of learning," recommended a traditional classical curriculum that included a course on the evidences of Christianity, Edward Wilkinson "offered a very strenuous objection" and refused to discuss the matter further. John J. McCaughan, who also had a strong interest in the university's curriculum, was not at that meeting, and the issue was laid on the table until the board's next meeting in February.

At its February meeting, the board again discussed the curriculum but took no action. Between the February meeting and a July 10 meeting in Oxford, the formality of designing a curriculum exploded into a public controversy. At the board's morning session on July 10, McCaughan presented a letter of resignation in which, according to Waddel, he made "a long and heavy assault upon religion . . . denouncing the whole Christian system." Edward Wilkinson, a member of the anticlerical faction on the board, read McCaughan's letter to the trustees. Wilkinson, again according to Waddel, added his own "assault upon the Ministry" and called for a new committee to design the university's curriculum. The board then named a new committee, chaired by Wilkinson, to design a course of study.

On July 12 the board reassembled to hear Wilkinson's report. Under Wilkinson's plan no ministers would be appointed to the faculty, and the course on the evidences of Christianity would not be offered. Instead, he recommended a course in mental and moral philosophy and the appointment of a university chaplain. The chaplain, who would rotate among the major denominations and be compensated by student fees, would say morning and evening prayers and conduct other religious services at the university. Isaac Davis, a member of the committee, presented a minority report recommending the course on Christianity and the appointment of ministers to the faculty. The board adopted Davis's motion only to reopen the entire issue two days later and revert to Wilkinson's original recommendation. The state press gave extensive coverage to the debate over the course on Christianity and the exclusion of ministers from the faculty. Mississippi's evangelical clergy viewed the spectacle "with sentiments of the strongest disapproval." Eventually, the board of trustees adopted the traditional classical curriculum, which included a course on Christianity. Even though the course on Christianity was a part of the curriculum, and ministerial students received tuition-free scholarships and four of the school's first five presidents were ministers, the state's evangelical clergy still characterized the university as a "regularly organized infidel institution."

When the trustees finally turned their attention from the curriculum to the faculty, they found a task only slightly less daunting. In the traditional American liberal arts college, the faculty included a president and four professors, and the board's original plan was to follow that model. The board of trustees opened the university with a president and three professors, however, because only four faculty houses were available. There was a "swarm of applicants" for those four positions, almost two hundred by one estimate. Most of the applicants submitted resumes and recommendations, or "testimonials" as they were called then, which had to be read and weighed. The primary responsibility for sifting through the applications fell to James Howry, secretary of the board. It is no wonder that he misplaced some of them, but John Waddel was most distressed to learn that Howry could not find Waddel's papers, especially since one of the letters recommending him came from William L. Sharkey, a board member.

Of the seventeen candidates for president, the leading contender was the Reverend Augustus Baldwin Longstreet, who was so certain of his appointment that he prematurely resigned as president of Emory College in Georgia. The anticlerical faction of the board of trustees, which included James Ventress, blocked his selection and engineered the appointment of George Frederick Holmes as president and professor of mental and moral philosophy. Ventress had read many of Holmes's publications and gave the twenty-seven-year-old scholar a "very flattering" recommendation. President Holmes was one of only twenty-six college presidents in antebellum America who was not a minister.

Holmes was born in British Guiana and came to America by way of Canada. After sojourning through Pennsylvania, Virginia, and Georgia, he settled in South Carolina, where he was befriended by John C. Calhoun. While living in South Carolina, Holmes published many scholarly articles in the *Southern Quarterly Review, DeBow's Review,* and the *Southern Literary Messenger,* where he came under the tutelage of William Gilmore Simms. Early in his literary career, when he was discouraged because his writing was rarely read outside the South and was bringing in almost no income, Holmes published a series of articles criticizing the American press for "pander[ing] to public taste [rather] than attempting to improve it." Simms wrote Holmes telling him not to be discouraged, reminding him that "[n]othing but the trashy survives."

Opting for a more regular, if only slightly more lucrative, livelihood, Holmes abandoned the literary world for academia. His first appointment came in 1846, as professor of classical languages at the University of Richmond. The next year he was appointed to the chair of history and political economy at the College of William and Mary. Following the death of William and Mary's president, Thomas Dew, a dispute developed between the board of visitors and the faculty over their claim that Dew's successor lacked the credentials and reputation to head the South's most prestigious institution and that his appointment was achieved through political connections. Holmes resigned in the spring of 1848 in protest over the appointment of Dew's successor, but he was without a position only briefly. In August he accepted the appointment as president of the University of Mississippi.

After a brief tenure at the University of Mississippi, George Frederick Holmes spent a ten-year rustication at Tanglewood, his mountain home in western Virginia. In 1857 he joined the faculty at the University of Virginia and enjoyed a distinguished career at Mr. Jefferson's university until his death in 1897. Holmes was a major Southern intellectual of the nineteenth century, but, as Harvey Wish observed in the *Journal of Southern History,* "Time has dealt ruthlessly with [his] once-brilliant reputation." Wish wrote, "His genius was expressed but too frequently in letters writ in sand, lost in the oblivion attendant upon the struggling Southern magazines of the antebellum and Reconstruction eras." Holmes also spent his genius defending the lost causes of slavery and states' rights.

Moments after naming Holmes president, the board of trustees appointed Albert Taylor Bledsoe to the chair of "Mathematicks and Astronomy," which made Bledsoe the senior member of the faculty. Although the basis for Bledsoe's appointment to the chair of mathematics over the other sixty applicants is not clear from the board minutes, for the "nomadic Bledsoe family the unbroken 6 year residence in Oxford was one of its most serene and secure." Bledsoe was a Kentuckian by birth and an 1830 graduate of West Point. Among his classmates were Jefferson Davis and Robert E. Lee. He was deeply religious, and throughout his academic career he considered theology the queen of the disciplines. In 1835 Bledsoe was ordained to the priesthood of the Episcopal Church. A year later he married Harriet Coxe of New Jersey.

In 1839 Bledsoe resigned from the Episcopal priesthood and moved to Springfield, Illinois, where he practiced law for several years before moving to Cincinnati. While living in Cincinnati, Bledsoe published his first book, a theological treatise on the freedom of the will. In 1847 he returned to Springfield and renewed his friendship with Abraham Lincoln. During their early days in Springfield, the Bledsoes and the Lincolns lived in the same rooming house and were close family friends. Bledsoe became Lincoln's confidant and moved freely among Lincoln's widening circle of friends. On an occasion when Lincoln was challenged, Bledsoe served as his second and persuaded Lincoln to choose broadswords rather than pistols. The selection of broadswords made the entire episode appear ridiculous, and both parties agreed to drop the matter.

Bledsoe's law partner in Springfield was Edward Baker, an ambitious English-born politician who is said to have wept when he read in the United States Constitution that "[n]o person except a natural born citizen . . . shall be eligible to the office of president." Lincoln called Baker the greatest orator of that age and said he would surely be president except for the accident of birth. On one occasion, Samuel Willard, a prominent Illinois politician, came to Baker's office to retain his services. It so happened that Baker, Bledsoe, and Lincoln were all in Baker's office. Willard recalled that day:

> In that office I saw at the same time three men—Lincoln, Baker, and Bledsoe—whose futures no one could have guessed, even with the wildest imagination enlisted for the task. . . . Had one who knew the three men been told that one of the three should become the President of the United States, and were he then bidden to point him out, he would have said: Baker is not the man, for he was born in England. . . . Lincoln will do for Sangamon County . . . but if the lightning of a presidential nomination hits him, it will hit the wrong man; he has more risk of being hit by the real article. Bledsoe must be the man!

Professor Bledsoe's heavy classroom duties at the University of Mississippi were reduced in 1850 by the appointment of L. Q. C. Lamar as adjunct professor of mathematics. Bledsoe boasted in later years that he taught Lamar everything he knew, especially how to think. In 1853 Bledsoe became the first professor to publish a book while on the faculty at the University of Mississippi. His wife, Harriet, recopied her husband's entire manuscript in a larger, more legible script required by the publisher. In the laborious process of copying the lengthy manuscript, her daughter remembered many years later, Mrs. Bledsoe lost the small delicate script that had been her customary style of writing.

A year after the publication of this book, *A Theodicy, Or Vindication of the Divine Glory,* Bledsoe accepted the chair of mathematics at the University of Virginia. On the day of his resignation, the board of trustees awarded Professor Bledsoe an LL.D., the first honorary degree given by the university. After two years at Virginia, Bledsoe published his third and best-known book, *Essay on Liberty and Slavery,* a stirring defense of slavery and states' rights. George Frederick Holmes, who had gone into intellectual exile after he lost the presidency at the University of Mississippi, praised Bledsoe's book in an article in *DeBow's Review.* Bledsoe wrote to Holmes thanking him for the review and telling him of an opening at the University of Virginia. Bledsoe offered to support Holmes if he decided to seek the position. Holmes did seek the post, and, largely because of Bledsoe's endorsement, he won the appointment.

After the Civil War, during which he served as assistant secretary of war and Confederate envoy to England, Bledsoe became the prototype of the "unreconstructed Rebel" and spent his considerable talent defending the "Lost Cause." In 1866 he published *Is Davis a Traitor, Or Was Secession a Constitutional Right Previous to the War in 1861.* Charles O'Conner, Mr. Davis's chief counsel, told Bledsoe's daughter without the facts marshaled in that book he could not have saved the life of Jefferson Davis. In the aftermath of the Civil War, Bledsoe was again ordained, this time into the ministry of the Methodist Episcopal Church South. For a short period of time he edited the *Southern Review,* the official organ of the Southern Methodist Church. In 1877, at the end of his long and exciting life, Professor Bledsoe could claim that he had served as Abraham Lincoln's second, taught L. Q. C. Lamar how to think, brought George Frederick Holmes out of exile, and saved the life of Jefferson Davis.

The third member of the original faculty was John Waddel, a Presbyterian minister, the son of Moses Waddel (president of the University of Georgia), and a nephew of John C. Calhoun. After failing as a cotton planter in Alabama, Waddel decided to buy some land in Jasper County and try again in Mississippi. In February 1841 he spent several days in Mobile, Alabama, finalizing the purchase. "On one of those lonely days of waiting," he recalled many years later, "I was walking the street, and passing a reading room, I stepped in to read the news of the day and to while away the heavy hours." A Jackson newspaper caught his attention because he would soon be living in Mississippi. As he read of the founding of the University of Mississippi, he was suddenly overwhelmed by a premonition that his personal destiny would somehow be linked to that institution. He was an old school Presbyterian of deep persuasion, and he did not take such moments lightly. After finalizing the land deal he gathered up his small family and meager belongings and moved to Mississippi. But he soon found that the drudgery and isolation of farming were not to his liking. After selling the farm for the second time in his young life, he established Montrose Academy in Jasper County, soon considered by many as the finest preparatory school in Mississippi.

"On a certain day [in 1844]," Waddel wrote, "as I stood in the doorway of the Academy building, I observed the Hon. Simeon Adams, the senator from the county of Jasper, passing, on his return home after the adjournment of the Senate." Senator Adams had dropped by to tell the headmaster of Montrose that the legislature had appointed him to the board of trustees of the University of Mississippi. After their conversation, the headmaster remembered his premonition in the reading room in Mobile. He was convinced that Providence had permitted "coming events to cast their shadows before." From his home in Montrose the headmaster journeyed on horseback two hundred miles "through a wild and desolate region" to attend board meetings in Oxford. In July 1848

Waddel resigned from the board of trustees and applied for the chair of Greek and Latin, a position he won and held until his resignation in 1857. Waddel was a favorite with the board, and he expected to be appointed president after Longstreet's resignation in 1856. To Waddel's mortification the office went to Frederick Barnard, and to Barnard's great relief Waddel resigned the next year.

Of the four original professors, the first to arrive in Oxford was John Millington, who was "duly appointed Professor of Natural Sciences, Chemistry, Geology, Mineralogy, Botany, and Natural Philosophy [physics]." Millington arrived in Oxford in mid-October, about three weeks before the session opened. He found the campus unfinished and in disorder. Scaffolding and scantlings were stacked in and around the buildings. Stumps and tree limbs were scattered across the campus. The main doors to the dormitories and the steps leading up to the entrances had not been installed. The condition of the campus, he recalled, was "unfavorable for the opening and the orderly conduct of the academical courses." Millington found the students "even less prepared than their habitation." In a sketch of Millington for the *William and Mary Quarterly,* George Frederick Holmes offers anecdotal evidence of the immaturity of the university's first class: "The first lectures in chemistry, being designed to attract attention . . . and to excite intelligent interest in the study, were illustrated with many simple, but showy experiments. These were intermitted during the discussion of the fundamental and abstract principles of the science. A disheartened pupil accosted the doctor before the opening of a lecture one day with the eager inquiry: 'Professor, when will you show us some more of your tricks?' "

At the time of Millington's birth near London in 1779, Mississippi was a Spanish colony, and when Mississippi became a state in 1817 Millington was lecturing at the Royal Institution with Sir Humphrey Davy and Michael Faraday. While Thomas Dudley Isom was living in a crude cabin among the Chickasaws, Dr. Millington was sharing the comforts of a gentleman's club in London with Sir John Herschel, the noted astronomer, and Charles Babbage, whose analytical engine made the computer possible. Professor Millington began his academic career in 1803 at the other Oxford. In 1806 he was admitted to the Royal Society, began lecturing at the Royal Institution in 1815, and was one of the founders of the Astronomical Society of London in 1820. After a brief stint as superintendent of a silver mine in Mexico, Millington traveled extensively in the United States. In Philadelphia he became ill and remained there for some time. During his recuperation he married for the second time, his first wife having died in Mexico.

In 1835 Millington was appointed to the chair of chemistry, natural philosophy, and engineering at the College of William and Mary. A series of "discords which divided the faculty, the students, and the town" forced him and his young colleague, George Frederick Holmes, to resign in the spring of 1848. Within a few months, he accepted the chair of chemistry and natural science at the University of Mississippi. Nearing the age of seventy, Millington would spend "his old age teaching the [new] sciences to the restless sons of the Old South." As Millington was by birth, judgement and sentiment a member of the Church of England, he naturally associated himself with the Episcopal Church and was a founding member and senior warden of St. Peter's Church in Oxford.

The board of trustees awarded the chair of science to Millington for two reasons in particular. First, Millington agreed to make his personal collection of scientific equipment available to the university, if the university would pay the shipping costs from Williamsburg. The board agreed to do so. Second, Professor Millington's interest in applied science as well as pure science made him attractive to Mississippi's planters who were entering an age of scientific agriculture and were seeking useful and practical knowledge. After a Millington speech to the Lafayette County Agricultural Association, which lasted almost two hours, an exuberant planter said he would cheerfully give a thousand dollars for Professor Millington's knowledge of agricultural chemistry. In 1850 Professor Millington initiated the first agricultural and geological survey of Mississippi, though he left the university before its completion. On July 13, 1853, Professor Millington, who also had a medical degree, accepted the chair of chemistry and toxicology at the Memphis Medical College. The board of trustees accepted his resignation with reluctance and passed a resolution commending him for his service to the university. The board of trustees also purchased the scientific apparatus he had brought to Oxford, some of which had been used in Davy's experiments at the Royal Institution in London.

Shortly before the Civil War, Millington built a "beautiful and romantic" mansion at LaGrange, Tennessee, where he hoped to live his final years in quiet seclusion. Unfortunately for Millington, LaGrange was near the grand junction of the Mississippi Central and the Memphis and Charleston Railroads from which Union Colonel Benjamin Grierson launched one of the most destructive cavalry raids of the Civil War. After federal troops occupied Millington's home, he journeyed to Richmond to live with his daughter Catherine, who had lived with her father in Oxford when she was thirteen. In 1868 at the age of ninety-one, Millington died in Richmond and was interred at Williamsburg.

Because the election of President Holmes and the faculty occurred so late in the summer, the board worried that all four professors might not arrive at Oxford in time for the opening ceremony. To the board's relief, they were all present, and the university opened its first session on November 6, 1848. President Holmes and Jacob Thompson delivered the usual orations that such an auspicious occasion demanded. The ceremony was held in the chemistry lecture hall in the Lyceum, which President Holmes called "one of the most elegant structures in the South." William Nichols patterned the Lyceum after an Ionic temple on the Illysis near Athens. The campus was in a setting of great natural beauty, with the buildings arranged in a semicircle at the crest of a slight eminence. The six original buildings, not counting the appurtenances, included the Lyceum, two dormitories, two faculty houses, and a steward's hall located west of the Lyceum. The three-story faculty houses included twelve rooms and were divided in a manner to accommodate two families. President Holmes and John Millington shared one residence; Professor Bledsoe and John Waddel shared the other.

The two dormitories, which were also three-story structures and similar in appearance to the faculty houses, accommodated only seventy-two residents, and some students took lodging in Oxford and its vicinity. Off-campus students created such mischief that the board of trustees decided to build another dormitory in 1851. Before construction began, however, the board decided to build "a large commodious hall" for student assemblies and commencement exercises instead of the dormitory. Several months of severe drought and other problems delayed construction of the assembly hall, which was identified in the board minutes and university publications as the "Chapel," but it was completed in time for the opening of the 1853 session. The three-story building included a large auditorium with balconies on three sides and a large raised stage. The third floor included several small rooms, two of which were assigned to the literary societies that had been meeting in the Lyceum.

The University of Mississippi's first student body included only freshmen and sophomores, with junior and senior classes added over the next two years. Tuition for the ten-month session was thirty-seven dollars, payable in advance. Room and board was eight dollars per month, payable quarterly in advance. Students could either provide their own dormitory furniture or rent it from the steward. The cost of laundry and stove wood was an additional expense. Dormitory students paid a four-dollar fee for servants, who made their morning fires, brought bath and drinking water from the university's artesian well, and cleaned their rooms. The term "servant" was a euphemism Southerners often used for slave. In 1852 the board rescinded the servant fee and allowed students "the privilege of hiring or not their own servants as they may deem advisable," but reserved "the power to dismiss any servant for misconduct." The trustees rescinded that policy in 1856, and assessed all dormitory students a five-dollar fee "to cover Servant hire." The university regulations of 1857 stated that no undergraduate student could "keep a horse or a servant at the University, or in the vicinity." That restriction did not apply to law students. After 1856 the university hired slaves from local slave owners, and in some cases from faculty members, to build fires, carry water, clean dormitory rooms and maintain the campus buildings. The university provided the slaves with quarters on the campus, and they could not leave the grounds without permission.

To counter the charge that a state university would perpetuate a landed aristocracy, the university's board of trustees established a policy of free admission for "any young man desirous of entering the University but unable to pay for tuition." The drawback to that otherwise generous policy was that an application for this exemption must include a statement signed by a local minister or public official certifying that the prospective student's father was unable to pay the tuition. Although the university catalog stated that "strict secrecy [would] be observed, and there [would] be no difference in the treatment of different *classes* of students," few men in antebellum Mississippi would admit to such an embarrassing situation.

By the end of the first session in July 1849, eighty students had enrolled at the university. All but two members of the university's first class were Mississippi residents; the non-residents were from Coosa, Alabama and Memphis, Tennessee. Members of the university's first class were enrolled as either "regular" or "irregular" students. Regular students took the four-year classical course that led to a bachelor of arts degree. An irregular, or "partial course student," could attend "such lectures as he may elect to attend." The board organized the faculty too late in the summer to administer entrance examinations, make character checks, and all who applied gained admission. The only admission requirement for the university's first class was that students be at least sixteen years old at the beginning of the fall term, though by special permission boys under sixteen could be admitted. This open admissions policy created both academic and disciplinary problems, but it was important for the university to have a substantial enrollment in its first session to counter the claim that the state's private institutions were meeting the educational needs of Mississippi's youth and that a public university was not necessary. When the first session opened, some of the classrooms were without desks, chairs, and benches, the board had not ordered textbooks, the university had no library, and the two dormitories were overflowing.

President Holmes compounded those problems by implementing an honor system. In his speech opening the fall session, Holmes asked the students to "pledge your honor that you will not violate" the rules of the university, and he promised them in return not to allow the faculty to conduct "espionage" against them. President Holmes's adoption of an honor system was a rare innovation in the collegiate system, and it proved to be a disastrous experiment. Professor Waddel described the university's first class as "disorderly and turbulent, idle, uncultivated and ungovernerable." Of that now legendary class of eighty, only forty-seven remained through the first full term. By July 1849 five had been expelled, eight were suspended, twelve were allowed to withdraw, and eight had absented themselves from the university, their whereabouts unknown.

As President Holmes was trying to keep his young charges under control and teach his classes, he was undergoing a family crisis. His wife, Lavalette, was with him in Oxford, but she did not conceal her wish to be back home with her family in Virginia and to take her sick child, Mary Anne, with her. Having lost his oldest son within the last year, and now fearing the loss of his daughter, Holmes left Oxford in March 1849 to take his family back to Virginia. Holmes told Professor Millington, with whom he shared a faculty house, that he would return as soon as he could. In his absence, Professor Bledsoe, the senior member of the faculty in date of appointment, became acting president. While Holmes was in Virginia, he also became ill, and his return to Oxford was delayed beyond his original intentions. He addressed a letter to Alexander Clayton, president of the board of trustees, explaining his situation and informing Clayton that he would return to Oxford as soon as his health permitted him to do so. Holmes entrusted his letter to a friend who agreed to deliver it to Clayton. For some reason that is still a mystery, the letter was never delivered.

In July 1849, having heard nothing from President Holmes since March, the board declared the office vacant and appointed Augustus B. Longstreet. Sometime later Holmes wrote to Clayton explaining his situation and asking for reinstatement. When this proved impossible, Holmes petitioned the board for compensation for the time of his illness. The board also declined that request, but stated that Holmes's separation from the university was not a reflection on either his character or his scholarship. That character reference proved to be of benefit to Holmes a decade later when he applied for a position at the University of Virginia.

After enduring its first academic year, the university held its first commencement exercise in the second week of July 1849. Although there were no graduates, the commencement was a gala celebration. The four-day festival included sumptuous banquets, a commencement ball, and many speeches. Every public room in Oxford was filled, nearly every family had guests, and throngs of people swelled the little village, which was one mile distant from the state university. Alexander H. Stephens, vice-president of the Confederacy, described the special character of college commencements in the Old South. Greece had its Olympic Games, Rome its circus, Spain its bullfights, and Native Americans their stickball. "But with us," he said, "the great gala day in country, village, and town — the day when all business is suspended, and the whole people turn out to catch and enjoy the prevailing spirit of the occasion — is the day of... the college commencement."

On Monday and Tuesday the faculty administered public examinations to the freshman and sophomore classes, and the proud editor of the Oxford *Organizer* reported, "We learn from more than one person fully competent to judge, that the Students acquitted themselves very creditably indeed." Over the next two days, eight student orators, selected by the two literary societies, declaimed on such themes as "The Age in Which We Live," "Ambition," "America," and "Republicanism: The Spirit of the Age." Other speakers included United States Senator Henry Stuart Foote, Alexander Clayton, and Professor Bledsoe.

As acting president, Bledsoe was expected to speak at commencement, and he did so with thundering effect. In his address, entitled "If Human Nature Be Really Fallen," he blamed the recent student disorders on the students' attitude that college life was "a sort of farce or comedy in which each actor is expected to display the brilliancy of his parts, and to signalize his genius in freaks of mischief and scenes of dissipation." He added that "there is a fountain within—in the profoundest depths of man's nature—continually sending forth its streams of pollution to disturb . . . every good thing on earth." Bledsoe then excoriated and abrogated the existing honor system:

> We have endeavored to impress it upon the Students of the University—that if young men come here . . . to cultivate their minds, then shall they be most affectionately welcomed and most kindly treated. . . . But . . . if they come here to . . . squander their parents' money in dissipation [we will not] permit them to fix a stain upon the character of this infant institution. We care not, whether their parents be high or low, rich or poor, mighty or weak, we cannot permit them to enact their obscene comedies in this holy temple of learning, nor to set their cloven feet upon the blossom of Science.

Bledsoe also attributed some of the misconduct to the absence of entrance examinations. The board of trustees admitted many unprepared students and the faculty did know the level of their academic readiness or the class in which they should be enrolled. Most students, he said, required individual and daily tutoring by their learned professors. By the spring the faculty had dismissed many of the younger and unprepared students, and those who remained were older and more serious about their studies. Bledsoe reassured his audience that the university had closed its first session in "perfect order" under his firm leadership.

The importance of the university's first commencement and the conclusion of the session in "perfect order" was not lost on the Jackson *Mississippian,* the state's largest and most widely circulated newspaper. "In the success of this University," the newspaper declared, "the people of Mississippi have a very deep interest." Many southern colleges "with flattering prospects for success" had failed because of the "short-sighted policy of sending our young men abroad to be educated." The *Mississippian* challenged both the press and the people to support their university: "It is the duty of the enlightened press of Mississippi . . . to support and advance this institution, and no less the duty of our citizens who have sons to educate . . . to give it preference."

In contrast to the *Mississippian*'s sense of duty, the religious press and the protestant clergy considered it their duty to condemn the godless institution. The relentless "*crusade* of the *sectarians*" against the university provoked the wrath of Benjamin Dill, editor of the Oxford *Organizer.* Dill admitted that he had been "persuaded by friends" to allow certain "misrepresentations" to pass because the mere mention of them "would enure to the benefit of those who are unfriendly to our institution." He would not, however, allow the latest "ebullition of venom" to pass without comment. "It is the bounden duty of every friend to our infant University," he wrote, "to ferret out and expose to the public these *real enemies,*" or the university will be "fettered and fenced in by the narrow and intolerant sectarianism of the churches."

The "assault" that so provoked his ire was an unsigned letter in an out-of-state newspaper. The New Orleans *Baptist Chronicle* published a statement from "A Mississippian" who criticized the university for not having a Baptist or a Methodist on its faculty. "This insolent and ridiculous pretension," Dill explained, was based "upon the fact that these denominations are most numerous in Mississippi." He went on to say that "[s]uch an arrogant assumption is beneath refutation," and then proceeded to refute the assumption in a lengthy and bitter response. Dill attributed these "slanders" to a "pedo-Baptist minister" who was a "rejected applicant" for one of the chairs at the university. The fiery editor also defended the university against the charges of infidelity that "grossly misrepresent the character and conditions of the University." Those charges, Dill wrote, were "not the result of ignorance, but design." As the school celebrated its first commencement in July 1849, Dill informed his readers and the public at large that the University of Mississippi was flourishing and that "nothing but the most *narrow* and *intolerant sectarianism* can prevent its success."

In the late summer following the university's first commencement, notices appeared in newspapers throughout the state announcing the opening of the second session in October 1849, listing Augustus Baldwin Longstreet as president and stating the new admission standards:

"No student will be admitted without a rigid examination . . . on English grammar, Composition, Arithmetic, and Geography; also in five books of Caesar, the Eclogues, and six books of the Aeneid of Virgil, and Cicero's Orations, together with the Greek Reader, and must be well versed in the Latin and Greek Grammars, including Latin Prosody."

Longstreet's appointment as president of the university, an alumnus recalled a decade later, came in the "darkest hour in her glorious history, when intemperance unbridled, ran rioting in [her] hall." It was "a critical period," and friends of the university contemplated that first year with "fear and trembling." The alumnus remembered how the "devoted mother and affectionate father heaped vituperation upon the institution, when they saw their lovely boy, whom they had consecrated with a kiss to Minerva, returning home Bacchanalian devotees. . . . But for the timely selection of [Longstreet] the name of the University ere this, would have been as 'sounding brass and tinkling cymbal.'" This alumnus was not alone in his assessment of the importance of Longstreet's appointment. When Longstreet arrived at Oxford in the fall of 1849, friends of the university hailed him as the savior of the fledgling institution. His steadying presence, and especially his rapport with the state's protestant ministers, enabled the university to repair its damaged image. The student magazine credited President Longstreet with fostering the institution into life and hailed him as the "father" of the university.

Augustus Longstreet was one of the best-known and most-admired Methodist ministers in the American South. Tutored by Moses Waddel (president of the University of Georgia), he graduated from Yale and studied law at Litchfield, Connecticut, one of the leading centers of legal studies in the United States. He had also served on the Georgia Supreme Court, edited the Augusta *Sentinel,* published a book of folk tales entitled *Georgia Scenes,* and served as president of two Methodist colleges, Emory in Georgia and Centenary in Louisiana. Mississippi's Protestant clergy admired President Longstreet because he shared their belief that "education [was] the loyal handmaiden of religion." And like his fellow clergymen, Longstreet regarded "the encroachment of scientific discoveries upon sacred mysteries with profound intolerance." If Longstreet thought "the intellectual culture fostered at his college," endangered the "spirit of primitive Methodism" he would have the college "demolished immediately." The ideal college president, Longstreet believed, was one "whose textbook in morals was the Bible, and whose lessons in physics all begin and end with its author." He did not even like the term "nineteenth century" because it was "dangerously suggestive in the age of science and reform." The Civil War, President Longstreet claimed, was a conflict between a Southern "Christ-taught band" and a Northern "science-taught band."

Longstreet was a cleric, not a scholar, a moralist, not a scientist. He was not oblivious to the intellectual revolution occurring all around him, but he was powerless to stem its tide. Reverend Longstreet was an old-time college president who found himself head of a state university, an institution in transition, and he was out of his element. When the board reprimanded him for spending too much time on church matters and neglecting his academic duties, Longstreet told the board if he could not "attend the sick" he would resign. The tension between Longstreet and the board of trustees intensified in the latter stages of his seven-year tenure, in part because he continued to devote so much of his time to his church duties, and partly because he became so actively involved in state politics.

President Longstreet began his tenure in October 1849 under the most favorable circumstances. The university's admission requirements were much higher, textbooks were available, and all students were under the daily supervision of the faculty, who visited the dormitory rooms at least once every day. Even with these changes and improvements, the drop-out rate in the second session was only slightly better than it had been in the first session. Of the seventy-six students enrolled in the 1849–50 session, only fifty-five were in attendance at the end of the term. Although none were expelled, three were suspended, and two were privately dismissed. Thirteen were called home by their parents, and there were three deaths, though only one occurred on campus. Of the fifty-five in attendance at the end of the second session, forty-five were regular students and ten were irregulars. During its second session, the university adopted a new public relations strategy, giving wayward students the option of withdrawing privately to escape public dismissal. President Longstreet also replaced Holmes's honor code with a more traditional disciplinary system and gave his faculty extensive police powers over their students. The first official publication of the University of Mississippi was the *Laws and Regulations of the University,* which appeared in 1850. Under the new rules of discipline, "no student shall go to Oxford or absent himself from the University without permission from some member of the faculty" or leave the campus "to go home or to other remote places without the written request of his parent or guardian to the president." If a professor encountered a student off campus during study hours, the student had to say "permission" (if he had permission to be off the campus) without the professor having to ask him; otherwise, the professor would assume the student did not have permission, and would issue demerits. A "strict observance of the Sabbath [was] enjoined upon every student, and it [was] his duty to attend divine service with punctuality every Sunday."

University regulations strictly prohibited students from bringing spirituous liquors to the campus. As Professor Waddel recalled, however, "the appetite for strong drink [was] so imperious as to bid defiance to law or public sentiment." Students "who desired to have the poison availed themselves of the [opportunities] offered by the wagons bearing cotton to the [Memphis] market, and, in return, bringing all goods ordered, and this among other articles." Other serious offenses were gambling, keeping and threatening to use firearms in a quarrel, and participating as principals or seconds in a duel. These offenses were punishable by expulsion. Students suspended or expelled from the university were required to leave the grounds within twenty-four hours and Oxford within forty-eight hours. Students were also enjoined from associating with anyone who had been suspended or expelled from the university, "or any other person of notoriously bad character *at any time* in Oxford, or its vicinity."

The regular exercises of each day began with prayers at sunrise and closed with evening prayers at vespers. The faculty attended morning and evening prayers, called the roll, and recorded the names of students who were absent. Most classes met five or six times a week, including Saturday mornings, and students were called in turn to recite from the assignment for that day. Professors made every effort to call on each student at each class meeting, and issued demerits to students who were unprepared. A notation was made each time he was unprepared. The faculty reprimanded or punished, and in some extreme cases, expelled consistently unprepared students. At the end of the academic year, the faculty administered public oral examinations for all classes and published each student's rank in his class. Near the end of the antebellum period, written examinations replaced the public oral examinations, though grading in the modern sense was not part of the academic practice at the University of Mississippi until after the Civil War.

The hours of recitation and study were from after morning prayers until breakfast, from nine o'clock to noon, and from two in the afternoon until five. The "residue" of the day was free time for recreation and supper. At early candlelight the college bell rang and each student was "required to repair to his room and occupy himself diligently in his studies until 9 o'clock." During "the hours of study every student [must remain] in his room and attend to his business without noise, or performance on any musical instrument; no excuse for absence from his room, except on absolute necessity, during those hours [would] be accepted."

Even young boys who might be afraid of the dark got little sympathy from their stern professors. One regulation stated: "Any student who shall lie down on his bed leaving a light burning within two feet or less of his bed, shall be fined five dollars." To enforce this regimen, it was "the duty of one member of the faculty to visit the room of each student daily at such times as he may deem proper." It was "the privilege of any member of the Faculty to enter the room of any student at pleasure." If a student did not permit the faculty member entrance to his room, "the officer [could] break it open, and the expense of repairing [the door would] be defrayed by the student, who [would] also be punished for disobedience."

The Southern gentry sent their sons off to college to be molded into men, and recreational activities were not a part of that regimen. The board of trustees considered one party a year sufficient recreation for the young scholars under their charge and prohibited students from attending "any public Ball or other public dancing party (always excepting the Annual Commencement Ball)." Students were also expressly prohibited from going to bowling alleys or ten pin alleys in Oxford "either as spectator or participant." The first violation of the rule was punishable by twenty demerits. The second offense resulted in suspension from the university. The board of trustees directed the faculty to make nightly rounds of the bowling alleys and private parties in Oxford, recording in their book of misdeeds the names of students partaking of those forbidden pleasures.

The university trustees were as unbending in their opposition to the proliferation of student organizations as they were vigilant in guarding their young charges from the influence of frivolous pleasures. On March 17, 1851, students from Monroe County asked the board of trustees to allow them to have a "social supper-party" every Saturday night after nine o'clock "for the purpose of cementing ties of friendship more strongly." Although similar organizations were routine at other colleges, the university's board declined their request. A month later several students petitioned the board for permission to establish a society called "The Moral Rectifier." The purpose of that lofty-sounding society is not known, but the board again rejected the students' request. The board even turned down a request from students who wanted to form a voluntary militia company.

If the board of trustees would not allow the students to meet in the open, they would assemble in secret. Students established several social fraternities and Greek societies, including the Mystic Seven, with President Longstreet's permission and encouragement. Longstreet had been a member of the Mystic Seven chapter at Emory College and probably helped organize the chapter at the University of Mississippi. Among the Greek fraternities organized at the university before the Civil War were Delta Kappa Epsilon (1850), Delta Kappa (1853), Delta Psi (1854), Epsilon Alpha (1855), Sigma Chi (1857), Phi Kappa Psi (1857), Chi Psi (1858), Phi Kappa Sigma (1859), Alpha Kappa Phi (1859), and Tau Eta Phi (1861). Since they were sub-rosa organizations, the fraternities met off campus in Oxford.

The only student organizations the board of trustees sanctioned were the two literary societies. In February 1849 university students organized the Hermaean Society, named for the Greek god of cunning, wit, and oratory, and established the Phi Sigma Society in May of that year. Phi Sigma are the Greek letters for "lovers of distinction." All students belonged to one of the societies, and attendance at the weekly meetings was mandatory. The societies met in the Lyceum until the Chapel was completed in 1853. Through the assistance of James Ventress, each society had a "large finely furnished" room in the new building. In a letter to Ventress thanking him for his support of the literary societies, James L. Smiley, class of 1851, wrote that "alone of all the college exercises" he found the literary societies the most enjoyable and the most beneficial. The board of trustees frequently changed the meeting times of the literary societies until Ventress persuaded the board in 1854 to allow the students to decide for themselves when it was most convenient to meet.

In April 1856 John A. Humphries and other members of Phi Sigma founded *Phi Sigma Magazine,* the first student publication at the University of Mississippi. A year later the two societies began jointly publishing the *Mississippi University Magazine.* The literary societies were both social and intellectual organizations. At their meetings, students were free from the tutelage of their professors. They could relax and have fun, as well as question the theories, values, and mores of their time, which is the right if not the duty of youth. With the *Mississippi University Magazine,* students could now give voice to their questions.

Students attending a university built on land "purchased" from the Chickasaws asked, "Were the Indians rightfully dispossessed of this Country?" Student writers applauded Professor Bledsoe's book *Essay on Liberty and Slavery,* and commended him for exposing the "glaring absurdity" of abolitionism, but they also blasted the board of trustees for rejecting popular textbooks critical of slavery. "We object to the principle which controls the members of the board," the *University Magazine* declared. "If the institution of slavery is wrong, we ought to be willing for the wrong to be exposed, and the truth of its criminality forced into our minds." The student writer continued, "[i]f slavery is tolerable on the principle of morality and religion, which we believe, to reject a textbook, in other respects of high merit, for the reason that it contains something against slavery [is] a tacit admission of the weakness of our cause."

Youth also have a duty to dream. After lamenting the "deadly spirit of religious intolerance, which sets like a nightmare upon a large portion of the world," a student writing in the May 1857 issue of the *Magazine* called for "universal peace and universal emancipation." In an article entitled "A Confederacy of the World," he wrote, "A confederacy of the enlightened nations of the world would do much to advance the progress of all; it would crush out, by the force of public opinion, the evil of bad governments, adjust, by honorable arbitration, the disputes of independent states, and bind them together, in one vast brotherhood, different nations, kindreds and tribes."

In the late 1850s, two of the university's most distinguished traditions were established. The first, which began with the appearance of the *Phi Sigma Magazine,* is the tradition of outstanding student publications. The other is the literary renown achieved by the university's alumni. A member of the class of 1857, Robert Haskins Crozier was the university's first published alumnus. Crozier published several novels, including *The Confederate Spy* (1866) and a popular account of Lincoln's assassination, *The Bloody Junto* (1869). After his ordination as a Presbyterian minister, Crozier wrote several volumes with religious themes to counteract "the corrupting effect" of the dime novels so popular in the post-Civil War period.

Writing and rhetoric were important elements in the university's antebellum curriculum and essential ingredients in a Southern gentleman's education. Every Monday, two seniors, in alphabetical rotation, delivered original orations in the presence of the faculty and the student body. The underclassmen, also in alphabetical rotation, declaimed and exhibited original compositions on the first Monday of every month to their professors and other members of their class. Oratory was more than an academic exercise at the university; it was also a form of recreation and entertainment. An 1857 issue of the student magazine included a notice that the two literary societies marched in a procession to the Methodist Church "where they were entertained by a speech from Mr. A. Y. Harper."

Students were especially enthralled by political oratory. In that pristine age, political speeches lasted two or three hours, and rival candidates often engaged each other in stern and vigorous debate. On November 5, 1849, thirty-seven students petitioned the board to dismiss classes so they could attend political speeches in Oxford. The board declined their request. During the secession crisis of 1851, however, the board dismissed classes on several occasions so the students could hear some of Mississippi's grand statesmen, including William L. Sharkey, Jefferson Davis, Henry Stuart Foote, and L. Q. C. Lamar.

In the 1851 governor's race Senator Foote, a unionist, and John Anthony Quitman, a secessionist, held several debates across the state. Foote, a veteran campaigner and one of Mississippi's great orators, overpowered General Quitman on the stump. On one occasion, Foote's biting sarcasm caused the aging Quitman, the "Hero of Mexico," to physically assault Foote on the speaker's stand. Quitman later withdrew from the governor's race, and the states' rights Democrats drafted a reluctant Jefferson Davis. Because he was recuperating from an illness at his Brierfield home near Vicksburg, Davis could not conduct an active campaign and other Democrats campaigned on his behalf. Among them was twenty-six-year-old L. Q. C. Lamar, adjunct professor of mathematics at the state university.

When Foote, the renowned, met Lamar, the unknown, all of Oxford, Lafayette County, and the university turned out to see David and Goliath. President Longstreet, a states' rights Democrat, dismissed classes so the students could see their mathematics professor (and his son-in-law) in action. Lamar did not best Foote, but he held his own, which was about all anyone ever did with Foote. That Oxford debate launched the political career of one of Mississippi's most famous statesmen. Edward Mayes, Lamar's son-in-law and post-Civil War chancellor of the University, described the students' reaction to Lamar's speech: "The college students . . . were wild with excitement and pride and bore him away from the hustings upon their shoulders." It was "the flood which led on to fame, albeit not to fortune." Until 1857, classes were routinely suspended on important political occasions such as the election of Franklin Pierce on November 2, 1852. Jefferson Davis and Pierce were close personal friends, and President Pierce appointed Davis secretary of war. Chancellor Barnard discontinued this tradition, and the *Laws of* 1857 specifically stated that the university would not suspend classes for politics.

L. Q. C. Lamar, who married the president's daughter, was the first addition to the university faculty. The trustees appointed the future congressman, senator, secretary of the interior and supreme court justice adjunct professor of mathematics in 1850. The following year, with enrollment up to 147, President Longstreet, who was teaching mental and moral philosophy, rhetoric, logic, political economy, and evidences of Christianity, in addition to preaching in several Methodist churches, asked the board to enlarge the faculty. The most immediate need was a professor of modern languages. Because John Waddel was proficient only in Greek and Latin, the university did not offer courses in the modern languages. On July 17, 1851, the board appointed William A. Strozzi to the chair of modern languages. He taught French, Spanish, and German. After Lamar returned to Georgia in 1852, Jordan M. Phipps, an honors graduate of the class of 1851 and the first alumnus to serve on the faculty, was appointed adjunct professor of mathematics. When the university closed in 1861, the faculty had grown from the original four to ten professors and enrollment had increased to 261.

The university's curriculum was in keeping with the classical tradition, but neither the board of trustees nor the state legislature was reluctant to add new chairs and new courses. Southern legislatures were much more pragmatic about higher education than their northern counterparts. *DeBow's Review,* a business journal published in New Orleans, attributed that pragmatism to the South's "continual struggle with the forest." By the 1850s, Mississippi's practical-minded planters wanted more information about soil chemistry and the science of agriculture. As they looked to the state university for this information, they encountered a faculty that was opposed to "grafting" experimental science onto the classical curriculum. Such courses, the traditionalists argued, were incompatible with the role of the university, which was to provide a liberal education, build character, and produce Christian gentlemen.

With disregard, if not contempt, for the classical tradition, the state legislature in March 1850 directed the university to conduct an agricultural and geological survey of the state. The legislature also appropriated three thousand dollars to purchase equipment and to pay the salary of an "assistant professor of agricultural and geological sciences." The geological survey and the assistant professor, who would actually conduct the survey, were under the supervision of Professor John Millington, whose title was changed from professor of chemistry to professor of chemistry and agriculture. President Longstreet and most of the faculty did not consider the geological survey a legitimate function of a university and did nothing to promote the survey while it was attached to the university. The state's farmers may have derived some small benefit from the two reports published before the Civil War, but the survey was disruptive and created serious personnel problems for the faculty and the board of trustees.

Some of the applicants for assistant professor of geology, according to James Ventress, "could not distinguish between a sapphire and a pudding stone." Ventress's close friend B. L. C. Wailes applied for the position, but the appointment went to Oscar L. Lieber, the son of Francis Lieber, a renowned scholar at the University of South Carolina. Oscar Lieber assumed the position on July 15, 1851, but resigned six months later due to an "unfortunate misunderstanding between [Professor Millington] and myself." Largely on Ventress's recommendation, the board then appointed Wailes.

Wailes and Millington worked well together, and they had nearly completed the survey when Millington resigned in 1853. Wailes presumed the board would elevate him to the chair of chemistry and agriculture, but the appointment went to a Baptist minister, Reverend John C. Keeney. Mississippi Baptists, who had complained since 1848 that their denomination was not represented on the faculty, virtually dictated the appointment of Keeney. He was an unfortunate choice. His "want of qualifications" was so evident that his students "invited" him to resign at the end of his first year. After Keney declined their invitation, the board dismissed him in 1854.

The dismissal of Professor Keeney and the resignation of Albert Bledsoe in 1854 created two vacancies on the faculty. The board appointed Frederick Barnard to Bledsoe's chair of mathematics and astronomy and Francis J. Mettaner to the chair of chemistry. When Professor Mettaner arrived on the campus in the fall of 1854, he was so disappointed in the chemistry laboratory and the lack of scientific equipment that he declined the appointment, leaving the university without a professor of chemistry for the 1854–55 academic year. In 1855 the board of trustees appointed Edward C. Boynton, "an accomplished chemist but a profane swearer," to the vacancy. Boynton was a West Point graduate and remained on the faculty until 1861 when the board dismissed him for "a want of attachment" to the Southern Confederacy.

Following Millington's resignation and the unfortunate appointment of Professor Keeney, the board established a new chair of agricultural and geological sciences independent of the chair of chemistry. Wailes applied for the new chair but the board again passed over him, this time for Lewis Harper, whose appointment was to prove even more troublesome than Professor Keeney's. Though disappointed that he did not get the appointment, Wailes completed the draft of his agricultural survey and stayed on long enough to see it published in the fall of 1854. John D. Easter, the first University of Mississippi professor to hold a Ph.D., briefly filled the position of assistant professor of geology. Easter stayed only six months, resigning on July 9, 1855. The circumstances of his resignation are not clear, but it seems likely that Easter could not work effectively with Professor Harper. After Professor Easter's resignation, the board authorized Barnard, who was then in the North attending a scientific meeting, to employ an assistant professor of geology. In August 1855, Barnard offered the position to Eugene Woldemar Hilgard, who immediately accepted and arrived on the campus in September. Hilgard joined Harper on a whirlwind tour of the state in preparation for Hilgard's field work.

Professor Harper, who was sometimes vituperative toward his students and uncooperative with his colleagues, became a disruptive element at the university. Harper accused Hilgard of not filing his field reports, thus preventing him from completing the survey on time. Hilgard accused Harper of plagiarizing the field notes he did submit. When Harper requested a special allocation from the board of trustees for the purchase of a telescope, Frederick Barnard, the professor of astronomy, considered the request an encroachment into his academic domain, and their relationship degenerated into an ugly public affair. Mrs. Harper was especially bitter toward Barnard and criticized him publicly. Some members of the faculty accused Harper, who claimed to have an LL.D. from an unspecified institution, of falsifying his credentials and plagiarizing the work of a colleague. These are the two inexcusable trespasses in academia, and Harper's colleagues charged him with both. A professor does not have to be proven guilty; the accusation alone can end a career. Eventually, the board of trustees dismissed Harper and detached the geological survey from the university.

Although the university's introduction of applied sciences into the curriculum was a failure, its venture into the social sciences was highly successful. "It is well known," Jacob Thompson told the Mississippi legislature in 1854, "that for a period of a thousand years the Bar has been the road to the titles [and] the power of the politician." Unfortunately, there was no southern road leading to the titles and the power. "Our ambitious youth go to the East for instruction in this department," Thompson told a chamber full of politicians, "for it is to be found there alone." The University of Mississippi should have "a professorship of law [but] not of law alone." The philosophy of government and the nature of the federal union should be taught along with law, he said, because instruction "in the science of government we think of high importance to the Southern youth." Though hardly necessary in those times of bitter sectional strife, Thompson reminded the lawmakers that "we live in a confederacy of states" and the "political relationships of the states to each other are looked at in somewhat different light according to the geographic points of view." Couching his call for funds within the framework of states' rights, Thompson found great favor with the legislature, which granted his appeal and created the Deep South's first state-supported law school.

The board of trustees offered the chair of law to Edward C. Wilkinson, an eminent jurist and a member of the board, but he declined. The board then appointed Caswell R. Clifton, a prominent Jackson attorney, but he, too, declined. On its third try, the board offered the position to William Forbes Stearns, who accepted the appointment and served as law professor until the Civil War. In 1860 the board added a second law professor. That appointment went to James F. Trotter, a former United States senator and former justice of the Mississippi High Court of Errors and Appeals.

In the fall of 1854, the university admitted its first law class, consisting of seven students. The enrollment increased to twenty-two in the second year, fell to seventeen in 1857, then increased to thirty-five in 1860. No previous academic training or entrance examination was required for admission to the law department, but applicants had to be nineteen years old and of "good moral character." International and constitutional law was transferred from the collegiate course to the law department, and all seniors "recited in those studies" to the law professor. Law students had access to the university library "upon the same terms as the undergraduate; but in all other respects [the law department] shall be disconnected with the college, save as to moral government." Professor Forbes taught his classes and maintained the school's meager library in a building on the Oxford square leased from William A. Avent.

In 1857 Professor Stearns addressed a circular letter to the state's approximately six hundred lawyers encouraging them to contribute to the school's library. "The books of law are annually multiplying with such vast rapidity," he wrote, "that soon none but a Croesus can afford himself a legal library, and only Methuselahs find leisure to pursue them all." More books were needed, he said, to aid his students "through the mazes of the legal labyrinth." Students who successfully navigated the mazes of the two-year course received a bachelor of law degree and, after 1857, were exempted from the state bar examination. In spite of this advantage, the law course did not supersede the apprenticeship system, and in its early years the law school trained more politicians than practitioners.

Although the university prospered under President Longstreet's leadership, and he was revered by his students and the state's protestant clergy, he eventually fell out of favor with the board of trustees. A major source of the board's displeasure with Longstreet was his frequent absences from the university and the neglect of his teaching duties. Longstreet considered his ministerial duties to be as important as his academic responsibilities, if not more so. One historian described Longstreet as "the Methodist minister who doubled as President of the University of Mississippi." Both Longstreet and his old friend Waddel, also a minister, were frequently absent from the university on church business. Their persistent absences prompted the board of trustees to adopt a policy in January 1854 stating that "absences from the college can only by justified in cases of absolute necessity." The new policy required the faculty to report the number of days they were absent to the board treasurer before receiving their salaries. The treasurer deducted ten dollars from a professor's salary for each unexcused absence.

On July 11, 1854, the faculty petitioned the board of trustees to repeal or modify its policy on absences. Governor John J. McRae, a member of the board of trustees, moved to repeal the ten-dollar penalty for each absence in favor of a statement that the primary obligation of every faculty member was to the university. Under McRae's policy, faculty members would still report the number of absences to the board treasurer. Isaac Davis, who had supported the appointment of ministers to the faculty, favored outright repeal of the policy. Edward C. Wilkinson wanted to strengthen the policy by adding a statement that excessive absences "would be sufficient cause for removal from their professorship." To the consternation of the faculty and President Longstreet, the policy's most serious offender, no substantive change was made and the board's policy on absences remained effective. When the issue of faculty absences was first raised, James Howry, the secretary of the board and an Oxford resident who knew Longstreet well, advised Governor McRae to disregard Longstreet's threat to resign because he was making too much money to leave. Longstreet's biographer wrote of his years in Oxford, "True to his fixed custom, Longstreet did not let slip any good chances of turning an honest dollar."

In his 1855 annual report to the board, President Longstreet advised the trustees that "the law which requires the faculty to report their absences from College" was "odious" to the faculty, who considered it a denigration of their status as professors. Longstreet again threatened to resign if the board did not modify the policy. He also complained about the authoritative and overbearing attitude the board assumed in its relationship with the faculty. The trustees did not "feel it obligatory to make any response" to President Longstreet's complaints, but they were "not unwilling to give expression to their views on the subject presented." After presenting a detailed explanation of how the legislature intended for the board to govern the university, and not to be "the mere automata supposed by President Longstreet," the board relented and repealed the policy Longstreet had placed in "so odious a light." The board did so "to cultivate relations of cordiality and harmony" between themselves and the faculty.

The dispute over faculty absences was only one of the sources of increasing tension between President Longstreet and the university's board of trustees. Longstreet and his son-in-law Lamar, who were high-ranking members of the states' rights Democratic Party, engaged in rhetorical warfare with Mississippi's pro-Union Whig Party and its short-lived successor, the American Party, whose members were called "Know Nothings." The American Party was a secretive political organization whose members responded to questions by saying they knew nothing about the party's platform or candidates. The American Party espoused strong nativist principles that often found expression in anti-Catholic and anti-immigrant sentiments, especially among Southern Methodists. One historian has estimated that seven of ten Mississippi Methodists were Know Nothings or active sympathizers. The most outspoken Know Nothing in Mississippi was William Winans, a popular Methodist minister, sometime politician, and a "remorseless anti-Catholic." President Longstreet was one of the few prominent Methodists unsympathetic to the nativist principles of the Know Nothings.

In 1854 President Longstreet advised the university's graduating class to reject the Know Nothings, and he called on the Methodist Church to condemn the American Party as both unchristian and un-American. In a lengthy newspaper article, Reverend Winans condemned Longstreet's proposal in the strongest terms, saying if the church took a stand on a purely political issue the democratic process "would be poisoned by the union of church and state." Longstreet fired back in an open letter to Winans published in the *Memphis Daily Appeal.* After recounting a number of assaults on foreigners and the bombing of several Catholic churches, Longstreet said to Reverend Winans, "Papal supremacy would be a luxury compared to your government, brother, if this be a specimen of it."

Winans and other members of the secret organization, many writing under pseudonyms, stepped up their attacks on both Longstreet and the university. The *Yazoo City Banner* wrote that Longstreet held the "Chair of Broken Languages" at the university. The criticism of President Longstreet prompted the alumni association, established in 1852, to pass a resolution in 1855 defending the university against the "unfounded and malignant slanders . . . promulgated by certain newspapers." At the 1856 meeting of the association, J. B. Herring moved that the resolution adopted the previous year in support of Longstreet and the university be "re-enacted and spread upon the minutes."

The Know Nothings assailed President Longstreet "from all sides and in all modes." They referred to him in the most demeaning terms, calling him a "dotard and fool," likened him to a clown, charged him with "falsehood and turpitude," and accused him of indoctrinating the university's students. Longstreet met every charge with a countercharge. "They tell me," he wrote, "as a minister of the gospel I have no right to meddle in politics. I reply then that the hundreds of preachers who are in should come out of it." President Longstreet also accused the Know Nothing Party of "whispering the students of my charge into midnight gatherings, and there binding them by oath upon oath to everlasting fidelity to its own creed."

The spectacle of the president of the state university trading epithets with a secret society was an unseemly sight, even to Mississippi's states' rights Democratic Governor John J. McRae. Longstreet's political entanglements, among other things, convinced Governor McRae that the state had conceded too much independence to the university's self-perpetuating board of trustees and had virtually forfeited its role in the management of the university. As a remedy, the governor recommended the establishment of a board of visitors, in addition to the board of trustees. Since the university was a state institution, he reasoned, it should be subject to the visitation of the state through its regularly appointed agents. A board of visitors would have a beneficial effect on the management of the university, and its attendance at public examinations would encourage students to better prepare themselves. Finally, the governor said, the affairs of the university "would be brought into public notice" by the various reports a board of visitors would publish from time to time.

The university's charter did not require the governing board to make any kind of public report or otherwise account for its actions except in an annual report to the state legislature. As a consequence, news of the university disseminated by word of mouth, editorial commentary, Sunday morning sermons, campaign speeches, gossip, rumor, and innuendo. Governor McRae believed that annual published reports issued by a board of visitors would reduce the damage done by rumor and innuendo, some of which he admitted was calculated by its enemies to undermine the university. Governor McRae's proposal for a board of visitors, which the legislature rejected, was the first effort in a continuing search for a structure of governance that would protect Mississippi's public colleges and universities from political intrusion but would also make them responsive to the body politic.

Governor McRae's effort to expand the role of the state in the university's affairs was followed six months later by President Longstreet's resignation on June 10, 1854, but there seems to be no connection between the two circumstances. President Longstreet was sixty-six years old, financially independent and tired of the bickering. He told his family and friends that he wanted to spend his last years enjoying the quiet life of a country gentleman. Longstreet's chief antagonist among the faculty was the ambitious Barnard, an Old Line Whig, who may have undermined Longstreet with the Whig members of the board of trustees. No doubt some trustees would have been glad to be rid of Longstreet, but the realization that he had stabilized the university after President Holmes's dismissal and that the university had prospered under his leadership made the board cautious about starting over again with a new president. When President Longstreet tendered his resignation, the board unanimously rejected it. After Longstreet declined their request to reconsider, the board accepted his resignation and awarded Longstreet an honorary doctor of divinity degree.

Chapter 4

UNIVERSITAS SCIENTIARUM, 1856–1861

I have done some work here which will not die with me.

Chancellor Frederick Barnard, 1859

President Longstreet's resignation excited "a great scramble" for the presidency. The Methodists supported Reverend George W. Carter. The Presbyterians thought Reverend John Waddel should be and would be appointed. The Episcopalians endorsed Reverend Frederick Barnard, the parish priest of St. Peter's in Oxford. Though small in number, the Episcopalians dominated the board of trustees, which gave Barnard an advantage over Carter and Waddel. The primary obstacle to Barnard's appointment was Lewis Harper, professor of agricultural and geological science. As the board was considering various candidates, Harper published a pamphlet questioning Barnard's credentials as a scientist and accusing him of immoral conduct. Barnard was in New York buying laboratory equipment, on his way to Glasgow to attend a scientific meeting, when he learned of Longstreet's resignation and Harper's accusations. L. Q. C. Lamar and Eugene Hilgard telegraphed Barnard in New York telling him of Harper's pamphlet and urging him to return to Oxford as soon as possible. They concealed their identity by inverting the letters of their last names.

Harper's attack so angered Barnard that he sent a letter of resignation to Jacob Thompson, chairman of the board of trustees and a parishioner at St. Peter's, with instructions to submit it to the board of trustees if they did not elect him president. If the board did not elect him, he told Thompson, that would be tantamount to an endorsement of Harper's charges against him. Barnard also wrote Hilgard lamenting that he was "born under an unlucky star." He had not completed the purchase of the laboratory equipment, and now he had to cancel his trip to Europe. Barnard assured Hilgard that he would never hear another recitation at the university if he were not elected president.

On August 19, 1856, the board met in Oxford to elect a successor to President Longstreet. Several recommendations were "laid before the Board." The board also received a copy of Professor Harper's pamphlet attacking Barnard. After much discussion, the board elected Barnard, dismissed Harper, detached the geological survey from the university, and declined the resignation of Professor Waddel, which he presented in heat and haste following the election of Barnard. The next July, the board accepted Waddel's resignation.

Frederick Augustus Porter Barnard was born in Sheffield, Massachusetts, on May 5, 1809. Under the influence of his mother, Barnard developed a fondness for music. He played the piano and the flute, enjoyed singing, and even tried his hand at song writing and poetry. While at Yale, where he graduated second in his class in 1828, Barnard drifted away from his Congregationalist upbringing and formed an enduring attachment to the Episcopal Church. Barnard's first teaching position was at the Hartford Grammar School. In his memoirs Barnard recalled his first day: "Through all this distress of time I can still recall the feeling of painful diffidence with which I stood up before the little handful of small boys to whom I had undertaken to speak in the tone of a master. I have since addressed great and imposing audiences [of] every variety of age, intelligence and culture; but I have never under any circumstances felt again the inward tremor with which I presented myself the first time before that squad of boys."

By 1832 Barnard had decided teaching was not a career option because of his severe hearing impairment. He spent the next six years working with his friend Harvey Peet at the New York State Institute, a school for the speech and hearing impaired. Though he was doubtful about his future, Barnard was intellectually active during his years at the institute. He published several articles on hearing impairment and developed methods of teaching concepts with sign language. In his writings he assaulted the lingering superstitions about deafness "in the present enlightened era." He especially criticized the theologians who opposed, on theological grounds, the L'Eppe method of signing.

In the autumn of 1837, Barnard went to Yale to use the library of his friend and mentor Professor Benjamin Silliman. On the way back to New York, Barnard met Basil Manly, president of the University of Alabama. President Manly had been to Providence to visit Francis Wayland, president of Brown University and one of the nation's distinguished figures in higher education. Manly had come to see Wayland for advice on how to reorganize the University of Alabama, which had recently closed following a student rebellion. As a result of this chance meeting, Manly offered Barnard the chair of mathematics and natural philosophy at the University of Alabama and Barnard accepted.

During his sixteen years at Alabama, Barnard became a charter member of America's emerging scientific community. His writings appeared in prestigious journals. His experiments with photography and his attendance at scientific meetings brought him in contact with the best minds in America. Barnard remembered those years as some of the happiest of his life, but they were not all serene. During the first year, President Manly wrote to a friend that Barnard "wants dignity, and more serious still, he is dull of hearing." Manly presumed the board of trustees would dismiss Barnard at its next meeting.

The main problem between the president and his star professor was Barnard's penchant for partying and drinking. Barnard was an exuberant person by nature and strong drink "unclothed his eccentricities and led to hilarious behavior." President Manly's journal contains several references to Barnard's binges. On one occasion he wrote, "Barnard was very drunk at a party at Judge Peter Martin's." On another he wrote, "Barnard, with Barr and Walker, spent the governor's fast day in a drunken frolic in Barnard's house. They got so drunk by [lunch] time that they could not eat. They slept till sun down, I have heard." Barnard, according to his biographer, had a low tolerance for alcohol. A letter from President Manly and two faculty colleagues seems to corroborate that presumption: "We implore you, by the concord subsisting among us . . . forbear; for God's sake forbear! You can have no safety but in entire and perpetual abstinence from every thing that can intoxicate." But Barnard did not forbear, and Manly's journal would from time to time include a notice that Barnard was drunk again.

What Manly's admonitions could not do for Barnard, Margaret McMurray could. Born in England and reared in Ohio, Margaret McMurray came to Tuscaloosa for an extended visit with a cousin who was a social friend of Barnard's. She was twenty-three, and Barnard was thirty-six. After a short romance, they married on December 30, 1847. The new Mrs. Barnard persuaded her husband to join the Sons of Temperance and mend his ways. Strangely, Barnard, an Episcopalian, asked Manly, a Baptist minister, to perform the nuptials. Perhaps it was a gesture of atonement for Barnard, and Manly must have "rejoiced to know that the wanderer in the roadless land of sin had come home." Marriage and middle age sobered and quieted Barnard but did not diminish his energy.

In the summer of 1854, Wilson G. Richardson, Barnard's former student at the University of Alabama who then held the chair of Latin at the University of Mississippi, informed Barnard that the chairs of chemistry and mathematics were vacant and urged him to apply for one of them. Although Barnard says in his memoirs that he had no intention of seeking either position, he made a long and arduous journey from Tuscaloosa to Oxford. He made the trip as a favor to a friend who was seeking the chair of chemistry. Barnard was so surprised and flattered by the attention he received at Oxford, especially from the board of trustees, that he accepted the chair of mathematics, astronomy, and natural philosophy. His decision to move to Mississippi delighted President Manly, who wrote a friend, "One great incubus thrown off—Barnard is gone." But his decision disappointed Margaret, who was happily situated at Tuscaloosa among her relatives and her expanding circle of friends. One of Mrs. Barnard's objections to moving to Oxford was that Mississippi had repudiated its state bonds in 1841. She told Barnard she did not want to rear her children in a "repudiating state." As it turned out, the Barnards had no children and throughout their long and loving marriage Margaret's "only pride was in her husband."

The Barnards packed up their chattels, his books and papers, and sent them down river four hundred miles to Mobile, by sea two hundred miles to New Orleans, up the Mississippi five hundred miles to Memphis, and then by wagon to Oxford. They traveled by horse and buggy from Tuscaloosa. Barnard's journey was uncomfortable but not because of the hardships of travel through what he called the "primeval forest" of north Mississippi. Recalling the trip years later, he wrote, "We made our trip without accident, but at the places where we stopped it was not encouraging to me to hear the professor whose place I was to fill [Albert Bledsoe] constantly mentioned as a man whose loss to the University was simply irreparable."

When Barnard arrived in Oxford, there was no faculty housing available so he and Mrs. Barnard took rooms in the Butler House, and he "plunged" into his work. He would "console the authorities for the loss of my predecessor." Barnard was linked to Oxford by more than his residence in the village. Soon after his arrival Bishop William Mercer Green, who would become a lifelong friend, ordained Barnard into the Episcopal priesthood. The ordination took place in Holly Springs, because there was no Episcopal church in Oxford. Before St. Peter's was built, Barnard and his flock met in the Presbyterian church at the sufferance of Reverend John Waddel. Barnard's association with the Episcopal Church brought him in contact, he said, with the "best class of people" in Mississippi, such as Jacob Thompson, president of the board of trustees.

After his appointment as president in 1856, Barnard received the congratulations of his parishioner, Jacob Thompson, who considered his election a "signal triumph" over the "combination against you," and the condolences of his bishop, who wondered if Barnard really knew what he was getting himself into. Bishop Green told Barnard the story of a man recently offered a college presidency. "If it should please God," the man said, "to give me my choice among all the occupations of the world, I would beg him to make me anything but an old stage-horse or the president of a college."

For several months after Barnard took office, Lewis Harper (who was now the state geologist) and the "Waddelites" (the disgruntled supporters of John Waddel) continued to circulate rumors about Barnard's moral character and his Yankee ideas. The Methodists were disappointed that one of their most popular preachers was passed over for an Episcopal priest. The Presbyterians felt slighted because they were not represented on the faculty after Waddel resigned. The Baptists, who were still steaming over the dismissal of Reverend Keeney, became even more upset when one of their favorites, Reverend William Carey Crane, was passed over for an appointment to the chair of ethics and metaphysics. To the protestant clergy, Barnard was a secular president of a godless institution, and they accused him of emphasizing academic excellence over moral character. Most of them agreed with the old-time college president who complained, "At college we tend to exaggerate the importance of the intellect." Despite the carping and complaining, Barnard devoted his every effort to making the University of Mississippi one of the premier institutions of higher learning in America. A man of great ambition and enormous energy, Barnard once compared himself to "the stick that was so crooked it could not lie still."

Barnard's creative response to the problem of student discipline was one of his most important legacies. In the 1850s few collegiate institutions offered their students any recreational or extracurricular activities. Instead, colleges corralled young boys away from home and out from under parental control for the first time into crowded dormitories, rousted them at sunrise, and placed them under the constant surveillance of their professors, who invaded their privacy at least once daily. Barnard, like his predecessor Longstreet, opposed the dormitory system. As president of Emory College, Longstreet converted the steward's hall into a classroom, closed the dormitories, and took boarders into his own home. When John Waddel became president of LaGrange College in Tennessee, he, too, abandoned the dormitory system, calling it an "unnatural assembly of immature young boys." But tradition prevailed at the University of Mississippi, and the board of trustees, citing the lack of available rooms in the village of Oxford, required all students to live on the campus. Under a new set of rules President Barnard implemented, dormitory students could no longer bring their personal slaves to the university. In lieu of that privilege, the university assessed each dormitory student a fee for servant hire that entitled the student "to the attendance of a servant to sweep his room, make his bed, carry his water and wood" and make the morning fires. Students could not "demand of any college servant the performance of any service not here specified."

Especially obnoxious to Barnard was the board's mandate requiring daily room inspection, and he often skipped his turn. When the board chastised Barnard for shirking this duty, he admitted that he did not conduct daily room inspection because he did not "believe in its utility," and he complained that his "police duties" interfered with his teaching and research. "The best instruction was often sacrificed in a vain attempt to secure good government," Barnard said, "under a defective system." Collegiate authorities took the "March Devil" that "invades every college in the spring" far too seriously, he believed, and student discipline was much too strict. In all of nature, he said, and especially in human nature, force is repelled by a corresponding force. Barnard attributed student pranks to the "giddy impulses of youth," not to a fountain of depravity deep within mankind. He believed students should be governed like the French, as Napoleon suggested, by "a hand of iron in a glove of velvet."

In the classroom, Barnard's friendliness and flexibility won him the devotion of his students. He preferred their respect and affection to their fear and dread. As president of the university, Barnard installed a firm but fair system of student discipline. He also understood that college students needed some form of recreation, a way of working off their energy, and a respite from the drudgery of their studies. In November 1857, Barnard, with the support of James Ventress, persuaded the board of trustees to fund the construction of a gymnasium "for the encouragement of healthful bodily exercise." The University of Mississippi was one of the few collegiate institutions in antebellum America to provide such a facility to its students.

Barnard also gave his active support to the university's literary societies and their joint publication, the *Mississippi University Magazine.* Barnard fully understood how important those organizations were in the development of a student's intellectual powers. Of his own days at Yale, he wrote, "No part of my training at Yale College seems to me to have been more beneficial than that which I derived from the practice of writing and speaking in the literary society to which I belonged." Phi Sigma inducted Barnard as an honorary member one month after he joined the faculty in 1854.

Two articles, one published and one rejected by the *Mississippi University Magazine,* speak to President Barnard's relationship with his students. In the published article the student magazine called him a "genius of the most versatile talents" and wondered "whether to admire most his native strength of intellect, or that incessant labor by which he has elevated and adorned its superior powers." The magazine also praised him for "endeavoring to infuse into the minds of the students a love for... profound critical scholarship and high toned unblemished moral character." A student editor refused to publish an article "on account of its bitter vituperations against northern men." On the eve of the Civil War, when disunionists directed their "bitter vituperations" at Barnard, the pampered sons of the Southern gentry came to his defense with letters, petitions, and other expressions of support. One of them persuaded his father, a member of the board of trustees, to change his mind and support Barnard's reorganization of the university. Chancellor Barnard said years later that he could not have made it "without my boys."

Barnard understood that student discipline was more than just being fair and firm. He saw a correlation between misbehavior and admission standards. Barnard formed his admissions philosophy during his days as a tutor at Yale. Along with other tutors, he conducted the entrance examinations for prospective students. From that experience Barnard formed a lifelong educational tenet: "[Y]oung men should never be accepted into institutions of higher education conditionally, or on a half-way admission." He said, "I had as leave cut my tongue out as to send a poor boy back to his anxious parents, after grinding him for three hours in the bark mill of examination, but then, you know, if I didn't do it, somebody else would, as the grog-shop people say."

The first catalog issued under Barnard's administration announced that the University of Mississippi was under new leadership, and the rules had changed. The most dramatic change was a new, more demanding admissions policy. As stated in the catalog, the "frequency with which young men desiring to become members of the University are found to be but imperfectly possessed of even the very moderate attainments required for their admission" prompted the new standards. In the future, students must meet the most rigorous standards for admission. Barnard stated categorically that there would be no exceptions, because that "only serves to open the way for a multitude of applications for similar indulgence." Barnard considered the freshman year, as it was then organized, below the level of collegiate work and announced that admission standards would gradually be raised until "all the studies heretofore taught during the Freshman year shall be excluded from the college course." He also discouraged the admission of irregular or partial course students and decreed they would not be "entitled to graduation."

These new admission requirements caused a precipitous enrollment decline, from 285 in 1856 to 177 in 1858. Barnard was a dreamer, but he was also a realist, and he compromised his admissions philosophy to compete for the small pool of students in Mississippi. If he did not take them, they would go to the small denominational colleges. He would then hear more criticism that the university was in decline because he was a Yankee, and Mississippi's gentry would not expose their sons to his abolitionist notions. Under these circumstances, Barnard designed an admissions policy that admitted unprepared students and allowed them to take courses and participate in all other activities; then when they were adequately prepared, they could matriculate and become members of the student body in full standing. Even after the establishment of a preparatory school in Oxford, Barnard continued this system of probationary admission. Barnard also introduced a forerunner of the modern grading system. Under this policy, faculty members sent letters, at "convenient intervals," to the parents of all undergraduates stating the academic standing of each student, his class attendance record, and the number of demerits he had accumulated thus far in the session. Barnard's new rules also made final written examinations mandatory in all courses.

The new academic regulations Barnard promulgated in 1857 extended far beyond student discipline and admissions. They went to the core of college governance, and Barnard achieved them only after great travail. The university's board of trustees, like most antebellum college boards, held absolute authority over the institutions they governed, and they exercised that authority with a jealous regard. Barnard complained that the board had authority over the most trivial detail of college government, even to the assignment of meeting rooms for the literary societies. During the first year of his administration, Barnard was criticized for a general lack of discipline and for misbehavior among the students. Parents and students also complained about faculty absences from recitations, the generally poor condition of the campus with its muddy walkways, unkempt and ill-equipped laboratories and lecture rooms, the food in the steward's hall, and the difficulty of obtaining firewood and water for the dormitories. Barnard did not deny the legitimacy of these complaints. He did maintain, however, that he was without the power to address them. He had responsibility but no authority. Like most college presidents in antebellum America, Barnard was a surrogate for the board of trustees, which held the actual power. President Longstreet tried several times, without much success, to persuade the board to relinquish or at least share some of its authority with the president and the faculty.

At the July 10, 1857, board meeting, Barnard submitted a draft for a new code of university regulations along with a memorial from the faculty "praying for various reforms" in the governance of the university. After discussing the recommendations, which the trustees considered too sweeping and radical, the board summoned the faculty to a late afternoon meeting at the Masonic Temple in Oxford. Following an unpleasant confrontation with the faculty, the board rejected Barnard's recommendations and ordered a reprinting of the existing rules and regulations.

President Barnard was sensitive to the board's rejection of his recommendations and their treatment puzzled him. After that eight-day board meeting ended, he wrote Hilgard, "there were three or four star chamber days." He went on, "Before I was President I was influential [but now] they treat me as they did Longstreet. If I hear from them at all, it is in the form of some official interrogatory, behind which lurks some contingent censure." As usual, when he did not get his way, Barnard began looking for another position. Less than a month after this "star chamber" meeting, his brother John Barnard wrote, "I know how you yearn for the north," but "I don't think you ought to leave Mississippi." President Barnard was interested in a job in the patent office. His brother discouraged him from seeking that position because it was a patronage appointment, and he could not count on it for "any length of time." A short time later, Barnard applied for what he thought was a vacant position at the Smithsonian Institution in Washington. "I feel a little ridiculous," he confessed to Hilgard. Barnard had misread a news article and thought the person holding the position had died; it was the man's wife who had died. Barnard considered several other positions, but none of them materialized. The most promising was the presidency of St. John's College in Annapolis, Maryland. Although Mrs. Barnard prayed that he would get the appointment, he was ill and unable to make the trip to Maryland for an interview.

At a called meeting of the board of trustees on November 5, 1857, Barnard again submitted a recommendation for sweeping reform in the governance of the university. In a stunning turn of events, the board approved virtually all of his recommendations, and ordered the printing of a thousand copies of the new rules. The board's reversal was due in part to Barnard's perseverance, his persuasive powers and possibly to his threat of resignation. In addition, Governor John J. McRae, who was now the ex officio chairman of the board, supported his reforms. The influence of James Alexander Ventress, the most learned member of the board, was also crucial in the board's reversal. The board was in such an expansive and generous mood at the November meeting that they authorized a gymnasium for the students, an electric clock for Barnard, and a "suitable stable" for each faculty member. After the November board meeting, an exuberant Barnard wrote Hilgard, "They gave us money to buy books, provided for a gymnasium, public clock, stables, etc—I am beginning to think we will make this institution something after all."

But Barnard could not be content just to make something of the university; he would make it a great university. During the winter months of 1857, he drafted a comprehensive plan to transform the University of Mississippi into "a true university in the largest acceptation of that term." He had been working on this essay for several years and was now ready to place it before the board of trustees and the people of Mississippi. In March 1858 he published his now famous *Letter to the Honorable Board of Trustees of the University of Mississippi.* In this 112-page essay, Barnard sketched the details of a *universitas scientiarum,* an institution that would include all the branches of science, medicine, agriculture, law, classical studies, civil and political history, and oriental learning. The new University of Mississippi, Barnard said, would stand in solemn defiance of the monarch's criticism of democracy "that letters wither [and] science perishes beneath the mephitic breath of republican institutions."

The primary function of the American collegiate system in the 1850s was to discipline the mind, not to disseminate information. A rapidly changing world, and one of increasing complexity, Barnard said, demanded that colleges and universities not only "diffuse knowledge among men" but by original investigation "add to the priceless mass." To meet that imperative, Barnard would radically reorganize the University of Mississippi. President Barnard's design for a *universitas scientiarum* was not original. Nor was he the first to seek its implementation. Columbia College had already adopted a similar plan, and Francis Wayland, Philip Lindsley, Bishop Leonidas K. Polk, William Mitchell, and others had discussed the need for reforms in the collegiate system for several years. Barnard's design was different because he modeled his new university on the German universities, an influence no doubt of his friend Hilgard, who at the age of twenty earned a summa cum laude Ph.D. at Heidelberg University. Barnard addressed his letter to the board of trustees, but it was really to the people of Mississippi. He published the letter six months before the board's July meeting, and Barnard's allies and friends of the university circulated it throughout the state. The sweeping dimensions of his recommendations dazzled most Mississippians, though few would actually read his *Letter.* Some, he said, could not be paid to read it.

Barnard conceded that some might object to the cost of the reorganization because Mississippi was a young state, "in her infancy," and could not "undertake labors as have marked the history of other communities . . . in the maturity of their powers." To liberate the people from their habit of thinking slow and small, Barnard first praised and then prodded them. He reminded Mississippians that their forebears were "not a class of ignorant and needy adventurers who planted themselves upon these fertile valleys." They were intelligent and enlightened men, and no frontier community anywhere, he continued, was "more respectable in an intellectual point of view." Having appealed to their pride of place and past, Barnard then linked the future of Mississippi to the fortunes of the university. "Regarding the University," Barnard said, "as its own intellectual position is assumed at a higher or lower level, the repute in which the state itself is held abroad will also be higher or lower."

To justify the need for his new university, Barnard advanced a devastating critique of the existing collegiate system in Mississippi. "If we trust the testimony of our presses," he said, "we shall be slow to admit that there are anywhere to be found educational advantages superior to those which we possess." The state's press and public officials had no disposition to test the "claims or merits of our institutions" and that, he said, had a "pernicious" effect on the state's collegiate system. If the colleges can "so cheaply win the guerdon of superlative praise," they will not strive for that "substantial merit which nobody appreciates." The practice of "universal laudation" of the state's colleges by the Mississippi press, Barnard said, misleads the public mind to presume a merit that is "more imaginary than real" and exempts the institutions from "that outside pressure which is the most effectual stimulus to internal improvement."

It was obvious to Barnard, and he thought it should be obvious to the university's board of trustees, that the thoughtful citizens of Mississippi were "disgusted with hyperbole" and were "anxious for a little honest fact." Many people saw through the "universal laudation" and realized they must send their children out of state for an adequate education. The trustees, therefore, should provide them and their sons a first-rate institution. If the board would implement his proposals, he promised them, the University of Mississippi would soon rank among the finest institutions in America. Barnard ended his letter with an assurance to the trustees that a true university "will be your noblest monument."

Barnard's letter stirred deep resentment in the college community, especially at the church schools, and among the state press, which he accused of misleading the people. Those two powerful constituencies reacted quickly, but not calmly, to Barnard's criticism. Both groups "gave vent to their spleen by heaping denunciatory epithets upon the University." The evangelical clergy renewed their charges that the university was a "citadel of atheism" and the press called it "a hotbed of abolitionism."

Two months after Barnard published his *Letter,* he journeyed to New Haven to deliver the annual alumni address at his alma mater. This was a signal honor for Barnard, one he cherished for the rest of his life. The honor of addressing Yale's illustrious alumni was enhanced by the special recognition given to the University of Mississippi's law professor, William Forbes Stearns, Barnard's friend and ally. Yale College awarded Professor Stearns an LL.D., primarily because of Barnard's glowing tribute to Stearns's intellect. In a letter recommending him for the degree, Barnard said that Stearns, who had no formal schooling beyond the primary level, was the best-read man he had met in the South. Embarrassed by his lack of a collegiate education, Stearns at first declined the honor, but Barnard persuaded him to accept it.

When President and Mrs. Barnard returned to the campus on May 17, 1858, he learned that some of his colleagues on the faculty had advanced several objections to his *universitas scientiarum,* and accused him of using the university to advance his own career. Only Boynton and Stearns endorsed Barnard's proposal to remake the university. Barnard was indeed ambitious, and there was something of the academic entrepreneur in him. Like most men of great talent and vision, Barnard was impatient with lesser men who would not enlarge their vision or concede the limits of their talent. He was not at all reluctant to point out what he considered faults and weaknesses in his colleagues. In addition to the criticism of his academic reforms, rumors questioning Barnard's soundness on slavery and states' rights were circulating around the state.

This was the opening salvo of a thunderous attack on President Barnard and his plan to reorganize the University of Mississippi.

A controversial appointment to the chair of ethics and metaphysics generated some of the dissension on the campus. William Carey Crane, a Baptist minister, "made an active campaign" for the chair. The Baptists, who were not represented on the faculty, thought they were "entitled" to the chair. The appointment, however, went to Reverend George W. Carter, a popular Methodist minister and one of Barnard's rivals for the presidency in 1856. Professor Carter soon aligned himself with J. D. Stevenson, editor of the Oxford *Mercury,* and Henry Branham, an Oxford physician who accused Barnard of being at least a "free soiler," if not an outright abolitionist. Wilson G. Richardson, professor of Latin and Barnard's former student, was also a member of this coterie.

The sweeping proposals President Barnard recommended in his letter to the board dazzled the trustees, who were predisposed by years of defending the status quo to reject it. A small group of dissidents led by Isaac Davis criticized Barnard for making his letter public and accused him of trying to dictate board policy. The board as a whole, however, endorsed the spirit of Barnard's letter and appointed a committee to devise a plan for implementing his recommendations. The board also authorized the printing of a thousand copies of the essay. During the summer and fall of 1858, Barnard's letter was discussed with interest and intensity in the pulpit, in the press, and on the hustings. In its annual report to the legislature, the board of trustees stated, "Finally, it can not be questioned that the sense of the people of Mississippi favors and demands the elevation of the University of Mississippi to a school of universal instruction."

Realizing that the state's secondary school system could not produce enough adequately prepared students to meet the admission standards of his *universitas scientiarum,* Barnard asked the board to establish a primary and secondary department at the university. Barnard would build his own education factory, and good students, eligible for admission to the university, would be its product. He also asked for funds to establish a normal department (a teacher training program), which he said would be a "grand thing for the state." The board was amenable to his recommendations but considered it financially inexpedient to establish a normal school and a primary department without additional state appropriations. The board authorized Barnard and the Oxford board members to establish a preparatory department, however, if they could do so within the university's existing budget. Eventually, several university alumni established a preparatory school in Oxford, but it was a private venture and not associated with the university.

The board of trustees also declined Barnard's request for schools of engineering and agriculture. The board held "itself in readiness to do so whenever circumstances may seem to render it practicable [but] in view of the present pecuniary means of the University" it was "inexpedient" to establish the two new schools. The board had already committed the only funds at its disposal, student tuition fees and a twenty-thousand-dollar annual appropriation, to the purchase of scientific equipment and the construction of several new buildings.

The board was, however, amenable to Barnard's recommendations that did not require large additional expenditures. The trustees allowed him to establish a chair of pure mathematics, independent of the chair of physics and astronomy. Professor Jordan Phipps, an assistant professor of mathematics, was appointed to that position. Barnard was also allowed to create a chair of English literature, which was perhaps the first in the South and one of the first in the nation. Professor William D. Moore held the first chair of English literature at the University of Mississippi. This four-year program included a study of Anglo-Saxon during the sophomore year and English history and literature in the senior year. Grammar, elocution, and composition were taught in the freshman and junior years.

The board also granted Barnard's request to change his title from president to chancellor. Barnard believed the term chancellor was more prestigious, and its use would be advantageous for the person who held the office, for the university, and for the state at large. Though he never made the trip, Chancellor Barnard planned an extensive visit to every part of the state "during the times when people are at home—spring and fall, to recommend the [University of Mississippi] in personal conversation or in addresses, and to endeavor to do something to build up the cause of education among the people." Barnard wanted to make the new office of chancellor "a more useful and honorable one than a mere school master."

The board of trustees appreciated Barnard's vision of an enlarged role for the chancellor and created the office of "assistant to the professor of physics" to relieve him of some teaching duties. In addition, the board established the office of proctor to relieve Barnard of his administrative chores. The proctor had been a part-time position held at various times by board members or faculty members. W. J. Molloy, the university's first full-time administrator, was appointed proctor in 1859. His duties included collecting student fees, maintaining the register of students, supervising the slave laborers employed by the university, and overseeing the buildings and grounds.

Although Chancellor Barnard continued to hear recitations and to lecture in physics, astronomy, civil engineering, and electromagnetism, his teaching assistant, Burton Norvell Harrison, relieved him of much of the paperwork and other mundane duties of his office. Barnard badly needed relief from his official and academic duties. On October 23, 1858, he apologized to Hilgard for not writing more often, explaining that he was "nearly crushed by official work." Six months later Barnard complained that his "ability to labor was so near zero" that he feared "the machine is wearing out." He had "cut into the night heavily several times already." At least he did not have to work by candlelight. The university installed oil lamps on Barnard's recommendation in 1856. At the rate he was working, he did not think he would last "four years longer." Barnard, truly, did not know his own strength. He would last forty years longer.

In addition to his teaching and administrative duties, Barnard was writing the *Report of the Coast Survey* (1858), an ongoing study of America's coastline conducted under the direction of the American Association for the Advancement of Science. He was also writing two scientific articles, both of which were published in 1859. In his report of the coast survey, Barnard used the term "physicist" rather than the antiquated "natural philosopher." He was one of the first members of the international scientific community to use the new term.

Although he was overworked and often unappreciated, he thought, Barnard gladly accepted almost total responsibility for the expenditure of a special one-hundred-thousand-dollar appropriation in 1856. The legislature allocated this special appropriation to the university in twenty-thousand-dollar annual installments for a period of five years beginning in 1856. As the image and esteem of the university ebbed and flowed in the late 1850s, the legislature threatened on several occasions to withhold the current installment. The university became a supplicant, and its officials practiced the indelicate art of pandering to the whims of state legislators. Thus was born another of the university's enduring traditions.

With some help from Professor Stearns, Barnard determined how the university would expend the special appropriation and what to buy. With this largess, Barnard assembled a collection of scientific apparatus and built an astronomical observatory that placed the university "in the front rank of American seminaries of learning." The university's mechanical apparatus included "not only every article which is usually found in such collections, but many which [were] less common." The "machines of Atwood and Morin for demonstrating the laws of falling bodies, lately purchased from Paris [were] unsurpassed in finish and accuracy, and provided with all the more recent improvements." To illustrate "the laws and properties of elastic fluids," Barnard purchased "a powerful air pump" constructed for the university by E. S. Ritchie of Boston. The air pump had "all the latest improvements . . . capable of carrying exhaustion to the highest attainable degree." Lectures on the construction and theory of the barometer were explained and illustrated by an instrument made "expressly for [Barnard's] Observatory." The "theory of music and the mathematical principles of harmony" were illustrated by "every instrument in the catalogue of Marloye of Paris."

The university's electrical apparatus, including a unique electrical machine constructed by Ritchie, was "superior to any similar collection in the United States." For research and instruction in his favorite field, Barnard designed and built an observatory to house the largest telescope in the world. Unfortunately, as the manufacturer was preparing the telescope for shipment to the university, the Civil War began, and the instrument was not delivered. The "celestial motions [were] beautifully represented by Barlow's magnificent planetarium, eleven feet in diameter—a piece of mechanism unrivaled in ingenuity, accuracy and elegance." The university's "thirty six globes of Malby of London [afforded] a very useful aid to the conception of astronomical problems."

At Chancellor Barnard's urging, the board of trustees accepted the invitation of Professor Alexander D. Bache to participate in the United States Coast Survey and allocated funds for a small building to house the magnetic instruments used during the survey. In its 1859 annual report to the legislature, the board of trustees boasted that the invitation to participate in the coast survey "indicates more decidedly than any mere language of compliment can do, the esteem in which the University is beginning to be regarded by the scientific men of the country."

The university's geological laboratory and its variety of specimens were, according to Barnard's biographer, "without superior in the United States." The Markoe Collection, "embracing a rare and elegant collection . . . of rocks, minerals and fossils," was purchased from Francis Markoe of Washington City. The collection was "pronounced inferior to none in the world." The Budd Cabinet, purchased from Dr. B. W. Budd of New York, contained more than five thousand species and more than twenty thousand individual shells, "many of which have never yet been described in works of Conchology."

When Chancellor Barnard scolded Professor Edward Boynton for teaching chemistry as a lecture rather than an experimental course, Boynton complained that he had no laboratory. To remedy that problem, Chancellor Barnard built a thirty-six-foot addition to the Lyceum for a chemistry laboratory and lecture hall. He designed the laboratory and lecture hall himself, proudly sketching it out in a letter to Hilgard. After the completion of this addition and the purchase of laboratory equipment, the facilities for instruction in chemistry were "second to none in the country." In 1859 *DeBow's Review* described the university's laboratories and scientific apparatus as "the most perfect in . . . arrangement and appointments now existing in the Union." Even given the Southerner's use of hyperbole in describing Southern men and institutions, that was high praise, and it was largely deserved.

Although Barnard had placed the university in the front ranks of American collegiate institutions, one area still needed significant improvement. To raise the university to the next level required a major expansion of the general library. When the university opened in 1848, it had no library at all, a situation President Holmes said was analogous to "Polyphemus without his eye." At the end of the first session, Jacob Thompson donated funds and a small collection of books from his personal library to the university and the board allocated five hundred dollars for the purchase of additional books. In the school's early years, a student who received a tuition-free scholarship operated the library, which was open only about two hours each Saturday morning. Students could check out two small books or one large book at a time. The librarian assessed a fine of ten cents for the first week and twenty-five cents a week thereafter for overdue books, and professors strictly enjoined the students from turning down the pages to mark their place. When Barnard joined the faculty in 1854, the university's library, plus the holdings of the two literary societies, included approximately three thousand volumes.

At its first meeting after the special $100,000 appropriation in 1856, the board of trustees allocated $32,075 for various campus improvements, construction projects, and special purchases. Of that sum, the board designated $2,000 for the law library and $9,200 to the general library. The board stipulated, however, if other campus improvements exceeded the allotted budgets, the cost overrun would be deducted "from the item of $9,200 appropriated to the general college library." Some of those improvements and purchases did exceed their budgets, and library funds were diverted to other projects. Barnard complained to the board of trustees in 1859 that the libraries of most "respectable colleges" outnumbered the university's library and those of the institutions that "claim to stand in the first class" of American universities vastly outnumbered the university's "humble collection of books." A college without "a copious library," Barnard said, "can rarely count on the great advantage of embracing in its faculty a man whose name is familiar to the learned world." In the board's 1859 report to the legislature, the trustees cited Barnard's description of the library and asked the lawmakers to renew the twenty-thousand-dollar annual appropriation, especially in view of the needs of the university's library.

The continuation of the special appropriation was a matter of great concern to the board of trustees and to Chancellor Barnard in 1859. Amid the tirades against the university over the previous year, were rumors that the legislature might not renew the annual appropriation. Barnard thought the university's loss of that appropriation was likely, and that "possibly a successful assault might be made on the charter itself." The support for revoking the university's charter outright was not significant, but there was support for relocating the university to Jackson.

Under the caption "Removal of the University of Mississippi," the *Pontotoc Examiner* reported that a "strong feeling is manifesting itself... favoring the removal of the State University from its present location either to Jackson or to Canton... where its officers might be better under the rigid surveillance of the Legislature." The *Examiner* continued,

"We know that a majority of the board of trustees have been such sycophantic fautors of the wealthy that . . . a youth, who is poor and not having influential parents, stands but little chance of reaping the honors of the Institution, how well soever his talents, acquirements, and moral conduct may merit them." The university's problem, according to the *Examiner,* was not its students but the "malfeasance and nonfeasance of duty" on the part of the trustees and faculty. Consequently, the newspaper continued, "these officers must be watched more closely, and—but hold we forgot the 'M. C. Railroad,' the great hobby of Oxonians. We suppose the Legislature will run up on that, every six months, to nurse this puny child of hers—the University; for they seem to think that everybody can reach their village by that road." The *Examiner*'s report concluded with a statement that its support for the relocation of the university to Jackson was "not dictated by any ill-will to Oxford, (which town we hope will soon reform its morals) nor any desire to injure the University." The editor assured his readers if it were moved to Jackson, "the University would in a few years become the pride of the state—equal at least to other Colleges of the South." There was no formal effort to move the university to Jackson, but an 1861 amendment to its charter empowered the legislature to appoint its trustees.

For all of his accomplishments, Barnard was growing increasingly impatient with his detractors. He wrote to Hilgard, "The misery of a situation in Mississippi [is] the destructive tendencies of its people." Unlike his happy years in Alabama, Barnard remembered his time in Mississippi as "the dreadful years." After Mississippi, he said many years later, the rest of his life seemed uneventful. The disheartened chancellor concluded that the University of Mississippi "was a thing too far above the ruling stupidity of the day to be a success," and he began looking elsewhere. A promising situation developed for Barnard in the summer of 1859. When he was in New Haven to receive an honorary degree from his alma mater, some of his friends encouraged him to apply for the vacancy created by the death of Professor Denison Olmstead. His northern friends and supporters assured Barnard that he could have the appointment if he wanted it. Barnard was so confident that he would get the Yale position that he submitted his resignation to James Howry in June 1859, to become effective January 1, 1860, but he asked Howry not to make the letter public. When Barnard did not get the Yale appointment, he was crushed. Fortunately, Howry had not made the letter public, and Barnard withdrew his resignation.

Barnard was almost as disappointed by the reaction of George Hampton Young, his friend and patron, as he was by the Yale rejection. Barnard told Young that he might get an offer from Yale, but he would not accept it if Young thought he should stay in Mississippi. Young was not optimistic about the university's future and advised Barnard to act in his own best interest. Barnard had hoped that Young would plead with him to stay and promise to work with him to achieve his goals for the university. He was sad and hurt, he wrote Hilgard, by Young's response.

Though disappointed by Yale and by Young, Barnard was consoled by Bishop Green. When the bishop visited Barnard at Oxford in July and learned that he was considering a move to Yale, Green encouraged Barnard to stay at Oxford because he was "the [premier] man of science in the South." The bishop reassured the sensitive scholar that the people of Mississippi were "learning to judge him more fairly." Bishop Green probably mentioned the accolades the Jackson *Mississippian* and the *True Southron* were giving Chancellor Barnard and the university. Calling the university the "literary Gibraltar of the South" and Barnard a scholar with "no superior" in the country, the *Mississippian* denounced the criticism of the institution as calculated to undermine its public image and to "sting a sensitive mind, such as we know Dr. Barnard to possess." Rather than criticize their university, wrote the *Mississippian,* people from all across the state ought to pay a visit to Oxford to see "the pride and ornament of our commonwealth."

In addition to soothing Barnard's sensitive soul, Bishop Green dangled before the chancellor's ambitious eyes the presidency of the University of the South at Sewanee, which was in the final planning stages and would soon open. Bishop Green assured Barnard that he would be the first president of Sewanee "if I can make it so." The wily bishop's visit was a tonic for Barnard, who was back on top again emotionally. A gleeful Barnard wrote to Hilgard, told him about his talk with the bishop, and asked him if he would like to have the chair of chemistry at the University of the South when he became its president. Barnard considered Hilgard the finest chemist in America.

Six months later Barnard's mood was somber, and he was again dejected. In November 1859 he wrote Hilgard, "I would take up any mechanic art, I would even be a private soldier, or a day laborer, before I would again be an officer in a southern college." He asked Hilgard, "Did you ever know such a target for the shafts of the malevolent as I have been?" He then ticked off the shafts that had been aimed at him: "In Alabama Dr. Manly tried to destroy me once. Here Harper assailed me—then Wilson [Professor Wilson G. Richardson]—then Harper again—then I. N. Davis—then incidentally Carey Crane—then Carter and Branham (without my knowledge) last summer and now, finally, the same *par nobile* in an open, fatal death struggle."

The "fatal death struggle" Barnard mentioned is now known as the "Branham affair." Dr. Henry B. Branham was an Oxford physician, a staunch pro-slavery, states' rights Southern Methodist, a son-in-law of A. B. Longstreet and the brother-in-law of L. Q. C. Lamar. He was a former partisan of Lewis Harper and an ally of Professor George W. Carter. Branham believed Barnard undermined Longstreet with the board of trustees and was instrumental in his leaving the university. Angry and unforgiving, Branham was waiting for the right moment to drive Barnard from office. Just such an opportunity presented itself in the fall of 1859. Branham, in league with editor J. D. Stevenson of the Oxford *Mercury,* Professor Carter, and Professor Richardson (Barnard's most vocal critics on the faculty), prompted a bitter controversy, which the *Mercury* called an "Irrepressible Conflict."

The Branham controversy began in early May 1859 when the Barnards were in Vicksburg attending the Southern Commercial Convention. Barnard had gone to the convention at the request of James Howry to make peace with board member Isaac N. Davis. When the Barnards returned on May 17, Professor Boynton, who lived in the other wing of their faculty house, told Barnard that two students, J. P. Furniss and Samuel B. Humphreys, had entered his residence on the night of May 12 "with shameful designs" on one of his "defenseless female servants." Jane, at twenty-nine the younger of the two servants, was apparently raped and in defending herself was badly beaten. Professor Boynton, after hearing a scuffle and loud noises, went outside to the fence separating the yards. He saw the two boys leave the residence and learned their identity from other students several days later. Mrs. Barnard also told the chancellor that Jane had identified Humphreys as the assailant. Furniss was a bystander and not involved in the altercation.

The faculty summoned Humphreys to a called meeting on May 23. He pleaded not guilty to entering the chancellor's residence and assaulting Jane. After taking testimony from several students, the faculty found Humphreys not guilty. Barnard, Boynton, and Moore voted guilty. Richardson, Carter, Phipps, Henry Whitehorne (professor of Greek), and Stearns voted not guilty. On a second vote, a majority of the faculty declared Humphreys "morally convicted" but did "not consider the evidence . . . sufficient, legally, to convict him." Under Mississippi law, a slave could not testify against a white person in court. A majority of the faculty believed Jane's identification of Humphreys was not admissible in the proceedings against him. Therefore, the faculty took no action against Humphreys.

After the faculty declined to expel Humphreys, Barnard wrote his parents and asked them to withdraw him from the university, which they did. When Humphreys reapplied for the fall session, Chancellor Barnard rejected his application. His refusal to allow Humphreys's readmission spawned a small student rebellion and provided Branham a pretext with which to challenge Barnard's soundness on slavery and states' rights. In protest of Barnard's action, several students withdrew from the university and transferred to Cumberland University in Lebanon, Tennessee, but most of them returned the next year.

Branham, Carter, and Richardson soon began a "whispering campaign" against Barnard accusing him of dismissing a student on the basis of "negro testimony." Professor Carter leaked the proceedings of the May 23 faculty meeting and insinuated that the faculty vote was sectional, the Northern men voting to convict and the Southern men voting not guilty. Stevenson printed every rumor and charge in the *Mercury* and denounced Barnard and the university's other Northern-born professors. The rumors and accusations became so serious and so persistent that Barnard wrote to Governor John J. Pettus, ex officio chairman of the board of trustees, asking for "the fullest and most searching investigation" of the charges against him, especially the accusation that he was unsound on slavery. Governor Pettus called a special meeting of the board of trustees at Oxford for March 1, 1860. James Ventress hastily wrote to William Sharkey, urging him to attend the Oxford meeting to help him defend the chancellor.

For two days, March 1 and 2, the board heard the testimony of seventeen witnesses called by Branham and Barnard. The most influential witness was Barnard himself. He testified that he had never discussed the assault with his slave, Jane, and that he had relied on evidence furnished by other sources to determine the guilt of Humphreys. Furthermore, he argued, because the governance of the university was parental, not municipal, the testimony of a slave, though he did not use it, was admissible and valid in the proceedings against a student. As to the question of slavery, Barnard declared, "I am as sound on the slavery question as any member of this board." It was a convincing argument but not altogether a true statement. Barnard owned slaves, but he had misgivings about the institution and would soon renounce it.

Shortly after dark on the second day of testimony, the board of trustees retired to its meeting room in the Lyceum. After considering the two days of testimony, the board unanimously absolved Chancellor Barnard of all the charges against him and ordered the proceedings, including its resolution clearing Barnard of all charges, printed and distributed throughout the state. The board exonerated Barnard, but did not vindicate him in the minds of the evangelical clergy or his critics in the press, who continued to criticize him and the university. Even Governor Pettus, though he heard all the testimony and voted to exonerate Barnard, had reservations about the chancellor and some of his Northern-born professors. One of the results of the Branham affair and the *Mercury*'s assault on Barnard and the university was the establishment of an alternative newspaper in Oxford. Howard Falconer, a member of an old Holly Springs family of journalists, an 1859 graduate of the university, and a friend of Barnard, established the Oxford *Intelligencer* in June 1860. The *Mercury* dismissed it as the "organ of the University clique."

Soon after the board of trustees exonerated Chancellor Barnard of the Branham charges, Jefferson Davis visited Oxford. "As most of the principal people of Oxford called on Mr. Davis at his hotel," Barnard recalled years later, "I went among the number." When the Oxford dignitaries entered Davis's room, they arranged themselves in a semicircle with Barnard "in the middle of the crescent." In his memoirs Barnard explains what happened next: "Mr. Davis glanced from one end of the row to the other, and then, instead of beginning at either end, he came straight to me in the middle, and offered me his hand. The incident was a trifling one, but to the company there assembled it had a profound significance." By this public display, Mississippi's favorite son validated the board's exoneration of Chancellor Barnard.

In addition to Davis's public gesture, Barnard received many letters of support following the board's investigation. James Gordon, class of 1855, thanked Barnard for his aid several years earlier when that "vile old Harper spewed venom at me" and promised to write a letter in the chancellor's defense to the Okolona *Prairie News,* one of the newspapers most critical of Barnard. Gordon explained to Barnard that John Richardson, "a cousin of the serpent [Professor Wilson G. Richardson] you once took to your bosom," edited the *Prairie News.* Jacob Thompson also congratulated Barnard and assured him that no self-respecting slave owner would fault him for protecting his servants. L. Q. C. Lamar wrote Barnard expressing his deep sorrow that any criticism of him emanated from his own household.

Barnard was a sensitive man who needed almost constant reinforcement, and he appreciated all of these letters. He was most pleased, though, to hear from William Sharkey, who offered his ringing endorsement of the board's decision, which he would have supported had he been at the meeting. Even more important to the chancellor, however, was Sharkey's promise to support Barnard's request for a paid leave of absence so he could join the Labrador expedition to view a solar eclipse. At its June 1860 meeting in Oxford, in an unusual display of generosity, the board agreed to pay Barnard's expenses for the expedition and granted him permission to miss the university's commencement. Alexander D. Bache, director of the coast survey, led the Labrador expedition, which was sponsored by several organizations, including the American Association for the Advancement of Science. At a meeting held in conjunction with the solar expedition, Barnard was elected president of the association.

At the June 1860 board meeting, Professor Carter resigned his chair of ethics to accept a position at another institution. Professor Richardson also resigned, but he apparently had no other employment because he later asked permission to withdraw his resignation. The board declined his request and appointed Alexander J. Quinche professor of Latin and modern languages. L. Q. C. Lamar, who succeeded Carter, joined the faculty for the second time, having previously served as adjunct professor of mathematics from 1850 to 1852. Lamar was a member of Congress at the time of his appointment and was given a leave of absence to complete his term. In accepting the appointment, Lamar told Barnard that he could do more good at a college than he could in Congress. Barnard engineered Lamar's appointment and wrote Hilgard about it several days in advance. He cautioned Hilgard to "be silent as the grave" and to "destroy this [letter] immediately." Hilgard may have been silent about it, but he did not destroy the letter.

When Barnard returned from his Labrador trip in the early fall of 1860, he found his family quarters in the observatory nearly finished. He and Mrs. Barnard moved into their new home in October. There was also great excitement in Oxford and at the university about the completion of the Mississippi Central Railroad. For the first time in the university's brief history students from the southern and central sections of the state could reach Oxford by rail. Oxford was now a stop on a great network of roads linking New Orleans with New York.

Almost as important as the network of railroads linking Oxford with the great cities of America was the boardwalk linking the campus and the square. The walkway had already been completed from the college to the corporate limits, and the town was completing its part of the walk in the summer of 1860. Howard Falconer, editor of the Oxford *Intelligencer,* was gleeful that "Oxonians" could walk from the square to the campus in comfort without "navigating . . . an expanse of mud which had no bottom" and adhered to shoes and clothing like "Spaldings Preferred Glue." But the editor was not happy — he was distraught — about the appearance of the university's classic groves. "There are hundreds of persons — former and present students of the University, and others," he wrote, "who will be sorry to learn that, of all the magnificent trees that once adorned the campus, and with which so many dear associations are connected, naught now remains save a few tall, unsightly stumps." Falconer explained that the trees had been "topped" and that "they will eventually be improved by the mutilation," though he feared "the promised improvement will not occur in *our* lifetime."

The thirteenth session of the university opened on September 17, 1860, in a time of great political excitement. The presidential election and the dread that Abraham Lincoln, the "Black Republican," might be elected was the consuming topic of conversation among the students, the faculty, and local citizens. Mississippi has been described as the "storm center of secession," and a majority of the state press, including both Oxford newspapers, favored secession. But neither the people of Mississippi nor the students at its state university were unanimous in their support for disunion. One month before their fathers voted, the sons of Mississippi's gentry cast a straw poll for president. John C. Breckinridge, the secessionist candidate, received 100 votes; John Bell, the Southern unionist, received 65 votes; and Stephen A. Douglas, an Illinois Democrat, got 4 votes. It is not clear if Lincoln was even a choice in the straw poll. He was not on Mississippi's official presidential ballot in 1860. On November 6, Mississippi cast 40,797 votes for Breckinridge, 25,040 for Bell, and 3,283 for Douglas. Though Abraham Lincoln did not receive a single vote in ten Southern states and received only 39.9 percent of the popular vote, he won a majority in the electoral college.

Southerners felt imperiled by Lincoln's election, and the prospects of "Black Republican Rule" alarmed even moderates like Jefferson Davis. The Oxford *Intelligencer* reported that the fourteen thousand black votes cast in Ohio elected Lincoln and asked, "Will Southern men submit to be ruled by negroes? We shall see." Following the secession of South Carolina on December 20, 1860, Mississippi seceded on January 9, 1861, from what the *Intelligencer* called the "United States of the North." At the secession convention, the professor of ethics and metaphysics at the state university, L. Q. C. Lamar, drafted the Ordinance of Secession, and a senior student, Francis A. Pope of Lexington, tallied the votes and kept a record of its proceedings. Several of the university's trustees were delegates to the convention, and all voted for secession. The final vote was eighty-five to fifteen in favor of disunion. William L. Sharkey was the only member of the board of trustees who publicly opposed secession. Even after the war began and throughout the conflict, Sharkey refused to give his allegiance to the Confederate States of America.

Secession was literally a "stop the presses" story. Under a bold caption, MISSISSIPPI IS OUT, Howard Falconer wrote that he had stopped the press at the *Intelligencer* at 8:00 P.M. on the night of January 9 to insert a bulletin informing his fellow citizens that Mississippi had seceded from the Union. Falconer reported that Oxford was brilliantly illuminated and people celebrated in the streets. "Three cheers for our gallant state," he wrote. While Oxford celebrated the news, a torch light parade wound through the streets of Mississippi's capital city to the stirring strains of "The Bonnie Blue Flag," which Harry McCarthy wrote at Jackson earlier that day. The celebrations at Oxford and Jackson, and similar ones across the state, were scenes more fitting for the end, rather than the beginning, of a war.

On the night of January 9, 1861, Chancellor Barnard was on a northbound train on his way to Washington to fulfill a longstanding lecture engagement at the Smithsonian Institution. Also on the train was J. D. B. DeBow, editor of *DeBow's Review,* who was in Jackson earlier that day when the fateful vote was cast. DeBow described for Barnard a "touching scene" in which "old men were moved to tears." The chancellor replied, "They might well weep on such an occasion." Barnard's reply surprised DeBow who asked, "What do you mean by that?" "I mean," said Barnard, "that to plunge a country into war may well be a subject of tears." DeBow again expressed surprise, "War! There will be no war." Barnard was astonished by DeBow's response and by "how almost universal in the South was the delusion that secession could be accomplished without war."

When Chancellor Barnard returned to the university from Washington on February 2, 1861, he found the campus draped in banners and consumed by the talk of war. From one dormitory flew the Bonnie Blue Flag, "which bears a single star." From another wafted Old Glory, bearing thirty-three. The flag of the Union continued to fly for several days, even after the establishment of the Confederate States of America in Montgomery, Alabama, on February 4. After the attack on Fort Sumter and President Lincoln's call for seventy-five thousand volunteers to put down the rebellion, however, Mississippi's secessionists and unionists formed an uneasy alliance. They did not settle their differences but sublimated them and closed ranks in defense of their native soil and the Southern Way of Life. Students who only a few years earlier criticized the board of trustees for censoring their textbooks now took antislavery books from the library and burned them on the college green. Book burning was not the only manifestation of Mississippi's closed society.

A man and his son were driven from Oxford for expressing antislavery sentiments. A local editor reported they had been seen in Pontotoc, and he was confident the good people there would "pass them on."

Now fifty-two years old, Chancellor Barnard was in a state of near depression brought on by the events that threatened the university to which he had given six years of his life and soul and energy. Barnard reveals his state of mind and his personal feeling about secession in a February 9, 1861, letter to a young Northern woman who sent him a miniature American flag. In thanking her for the flag, Barnard wrote, "I am for the Union, first, last, and forever." He assured her that he would cherish the flag, "at least in private." After the University Greys, a military company composed of university students, left for Corinth, Mississippi, on May 1 and most other students had gone home to enlist, Barnard wrote a Northern friend, "We are indeed inhabitants of a solitude. . . . Our University has ceased to have visible existence."

As foreboding as conditions were in the summer of 1861, the board of trustees would not close the university. During the week when commencement exercises were normally held, the board announced that the university was "temporarily arrested by the patriotic ardor of the students in rallying to the standards of their country." The board conferred the bachelor of arts degree on an absent senior class. Their diplomas would be presented when hostilities ceased and students returned to the campus. As a precaution, the trustees told the faculty that they could not guarantee their salaries beyond October and advised them to begin looking for other positions.

A few days before the university was scheduled to open its fall session, the board held an emergency meeting in Oxford and received a dismal report from Chancellor Barnard. Only four students were registered for the fall term. The board also discussed an allegation that Professor Boynton expressed a "want of attachment . . . to the Southern Confederacy." The accusation was based on statements he made to his father in a letter that was intercepted, opened, and made public by Confederate authorities in Memphis. Boynton acknowledged his authorship, and the board dissolved the connection between the accomplished chemist and the University of Mississippi. The trustees had high regard for Boynton and they offered him safe passage out of the Confederacy if he pledged not to take up arms against it. He accepted the offer and honored the pledge.

At the October meeting the trustees decided that keeping the university open under the present circumstances was useless and accepted the resignations of Barnard, Stearns, Trotter, Lamar, Quinche, and Harrison, and declared the other chairs vacant. The board placed Professor Quinche and Burton Harrison in charge of university property and authorized them to teach "such students as may apply." In the fall of 1861 approximately thirty Oxford boys enrolled in a primary school on the campus, but the school closed when the Confederates established a hospital at the university in early 1862. During the first year of the war, Burton Harrison, with his mother and sister, shared the living quarters in the observatory with Professor Quinche and his family. After Harrison moved to Richmond in 1862, to serve as private secretary to President Jefferson Davis, his mother and sister remained in Oxford and continued to live in the observatory. When the Civil War ended, federal soldiers arrested Jefferson Davis and Burton Harrison and imprisoned them on a charge of treason.

As a possible alternative to closing the university in the fall of 1861, the board of trustees asked Chancellor Barnard to study several Southern military academies and draft a plan for converting the university into a military school. Barnard conducted a study and filed a written report at a special meeting of the board of trustees on November 19 in Jackson. The board considered Barnard's report but concluded that it would not be feasible to conduct the university as a military school and closed the institution during the hostilities. At that meeting, the board of trustees awarded Chancellor Barnard a doctor of divinity degree, and his tenure with the University of Mississippi officially ended.

Chancellor Barnard had played no role in the sectional debate. He was a scientist, not a statesman. He was more interested in a republic of letters than a confederacy of states. He was a slave owner in fact but an abolitionist at heart, a Southerner in sentiment but a Northerner in temperament. Now, in the fall of 1861, he had to take sides. It was not an easy choice. He had developed a fondness for the region where he had lived for the last twenty-two years. "A residence in Oxford seemed to me undesirable," Barnard recalled years later, "for the reason that the place was on the line of the most probable advance of Federal forces." Because he preferred to "keep out of the way of active military operations," Barnard packed up his books, sold most of his other belongings (which probably included his two slaves), and moved to Tuscaloosa in December 1861.

Shortly after the establishment of the Confederate States of America, President Davis offered Barnard a position with the Confederate government, but precisely what that position was, or what Barnard thought it was, is not clear. Barnard declined the position and eventually asked President Davis to provide him a passport across the lines, which Davis agreed to do. By the time Barnard and his wife arrived at Norfolk, Virginia, however, Confederate authorities had suspended all passes, and the Barnards remained virtually under house arrest until the city was captured by federal troops on May 9, 1862. After Norfolk surrendered, Barnard wrote to his sister that he could "breathe at last once more the air of freedom."

Barnard spent the next two years in Washington working in various positions, none of which he considered worthy of his talents. In late 1863 he wrote a thirty-two-page letter citing the Northern antiwar movement as a greater threat to the Union than Southern secession and defending President Lincoln's conduct of the war. The letter was widely published in the Northern press and brought Barnard to the attention of the trustees of Columbia College, who were searching for a president. After the trustees contacted Barnard, he pursued the position with his characteristic energy and enlisted all of his friends in his behalf. On May 18, 1864, the board of trustees elected Barnard president of Columbia College. Of all the positions Barnard had considered over the years, according to John Waddel, this was the one he wanted the most. This appointment gave him one more chance to take a small college and transform it into one of the world's great universities. What Barnard did for Columbia, he might have done for the University of Mississippi.

CHAPTER 5

STUDENTS AND SOLDIERS, 1861–1870

In the memorable conflict on the plains of Manassas the University Greys covered themselves with imperishable glory.

BOARD OF TRUSTEES ANNUAL REPORT, 1861

"No one knows how the University Greys began. Most likely it was in a dormitory room in December 1860," writes Howard Bahr, "before a meager fire lit against the cold; a circle of lads . . . pledging fealty to one another and to a cause [that] would consume them all, one way or another in the end—but this was the beginning and they couldn't know that yet." The student soldiers first called their company the University Blues, but later changed the name to the Greys in favor of the color of the Confederacy. The Greys elected 19 year-old William B. Lowry captain, began collecting arms, and conducting close order drills. The motto of the Greys was *Ducit amore patria* (The love of my country leads me).

During the excitement following the establishment of the Confederate States of America on February 4, 1861, Chancellor Barnard and the faculty found it almost impossible to keep the boys in class and focused on their studies. Several times in the spring of 1861 the faculty suspended and readmitted Captain Lowry for excessive absences. After the firing on Fort Sumter on April 12, 1861, students who did not join the Greys or the Lamar Rifles, another Lafayette County unit, went home to enlist in companies being raised in their communities. Chancellor Barnard pleaded with the parents of university students to keep their sons in school and petitioned Governor Pettus not to muster the student units into military service. Confederate President Jefferson Davis endorsed Barnard's petition. Sending young boys off to war, Davis said, was like "grinding the seed corn of the republic." Imbued with a romantic notion of war, the student soldiers would heed neither their chancellor nor their president. On May 1, 1861, the University Greys boarded a train bound for Corinth, Mississippi, the "Crossroads of the Confederacy." A large crowd gathered at the depot to see them off. Old men wept, young ladies waved and blew kisses, and mothers wondered if they would ever see their sons again. By the end of the summer, several of the Greys would lie still and cold on the plains of Manassas, casualties of a war they feared would be over before they could join it.

At Corinth ten companies from north Mississippi, including the Greys (Company A) and the Lamar Rifles (Company G), formed the 11th Mississippi Volunteer Infantry Regiment. By mid-May the regiment was at Harpers Ferry, Virginia. The University Greys were an unruly lot, but they were well-dressed and good shots. The inspector general at Harpers Ferry noted that they "take much pride in their appearance." When a farmer complained that a member of the Greys shot one of his hogs, and that he heard it squealing, he was told that he must be mistaken. If a University Grey shoots a hog, he was advised, it doesn't squeal.

At Harpers Ferry the 11th Mississippi was brigaded with the 2nd Mississippi Infantry Regiment, under the storied Colonel William Falkner, the model for William Faulkner's Colonel John Sartoris. In a battle on the plains of Manassas near Bull Run Creek on July 21, 1861, Confederate General P. G. T. Beauregard, observing Colonel Falkner (with a large black plume in his hat) charging the federals, shouted to his own troops, "Men, follow yonder knight of the black plume and history will not forget you." During the First Battle of Manassas (also known as the First Battle of Bull Run) seven members of the University Greys were killed or died of wounds suffered in the battle.

In the heat of the First Battle of Manassas General Beauregard observed a column of troops approaching his position, but could not determine if the troops were Union or Confederate. In the early stages of the war some troops on both sides wore blue uniforms, and the first national flag of the Confederacy, known as the Stars and Bars, was so similar to the Stars and Stripes that it could not be distinguished from the American flag at a distance. Beauregard ordered his men to fire on the approaching column, only to learn that they were Confederate troops. After the First Battle of Manassas, General Beauregard adopted a new battle flag that could be easily and quickly distinguished from the American flag. The Confederate battle flag, also called the Beauregard battle flag, the Southern Cross and the flag of the Army of Northern Virginia, and is now generally identified as the Confederate or Rebel flag, was popular throughout the Confederacy and became a part of the second and third national flags of the Confederate States. In 1894 the Confederate battle flag became a part of the state flag of Mississippi and was added to the Georgia state flag in 1954.

After the Civil War, the Confederate Veterans organization, and subsequently the Sons of Confederate Veterans, adopted the battle flag as their official emblem. In the late 1940s the Confederate battle flag became an unofficial spirit symbol for the Ole Miss Rebel football team. At about that same time the Confederate battle flag also became identified with the Dixiecrats, Southern resistance to civil rights, and the Ku Klux Klan. When the University Greys and the 11th Mississippi Infantry followed this flag into battle and won imperishable glory, "it was the beginning and they couldn't know [any of] that yet."

After the First Battle of Manassas, both sides withdrew from the field, went into winter quarters, reorganized their armies, and prepared for the great battles to come. The University Greys were in most of those great battles, including Seven Pines, Gaines Mill, Fraser's Farm, Malvern Hill, Second Manassas (Bull Run), Sharpsburg (Antietam), Gettysburg, the Wilderness, Spotsylvania, Cold Harbor, Petersburg, and Appomattox. On that fateful day of July 3, 1863, at Gettysburg, the University Greys and the 11th Mississippi Infantry were on the extreme Confederate left flank during the Pickett-Pettigrew-Trimble charge of the federal forces deployed behind a stone fence along Cemetery Ridge. The three divisions of General Robert E. Lee's Army of Northern Virginia making the charge were under the command of General James Longstreet, the nephew of Augustus Baldwin Longstreet, the University of Mississippi's second president.

During the cannonade just before that now legendary charge, Jeremiah Gage, of the University Greys, was mortally wounded. From a field hospital he wrote his mother:

> This is the last you may ever hear from me. I have time to tell you that I died like a man.... Remember that I am true to my country and my greatest regret at dying is that she is not free.... This letter is stained with my blood.

Just before he died, Gage pressed the letter to his bleeding abdomen, took a cup of opium, feebly raised it to his comrades, and said:

> Come around boys, and let us have a toast. I do not invite you to drink with me, but I drink the toast to you, and to the Southern Confederacy, and to victory.

As Jeremiah Gage was dying, Color Sergeant William O'Brien called the 11th Mississippi Infantry into battle line. General Longstreet's assault against Cemetery Ridge began at 3:10 p.m. As the Confederate left flank crossed the Emmitsburg Road and charged the stone fence near a barn on Abraham Brian's farm, the 11th Mississippi met a withering volley of musket fire. They fell "like leaves in an autumn wind." After Sergeant O'Brien was killed, a private picked up the flag. He was killed as he charged the Union line. Another soldier retrieved the colors and he, too, was killed immediately. A lieutenant then picked up the colors and carried them to the stone wall where he collapsed and was captured along with the regimental flag. Every member of the University Greys in the charge at Gettysburg was killed, wounded, or captured. A Union general wrote, "The death angel alone could produce such a field." The captured Greys were taken at or beyond the stone wall at Brian's Barn, which is now known as the High Water Mark of the Confederacy.

Shelby Foote says the Civil War was the defining moment in American history, and many historians agree that Gettysburg was the turning point of the Civil War. It is one of the great ironies of American history that part of the battle that defined America and decided the war caused by slavery was fought on land owned by a black man. Abraham Brian, whose barn gave brief cover from the hail of bullets, and whose fields were nourished by the tears and blood of the men who died in that epic battle, was a free man, an American of African descent.

Following the Battle of Gettysburg, General Lee and the Army of Northern Virginia fell back across the Potomoc and fought on for two more years before finally surrendering to General Ulysses S. Grant. The University Greys and the Army of Northern Virginia stacked their arms and furled their colors at Appomattox Court House on April 12, 1865. After the war "none of the boys gathered around that dormitory grate [in December 1860] returned to their alma mater." Those who survived the war "wandered off into the 19th century [taking] with them the knowledge that they had done something extraordinary, that they had passed the watershed of their lives." But they are not forgotten. A Dale Gallon painting depicts the Greys and the 11th Mississippi at Brian's

Barn in the climactic moments of the charge; a monument to them stands watch on the field at Gettysburg; and on the Ole Miss campus in Ventress Hall "there remains, against all odds, a stained glass window dedicated to the Greys."

In the fall of 1861, when the board of trustees informed the Mississippi legislature that they had cancelled the fourteenth session of the state university, and that the institution would remain closed during the war, many alumni and friends despaired for its future. But as Frank Keyes wrote on the eve of the Civil War, the University of Mississippi was not born "to taste of life and pass away, it shall stand from generation to generation."

In the early months of 1862, as General Albert Sidney Johnston was massing his army of fifty thousand for the coming battle with General Grant that would be fought somewhere in north Mississippi, probably at Corinth, Governor John J. Pettus authorized T. W. Caskey to establish a military hospital on the campus of the university and allocated a hundred thousand dollars for that purpose. The capacity of the university hospital was one thousand, but as early as March 1862, a month before the great battle, which took place on April 6 and 7 at Shiloh rather than Corinth, Caskey already had five hundred fifty patients at the university. After Shiloh, perhaps as many as two thousand wounded Confederate soldiers were treated at the university hospital. Caskey set up tents across the campus, and shuttled soldiers to private homes as soon as they could be moved. In a report to Governor Pettus, Caskey inflated the number of wounded Confederate soldiers to three thousand, but he did not exaggerate when he said that the "whole country is overrun" with the sick and wounded.

Dr. Thomas Dudley Isom, the post surgeon, and fourteen physicians, including Dr. Henry B. Branham of Oxford staffed the hospital. Local slave owners provided eighty-five slaves as orderlies, and dozens of Oxford women served as nurses. Established and financed by the state of Mississippi, the university hospital was so efficient and well organized that the Confederate government decided to assume control of it and sent what Caskey called "a brass buttoned Jack Ass from Richmond" to take charge. Caskey informed Governor Pettus that he had sent the Confederate emissary back to Richmond, and that he was still in charge.

Though he quickly resolved his troubles with Richmond, Caskey faced a much more serious squabble at Oxford. W. F. Avent, the hospital quartermaster, ordered Professor Alexander Quinche and other occupants of faculty houses to vacate their premises because the hospital needed more room. James Howry, a member of the board of trustees who lived in Oxford, instructed Quinche to remain in the observatory and continue to oversee the university buildings. Mrs. L. Q. C. Lamar's residence in one of the faculty houses and the lingering bitterness between Dr. Branham and some members of the board of trustees complicated the "miserable controversy" over the use of campus buildings, as Caskey called the disagreement.

Howry complained in a letter to Governor Pettus that some people were trying to turn the soldiers against university authorities by telling them the board of trustees would not allow the wounded to use the university buildings. He suggested that A. B. Longstreet open his spacious mansion to the wounded Confederates. Why Mrs. Lamar, who was Longstreet's daughter, did not move into her father's large house is not clear. Apparently the Branham clique, which now included W. F. Avent, attempted to entangle Caskey and the hospital in an old controversy. Caskey remained above the fray, writing Governor Pettus that he would not move anyone in or out of their residences. But Howry was outraged by what he thought was a renewal of an old battle. "I think the vandals who would seek the present unhappy condition of our country to renew a warfare on the University," he wrote Pettus on April 12, 1862, "are worse than Lincoln & Andy Johnson & you know my opinion of them." Notwithstanding this distraction, Caskey continued to operate the university hospital with great success until the fall of 1862, when the approach of General Grant's army from Holly Springs forced him to move the hospital to the central region of the state.

In a cemetery behind the C. M. "Tad" Smith Coliseum, several hundred Union and Confederate soldiers who died while being treated in the university hospital are buried in unmarked graves. Sometime in the late 1870s, Martin W. Phillips, the university proctor, sent a crew of workers to mow the grass in the cemetery. The workers removed the markers to facilitate the mowing and stacked them in a pile along the edge of the cemetery. When it was time to put them back, the workers could not remember where to place each marker. The markers were then discarded, and now the soldiers sleep together in unmarked graves.

In early December 1862, as General Grant crossed the Tallahatchie River several miles north of Oxford, Colonel W. H. Jackson's cavalry and other Confederate forces fell back to the Yocona River, which is a few miles south of Oxford. The withdrawal of Confederate troops created a panic in Oxford, and many citizens fled the town. Some of Oxford's wealthiest and most prominent citizens, including several elected officials, evacuated Oxford in June when Grant captured Holly Springs and appeared to be headed for Oxford. Rebecca Pegues, whose husband was among those who took their slaves to safer locations in the summer, wrote of that first exodus, "It was discouraging to see so many of them running off—fearful of arrest—deserting their homes, and leaving the women at the mercy of the invaders."

General Grant arrived in Oxford on December 5, 1862, and established his headquarters in the abandoned mansion of James Brown, who had taken his slaves to Gainesville, Georgia, earlier that summer. On the eighth of December, Grant sent for General William T. Sherman, who was with his troops at College Hill about seven miles north of Oxford. Throughout the night of December 8 and in the early morning hours of December 9, two of the men who would decide the outcome of the Civil War talked tactics and strategy in a house on Depot Street in Oxford. Grant instructed Sherman to take his corps back to Memphis, sail down the Mississippi to the Yazoo River and attack Vicksburg from the high ground at Chickasaw Bluffs. In the meantime, Grant would lead the rest of his army overland and attack Vicksburg from the northeast. General Sherman liked the plan because he would have a major role in the conquest of the Gibraltar of the Confederacy.

On the way back to College Hill, General Sherman rode through the campus. "When I rode through the grounds of the college," he wrote his old friend Frederick Barnard, "I thought of you and asked where you lived." When Sherman was shown the observatory, he said he could see the hand of Barnard in that classic building. Sherman reminded Barnard that they had talked about the observatory when "we were traveling down the [Mississippi Central Railroad] which I have destroyed root and branch." Before the Civil War, Sherman was president of Louisiana Seminary in Baton Rouge, which became Louisiana State University.

He had often traveled through Oxford on the Mississippi Central to and from his home in Ohio. Sometimes Chancellor Barnard was on the same train. Sherman also knew Barnard's younger brother, General John Gross Barnard, former commandant of West Point and chief engineer of Washington's defenses during the Civil War.

While Sherman was moving his corps from College Hill to Memphis, General Grant's father, Jesse, brought several Jewish merchants from Cincinnati to see the general in Oxford. The merchants were seeking special trading privileges in the occupied territory and were particularly anxious to buy confiscated cotton, which they could then sell on the open market at great profit. They induced Jesse to intercede on their behalf with Grant, and agreed to share the spoils with Jesse. General Grant was so incensed by this duplicity in particular, and the profiteering of unscrupulous merchants in general, that he issued the infamous "Jewish order." General Order No. 11, dated December 17, 1862, Oxford, Mississippi, expelled all Jews from the territory under General Grant's command. The order created such controversy that President Lincoln directed General Grant to rescind it.

Three days after he issued General Order No. 11, Grant's strategy for taking Vicksburg was fundamentally altered by a daring cavalry raid under Confederate General Earl Van Dorn. Grant had stockpiled supplies for several months at Holly Springs in preparation for his Vicksburg campaign, but in the early morning hours of December 20, General Van Dorn's cavalry entered Holly Springs and, after meeting only light resistance, destroyed the Union base and its military stores. With the town in shambles, Van Dorn was gone by late afternoon.

The day before Van Dorn's raid, Mrs. Ulysses S. Grant, her four-year-old son, Jesse, and her personal slave, Jule, were guests in the Harvey W. Walter home in Holly Springs while on their way to Oxford to spend Christmas with the general. There was just enough warning of Van Dorn's raid to get Mrs. Grant out of Holly Springs in the late afternoon of December 19 before the Confederates captured the town in the early hours of December 20. Years later Jesse remembered the hasty evacuation of Holly Springs and recalled the image of his mother sitting in a chair in an otherwise empty boxcar during the nighttime trip to Oxford. In her memoirs Mrs. Grant does not refer to a hasty departure from Holly Springs, but she does recall that the movements of Van Dorn's cavalry created such a stir in Grant's headquarters that he did not meet her at the Oxford depot, and that she saw little of him during the night of December 19.

In 1901, nearly forty years after this event, John G. Deupree, a professor of Greek at the University of Mississippi who had served in the First Mississippi Cavalry under Van Dorn during the capture of Holly Springs, wrote an account of that legendary raid. In addition to the military details of the raid Professor Deupree's account included a reference to the wife of General Grant. Deupree wrote: "Mrs. U. S. Grant was in [Holly Springs] residing in the stately mansion of the late Harvey W. Walter. Of course, she was undisturbed and none of her personal property was touched. In consideration of the courtesy shown his wife, Gen. Grant gave this house a safe-guard and a guarantee during the remainder of the war against search or trespass or devastation by Federal parties." Deupree concludes his account, "This house . . . still stands as a monument of Grant's appreciation of Southern chivalry."

Professor Deupree's account of the courtesy shown Mrs. Grant was a written expression of an oral tradition that placed Mrs. Grant in Holly Springs on the day of Van Dorn's raid. The origin of that tradition may be a statement Confederate Colonel John S. Griffith made in his memoirs. On the day of the raid, according to Victor Rose, who published Griffith's memoirs in 1881, Griffith went to the Walter mansion "fearing some rudeness might be committed" against Mrs. Grant. When Griffith arrived at the Walter house, Mrs. Grant, "stepping forward," said, "'And you, sir, make war upon women, do you?' 'On the contrary, madam,' replied the knightly Griffith, doffing his plumed chapeau, and bowing profoundly to the lady, 'we leave that to our enemies.'" After this exchange with Mrs. Grant, Colonel Griffith placed a guard on the house "for the protection of the ladies" while his command remained in Holly Springs. The conversation between Mrs. Grant and Colonel Griffith, recalled with such specificity many years later, could not have taken place, because Mrs. Grant was in Oxford.

The myth of Colonel Griffith's chivalrous gesture toward Mrs. Grant and General Grant's mythical gratitude for the gesture has seeped into the mainstream of Southern history and illustrates how Southerners make use of historical memory. To Victor Rose, Colonel Griffith, and Professor Deupree, historical memory was a device of cultural survival. In 1862, having learned that Mrs. Grant was in Holly Springs but unaware that she had left the night before, the Confederates went to the Walter mansion undoubtedly to capture Mrs. Grant, a legitimate prize of war. In 1881 Mrs. Grant was an admired American woman, the former first lady and the devoted wife of one of the nation's aging heroes, and the knightly Griffith could not admit, nor would Victor Rose record, that he had gone to the Walter mansion to capture Mrs. Grant. So, as Griffith remembered the episode twenty years later and as Professor Deupree explained the event almost forty years later, Colonel Griffith had gone to the mansion to protect Mrs. Grant. It is said that truth is the first casualty of war. Perhaps memory is its final casualty.

After the loss of his supply base at Holly Springs, General Grant changed his plans for an overland attack of Vicksburg. He would take his army back to Memphis and then down the Mississippi for an amphibious attack against what the Confederates believed was an "impregnable fortress." As Grant was preparing to leave Oxford, he sent troops and wagons fifteen miles in every direction to collect all the food and forage they could find. He was astonished by the success of those foraging expeditions and learned a lesson that influenced his future campaigns. Grant told Adam Badeau, his aide-de-camp and the first to chronicle Grant's Civil War campaigns, if he had realized he could live off the land he would have pushed on to Vicksburg and perhaps could have prevented Sherman's defeat at Chickasaw Bluffs. The lesson Grant learned at Oxford was that with five days' rations his army could live twenty days off the land.

During Grant's occupation of Oxford and his use of the campus buildings as a hospital, the university suffered almost no damage. Except for a group of Kansas Jayhawkers who got drunk on alcohol they found in the chemistry laboratory and broke some furniture and shelving in the observatory, Grant's troops committed only minor depredations against persons and property. One Union soldier recorded in his diary that General Grant ordered the burning of Oxford as the federals withdrew but countermanded his order before any damage was done. That order, however, does not appear in any of the official records of the war and is not cited by any other federal soldiers.

In a June 1865 letter asking Frederick Barnard for assistance in securing a presidential pardon for his role in the rebellion, Alexander Pegues wrote that General Grant had done "little injury" to the town or the campus, but General A. J. "Whiskey" Smith in August 1864 burned all but one of the buildings on the square and several houses. Barnard received a similar letter in September from George Young, his old friend and patron on the board of trustees. Young told Barnard that "the candy shop—alone [is] left on all the square." Young also told Barnard that his son Beverly was "wounded at Gettysburg [and] sleeps among strangers at Davis Island [a Union prison]." "I am indeed poor," wrote the master of Waverley mansion. "Perhaps I deserve [my fate]. I fear I do," he said, and asked his old friend to write him "if there is no treason in it." On a happier note, Young told Barnard that the board of trustees recently met in Oxford and the university would soon reopen.

On July 31, 1865, three months after the surrender at Appomattox, Governor William L. Sharkey convened the board of trustees at Oxford. President Andrew Johnson had recently appointed Sharkey provisional governor of Mississippi. At its July meeting, the board elected John N. Waddel chancellor and John J. Wheat professor of Greek. The first native Mississippian appointed to the university faculty, Professor Wheat was a popular Methodist minister, considered by some as "the most eloquent preacher in the state." The trustees reappointed Alexander J. Quinche professor of Latin, and appointed Confederate General Claudius Wistar Sears, who had lost a leg in the Battle of Franklin, professor of mathematics. After Confederate General Alexander P. Stewart declined the chair of physics and astronomy, the trustees appointed Confederate General Francis A. Shoup, an Episcopal priest and rector of St. Peter's Church in Oxford, professor of physics and astronomy.

During the 1866–67 session, a substantial enrollment increase necessitated additional faculty. Landon C. Garland joined the faculty in 1867 and served until his appointment as the first president of Vanderbilt University in 1875. Stanford G. Burney, a Cumberland Presbyterian minister, was appointed professor of English literature, but for reasons that are not clear from the faculty minutes, Professor Burney was dismissed in 1872. On October 2, 1872, the faculty passed a resolution expressing appreciation for Burney's service to the university, but rescinded the resolution a week later. It is possible that he was a casualty of some denominational machination because John Lipscomb Johnson, a Baptist minister, succeeded him. A Baptist member of the faculty and a Baptist member of the board of trustees championed Johnson's appointment. These machinations prompted William Mercer Green, Episcopal bishop of Mississippi, to write his old friend Frederick Barnard that he was not "sanguine of [the university's] success, when everyone knows that its faculty was appointed more for denominational effect than for established reputations in the several departments."

In the fall of 1866, L. Q. C. Lamar joined the faculty for the third time as professor of ethics. Three months later, in January 1867, Lamar accepted the chair of law after Horatio Fleming Simrall declined the appointment. Lamar held the chair of law until his resignation in 1870. Eugene Hilgard, who had been "acting professor of chemistry" during the 1865–66 session, was appointed professor of chemistry in 1866. After Hilgard's appointment, Barnard wrote his old friend asking about the university and his former colleagues. Barnard was especially solicitous of Chancellor Waddel and hoped for his success. Waddel's friends had conspired against Barnard but never Waddel himself, Barnard wrote Hilgard, adding, "I sincerely trust the University will flourish under him as it ought to flourish."

Neither the board of trustees nor the faculty anticipated a large enrollment when the university opened in the fall of 1865. The Oxford *Falcon,* which expected no more than 50 students, reported that university authorities were both surprised and unprepared for the 86 who enrolled in November. During the next few months an additional 107 matriculated. Of the 193 students enrolled during the first session following the Civil War, 5 were juniors, 41 were sophomores, and 50 were freshmen; there were 40 partial course students and 57 preparatory students. The first session after the war was similar in some ways to the first session in 1848. No seniors enrolled, textbooks were in short supply, entrance examinations were not given, and many students were not academically prepared for collegiate courses. Students who could not meet collegiate admission standards enrolled in a preparatory class, which was created, in part, as an alternative to rejecting Confederate veterans. Tuition and fuel expenses were seventy-five dollars a year, with boarding approximately fifteen dollars a month. Realizing the financial condition of Mississippi's gentry, the board of trustees allowed students to board with Oxford families or prepare their own meals in their dormitory rooms. There was no servant fee, and the traditional services provided by servants were discontinued, though students "could procure such attendance or not, according to their own convenience."

A month after the fall session opened, the editor of the Oxford *Falcon* reported that he heard "the common remark of both professors and citizens" that the students now attending the university "are the most studious, quiet and gentlemanly body of students they have ever seen." In the same issue, the editor also congratulated the good people of Oxford for rebuilding the town. "In fact," editor Sam Thompson wrote on November 23, 1865, "we are more than rejoiced to see business resume again in Oxford, with such vigor, and new houses going up and new enterprises starting every day—new life infused into our people. It makes one almost forget the dreary past."

Chancellor Waddel and the faculty were pleased with the maturity of the postwar students. None was under sixteen years of age and some were as old as twenty-five; the average age in this first class after the war was twenty. But the chancellor and the faculty were dismayed by their lack of academic preparation. Although few of the postwar students could have met prewar admission requirements, Chancellor Waddel and the board of trustees admitted them. Waddel later explained that he would not reject "worthy young aspirants after knowledge because they were backward and ignorant." He believed it was his "duty to take them by the hand and raise them from the lower to the higher . . . departments of education." Some Mississippians ridiculed the decision to enroll students who could not meet admission standards and accused Chancellor Waddel and the university of "degrading the cause of higher education." A writer in the *Jackson Daily News* accused the university of engaging in "a mere scramble for numbers." There were students at the state university, this writer claimed, "who can not read [and] do not understand the elementary principles of arithmetic."

An indignant board of trustees, departing from its usual course of ignoring "recklessly false" criticism, published a formal statement in several state newspapers defending the university and its chancellor from this "unmanly personal" attack. The board conceded that the dislocations caused by the war had induced the university to adopt a "temporary expedient" of admitting students who were not "fully prepared." This policy was justified, the board asserted, because of the wholesome results it produced. Many of the students who were admitted under this temporary expedient, according to the board of trustees, had "by earnest and diligent application" overcome their academic handicap and were now good students in full standing. The board concluded its lengthy defense by reiterating its "inflexible determination . . . to maintain and elevate" the university's "dignity and to extend its sphere of usefulness."

Three weeks after the opening of the university, Chancellor Waddel had an opportunity to defend the admission policy in a speech before a joint session of the state legislature. Waddel outlined the deficiencies of the state's common schools and explained that under the present circumstances Mississippi's young men, especially its veterans, could not obtain adequate preparatory training. To provide a short-term remedy to that dire situation, the university opened a preparatory department and relaxed its admission requirements. As a long-term solution Chancellor Waddel recommended the establishment of "a thorough system of public schools" to be linked with the "reorganization of the University upon an enlarged scheme." Waddel's proposed statewide school system embraced elementary, secondary, and higher education. This system, Waddel said, would "complete the circle of education, as concentric, not antagonistic, but mutually auxiliary." The 1865 legislature rejected Waddel's recommendation because it was too expensive and too sweeping for those uncertain and troublesome times.

In spite of those difficult times, the university survived its first session after the Civil War in remarkably good fashion. There were virtually no disciplinary problems. Even the presence of black troops stationed in Oxford provoked only occasional and usually minor altercations between the students and the soldiers. The black troops were gone by May 1866, two months before the assembly of a large and potentially unruly crowd for commencement. In anticipation of a large commencement attendance, editor Sam Thompson of the Oxford *Falcon* brought to the attention of Oxford's city fathers a serious problem. In April 1866, Thompson wrote, "There are . . . festive youths who visit Oxford frequently, and indulge too freely in something stronger than lemonade, and when they start home, run their horses at full speed through our streets. Do our city authorities know anything of this?—if they don't we do."

The 1866 commencement at the University of Mississippi was unlike any other in its brief history. There were no graduates, but members of the class of 1861 who survived the war were invited to commencement to receive their diplomas. Captain Francis A. Pope spoke on behalf of his class. At one point during his emotional address, Pope turned and recognized a special member of the board of trustees—Charles Clark, the three-times wounded and disabled Confederate general who was elected governor in 1863 and imprisoned at Fort Pulaski in 1865. His gracious gesture "loosed the pent up emotions" of those in attendance and the "big college hall . . . rang with . . . applause."

Following his address, in a solemn and moving ceremony, Francis A. Pope, James Edward Wilson, Francis Fentress, Reuben Turner Pollard, Henry Gore Fernandez, William Lea, James Lufkin McCaskill, Duncan McCollum, and James Alexander Wiley accepted the diplomas they left behind in their youthful rush to war. After these nine young men were awarded their diplomas, critics accused the administration of giving diplomas to anyone and everyone who had ever attended the university. Chancellor Waddel, who awarded the diplomas and defended the university's decision to do so, must have had a special affection for those student soldiers who had survived the war. One morning soon after the Battle of Atlanta in 1864, Waddel recalled many years later, "I was awakened by a heavy knock at my door, and a dispatch was handed me, which I read by the grey light of early morning, containing these dreadful words: *'Your son, Gray, was killed this morning.'*"

The burden of the Lost Cause weighed heavily on students at the University of Mississippi, especially in the first few years after the Civil War. Burton Harrison's sister read his letters from prison to their mother in chapel. Scholarships were offered to Jefferson Davis's son and to the son of William B. Reed, Davis's chief counsel who volunteered his services to defend the president against the charge of treason. Although their sons did not enroll, the only son of Nathan Bedford Forrest, William M. Forrest, did enroll at the university when it reopened in 1865.

Commencement speakers, poets and politicians placed on the young shoulders of university graduates the burden of historical memory. As they were called on before the war to safeguard a way of life, they were now called on to keep safe the memory of that way of life. Reverend T. D. Witherspoon, class of 1857, implored the class of 1867 "to embalm in literature, and thus preserve in . . . memory [that] civilization which has been an ornament of the South." It was their duty, he said, "to prepare a peculiarly Southern series of textbooks for the youth of the South [and] transmit to posterity in permanent form a . . . record of the struggle which just closed." The "pen must win," wrote a Mississippi poetess, "what the sword has lost."

Most white Mississippians were emotionally and psychologically unprepared for military defeat and the consequences of emancipation, but circumstances beyond their control forced them to accept the "world remade by the Civil War," and the reconstruction of the union. There were two phases of Reconstruction in Mississippi. During the first period, known as Presidential Reconstuction (1865 to 1867), President Andrew Johnson implemented a cautious and conciliatory policy for the restoration of the union. The second phase, known as Congressional or Radical Reconstruction, began in 1867 when Congress took control of the process. Congress disfranchised a large portion of the state's white population for their participation in the rebellion and extended full citizenship to Mississippi's 436,000 former slaves, who were then called freedmen.

The Mississippi Republican Party, which included Northerners called carpetbaggers, Southern whites known as scalawags, and the freedmen, installed the new order in January 1870, and it lasted until 1876. The idea of their former slaves holding public office was a bewildering notion to most white Mississippians. The freedmen had a saying: "The bottom rail is now on top." The magnitude of change in post-Civil War Mississippi is difficult to measure in word, but the following letter does:

House of Representatives
Jackson, Mississippi
March 26, 1870

To His Excellency Governor James L. Alcorn:

Governor, I was a slave of Col. W. G. Henderson. Boys together as we were, he is the center of the tenderest associations of my life. Arrived at manhood's estate, I was still intimately connected with him. . . . When he was wounded at Upperville, . . . he languished in the valley of Virginia . . . until it was my privilege to take him away, secretly, through the lines to his own people.

> My friend and loving master is a candidate for . . . Circuit Judge . . . and a good republican.
>
> Now, Governor, I, by the mysterious providence of God, am a member of the Legislature . . . and I now place . . . my earnest prayer that you appoint to the Judgeship of the First District the playmate of my boyhood, the companion of my manhood, the generous friend of my whole life—my former master, Col. Henderson.
>
> /s/ Ambrose Henderson

To most white Mississippians the new order was an experiment doomed to failure and to be endured only as long as necessary. The words "carpetbagger" and "scalawag," were terms of hate and bitterness coined in a time of great social upheaval. Some carpetbaggers and scalawags were corrupt and incompetent, but most of them were like the Southern moderates in the 1960s who were willing to accept sweeping social changes they saw as desirable, necessary, and inevitable. Mississippians who could not or would not accept those changes used the terms in anger against the apostles of the new order.

One of the first measures passed by the Republican legislature in 1870 was a law establishing a statewide public school system. Another was a bill reorganizing the university with a new twelve member board of trustees. Under the new law the governor appointed the twelve trustees and continued as ex officio president of the board. Governor James L. Alcorn, a wealthy planter and former Confederate general, a Republican and by definition a scalawag, appointed a combination of Democrats and Republicans to the university's new board of trustees and enjoined them to "purge its halls [of] political factions, [a] vice that has haunted them so long." The Reconstruction board took office in June 1870.

In their "day of jubilee," Mississippi's former slaves craved the "stores and treasures of knowledge" that were secreted from them during their years in bondage. Their desire to know about "the world remade by the Civil War" left many white Mississippians uneasy. Edward Mayes, a tutor at the University of Mississippi in 1870, wrote about those anxious days of jubilee. "There was a strong undercurrent of nervous apprehension," he wrote, "lest at any time some aggressive negro student should . . . demand admission to the University, in which case an explosion was regarded as inevitable."

That undercurrent of apprehension prompted Judge Robert S. Hudson of Yazoo City to address an open letter to Chancellor Waddel asking him, "Will the faculty as now composed, receive or reject an applicant for admission as a student on account of color?" Waddel and the faculty responded that they would be "governed by consideration of race and color" and would "instantly resign should the trustees require them to receive negro students." The Mississippi press published the correspondence between Hudson and Waddel, and their letters prompted extensive comment. William L. Sharkey praised Chancellor Waddel, saying "the University was saved" by his decisive and uncompromising statement. The Jackson *Clarion* also praised the faculty: "We warmly endorse their stand." Governor Alcorn branded Hudson's letter as the "stuff of political hucksters" and chided the "obsequious faculty" for allowing "such a man as Judge Hudson" to intimidate them. He added that they were at liberty to resign at any time.

Robert W. Flournoy, a former slave owner and Confederate colonel, and editor of a Pontotoc newspaper called *Equal Rights,* believed the federal courts should settle the controversy over the admission of blacks to the state university. Flournoy encouraged black students "competent to enter the University" to seek admission and "test the question whether [Waddel] or the Constitution is supreme." No black students sought admission to the university, however, and only one Southern state university, the University of South Carolina, integrated during Reconstruction. Nearly a century later, a black student competent to enter the University of Mississippi sought admission. The federal courts ruled that "the Constitution is supreme" and ordered his admission. He enrolled, and the explosion, "regarded as inevitable," occurred.

As the Mississippi Republican Party installed the new political order in 1870, American higher education also entered a new era. According to one historian, 1870 was the *anno domino* of higher education in the United States. Two towering figures assumed college presidencies around that time: Charles W. Eliot at Harvard in 1869 and Noah Porter at Yale in 1871. Cornell and the University of California had recently opened; Frederick Barnard had just begun his career at Columbia; and Johns Hopkins University was on the drawing board. In his inaugural address at Yale, President Porter proclaimed that higher education was "convulsed by a revolution." By revolution's end, American collegiate education would be secularized, there would be few clerics among the academics, and the purpose of a college education would be to develop the student's intellect and have fun, rather than "to militate the condition of man and direct his heart to heaven."

Chapter 6

A REPUBLIC OF LETTERS, 1870–1887

The spot where we now stand, though not "holy ground," is invested with no ordinary interest to every Mississippian.

Chancellor John Waddel, 1873

In 1871 the University of Mississippi was transformed from a liberal arts college with a prescribed classical curriculum to a university with an elective curriculum, an undergraduate college, and several professional schools. That transition began with the inauguration of Chancellor Waddel. In his address opening the fall session of 1865, the chancellor urged the board of trustees to restructure the institution and make the university a "republic of letters." The board eventually accepted his recommendation, and in the summer of 1869 Waddel visited Harvard, Yale, Amherst, Princeton, Massachusetts Institute of Technology, Brown, Michigan, Georgia and other institutions of higher learning. He did not visit Columbia, because President Barnard was in Europe. At the board's fall meeting in 1870, Waddel recommended an organizational structure for the University of Mississippi based on the best features of Harvard and Michigan. After a year-long study, the board of trustees approved Waddel's recommendation and directed him to implement as much of the plan as the university's financial condition would allow. Under Chancellor Waddel's reorganization, which he implemented in the fall of 1871, the university's expanded academic program included three departments: a department of professional studies, a department of science, literature, and arts, and a preparatory department.

As the state emerged from the devastation of the Civil War, Chancellor Waddel considered preparatory schools "the great want of Mississippi" and reluctantly established a precollege course at Oxford. Initially, preparatory students lived on the campus but attended classes in a rented building in Oxford. The preparatory department was a three-year program open to thirteen-year-olds and was a highly successful operation.

In fact, success was its undoing. Private academies and high schools across the state objected to collegiate preparatory departments because they impeded the growth of public high schools. University officials acknowledged the validity of that complaint, and, in the interest of promoting high schools in the state, the preparatory department was superseded by a subfreshman class in 1883. The subfreshman class was a one-year course open only to students who would matriculate at the university upon completion of the remedial program.

The university's new department of science, literature, and arts, which eventually became the college of liberal arts, offered six courses of study leading to four undergraduate degrees and two graduate degrees. The bachelor of arts, bachelor of science, and bachelor of civil engineering degrees were four-year prescribed courses. The bachelor of philosophy degree, a three-year program, was an elective course. The two graduate degrees were the master of arts and the doctor of philosophy. The professional department included a school of law and governmental science, a school of medicine and surgery (which did not open until 1903), and a college of agriculture.

The university's college of agriculture, which opened in 1872, was to be financed by revenue from a federal land grant donated to Mississippi under the Morrill Land Grant Act of 1862. The legislature allocated two-fifths of that revenue to the university and three-fifths to Alcorn University, the nation's first agricultural and mechanical college established for African Americans. The legislature did not, however, immediately appropriate any of the land grant funds to the university. Consequently, the college of agriculture was initially funded by a five-thousand-dollar allocation from the board of trustees. There were no funds from any source for instruction in the mechanical arts. The four-year course leading to a bachelor of scientific agriculture opened on October 2, 1872, with Eugene Hilgard as professor of agriculture and Martin W. Phillips adjunct professor and superintendent of the demonstration farm. The university's ninety-acre demonstration farm included a small orchard, a botanical garden, a sizable pasture, and sixteen to twenty acres under cultivation. The university catalog announced that Professor Hilgard used the latest farming implements on the demonstration farm, and that current issues of several agricultural journals were available in the library reading room. Agriculture, so the catalog stated, was taught at the University of Mississippi "as a profession, requiring varied knowledge and a liberal education, and fully equal in dignity to other professions, usually so designated."

Shortly after the opening of the college of agriculture, a dejected Hilgard reported to Chancellor Waddel that a lack of funds and prejudice against scientific farming had stymied the program. Hilgard suggested an educational campaign to "dispel prejudice and misunderstandings" against "book farming." After the close of the second session, with only one student enrolled, Hilgard realized that the general public would never support his fledgling enterprise. Mississippi farmers and the state's agricultural press preferred their own agricultural college separate and independent from the old aristocratic state university at Oxford. In 1873 Hilgard resigned and accepted a position at the University of Michigan. After a short stay in Ann Arbor, Hilgard became dean of the school of agriculture at the University of California, where he enjoyed a long and distinguished career, earning the reputation as "the father of soil science." After Hilgard's resignation, the University of Mississippi's school of agriculture languished and the administration abandoned the enterprise in 1876. Two years later, the legislature established Mississippi Agricultural and Mechanical College at Starkville.

Professor Hilgard's departure was followed a year later by the sudden and unexpected resignation of Chancellor Waddel. On June 26, 1874, immediately after breakfast and under "divine inspiration," Waddel decided to resign. He was a sentimentalist who had a deep affection for the university and was loath to leave the institution that had been a part of his life for so long. A year before his resignation, Chancellor Waddel delivered the principal address at a ceremony commemorating the university's twenty-fifth anniversary. Though he did not realize it at the time, that speech was his last major public address as chancellor, and it was his affectionate farewell to the university. The closing sentences speak of his deep feelings for the institution: "This University has my heart's affections. She was my first love. . . . I may not stand upon the same lofty elevation whereon stand my predecessors, Holmes and Barnard; I may never reach the eminence of Longstreet . . . but I would fain carve my humble name upon the pedestal of the University Monument. When the touch of death shall lay me in the grave, then let me sweetly sleep beneath the shadow of her fame, amid these classic groves. Content shall

I be to know, and to have it known, that, with such men, I labored for THE GLORY OF THE UNIVERSITY OF MISSISSIPPI." A premonition had brought Waddel to the University of Mississippi in 1844, and an inspiration took him away in 1874.

Chancellor Waddel's resignation, at the age of sixty-one, was prompted by the desire to devote the rest of his life to his beloved Presbyterian Church. The resignation was precipitated, however, by an incident at the chancellor's annual reception a few days earlier. Several Republican members of the board of trustees indicated to Chancellor Waddel that they would attend his reception. "As I sincerely desired to have them feel at home and enjoy the evening," Waddel wrote many years later, "I [intended] to have those gentlemen introduced to the ladies who were present." A few days before the reception the chancellor "took the precaution to ascertain the personal sentiment of the ladies in this regard, and ascertain whether it would be agreeable to them to be presented in this way." Unfortunately for the chancellor, "Every lady whom I approached declined very quietly, but very promptly." Chancellor Waddel learned that the trustees "resented this neglect, and laid the entire blame to my charge." To Waddel, the affair was "one of those unavoidable circumstances . . . which could not be explained without making matters worse." When Waddel heard of the board's dissatisfaction, he took it as an omen confirming his inclination to resign. The trustees, genuinely surprised by his action, called him before the board and asked him to reconsider. Waddel agreed to do so but resubmitted his resignation a month later, and the board accepted it.

Chancellor Waddel had decided that he could do as much good for God and man in some other office with less "wear and tear of body and mind." The chancellor was no longer just a schoolmaster, as Barnard described the office in 1859. The chancellor was now as much a political as an educational official. Mississippians, Chancellor Waddel complained, have "manifested a greater enthusiasm in political contests than in all other matters, and in that vortex every other interest has been absorbed." Because he was the head of one of the most influential and important institutions in the state, John Waddel was inevitably caught up in the political fray, just as Longstreet and Barnard had been.

The increasingly political nature of his office disheartened Chancellor Waddel and he wearied of the constant need to defend the university against its critics, but his decision to resign was his own. It was not caused by political interference with his authority by the Republican board of trustees. The Reconstruction board did not intrude upon the administration of the university or disturb the faculty. Nevertheless, the Democrats railed against Governor Alcorn, Chancellor Waddel, the faculty, the trustees, and even the university itself. The Jackson *Clarion,* a partisan journal edited by Ethelbert Barksdale, claimed the university "had been ruthlessly seized by the Spoils men [Radical Republicans] who have determined to radicalize it."

Actually, the Republicans did not radicalize the university during Reconstruction. When the Republican board had its first meeting in June 1870, L. Q. C. Lamar was professor of law. He was extremely critical of Reconstruction, and, like Longstreet's attacks on the Know Nothings, Lamar's attacks on Republicans were often personal, always bitter, and sometimes violent. In federal court at Oxford, while defending several Ku Klux Klansmen, Lamar attempted to throw a chair at a witness and struck the United States marshal who restrained him. According to the historian of Reconstruction in Mississippi, Lamar wanted "to become a martyr at the hands of the Republicans," but the Reconstruction board scrupulously avoided a confrontation with him. Disappointed in the board's refusal "to cooperate in his scheme," Lamar resigned in the summer of 1870 and was soon after elected to Congress.

Thomas L. Walton, class of 1854, an 1857 graduate of the law school, and a Republican, succeeded Lamar. Walton's views on states' rights brought criticism to him and to the university. Professor Walton taught his law students that the federal constitution took precedence over the state constitution, laws, and judicial proceedings. In speeches, articles, and lectures, Walton insisted that Mississippi was bound by the Fourteenth Amendment and must abide by federal court orders based on that amendment. When Walton's views reached south Mississippi, the Crystal Springs *Monitor* called on Mississippians to take their sons out of the university where "their minds were being imbued with the worst principles of scalawag and carpet-bag politics."

The criticism of the university by Democratic partisans was evidence that Governor Alcorn's plea "to purge its halls [of] political factions" had gone unheeded. Moreover, most of the criticism was unfounded or fabricated. Jonathan Tarbell, an especially despised carpetbagger and a member of the board of trustees who was often singled out for special abuse, claimed that no "political question or consideration has ever intruded itself into deliberations of the trustees." Judge Tarbell made that statement during the bitter campaign of 1873, when Adelbert Ames, a carpetbagger, defeated James Alcorn for governor. The statement may have been self-serving, but there is evidence supporting Tarbell's claim that "the political bias of individual trustees" did not influence their decisions. On February 1, 1873, Professor Alexander Quinche reassured John Lipscomb Johnson, an unreconstructed Rebel who later claimed to be the author of Mississippi's Jim Crow law, that the Republican "policy towards the University has been much more conservative than any of us anticipated [and that] none of us have yet been molested on account of our political opinion." Quinche told Johnson, who was seeking an appointment at the University of Mississippi, that he did not believe the Republican board would remove "any professor . . . who faithfully discharges his duty." According to Quinche's count, there were seventeen Democrats and conservatives on the faculty and staff of the university, and only two were "loyal" to the party in power.

Edward Mayes, L. Q. C. Lamar's son-in-law and the first historian of the university, was a practicing attorney in Coffeeville during Governor Ames's administration (1874–76). He characterized Ames's policy toward the university as "thoroughly conservative and wise," adding that "he left it thoroughly alone." In his memoirs, Chancellor Waddel offered a similar assessment of Governor Alcorn's policy toward the university: "I sincerely believe that the policy of Governor Alcorn was directed to the advancement of the best interests of the University at all times." The University of Mississippi actually prospered under the Reconstruction government, and, during that volatile era, whatever damage it suffered came from those who claimed to be its friends.

The only circumstance in which the Reconstruction board became entangled in academic affairs involved student speeches at commencement, but that problem lasted well into the twentieth century. The first instance occurred in 1869 when a student heralded the Lost Cause in a speech entitled "Our Dead Heroes." His oration included several derogatory references to federal officials. Several Republican members of the board of trustees criticized General Francis Shoup, the faculty member assigned to read and approve student orations, for allowing the speech. The former Confederate general indignantly informed the board that the student added the offending references after he approved the speech. The board accepted Professor Shoup's explanation and considered the matter closed. Professor Shoup, however, believing that his honor was called into question, tendered his resignation. Another student speaker who criticized the United States Congress got Chancellor Waddel in trouble with the board in 1872, but those were the only two cases in which the Republican board of trustees intruded upon the management of the university.

Perhaps the best indication that the Reconstruction board was not ruled by political bias was the appointment of an ex-Confederate general to succeed Chancellor Waddel. The board must not be given too much credit, however, because the general was the only applicant for the office. On October 7, 1874, the board of trustees elected Confederate Lieutenant General Alexander "Old Straight" Stewart chancellor and professor of mathematics. An 1842 graduate and former professor of mathematics at West Point (among his students was Stonewall Jackson), Stewart enjoyed a distinguished academic career before the war at the University of Nashville and at Cumberland University in Lebanon, Tennessee. General Stewart was an Old Line Whig, who opposed slavery and secession, and a Cumberland Presbyterian of deep persuasion. Robert A. Hill, a fellow Cumberland Presbyterian, federal judge and Republican member of the board of trustees, induced Stewart to accept the appointment. The first chancellor to hold a formal inaugural ceremony, General Stewart was installed on November 10, 1874, in the Oxford Cumberland Presbyterian Church. Congressman Lamar was the featured speaker.

In the summer following his first year in office, Chancellor Stewart took an extensive tour of Mississippi to acquaint himself with the university's patrons, convince them that the school merited their support, and assure them that their sons would be safe there. In hailing Chancellor Stewart's appointment and reiterating his assurance that the young men of Mississippi would be safe at the university, the student magazine asked, "What Mississippian can not trust his son with the instructor of Stonewall Jackson?" The student publication also defended the university against the recurring criticism that the trustees favored certain denominations in the appointment of faculty.

Chancellor Stewart's most immediate challenge was to arrest the enrollment decline. From a postwar high of 302 in 1873, enrollment fell to 208 in 1874, to 131 in 1875, and to 125 in 1876. Among the causes of the decline during the 1870s was the drumbeat of criticism by the Democratic press and the recurring charge that the university was an elitist institution. Although the number of students was small, most were members of the few wealthy families who could afford to send their sons to college, and this circumstance revived the antebellum criticism that the state university was a rich boys' school.

During the summer of 1875, when Chancellor Stewart toured the state, Mississippi was engaged in the most exciting electoral contest in its history. Political rallies were measured in acres rather than numbers. That legendary election, known in Mississippi folklore as the "Revolution of 1875," restored the Democratic Party to political power and is without parallel in the history of election abuse. In the language of Mississippi politics, it was an act of redemption committed in the interest of white supremacy. The Democratic Party's strategy was to make Reconstruction seem so calamitous that its cause—secession and Civil War—would be obscured, and to make Negro suffrage appear so injurious to good government that the disenfranchisement of blacks would justify the use of fraud and violence. The color line was drawn in Mississippi politics, and membership in the Democratic Party was expected of all white Mississippians. The enlistment of blacks in the white man's party, especially in the predominantly black counties, indicates that power, not principle, was at stake.

Following the Democratic sweep in 1875, the legislature impeached the lieutenant governor, Alexander K. Davis (an African American), forced Governor Adelbert Ames to resign under threat of impeachment, and reorganized the University of Mississippi. The law reorganizing the university created a fifteen-member board of trustees who served six-year staggered terms. Under the terms of the statute five of the fifteen trustees must be alumni of the university. Governor John Marshall Stone, the president pro tempore of the state senate who succeeded Governor Ames, continued as ex officio chairman and appointed the new board of trustees. Restoration of public confidence in the university was one of the first and most important goals of the new board.

A first step in that process was the publication of five thousand copies of a brochure entitled "Where Shall I Send My Son?" Written by Judge H. H. Chalmers of the state supreme court, class of 1853 and an influential member of the board of trustees, the pamphlet included a brief history of the university, a description of the campus, and a discussion of the curriculum. The brochure referred in glowing terms to the high morals of university students and to the "strong religious element in the student body." The board cited a "weekly prayer meeting, wholly gotten up and sustained [by the students] themselves without suggestion from any quarter" as evidence of the spiritual atmosphere on the campus. "We have been assured both by the faculty and by the citizens of Oxford that since the war drinking, gambling, extravagance and dissipation of every kind," the board announced proudly, "has been yearly diminishing." The board also stated categorically, "There are no sons of rich men there." The trustees concluded this remarkable tract with a plaintive appeal: "We long to see the halls of our State University crowded to overflowing with eager, ambitious and studious young men . . . to see the [commencement hall] crowded with happy mothers and sisters and sweethearts smiling with tearful joy as the young men bid adieu to the scenes of *Alma Mater,* and step forth to meet the stern realities of active life. These are the scenes which are witnessed each year at Charlottesville and Cornell, and Yale, and Harvard, and Dartmouth. It depends on you, fellow citizens, to say whether they shall be witnessed at *the* University of Mississippi."

If numbers alone are a measure, this pamphlet was one of the most effective recruiting efforts ever made by the university. The enrollment jumped from 125 in 1876 to 471 in 1877. Far more important than the brochure in this enrollment explosion, however, was the elimination of tuition in 1876. Other factors in the increase were the enrollment of 259 students in the preparatory department and the reopening of the law school. In 1874 the board of trustees closed the law school to prevent its relocation to Jackson and its integration. Board member Charles Clark introduced a motion in 1872 asking the legislature to amend the university's charter and move the law school to the state capital. A year later the legislature passed a bill authorizing the relocation of the law school but went much further than Clark had intended. The 1873 statute authorized, but did not direct, Alcorn University and the University of Mississippi to jointly establish and operate a law school in Jackson. Because of an indefinite funding mechanism and the controversy that an integrated law school would excite, the two universities took no steps to implement the law.

When Professor Thomas L. Walton resigned the chair of law to accept a judicial appointment in 1874, the trustees did not replace him and closed the law school. After the Democratic Party regained control of state government and the threat of integration passed, the board reopened the law school but had some difficulty in securing a professor. After J. J. Hamm declined the appointment, Edward Mayes accepted the position, and the school reopened in the fall of 1877 with thirty-six students. In 1881 Professor Mayes reinstated the two-year course, which had been reduced to one year in 1872.

Another factor in the restoration of public support for the university and the enrollment increase was the endorsement of the Jackson *Clarion,* its former and most bitter critic. Editor Ethelbert Barksdale acknowledged that he had been accused of hostility toward the state university but said that was not a fair charge. He maintained that he waged war against the Republican board of trustees but not the university itself. Now that it was redeemed from carpetbag and scalawag corruption, this "noble institution [was] entitled to command the attendance of the rising generation of Mississippians."

Chancellor Stewart began his administration just as Mississippi was entering a long period of financial austerity. The legislature sharply curtailed salaries, services, and expenditures. Congressman Lamar even suggested to Governor Stone that he sell the Governors Mansion in Jackson. During this period of retrenchment, the legislature reduced the university's annual budget from approximately fifty thousand dollars in the 1870s to about thirty-two thousand dollars in the 1880s. In spite of these pecuniary conditions, and even though Allen Cabaniss in his centennial history of the university calls him the "forgotten chancellor," there were many lasting and significant developments during the twelve-year administration of Old Straight Stewart.

One of the most important of those developments occurred in 1880 when the legislature acknowledged the state's obligation to the university for the loss of the seminary funds. In a memorial, drafted by Oxford lawyer and board member Hampton M. Sullivan, the board of trustees asked the legislature to honor that longstanding obligation and informed the lawmakers that the recovery of the seminary funds was essential if the University of Mississippi was to become "a seat of learning whose renown shall attract crowds from all parts of the earth, as did Cambridge, Bologna, and Oxford of old." It is doubtful that the legislature expected the university to reach such renown, but it did acknowledge the university's right to compensation and established an annual appropriation of thirty-two thousand dollars, an amount equal to the interest the institution would have received if the seminary funds had not been lost.

One important first during Chancellor Stewart's administration was the appointment of a full-time professional librarian. In the 1880s the University of Mississippi had more students but fewer library books than any other Southern state university except Virginia, which had more books and more students. When the Democratic trustees took office in 1876, they combined the offices of janitor and librarian as a cost-saving measure. Soon after assuming his duties, the janitor-librarian issued a plea to the faculty to surrender their keys to the library and to return their borrowed books. The library was located in a room on the third floor of the Lyceum and was open only two hours a week on Saturday morning. In its 1880 memorial to the legislature seeking reimbursement for the loss of the seminary fund the board cited improvement of the library as one of the university's most pressing needs. A year after the establishment of the endowment, the library was moved from the Lyceum to a room on the first floor of Lafayette Hall, the southwest dormitory. The board allocated seven hundred dollars for the renovation and furnishing of the library, and encouraged students to use the facility, which was now open three hours every day except Sunday. In 1882 the board reestablished the office of librarian, and placed a faculty member in charge of the library and reading room.

Having been without a librarian for several years, the library was in chaos. The most immediate need was to shelve, classify, and catalogue the library holdings in a manner that would make them accessible to the students. In 1883 when it received a request from the faculty for two hundred dollars for this "urgent necessity," the board expressed some displeasure with Chancellor Stewart that he had not already classified the holdings, because it authorized the employment of two people to catalogue the holdings two years earlier. Nevertheless, the board allocated twenty-four hundred dollars for the project and directed Chancellor Stewart to move the library from Lafayette Hall to the rotunda of the observatory. The rotunda was not large enough to house the collection, however, and Stewart moved the library from Lafayette Hall back into the Lyceum. More important, the board established the university's first full-time librarian and appointed Julia Wilcox, who began her duties on July 1, 1884. Appointed a year before Sarah McGehee Isom's appointment as a tutor in elocution, Miss Wilcox was the university's first full-time woman employee. Within three years she increased the size of the library to twelve thousand volumes. The law library, which was not under her control, contained fifteen hundred volumes in 1887. Miss Wilcox also doubled as postmistress after the university post office opened in Calhoun Hall in 1887.

The most visible and significant change during Chancellor Stewart's administration was the admission of women students. Chancellor Waddel had considered the possibility of coeducation during his reorganization of the university in 1871, and he acknowledged that some of the nation's finest collegiate institutions had adopted coeducation "with fine effect." He opposed coeducation, however, because "the association of the sexes in such close quarters impaired the delicacy which was woman's adornment." Notwithstanding the chancellor's opposition to educating the sexes in the same institution, the Reconstruction legislature established "a female department at the University of Mississippi, for the education of females, on the same and equal privileges that the males have been and are now being taught." The Reneau Female University of Mississippi at Oxford was established on April 5, 1872. The statute, which created a separate board of trustees for Reneau University, named Sallie Eola Reneau principal of the female department and vice president of the University of Mississippi. Although he opposed the establishment of the female branch of the university, its charter designated Chancellor Waddel ex officio president of the faculty of Reneau University.

The law establishing Reneau University authorized its board of trustees to build a separate twenty-five-acre campus on university lands that could accommodate up to five hundred students. The funding for this new institution was contingent upon the grant of another township to

Mississippi by the United States Congress. When it became evident that Congress would not make the anticipated grant, the legislature repealed the law establishing Reneau Female University in February 1873. Miss Reneau, who had worked for the creation of a state-supported college for women since the 1850s, abandoned her effort in Mississippi and moved to Tennessee.

The repeal of the law founding Reneau University did not settle the issue of coeducation at the University of Mississippi. Coeducation was a popular topic in the *Mississippi University Magazine,* which was revived in 1874. In December 1875 a male student writing in the *University Magazine* conceded that some women liked to be treated as inferior, as an "upper servant," but he predicted the day was coming when "women will take their place as equal of men." Typical of the arguments against coeducation was an assertion in the January 1876 issue that women's "reasoning powers . . . can not sustain long and intricate trains of thought."

By the early 1880s the debate had run its course, and most state universities had adopted coeducation. Standing in favor of coeducation were Chancellor Stewart and most of the faculty, especially John Lipscomb Johnson, Alexander Quinche, and Claudius Sears, whose daughters were among the first women to enroll at the university. Alexander M. Clayton, one of the university's original thirteen members of the board of trustees who was reappointed by Governor Stone after Reconstruction, joined Hampton Sullivan in persuading the board to authorize the admission of women to the collegiate department on the same basis as men in 1882. Females were not admitted to the preparatory department or to the law school, and the board did not allow women students to dine in the boardinghouses or live on campus, except in the home of a faculty member. The eleven women who matriculated in 1882 attended classes with the male students but had their own separate study rooms in the Lyceum. The university did not modify or expand its curriculum, and women students took "the severe classical, scientific and philosophical courses offered to the boys."

In the class of 1885, the first class with women graduates, highest honors went to Sallie Vick Hill. Mattie James Smythe won highest honors in the class of 1888. In their valedictory addresses, Miss Hill and Miss Smythe demonstrated that women could "sustain long and intricate trains of thought." In 1890 five of the university's twelve women graduates were college professors, one of whom was Sallie Vick Hill, a professor at the Industrial Institute and College at Columbus. In 1888 Professor Hill was a featured speaker at the University of Mississippi commencement. Despite the apparent success of coeducation, there were detractors, some of whom were bitter. The *Memphis Appeal* reported on June 1, 1886, that the board of trustees would likely abolish coeducation at its meeting later that month. The Memphis paper cited the opposition of male students, "almost to the unit," and their intention to "make every effort to have the young ladies excluded hereafter." The predicted repeal did not occur; the matter did not even come before the board at its June meeting.

Even after the state university began admitting women students, advocates of a state-supported college for women did not abandon their cause. Since the university did not offer the industrial and vocational training women needed to enter the expanding job market, Annie Coleman Peyton and others continued their support for an institution that would provide this kind of training. In 1884 the legislature established the Mississippi Industrial Institute and College at Columbus, which became Mississippi State College for Women and later Mississippi University for Women. In justifying the establishment of this new institution, a writer in the Jackson *Clarion* explained that "each school (the university and the industrial institute) occupies its own field . . . neither can do the work of the other."

With the adoption of coeducation and its immediate success, the appointment of a woman professor was simply a matter of time. Again, it was Hampton Sullivan who first broached the subject with the board of trustees. Before he brought the matter to the board, however, Sullivan wrote to Frederick Barnard asking for his advice. "The question as to female capacity for teaching in any branch," Barnard replied, "was practically settled in the Italian universities two centuries ago, and the University of Bologna still shows with pride the portraits of its female professors of the seventeenth century." In the fall of 1885 a month after receiving Barnard's response, which he may have read to the board, Sullivan recommended the appointment of Sarah McGehee Isom as a tutor of elocution. The daughter of Thomas Dudley Isom, Sarah Isom studied at Augusta Seminary at Staunton, Virginia, at the Philadelphia School of Expression, and with noted elocutionists in Boston. Several of her contemporaries believed Miss Isom could have been a great dramatic actress. Instead, she spent twenty-five years on the university faculty teaching speech and elocution. She was not involved in the feminist movement, which was led by Mississippi's Belle Kearney and others, but she did enjoy, according to Stark Young, a good cigar. The editors of the 1905 *Ole Miss,* dedicated the college yearbook to her, and in 1929 a new women's dormitory was named in her honor. In 1979 the university established The Sarah Isom Center for Women's Studies. Joanne V. Hawks was director of the Isom Center from 1979 until her death in 1998.

Through the closing decades of the nineteenth century, an era historians call the Gilded Age, the University of Mississippi was in a state of a transition from an old-time liberal arts college to a modern secular university. In the 1880s and 1890s the social functions of collegiate institutions became increasingly important, and American colleges initiated primitive versions of today's sophisticated recruitment programs. During the summer months, the board of trustees dispatched Chancellor Stewart and his learned professors to the four corners of Mississippi to recruit students. The board paid their travel expenses, and the university sometimes spent as much as seven hundred dollars a year in newspaper advertisements touting its advantages over Mississippi's other collegiate institutions.

During the industrial and cultural revolutions spawned by the Civil War, college students across the country created new forms of amusement and entertainment. In the Gilded Age college athletes displaced student orators as campus celebrities, and social fraternities eclipsed the literary societies. The postwar rise of the Greek system at the University of Mississippi began during the first session after the Civil War. In May 1866 a chapter of Sigma Alpha Epsilon, founded at the University of Alabama in 1856, was the first of many postwar fraternities established at the University of Mississippi. In June 1881 when the board of trustees voted to abolish the fraternity system in a crackdown on student misconduct, there were twelve active Greek societies at the university. The board minutes do not indicate a direct connection, but the crackdown occurred on the same day that a "lewd woman" was discovered in a boy's dormitory room. Later in the day the board rescinded its action abolishing fraternities. Although there is no direct evidence, it is probable that Hampton Sullivan, class of 1870, an active member of Delta

Psi and an influential member of the board of trustees in 1881, persuaded the board to repeal the ban on fraternities.

Paralleling the rise of fraternities was the rise of college sports. Athletic contests between the university and other collegiate institutions did not begin until the establishment of a football team in 1893, but students organized a baseball club in the early 1870s. The origin of the university's athletic program can be traced to an 1867 student request for courses in "physical culture" and the appointment of an instructor in calisthenics. The board of trustees declined that request but did agree to make repairs to the gymnasium. Ten years later students were still asking for courses in compulsory exercises. They also asked the board for a new and larger gymnasium. In the late nineteenth century a gymnasium was a room where gymnastic exercises were performed. It was not until much later that the term was used in reference to a basketball arena.

After the board declined the request for a physical education program, students organized a baseball club. The first mention of the club in official university records appears in the faculty minutes of April 18, 1871, when the faculty granted the baseball team permission to play a game in Holly Springs. Four years later, as the team became increasingly popular and the student body more sophisticated in its relationship with the administration, the secretary of the baseball club notified the faculty that the players had elected them honorary members of the team. The faculty graciously accepted and thanked the team for the honor.

Mississippi Agricultural and Mechanical College also had a baseball team in the 1880s, but there is no evidence that the state university and the agricultural college played each other. The university's baseball club, like A & M's team, played neighboring towns rather than other collegiate institutions. The university club probably played several games each year with the Oxford team known as the "Lamars." On March 27, 1883, the baseball club asked the faculty for permission to go to Water Valley for a Friday night game. The team members promised they would behave like gentlemen, would not drink any whiskey, and would be back on Saturday and ready for classes on Monday. The faculty approved the trip but sent along a professor to chaperone the team.

As some students were drawn to sports in that period of expanding interests and opportunities, others were drawn to music. In June 1874 a group of students asked the board of trustees to add music courses to the curriculum and for funds to buy musical instruments. The introduction of musical education and the purchase of instruments would result in a savings for the university, the students assured the board, because the student band could provide music during commencement week and save the board the expense of hiring musicians for that purpose. The Reconstruction board responded favorably and authorized five hundred dollars for the purchase of instruments and the employment of a part-time instructor. Unfortunately, the university's nascent music program was an early casualty of the Democratic board's austerity program.

Among the early signs of the secularization and modernization of the University of Mississippi was Jonathan Tarbell's recommendation in 1871 that literary men rather than ministers be invited as commencement speakers. Other signs included the university's discontinuation of the honorary doctor of divinity degree in 1883 and, after 1884, the printing of diplomas in English rather than Latin. According to Allen Cabaniss, the change from Latin to English diplomas was a sign that "the old learning which had dominated the schools of western civilization ever since the Renaissance was in decline."

For some members of the board of trustees, the old learning was not declining fast enough and the university was not modernizing quickly enough. Judge H. H. Chalmers, one of the board's strongest advocates of modernization, wrote a long letter to Barnard in August 1880 asking his advice on a wide range of topics. The university's operating budget was about thirty-two thousand dollars a year, which in those times of retrenchment seemed excessive to Chalmers. Could the budget be reduced without comprising the university's academic integrity, he asked Barnard. Chalmers also thought there were too many students and too many courses in some subjects, while other courses had low enrollments. Should English literature be combined with some other department, he asked, and should the number of Greek and Latin courses be reduced. Barnard's reply to Chalmers, if one was made, has not been found.

With or without Barnard's assistance, Chalmers presented a lengthy report to the board of trustees on June 20, 1884, recommending several changes in the operation of the university. Chalmers proposed a tuition fee of fifty dollars a year to be divided among the faculty and, because the faculty-student ratio was too high, he recommended a reduction in the teaching staff, which would also enable the board to substantially raise faculty salaries. His proposal included six-year contracts and the classification of the faculty in such a way that one-third would be up for contract renewal every two years. Chalmers also recommended that the faculty be given a primary role in faculty appointments. Under his proposal the faculty would present three names to the board of trustees along with accompanying documents and recommendations. The board would make the appointment from the three names submitted by the faculty. Chalmers also recommended that the board place five thousand dollars of the university's thirty-two-thousand-dollar annual appropriation in a trust fund each year to build a permanent endowment, and to allocate the interest from the endowment to the library and capital construction. The principal would remain intact. Finally, Chalmers recommended shortening the seven-day commencement to three days and the discontinuation of most of the fifteen student orations.

Two months after Chalmers's report, the board voted on his recommendations. The board combined and abolished some chairs, but did not give the faculty a raise or long-term contracts. Instead, the board ordered a 10 percent across-the-board reduction in salaries and restated its long-standing policy that the faculty serve at the pleasure of the board. This stern action reflected the board's growing dissatisfaction with Chancellor Stewart and the faculty. In a section of his letter to Barnard marked "private and confidential," Judge Chalmers asked Barnard if he knew enough about the university's current faculty to suggest any changes. Chancellor Stewart and the senior members of the faculty had come of age under the influence of the classical curriculum and the "genteel tradition." Judge Chalmers and his allies on the board believed that the faculty, some of whom had been at the university for twenty years or more, did not sense the seismic shift that was occurring in American higher education and were not much interested in modernizing the institution.

The board's dissatisfaction with the faculty was not a well-kept secret, and there were several public manifestations of that displeasure. On February 11, 1886, Joshua Kilpatrick, class of 1875 and former tutor at the university, wrote a long letter to his friend Louis McInnis, class of 1876 and also a former tutor. Kilpatrick told his old school chum he had read in the Oxford *Falcon* that August Blomgren, the university proctor, had been fired, and he predicted there would be others. Kilpatrick wondered how much longer the university could "hold together without an explosion."

Kilpatrick also advised McInnis not to enroll in the university's Ph.D. program because the degree had been "shorn of its honor." The board of trustees awarded Robert H. Loughridge an honorary Ph.D. in 1877 without the approval of the faculty. Kilpatrick told McInnis that Hampton Sullivan, a Delta Psi, arranged for Loughridge, a fraternity brother, to get the degree. There may be some truth to that, but Loughridge had done work toward the degree under Professor Hilgard before he left the university. After receiving his Ph.D., Loughridge was associated for many years with Professor Hilgard in the school of agriculture at the University of California.

The explosion Kilpatrick predicted in February 1886 occurred six months later. At its June 24 meeting, the board of trustees declared all chairs vacant, "with a view to a thorough reorganization of the faculty." This drastic action was the culmination of nearly a decade of the board's frustration with the general state of affairs at the university. In June 1880 the board created a special committee to investigate the "entire operation of the University." Nothing would be "beyond the scope of their investigation." In 1881 the board complained about students who were absent from classes "on the plea of sickness" and directed the faculty to "repair this evil." An article in the *Mississippi University Magazine* accusing Professor John Lipscomb Johnson of being prejudicial and subjective in his grading method sparked a protracted controversy about the "marking system" at the university. The faculty censured A. S. Meharg, the author of the article, and G. R. Price, editor of the magazine. The faculty also demanded and received an apology from Meharg for the strong language he used in the article. Eventually, the board directed the faculty to draft a new and more objective marking system, and, on November 11, 1884, the faculty adopted the following grading scale: 90–100, Excellent; 75–90, Good; 50–75, Passable; below 50, Deficient.

Though it is always difficult to judge the validity of student complaints, some students and alumni accused the faculty of maintaining an "icy reserve" and cited a lack of rapport between the faculty and students. The senior class appeared twice before the board to express their general dissatisfaction with the faculty. Student grievances against the professor of mathematics were so insistent that the board of trustees directed the professor "to give more time to oral explanations in the lectures." Johnson, the professor of English, "had the honor to be called before the board" to answer various complaints about him. On one occasion, Johnson removed his coat and challenged a student to a fist-fight. The student was the son of the professor of modern languages.

An "Alumnus" wrote a lengthy letter to the Jackson *Clarion* on June 30, 1886, calling for a wholesale shake-up of the faculty. This writer dismissed the debate about coeducation at the university as irrelevant because professors would soon outnumber the students if the enrollment decline continued. The enrollment in 1886 was 185. To call the college at Oxford a university, this writer said, was a "burlesque." What the university needed was "an infusion of young, progressive and vigorous blood."

There were rumblings of dissension among the faculty as well. These complaints are also difficult to assess from this great distance of time, but there is evidence that General Sears, a West Point graduate and professor of mathematics, detested General Stewart, his old commander in the Army of Tennessee. In his memoirs, Professor Johnson recounted a conversation with Professor Sears, who lamented: "I was under him at West Point; I was under him in the Army; I am under him now; and I reckon I will be under him in h–ll." Professor Johnson, a Baptist minister, excused Professor Sears's unparliamentary language on the grounds that he was an Episcopalian and, consequently, had a "license for free speech." Johnson referred to Professor Sears and Professor Wheat as the Big Two who "had their way in the conduct of the institution" except when he challenged them, which he often did, and, by his own estimate, successfully.

Professor Johnson also had a low opinion of Chancellor Stewart. He referred to General Stewart as "a stern West Point martinet" and "a religious crank {who} read his little New Testament as he walked about the campus." Johnson ridiculed Chancellor Stewart for kneeling in prayer with students he was disciplining, and as a Baptist minister, Professor Johnson disagreed with the Cumberland Presbyterian's theology. Stewart "preached the Christian's power to get anything he wished for the asking." "One evening," Johnson recalls, "when he and I were sitting on my front porch . . . I {asked}: General, if you believe that . . . why do you let General Sears go stumping it around here on a wooden leg, when you, by asking for it, could get a new leg to grow out for him? You are the worst man I know, if you can do it and don't do it." To Professor Johnson, it was "easy to see that such a man would be unpopular in a State University."

Of all the reasons Chancellor Stewart and the faculty might incur the displeasure of the board of trustees and the public at large, the most egregious was the continuing problem of student discipline. The elimination of tuition fees, an increasing number of students pursuing "select studies" and the competition for students between the university and the agricultural college generated a corresponding pressure to relax admission standards, which in turn led to discipline problems. The faculty minutes for the 1880s are replete with appeals from students with academic deficiencies for admission to the collegiate course. Rarely did the faculty reject those appeals. Students admitted on probation were allowed to correct their deficiencies before moving up to the sophomore class; if they were unable to do so, they could remain at the university and pursue an entirely elective course identified in the catalog as "select studies."

To keep students in school and to shield the university from criticism for its declining enrollments, the administration and faculty devised a system of departmental diplomas and certificates. Students who could not meet the graduation standards for baccalaureate degrees received diplomas from various departments in the school of arts and sciences or certificates of proficiency in one or more subjects. These diplomas and certificates, awarded at commencement, compromised the integrity of the degrees given by the university, and some graduates objected to the recipients of these awards being classified as alumni. The issue became so contentious that the legislature passed a resolution stating that students receiving degrees, diplomas, or certificates were alumni of the University of Mississippi. Some trustees opposed departmental diplomas and certificates but accepted them as a necessary evil as the university was inexorably drawn into a "mere scramble for numbers." On June 21, 1899, the board of trustees changed departmental diplomas to "certificates of proficiency" and discontinued the practice of awarding them at the commencement ceremony. The chancellor presented them privately to the recipients, and the 1904 catalog states that the holder of a certificate "shall not be considered an alumnus of the University."

With the Confederate veterans gone and the enrollment of so many "little boys" in the preparatory department, some of whom were only thirteen years old, student misbehavior became a matter of public concern and controversy. Railroad authorities complained that students were throwing stones at the cars as they passed beneath the bridge across Hilgard's Cut and that students sometimes annoyed passengers at the Oxford depot. Judge Robert Hill, a university trustee, complained of card playing and introduced a resolution to expel any student caught playing cards for money. In the spring of 1876, the *Mississippi University Magazine* reported that "tying balls of fire to the tails of calves on dark nights to see them run across the campus" was a favorite amusement that spring. That was one type of mischief that could be easily remedied. The board decreed that faculty could no longer keep cows, hogs, or chickens on the campus. They could, at their own expense, enclose portions of the university lands for their personal use and keep their livestock in those designated areas.

Student hazing, kangaroo courts, gambling, drinking, cheating, and disrespectful behavior toward the faculty were serious problems and were given wide currency in Mississippi newspapers, in pulpits across the state, and on the hustings. Reports of misconduct, such as a sixteen-year-old student boasting that he had voted in an Oxford election, received wide press coverage. On October 8, 1880, Judge Chalmers wrote to the faculty concerning the "many undesirable reports [of] immorality and intemperance" among the students. Judge Chalmers and other board members were especially embarrassed that special police were required, at three dollars a day, "to preserve order . . . at the Commencement Ball."

According to the faculty, the dormitory system was the major cause of student mischief. In the first few years after the Civil War, Confederate veterans, thirteen-year-old preparatory students, undergraduates, and law students were housed in common quarters. The veterans of Shiloh, Sharpsburg, and Spotsylvania would not submit to a curfew. Law students were not subject to the general regulations that governed undergraduates and had much more freedom of movement to and from the campus. Chancellor Waddel, who opposed the dormitory system on general principles, was especially averse to this mixture of students. It was, he told the board of trustees, "unwise to throw together in the same community parties whose privileges are not the same." In 1870 Waddel and the faculty recommended the abolition of the dormitory system. The faculty made a similar request in 1886, but the board rejected those recommendations and issued a directive that students would not be allowed to take their meals in Oxford and that all students must live in the dormitories even if three to a room. This "unnatural assembly" of young men was a source of continuing problems.

In the spring of 1881 the "faculty was mortified" by an incident in one of the dormitories. A "lewd woman" was found in a student's room. Before she was discovered, the faculty learned, several students had "visited" her. This incident resulted in the expulsion of five students and a stern warning to the postmistress of Oxford. Although the faculty minutes are not clear, it appears that the "lewd woman" might have been a mail carrier for the Oxford post office. During a discussion of this matter, the faculty passed a resolution complaining about the conduct of an employee of the Oxford post office, and Chancellor Stewart threatened to inform the postmistress's superiors in Washington if she did not correct the problem.

In response to increasing pressure from the board to deal more effectively with student misconduct, Chancellor Stewart initiated a weekly inspection of the dormitories "as is customary at West Point and other military schools." He also authorized faculty members to visit dormitory rooms at any time of the day or night. Several faculty members objected to this procedure, and Professor Johnson refused to "act as policeman and spy." Some professors were better disciplinarians than others, and some considered the military style regulations incompatible with the atmosphere of a college campus. Inconsistent enforcement of the rules, no doubt, encouraged misconduct.

The problem of making unruly teenagers behave was also exacerbated by influential parents who interceded for their sons. In a celebrated case, Judge J. A. P. Campbell, one of Mississippi's most prominent attorneys and a member of the state supreme court, pleaded with the faculty not to dismiss his son but to "indulge him for a time . . . say a month or two." His son had been previously dismissed from Mississippi College at Clinton for academic and disciplinary reasons. His son was not entirely at fault, the esteemed jurist explained; he was really a fine boy ruined by a college. Judge Campbell knew "what nurseries of evil colleges can be." His only desire was to do what was best for his "wayward son," and if the University of Mississippi could save him, the judge would "rejoice in its efforts." The faculty permitted Judge Campbell's son, who had an average of 40 in mathematics and 30 in English, to remain at the university, but he did not graduate.

In the interest of improving student discipline, the board decided not to hear any appeals from students except in cases of expulsion and empowered Chancellor Stewart with full authority over disciplinary matters. If any faculty member did not give the chancellor his full cooperation in disciplinary matters, that professor would be called before the board to account for his actions. The board also reestablished the compulsory dormitory visitation system that had been in place during the antebellum period.

After these measures produced no significant improvement in student conduct, the board of trustees, under pressure from the public to do something, declared all the university chairs vacant on June 24, 1886. The board's action was more an act of frustration than a blatant disregard for the university's integrity. Actually, the board had taken the same action two years earlier. At its June 1884 meeting the board declared all chairs vacant. The secretary of the board then called the roll of the faculty, and, as each name was called, the trustees voted by secret ballot to reelect that professor or request his resignation. As the roll call proceeded in 1884, the board of trustees reelected all professors.

In 1886 the results were quite different. As the board proceeded through the roll call, Chancellor Stewart and seven of the thirteen professors and tutors were reelected. The five professors not reelected were John J. Wheat, Claudius Wistar Sears, Alexander J. Quinche, George Little, and John Lipscomb Johnson. The board announced those chairs would be filled at a special meeting in July and invited applications for the five positions. According to one count, there were more than four hundred applications.

Two weeks after this shake-up, Alexander Clayton wrote a long and plaintive letter to Barnard explaining the board's action and asking for recommendations for new faculty members. Clayton reminded Barnard that he had been on the board of trustees when Barnard was chancellor. "You will say this is a . . . radical change. I think so myself," Clayton wrote, but some change "seemed a necessity." This drastic action, he explained, was not prompted by an "outbreak of feeling . . . but a pervading dissatisfaction." Clayton added that two of the five dismissed professors, Sears and Johnson, might be reappointed. One factor that influenced the board's action, he wrote, was the emerging rivalry between the agricultural college and the state university. An honest comparison between the two, Clayton confided to Barnard, was "not at all to the credit of the older institution." In 1880, the year Mississippi A & M opened, the university's enrollment was 414. Enrollment had dropped to 185 by 1886, the year of the faculty shakeup. Amid the many newspaper reports condemning or condoning the board's dismissal of the five professors was a letter praising the agricultural college at Starkville. According to this writer, the enrollment at Mississippi A & M in 1886 was 224 and he anticipated an enrollment of 300 the next year.

The dismissal of the five professors, affectionately called "old landmarks" by their supporters who pleaded with the board not to turn them out in their old age, caused a lot of comment and some serious maneuvering. One writer suggested keeping the faculty and getting rid of the "old fossils" on the board of trustees. Between his dismissal in June and the special board meeting in July, Professor Johnson laid his case before his larger constituency, the Mississippi Baptists. At the state convention in Meridian, Johnson and his allies maneuvered to have him elected president of the Mississippi Baptist Convention, which they believed would almost guarantee his reinstatement. Since his opponent "was a very popular man and it was by no means certain that I could be elected," Johnson wrote, "I determined to avoid the possibility of defeat by declining the nomination." He did, however, ask all of his Baptist friends to write letters to the board of trustees supporting his reelection.

When the trustees convened in July to fill the vacant chairs, they bowed to public pressure and reelected all five professors. At that meeting, Chancellor Stewart, now sixty-five, weary of the infighting among the faculty and tired of trying to make his students behave, submitted his resignation, and the board unanimously accepted it. Thinking it unlikely that they could find a suitable replacement for Stewart before the opening of the fall term, the board directed the faculty to elect a chairman who would exercise the power and authority "heretofore invested in the Chancellor." On July 29, 1886, Edward Mayes was "unanimously elected by acclamation" chairman of the faculty.

Chapter 7

OLE MISS, FOOTBALL, PRETTY WOMEN, AND RHODES SCHOLARS, 1887–1904

I hope the University is getting along fine. I didn't know that I did think so much of it until I got away from it.

FRANK ROBERTSON TO ELIZABETH M. HUNT, LIBRARIAN, FROM THE PHILIPPINES, 1901

At its commencement meeting in June 1887, the board of trustees commended the faculty for their cooperation during the difficult year following Chancellor Stewart's resignation. The trustees were especially pleased with the harmony and good will displayed by the faculty, at least on the surface. The student magazine also commended their professors, saying, "and last of all, there seems to be no discord." The magazine attributed that good will to Chairman Mayes and suggested that he be named chancellor, but the professors preferred the new administrative arrangement and reelected Edward Mayes chairman of the faculty. Even in this harmonious state of affairs, the board of trustees meant for the faculty to understand that they held their appointments at the will of the board. On the day after commending them, the board asked each professor to sign a statement acknowledging that he was employed at the pleasure of the board.

Chairman Mayes's efforts to maintain harmony with his faculty and board of trustees was complicated by a public dispute in 1887 with James Z. George, Mississippi's senior United States senator and a member of the board of trustees of Mississippi A & M. Senator George challenged the validity and the fairness of the legislature's 1880 special appropriation compensating the university for the seminary funds that were lost during the banking crisis of 1837. The original funds, he argued, were not designated to one particular "seminary of learning," and Mississippi A & M should receive a share. Senator George called the special appropriation "a fraud on the people of the State" and accused the university of making "forays on the treasury whenever it suits its convenience or its tastes to do so."

In a rejoinder, Chairman Mayes accused the senator of viewing the matter with "a jealous eye" and of being "anxious to find fault." A running debate between Senator George and Chairman Mayes, conducted in the press and in pamphlets, went on for several months. The ugly exchanges between George and Mayes reveal much about the origins of the rivalry between Ole Miss and Mississippi State. The dispute was ostensibly about money, but there was more to it than that. Senator George not only represented Mississippi A & M, he personified the "people's college." He was a son of the industrial class, and his admirers called him the "Commoner" with the same pride that the Populist followers of William Jennings Bryan hailed him as "the Great Commoner."

Senator George's aristocratic detractors chided him for his country manners and his unkemptness. He chewed tobacco, and its traces could be seen on his chin and sometimes on his shirtfront and vest. Without the benefit of a college connection, Senator George was a self-made man in a time when lineage was prized above self-reliance, and the gentry often taunted him for his lack of ancestry. Senator George's official congressional biography does not list his father's name or any of his forebears and states only that he "moved to Mississippi with his mother when a lad."

Edward Mayes was a study in contrast. He had a distinguished Virginia ancestry. His father served in two branches of government and held the chair of law at Transylvania University. Mayes began his college education in Virginia and earned two degrees from the University of Mississippi. He married L. Q. C. Lamar's daughter and through her he entered the lineage of the Longstreets. In his dialogue with Senator George, Chairman Mayes betrayed a contempt for his adversary and a condescension that smacked of class. That contempt was directed not just at George but also at the institution whose interests he defended.

The university was the state's "most precious possession," Chairman Mayes said, and, as such, it warranted the special appropriation. His logic was simple and unassailable; if the university were the state's most precious possession, the agricultural college was less important and therefore must occupy a lower level in Mississippi's educational hierarchy. In the minds of the alumni and friends of the agricultural college, the special appropriation was evidence that a hierarchy did exist, and they were incensed by it. Again, it was more than just a matter of money; it was the insinuation that the university's rich kids, the sons of the old aristocracy, still came first, that they were better than everyone else. To the sons of the gentry, Mississippi A & M was just a "cow college."

A legislative committee articulated in 1886 the popular notion that the university was the preeminent institution of higher learning: "Nothing is better calculated to detract from the merits of the [University] than unfriendly remarks. . . . It should not be regarded by other schools or colleges as a rival, but looked up to as . . . pre-eminently superior to all others, and to which all others should be tributary." The legislature's reference to the university as the state's superior institution and the call for an end to any criticism of it confirmed the claims of the industrial classes, in their minds at least, that the university was the last standing bastion of the old aristocracy.

The dispute between Senator George and Chairman Mayes was not resolved; it just ran out of steam. But that controversy was quickly followed by others. The most bitter dispute, and the one that may have eventually prompted Mayes's resignation, stemmed from his dismissal of five professors. In his 1889 annual report, Chairman Mayes recommended a major restructuring of the curriculum and the dismissal of professors Charles W. Hutson, John Lipscomb Johnson, Alexander J. Quinche, Claudius W. Sears, and Woodville Latham. Although the university awarded Professor Quinche severance pay for his years of long service, his dismissal was traumatic and aggravated a severe insomnia that had been troubling him for weeks. Two months after his dismissal, he took his own life.

The Oxford *Globe* was harshly critical of Mayes and the trustees for dismissing the five professors, especially Quinche and Sears, who had been at the university for many years. Two weeks after the shakeup, the *Globe* wrote, "If these changes were pending months ago, as appears to be the case, simple justice would have required that some warning should have been given to those whom it must have concerned." The editor did not mention that Quinche, Sears, and Johnson were fired and rehired in 1886, and he did not necessarily disagree with the action taken by Mayes. He admitted that the university was "going down on the shady side of the hill." What he did not like was the way Mayes handled the dismissals, but there was no easy or right way to dismiss a professor who has given many years of service to an institution and who may have stayed beyond his time.

On the day after dismissing the five professors, the board of trustees reinstated the office of chancellor and appointed Edward Mayes. The editor of the *Globe,* who thought there had been "too many bosses" at the university during the last few years, applauded his appointment. A native of Hinds County, a member of the class of 1868 and the law class of 1869, Edward Mayes was the first Mississippian and the first alumnus to hold the office of chancellor. After serving as a tutor in English in 1870, Mayes practiced law in Coffeeville until his appointment to the chair of law in 1877. In addition to reinstating the office, the board augmented its authority. The chancellor would have broad authority over the course of instruction, class schedules, textbooks, and student discipline.

During his first year in office, Chancellor Mayes increased the number of departments in the undergraduate college from ten to twenty-one. The increase resulted from the creation of several new departments, such as history, belles lettres, and elocution, from the division of the department of natural history into zoology, botany, and geology and by the division of the department of modern languages into the departments of French and German. Chancellor Mayes also established a philosophy department, a highly innovative move in 1889. In keeping with a national trend in American higher education, Mayes's new curriculum de-emphasized Latin, Greek, and classical studies.

As Chancellor Mayes was installing his new curriculum, he also began the construction of the university's first library building. The library holdings, which included approximately twelve thousand volumes, were in an unattractive and inaccessible room on the third floor of the overcrowded Lyceum. In 1889 the board of trustees authorized Mayes to retain an architect and allocated $10,000 for the construction of a building that could house approximately fifty thousand books. Mayes's new library building, designed by C. G. Rosenplanter of Memphis and built by W. F. Worley of Oxford, was constructed at a final cost of approximately $12,000.

One of the most interesting features of the library was the memorial window to the University Greys located on the north wall of the lobby.

The window depicts the Greys in parade formation in front of Barnard Observatory and in various battle scenes. The Tiffany stained-glass window was originally proposed by the Delta Gamma Sorority. When the Delta Gammas learned that they did not have sufficient funds to purchase the window, they asked for and received additional financial support from the alumni association. In accepting the financial support of the alumni, the Gammas agreed that the window would be a memorial to all university students who had served in the Confederate Army.

The great task confronting Miss Alice Beynes, who succeeded Julia Wilcox as librarian on October 11, 1887, in addition to moving the holdings down three flights of stairs and across the campus into a new building, was the classification of twelve thousand books, magazines, and journals under the new Dewey decimal system, designed by Melvil Dewey in 1876. The *University Magazine* was especially proud of the new library and explained the classification system and the process of checking out books. It was a simple and enduring method. A student wrote the call number on a checkout slip, signed the form, and handed it to Miss Beynes, who retrieved the requested book. (When the author joined the University of Mississippi faculty in 1970, that simple system was still in use.) Chancellor Mayes's library, which now houses the college of liberal arts, was named Ventress Hall in 1985 and restored in 1998.

After persuading the board of trustees to build a new library and to adopt his academic program, Mayes made an extensive tour of the state to defend his dismissal of the five professors and to explain the advantages of his new curriculum. He also published several lengthy letters in newspapers across the state. One letter filled six columns in the *Clarion-Ledger.* The *Meridian News* and the *Tate County Record* printed his letters, praised the chancellor, and offered their strongest endorsement of him and the university. The *Globe* commented, "Hardly an exchange [other state newspapers] do we pick up, but what we notice complimentary sayings concerning Chancellor Mayes."

Chancellor Mayes's tour improved the image of the university and widened his own popularity, and he soon became the topic of some political speculation. The Oxford *Globe* reported that Mayes was being touted for the United States Senate to succeed Edward Carey Walthall. It is not clear who was sponsoring Mayes, but he did not encourage the movement and asked his friends not to place his name in nomination. A short time later the Batesville *Panolian* reported that university students were urging Chancellor Mayes to run for the Mississippi Supreme Court. Again, there is no evidence that Mayes encouraged these maneuvers, but the speculations indicated that he was being drawn more deeply into the thickets of Mississippi politics. The more involved he was politically, the more vocal and relentless were his critics. Actually, Chancellor Mayes never got beyond the anger and controversy generated by his dismissal of the old professors in 1889. Their unforgiving friends and supporters, and the clerics—especially the Baptists (two of the five professors dismissed were Baptists)—never let up in their criticism of Mayes and the university.

Mayes eventually decided that being chancellor of the state university was not worth the price he had to pay or the pressure he had to bear. On June 23, 1891, Chancellor Mayes advised the board of trustees that he would resign in June of 1892 and advised them to begin the search for his successor. "I have come to a parting of the ways," he said. He would return to the practice of law. Mayes did not elaborate on his decision, but the lingering ill will over the faculty dismissals and the wearying demands of the office were factors in his decision. As chancellor, Edward Mayes also held the chair of law, disciplined the students, and fought a steadily declining enrollment. When he was appointed chancellor in 1889, the academic enrollment was 191. The next year it was 163, a drop of 15 percent, and the next year it went down another 10 percent, to 146. The low enrollment, said the *Port Gibson Reveille,* was proof that the University of Mississippi was a school of "elitists." It may be that Chancellor Mayes, after reorganizing the faculty and the curriculum and building a library, felt that he had done all he could do for the university and did not want to stay beyond his time.

Although Mayes had agreed to remain until June 1892, in December 1891 he informed the board that he would be leaving immediately. The death of Wiley P. Harris, the senior partner in a prominent Jackson law firm, prompted that unexpected announcement. After Harris's death, on December 3, 1891, Mayes decided to associate himself with the firm and resigned from the university in January 1892. Following Mayes's departure, the trustees appointed Albert Hall Whitfield to the chair of law and named Vice Chancellor Robert Fulton acting chancellor. At its next annual meeting, on June 28, 1892, the board of trustees elected Robert Fulton chancellor over former Lieutenant Governor Garvin D. Shands by a vote of five to four. Two years later, Shands was appointed to the chair of law when Professor Whitfield was elected to the state supreme court.

Chancellor Fulton, the second graduate of the university to serve as its chief administrative officer, was thoroughly familiar with the school's history and traditions, having graduated first in his class of 1869. Fulton was appointed tutor in the department of physics on March 5, 1871. At the time of his appointment as chancellor, Fulton was professor of physics and astronomy, a position he had held since 1875. One of Robert Fulton's first initiatives as chancellor was the elimination of the subfreshman class. In his 1892 annual report, Fulton recounted the problems created by that department and recommended its discontinuation. The board of trustees accepted his recommendation, and phased out the department by the end of the 1893 academic year. The *University Magazine,* which had published a mock curriculum for the "preps" that included Mother Goose and other nursery rhymes, praised the chancellor's action and enjoined the students, "Remember boys, this is . . . a University." With the "preps" gone, the university "assumed a new dignity."

Chancellor Fulton was a man of great energy and tenacity, and, like Barnard, he devoted his life and energy to the advancement of the University of Mississippi. Among his most notable achievements was the acquisition of a second federal land grant. After Fulton's third request, the United States Congress in 1894 awarded Mississippi 23,040 acres from the naval reserve land in Harrison and Jackson counties along the Gulf Coast. One of Chancellor Fulton's enduring legacies, the 1894 land grant provides a continuing source of income for the university.

Another of Chancellor Fulton's legacies is the beauty of the university's physical landscape. He lavished great care on the campus and is responsible for creating the university's most enduring and endearing landmark. When the library was built in 1889, the inner circle of the campus was enclosed by a wooden fence. After the completion of this new building, which was just outside the enclosure, Chancellor Fulton removed the wooden fence and extended the campus eastward to the railroad. He planted trees and ornamental shrubs in this area and privet hedge around its perimeter. To generations of Ole Miss students, this beautiful landscape would be known as the Grove.

The university's great natural beauty often drew praise from visitors. A Jackson reporter who covered the 1892 commencement noted that the "March Devil" that invades most college campuses in the spring "did not put in an appearance" at the university that year. This reporter called the campus "the loveliest landscape in the state." University students also took great pride in their campus. An article in the October 1894 issue of the *Magazine* shows how extravagant was their praise:

> Imagine your self this beautiful October day, a visitor who is approaching, for the first time, the campus of the University of Mississippi. . . . You approach from the town of Oxford, and as you approach through University Street you see the heads of the giant oaks on the campus just in front. The spire and roof of the Library building is the only thing visible above the dense foliage that wraps up all the other buildings; and so regular and green do the tops of these ancient trees present themselves to your view that you might fancy yourself nearing an elevated lawn all covered with the greenest grass and shrubbery. . . . You cross the railroad bridge and find yourself beneath the spreading arms of these matchless trees and passing over grounds that exhibit some of nature's best handiworks. . . . Here and there, in artistic order, a dignified old building of venerable style reaches up into the lofty trees as if to dispute a question of height with the sturdy hickories. . . . There at the end of the main walk stands the grand old Lyceum with its Doric columns and classical outline. How serenely and grandly does it look down upon you and how suggestive its towering grandeur.

Writing in the campus newspaper on May 7, 1902, a student called the campus the "prettiest place I ever saw." Spring is "busting out," he wrote, and the "magnificent oaks are beginning to cast an inviting shade [on] those hot spring days." Students could not "resist the temptation" of "passing a ball," playing "leap frog," and "lounging upon the green sward." The serenity of the university's expanding landscape was unexpectedly disturbed in the late 1880s by a newfangled machine. On March 29, 1889, the faculty bicycle committee recommended, and the faculty adopted, a set of regulations governing the use of bicycles on the campus. Riding bicycles on campus walkways or within three feet of sidewalks was "strictly prohibited." Riding on footpaths was allowed, but only at "moderate speeds." All bicycles had to have a bell that must be rung when the rider came within three feet of a pedestrian, and bicycles ridden at night were required to have a headlight. The faculty was enjoined to take the names of students violating these regulations and report them to the chancellor. Demerits were given for first offenses. A second offense could result in suspension.

In 1896, as Chancellor Fulton began the process of modernizing the campus, he replaced the cisterns that had been in use for many years with a deep well, and within a decade a metal tower replaced the wooden water tank. Two years after the construction of the new water tower, the university installed a sewer system and added water closets to the dormitories and most of the university's other buildings. In early 1901 steam heat and electricity were extended to the dormitories and classroom buildings. The communication revolution reached the university in 1904 with the installation of telephones in the Lyceum, the power plant, Ricks Hall (a women's dormitory), and the library. The finance committee of the board of trustees questioned the need for so many telephones and asked the chancellor if the university could get along with fewer. Apparently, Chancellor Fulton convinced the committee that they were all necessary, as the records do not indicate that any telephones were removed.

The finance committee did, however, draw the line on pianos. The university owned one piano, located in the chapel and used for daily religious services. When it learned that the university rented another piano for Ricks Hall, the finance committee directed Chancellor Fulton to return the rented piano. The committee could not justify such a frivolous expenditure of university funds. Exercising the art of gentle persuasion, Chancellor Fulton convinced the full board that the piano was a source of wholesome entertainment for the boys and girls who visited in the lobby of Ricks Hall. The board authorized the chancellor to purchase another piano.

One of the most visible and controversial additions to the university's physical landscape was the construction of two wings on the north and south exteriors of the Lyceum in 1903. In a section called "Pertinent Questions," the *University Magazine* wrote that it did not wish to be disrespectful of Chancellor Fulton, but felt compelled to express its opinion that the attachment of the two annexes compromised the classic lines of the Lyceum. After the new gymnasium and swimming pool, located in the south wing, opened in February 1904, the *Magazine* made no further complaints about stylistic compromises. The journal was soon complaining that the gymnasium and the swimming pool were too small and recommended the construction of a larger sports facility. The swimming pool was actually a small natatorium, or plunge bath, and not a swimming pool in the modern sense.

Of the several new buildings constructed in the early 1900s, the most imposing was the Science Hall, a four-story brick structure that housed most of the science departments and the university's medical school. The Science Hall was located on the site now occupied by Hume Hall. Another important addition was the infirmary, a one-story brick building named Brady Hall in honor of Minnie Brady, the university nurse. Brady Hall also housed the journalism department for many years, before it was razed in 1977 to make room for Coulter Hall. To meet the housing needs of an expanding faculty, the university built several new faculty houses in the early 1900s. A wholly unexpected need for specialized student housing developed in the early twentieth century with the increasing enrollment of married students. Though it is difficult to determine the number of married students, the university recognized this new dimension of collegiate education in August 1904, building two new cottages and repairing two existing cottages. Those four apartments, located in a small grove south of the Lyceum, were rented to married students.

The construction of Ricks Hall in 1903 temporarily relieved one of the university's most pressing needs in the early twentieth century—dormitory space for women students. The student newspaper noted that the new girls' dormitory, named for Fanny J. Ricks, one of the university's early benefactors, was "in a retired and convenient location on the campus." Student publications often referred to Ricks Hall as the "Coop," and for several years following its construction the campus newspaper carried news of women's activities in a column entitled "News From the Coop." Ricks Hall was demolished in 1976 to make room for the Ole Miss Union.

The construction of Ricks Hall was a milestone in the history of the University of Mississippi. Along with the appointment of a dean of women and the founding of a women's literary society in 1903, the opening of Ricks Hall symbolized the acceptance of coeducation as a legitimate function of the state university. The last serious effort to abolish coeducation occurred in 1906 when a state representative denounced the practice of educating both sexes at the same institution and called for its discontinuation. After that effort failed, there was no other major challenge to coeducation, and pretty women became an Ole Miss tradition. As this new tradition was evolving, the editor of the student newspaper reported that the rising generation of American women, including Ole Miss coeds, were slaves to beauty, but he noted that none were crying out for freedom.

In 1909 there were so many pretty women at Ole Miss that students held a contest to select the most beautiful. They voted Marguerite Rhodes of Oxford most beautiful in 1909 and again in 1910. Beginning in 1918 the college yearbook annually celebrated, in a special Parade of Beauties section, some of the university's beautiful women. The yearbook featured eleven coeds in 1918, nineteen the next year and in 1920 the *Ole Miss* featured twenty-four coeds in the Parade of Beauties section. The 1920 yearbook also included a William Faulkner tribute to the now legendary beauty of Ole Miss's pretty women:

TO A CO-ED

The dawn herself could not more beauty wear
Than you 'mid other women crowned in grace,
Nor have the sages known a fairer face
Than yours, gold-shadowed by your bright sweet hair[.]
Than you does Venus seem less heavenly fair;
The twilit hidden stillness in your eyes,
And throat, a singing bridge of still replies,
A slender bridge, yet all dreams hover there.
I could have turned unmoved from Helen's brow,
Who found no beauty in their Beatrice;
Their Thais seemed less lovely then as now,
Though some had bartered Athens for her kiss.
For down Time's arras, faint and fair and far,
Your face still beckons, like a lonely star.

W. Faulkner

In 1903, even after the opening of Ricks Hall, the editor of the student magazine wrote that the lack of housing and dining facilities remained "one of the [University's] greatest problems." The two boys' dormitories, with a capacity of 120, were full. The makeshift living quarters in the Lyceum and chapel were "quickly filled," and some professors took in boarders. In a dining hall designed for forty, Mrs. M. H. Crockett was feeding eighty students. Off-campus boarding houses, students complained, were expensive and inconvenient. The university obviously could not grow if it could not feed and house its students. In 1905 Chancellor Fulton and the board of trustees presented a comprehensive building plan to the legislature that included an additional men's dormitory and a dining hall to accommodate two hundred fifty students. The trustees also made the first formal request of university alumni to lobby the legislature. The lobbying effort on behalf of the building program was eventually successful and made possible the construction of Gordon Hall in 1909. This large and commodious building provided housing for two hundred male students and included a large dining hall.

Concerned as he was with enlarging the university's physical plant, Chancellor Fulton was also committed to enhancing its academic program. At the end of his second year, the chancellor advised the board of trustees that the University of Mississippi was not yet a true university and would not be until it established other schools of advanced learning in addition to the school of law. After several years of discussion and delay, the board of trustees finally established a school of engineering in 1900, which offered baccalaureate degrees in mining, electrical, and civil engineering.

The university's third professional school evolved from the 1893 summer seminar for Mississippi teachers, which brought together on the university campus the largest assembly of teachers ever held in Mississippi up to that time. More than one thousand teachers attended some portion of a month-long seminar financed in part by the Peabody Fund and taught by some of the South's premier educators. Following what the *University Magazine* called the "great summer school" of 1893, Professor James U. Barnard was appointed to the chair of pedagogy and began offering education courses ranging from school management to applied psychology. The increasing enrollment in the department of pedagogy prompted the university to establish the school of education in 1903. A decade later the school of education moved into a new forty-thousand-dollar building constructed with a grant from the Peabody Fund. The great success of the summer teacher institutes induced Chancellor Fulton and the faculty to expand the summer session to include academic courses leading to the various degrees offered by the university. A gift of fifteen hundred dollars from Fanny J. Ricks in 1900 enabled this expansion. In 1903 the summer school drew over 750 students, more than twice the number enrolled in the regular session.

In the year the school of education opened, the university also established a college of medicine under Dean Waller Leathers. During its early years the medical school was a two-year program. In a premature attempt to expand the medical school, the university entered into an agreement with the city of Vicksburg in 1909 to offer the third and fourth years at the state charity hospital, That arrangement was plagued by a lack of teaching facilities and laboratories, a competent faculty, and adequate funds. The Vicksburg branch of the medical school was in operation only two years and produced only four graduates. After that experiment failed, the medical school remained a two-year course until the founding of the University Medical Center at Jackson in 1955.

Five years after the establishment of the medical college, the university's fifth professional department, the pharmacy school, opened on September 24, 1908, with fifteen students. The school doubled its enrollment the following year to thirty-five. The two-year pharmacy program included 864 hours of lectures and 936 hours of laboratory work. In 1910 eight of the original fifteen students graduated with a bachelor of pharmacy degree. Professor Henry Minor Faser, the pharmacy school's first dean, and several other university professors held joint appointments in the department of arts and sciences, the college of medicine, and the school of pharmacy.

On June 1, 1907 the student newspaper applauded the establishment of the university's new professional schools. "The demands of modern times," a student writer proclaimed, "require something more of a university than classical and legal studies." Mississippi, he said, was losing many of its best people because they were going out of state for their professional training and not returning. This was one of the earliest references to the "brain drain," an outmigration that has robbed Mississippi of much of its talent, especially in the state's African American community.

The proliferation of professional schools in the late nineteenth and early twentieth centuries prompted a significant increase in academic research, a new and iconoclastic force in American higher education. College presidents across the country found it increasingly difficult "to find men who are strong intellectually and at the same time possessed by a distinct and aggressive interest in Christian work." As younger men with Ph.D.s gradually replaced the older Southern professors with their honorary LL.D.s, some presidents of Southern state universities viewed the intellectual detachment that pure research required as a threat to the region's belief system. The University of Mississippi awarded only three Ph.D.s in the 1890s and discontinued the doctoral program in the early 1900s.

This does not mean that Chancellor Fulton discouraged scholarship. He was one of the founders and first president of the Southern Association of Colleges and Schools, the regional accrediting agency that raised and standardized the curriculum in southern colleges and secondary schools. To upgrade the university's teaching corps, Fulton granted leaves of absence to young professors to work on their doctorates, and he encouraged faculty publications. Chancellor Fulton did not establish a policy of "publish or perish," but he did include in his annual reports the names of professors who published and the titles of their publications. "The highest type of university life," Chancellor Fulton wrote in 1906, "finds expression in the publications of its faculty."

In keeping with a national trend, Chancellor Fulton also implemented a system of professorial rank. Young professors, with Ph.D.s when possible, were appointed as assistant or associate professors at a lower salary than full professors. The promise of promotion and an increase in pay encouraged professional and academic development. The appointment at a lower rank allowed university officials to observe young professors for several years before conferring upon them the "element of permanence which is implied in a full professorship." The board of trustees approved Chancellor Fulton's system of professorial rank, but stated emphatically that, even though the term "full professor" might imply an "element of permanence," faculty of all ranks held their office at the will and pleasure of the board.

The *University Magazine* in January 1904 praised Chancellor Fulton for encouraging intellectual development and academic freedom, two traditions that any university worthy of the name would guarantee. "Education, if it means anything at all," the student editor wrote, "means freedom of intellect and freedom of speech. . . . There is nothing more pitiable than a college professor afraid to express his honest views for fear that they will not meet the approbation of the college president or the college board of trustees."

During the administrations of Mayes and Fulton, some of the university's best-known and most-admired professors joined the faculty. Among them was Eula Deaton, the university's first dean of women. She was also a graduate of the first class at the Industrial Institute and College and the first woman to earn a master's degree at the University of Mississippi. Perhaps the most popular and admired professor at the university at the turn of the century was Stark Young, assistant professor of English and the school's first writer of national prominence. A member of the class of 1901, Young was editor of the 1901 yearbook. While a young professor, he published *Guenevere* and *The Blind Man at the Window, and Other Poems.* The *University Magazine* took great pride in Professor Young, praised his work, and included some of his poems in the magazine. Other professors who joined the faculty during this period included Alfred Hume, Alexander Bondurant, Howard Odum, Thomas H. Somerville, David Horace Bishop, John Wesley Johnson, Paul Hill Saunders (the popular professor of ancient literature who received his Ph.D. from the University of Mississippi), and Franklin L. Riley, the university's first professionally trained historian.

All of these professors had lasting impact on the university, but Alexander Bondurant would fundamentally alter the character and function of the University of Mississippi. A Harvard-trained Latin professor, Bondurant introduced intercollegiate football to the university, served as its first coach, and nurtured the program through its early difficult years. In the April 1890 issue of the student magazine, Professor Bondurant wrote, "No phase of college life has had a more rapid development in American institutions than athletics, a name to which there was no corresponding fact for the students of a generation ago." The learned professor could also have said the same about the terms *college life, school spirit, student body, student press, extracurricular activities,* and *alumni affairs.*

Around the turn of the century, two new forces in American higher education appeared with enormous impact. Those forces, intercollegiate athletics and the alumni movement, intersected and interacted with each other. "The alumni movement," Frederick Rudolph wrote in his classic study of the American college and university, "had its own rationale, its own purposes, its own life, and how remote these were from the purposes of the professors was revealed by a great celebration at the New York Yale Club honoring the crew that had defeated Harvard." A Yale alumnus said on that auspicious occasion: "I would rather see the color of the blue-tipped oars first across the finish line than gaze at the matchless splendor of a masterpiece of Titian. I would rather watch the hats go over the cross bar after a Yale victory than the finest dramatic performance the world has ever known. I would rather in the midst of a titanic gridiron struggle hear 'March, march on down the field' than listen to the music of a great opera." Rudolph concluded, "Deeply imbedded in the structure of the American college and university were the values and apparatus that made such a speech possible and that henceforth could only confuse rather than clarify the nature and purpose of American higher education."

Writing in the 1930s Robert Maynard Hutchins, president of the University of Chicago, explained how such a speech could be made by a graduate of one of the world's great universities. "The emotional unity that the students fail to create in the college by making of themselves an intellectual community," Hutchins wrote, "is supplied by quasi-intellectual or nonintellectual activities, pre-eminently by intercollegiate sport. . . . Consider the alumnus. His college career represents one of life's climactic experiences, and it grows rosier in memory as it recedes in time. . . . As youth itself is overvalued, so also are the events that linger in memory. . . . In some as yet undefined way...renewed contact with intercollegiate athletics revives his youth as no other experience could."

By the turn of the century, the college campus was a self-contained community with its own customs, mores, and value system. There were so many nonintellectual and extracurricular activities at the University of Mississippi in the 1890s that the YMCA began publishing a handbook for new students. The handbook eventually became known as the *M-Book* and is still issued to new students each fall. A list of clubs and organizations compiled from student publications indicates the random nature of social organization at the university. Among the student groups were the YMCA, the Glee Club, the Mandolin and Guitar Club, the University Orchestra, and the Minstrels, a traveling musical troupe. Academic clubs included the Science Club, University Teacher's Club, Graduate (Students) Club, the Press Club for future journalists, the Sketch Club for art students, and the Dramatic Club.

Social and recreational clubs included the Kodak Club, the F.O.X. Social Club, and the Cotillion Club. The Stag Club, established in 1895, was a "gentleman's club" that admitted only seven select members of the law class. Its annual banquet was "a feast for the gods." The 1899 yearbook listed two shooting clubs. One was a gun club. Membership in the Shooting Club No. 2 was unrestricted and open to all "crap shooters." Among the many other organizations were the Delta Club, the Chess and Checker Clubs, the Boxing, Irish, and Jackson Hall Egg Clubs. Organizations for women students included the Talkatanti Club, the SSS Club, the YWCA, the Women's Athletic Association, the Tennis Club, and the Gymnasium Club.

The German Club, noted not for its study of language but for its annual levees, was one of the most popular social clubs on the campus. A minor crisis occurred in 1906 when rumors swept the campus that some of the boys at the German Club's annual ball were intoxicated and disorderly. The faculty summoned the officers of the club and ordered them to provide the names of the offenders. One by one, the officers testified that they had not seen anyone intoxicated or disorderly. Miss Deaton testified that her girls had seen no evidence of drinking or misbehavior. One coed did say that the "break down dance [was] a little rough," but, other than that, she had no complaint about anyone's behavior. The faculty accepted the testimony of the students and filed no charges of misconduct.

The popularity of social organizations took its toll on the university's oratorical tradition and the literary societies. Only about half of the students belonged to literary societies at the turn of the century, and some debates were canceled because no one entered the contests. This lack of interest confounded Sarah Isom, professor of elocution. "Why is it," she asked, "that a science and art like elocution . . . should now be comparatively disregarded as part of our education?" The editor of the student newspaper offered a simple explanation in the April 19, 1902, issue. First, most students would rather spend their time "loafing about" than debating the great issues of the day. Secondly, "we live in a cold, money making age [and] great orators like great poets are nearly all dead."

That "cold, money making age" was also a time of flux and change, when many old customs were giving way to new traditions, and the formal academic atmosphere of the college campus was changing to one of spontaneity and informality. In January 1905 the editor of the *Magazine* noted that the custom of students "touching the hat to a professor" was waning and he was sorry to see it go. Perhaps he was mollified by the introduction of the new tradition of wearing caps and gowns at commencement. The class of 1899, in celebration of the university's semicentennial commencement, was the first class to wear the traditional academic regalia.

One of the university's most distinguished academic traditions was established in 1905 with the appointment of the first Rhodes Scholar. Founded by a bequest of Sir Cecil Rhodes in 1903, Rhodes Scholarships are awarded to students in the former British Empire, the United States, and Germany to study at Oxford University. In 1904, the first year of competition, no Mississippian passed the qualifying examination. The *University Magazine* attributed that failure to "overconfidence, probably." That no Mississippian passed the examination, however, was a "disgrace," and the editor enjoined his readers to prepare for the next round of tests. Ebb J. Ford of Columbia took the editor's advice to heart, passed the examination and was named the first of the university's twenty-five Rhodes Scholars in the spring of 1905. In a December 30, 1905, letter to Chancellor Fulton, Ebb Ford wrote that he was having a wonderful time in the other Oxford and that he had supper with Rudyard Kipling on a recent visit to Berlin. Two years later Richard Capel Beckett of West Point was named the university's second Rhodes Scholar, and this proud tradition was well established.

Another honored Ole Miss tradition established in 1905 was the presentation of Taylor Medals. In honor of Marcus Elvis Taylor, class of 1871, Taylor Medals are awarded to students nominated by the faculty for superior scholarship in one particular academic discipline, combined with outstanding achievement in all other disciplines. The number of Taylor Medals awarded annually may not constitute more than 1 percent of the student body. The first three Taylor Medals were awarded in 1905.

The student press was important in establishing Ole Miss traditions and in shaping the university's identity, especially after the establishment of Mississippi Agricultural and Mechanical College. The first rivalry between Ole Miss and Mississippi State was not on the playing fields but in the pages of their student publications. In December 1895 the student magazine changed its name from *Mississippi University Magazine* to *The University of Mississippi Magazine* and chided the *College Reflector,* its counterpart at Mississippi A & M, for criticizing the university, for lacking dignity, and for bragging about its baseball team. The *University Magazine* said the best feature of the *Reflector* was its joke section.

Founded in 1856, the *University Magazine* was published monthly by the literary societies. It struggled financially through the years and was kept afloat by subscriptions, advertisements, and small grants from the board of trustees. In 1894 the editor chastised university students for not subscribing to the magazine: "If you are not patriotic enough to subscribe to it you are unfit to be a student at a great University like this. You had better be at home picking cotton." Anyone who would "not pay $1.00 for his own college magazine," the editor predicted, "will never amount to much."

The university's first student newspaper, *The University Record,* was established in 1898. Styling itself "A Journal of College Life," the *Record* was published every Wednesday to chronicle the exploits of the university's athletic teams. The *Record* also kept students informed of other campus activities and reminded them to remember the past. Under the caption "Our Confederate Cemetery," a student writer explained in the May 5, 1899, issue that several hundred Confederate soldiers killed at Shiloh were buried on the campus. "In a special sense," he wrote, "these . . . heroes [of] Shiloh, belong to us of the University, and . . . it is our duty to cherish their memory." Like the student magazine, the newspaper struggled financially and suspended publication after only four years. In May 1907 the YMCA and the student athletic association jointly established another weekly newspaper. The first issue of the *Varsity Voice* appeared on June 1, 1907. Editor C. R. Bolton announced that the *Varsity Voice* was published in the interest of the "Greater University of Mississippi" and for the "sons and daughters of Ole Miss both on the campus and away from the campus." The *Mississippian* superceded the *Varsity Voice* in 1911.

In 1897 the Greek societies established a college yearbook, which they titled *Ole Miss,* a name suggested by Elma Meek, a student from Oxford. The term "Ole Miss" was a title domestic slaves in the Old

South used to distinguish the mistress of the plantation house from the young misses of the family. The first volume of the yearbook was dedicated to the University Greys, and within two years students and alumni were referring to the University of Mississippi as Ole Miss. In the 1899 yearbook Durrell Miller celebrated his alma mater in song and verse:

A thousand leagues of prairie
Between my heart and bliss;
How can it then be merry,
Beloved Ole Miss?
How strong so'er I be
I needs must weep at this;
Thy hallowed groves I see
No more, Ole Miss.

* * * * * * * * * *

Let fortune smile on me,
Or o'er my failures hiss
As I am true to thee
Or false, Ole Miss.

* * * * * * * * * *

In his annual report on June 12, 1893, Chancellor Fulton informed the board of trustees that the faculty was now disposed to accept intercollegiate athletics, a phenomenon that was sweeping college campuses across the country. Many institutions, Chancellor Fulton said, had found that sports acted as "a safety valve to the exuberance of youthful spirits that would frequently find vent in some harmful way." During the thirteen years between Fulton's 1893 report and his resignation in 1906, the University of Mississippi would develop a complete program of "physical culture" and a full range of intercollegiate athletics. Ole Miss students received academic credit for courses in physical education that included gymnastics, cycling, swimming, boxing, and wrestling. Intercollegiate sports included baseball, tennis, women's basketball, track and field, cross country, and football. The student magazine was pleased to announce the addition of men's basketball in 1907 because it was a great game and, best of all, it came between football and baseball.

The centerpiece of the university's original sports program was football. Rutgers and Princeton played the first intercollegiate football game in the United States in 1869, though it was quite different from the present game. In the 1880s football evolved into the modern game and spread rapidly to colleges and high schools. Towns and cities across the country formed semipro teams and played other towns and even some college teams. It was a popular game, but there was widespread opposition to football because of its violent nature and the large number of injuries to the players, who wore practically no protective gear. After President Theodore Roosevelt threatened to ban football, the rules of the game were modified to make it less violent and to reduce the number of injuries.

In the early fall of 1893, Professor Alexander Bondurant, who became interested in football while in graduate school at Harvard, organized the university's first team and served as its coach. Dr. Chiles C. Ferrell, professor of modern languages, was assistant coach. In November 1893, as the first game approached, the student magazine reported: "All of our attention is now directed toward football. . . . The athletic fever has now taken full possession of the University." A week after the game the Oxford *Eagle* announced, "The athletic star is in the ascendancy."

The university played its first football game on November 11, 1893, at University Park on the campus. The Oxford *Eagle* reported on November 16, 1893: "The largest crowd that has gathered at the University Park for several years gathered last Saturday to witness the game of football between the University of Mississippi and the Southwestern Baptist University of Jackson, Tennessee." Several years later Professor Bondurant recalled that special occasion in the University's history: "The longed for day came at last, and a large body of students went to the station to welcome the visitors. . . . The square presented a festive appearance in its garb of crimson and dark blue bunting donned in honor of the day. . . . The afternoon was bright with just enough crispness in the air . . . and the crowd of vehicles and pedestrians that surged up University street . . . showed that the community was prepared to enter with zest the excitement attendant upon a football game." The first game was a lopsided 56 to 0 victory for the University of Mississippi.

About a week after the game, the *Eagle* received a letter from a lovestruck fan who saw "in your little city . . . the prettiest girl" in all the world and asked the editor to publish some verses he had written for her. The editor indulged his wish:

To An Oxford Beauty

Through all my travels in this world
I have just found the prettiest girl,
At the game of ball; what a charming sight
I beheld her there, with eyes so soft and bright.

So charming; pure, and sweet did she look
I drew from my pocket, an order book.
Her name; I would like to know says I.
When "Sarah" I heard come from a friend near by.
* * * * * *
Oh! How I wish that this was my home
That I might with this lady become well known,
But so long as abroad, it never can
Become the home of this traveling man.

The university's second game was in Memphis on November 18 against the Memphis Athletic Club. The excitement of the first victory caused the faculty to have a change of heart. The faculty had originally declined a student request that they be allowed to attend the game, but they relented and allowed the students to go to Memphis on the condition that each student pledge in writing not to drink any intoxicating beverages and to return to Oxford on the first train leaving Memphis after the game. During the game with the Memphis Athletic Club, Ole Miss fans assembled at a bookstore on the square where they received periodic reports of the game sent over the wires by the student manager. The *Eagle* reported: "Oxford celebrated her victory over the Memphis Athletic Club football team with great enthusiasm. A special telegraphic account of the game was received by Winchell and Davidson [the bookstore], and each bulletin brought forth greater crowds and louder yells. Nothing has created such excitement in Oxford since Cleveland's election. Bonfires were lit and crowds paraded the streets."

This report contains two interesting statements. First, the *Eagle* stated that "Oxford celebrated her victory" over the Memphis team. Oxford and the University of Mississippi have been almost interchangeable since the founding of the university, so closely are the two identified. The other reference of note is to Grover Cleveland, the first Democratic president elected (in 1884) since Abraham Lincoln. Southerners admired Cleveland for bringing many Southerners into his administration. He was especially admired for appointing Oxford's L. Q. C. Lamar secretary of the interior. Oxford is the only town in America that has produced two secretaries of the interior, the other was Jacob Thompson.

The 1893 game between the university and the Memphis Athletic Club was the first football game played in the "Bluff City" and drew a large attendance. The faculty generally opposed away games because they excited greater effort by the players, which often led to serious injury. The student athletic association convinced the faculty, however, that Oxford was too small to produce large gate receipts and the university would have to play some of its games in larger towns. During those early years the university often played in Jackson and other cities for that reason.

After another easy win in a rematch with SWBU, the football team traveled to New Orleans for a game with the Southern Athletic Club of New Orleans on November 30. The color and pageantry of college football was evident on that Thanksgiving afternoon. The Southern Athletic Club wore uniforms of light blue and white; the university wore red and blue. A large number of the three thousand spectators were University of Mississippi fans. The 24–0 loss to SAC was the only defeat suffered by the university in its initial season.

On Saturday, December 2, 1893, the University of Mississippi played its first game against Tulane University and won by a score of 12 to 4. The *Eagle* reported that "Oxford was ablaze with excitement Saturday... as the dispatches were coming from New Orleans....The excitement knew no bounds when the victory of the Oxford boys flew over the wire." According to another account, "Oxford is wild with enthusiasm. The citizens have turned the town over to the students.... College yells fill the air from all sides."

Two days before the Tulane game, just in case it was needed for a celebration, the Oxford *Eagle* printed one of the university's most popular yells: "Razzle, Dazzle, Gobble Gobble, Sis-Boom-Bah! 'Rah-'Rah-'Rah!!" This yell was not the official university cheer, which was "Ris! Ris! Ris! University of Miss! Hep! Hep! Hurrah!" In addition to the official university yell, each class had its own cheer. For example, the official cheer of the class of 1897 was "Sis-boom-bah! Hokey, pokey, yah! '97, '97, wah, whoo, wah!"

The university's first football team, which won four and lost one and graduated twelve of its sixteen players, presented few if any problems to the faculty athletic committee. But over the next several years, the complications that intercollegiate athletics generate in an academic environment became increasingly obvious. Players were given special permission to rearrange their schedules to avoid late afternoon classes. Some players who fell below the 70 percent grade requirement were given exemptions because of extenuating circumstances. The policy of discounting grades for absences was not applied to athletes, and eligibility forms were sometimes mysteriously signed by persons unknown.

Southern collegiate officials realized the importance of a regulatory agency and established the Southern Intercollegiate Athletic Association in Atlanta in 1894. By 1906 the SIAA included twenty colleges and universities in eight southern states. The announced objectives of the SIAA were "to reduce the evils of intercollegiate games to a minimum, . . . to keep college athletics free from any taint of professionalism [and] to regulate, supervise, and purify college athletics throughout the South."

The rules of the SIAA were few and simple: only students who registered at an institution within thirty days after the beginning of the fall session were eligible for team sports; anyone who had received pay to play any sport was ineligible; an athlete must sit out one year after transferring from one institution to another; and members of the association could play only collegiate teams. Professor Bondurant admitted that these rules were "exceedingly vigorous," but "they have been found necessary to keep men from being brought into an Institution for the primary purpose of participating in athletics." Bondurant believed that universities could follow these rules and "still develop winning teams."

Although the university had a winning season (6–1) in 1894, prospects for fielding a team in 1895 were not good. The student athletic association had no funds, and no one had volunteered to coach the team. The university magazine, which quoted Professor Bondurant as saying "the alumni demand a team," challenged the student body to support the football team or "submit to the humiliation of seeing the University of Mississippi take a very low standing in the department of athletics." At a pep rally on October 25, 1895, students agreed to raise the funds necessary to field a team and to hire a coach. With the help of Oxford supporters, and Professor Bondurant, the student body raised enough money to field a team, which played a three game schedule.

After surviving the 1895 season, an effort by Professor Alfred Hume to ban the game in 1898, and a loss in the first game with Mississippi A & M in 1901, football became an Ole Miss tradition. In a special 1903 commencement issue, the university magazine touted the benefits of college football to students, to the university, and to society. According to the student editor, "today's colleges and universities" because of their athletic programs produce "strong and vigorous men" instead of "the weak and sickly bookworms of twenty years ago." Football's "importance as a phase of college life is now universally realized and universities become widely known for their athletics. . . . Other things being equal the vast majority of students will select as their alma mater that institution which maintains a high athletic standing." Any institution of higher learning that does not recognize this, the editor concluded, is "blind to its own interest." In the spring following this article, Ole Miss students established the University of Mississippi Athletic Association and adopted, at the suggestion of Professor Bondurant, red and blue as the official school colors.

By the end of the first decade of the twentieth century, college football was America's game. In 1906 the *Mississippi Magazine* wrote that college football had "found a . . . unique place in the hearts of the American people. . . . Greece had the Olympics, Rome had its Coliseum and . . . American colleges will have the struggle of the gridiron." Ole Miss students cheered for the Red and Blue, and, like students across the country, they lionized "Autumn's Hero":

> Hero of the gridiron! Who has sung your praise?
> Who has lined in marble the beauty of your ways?

Chancellor Fulton's supposition that college sports would act as a harmless vent to "the exuberance of youthful spirits" was true at least through the 1890s. During that decade most disciplinary problems were relatively minor, and the university enjoyed a measure of success in repairing its reputation as a "Sodom or Gomorrah." In 1899 the student magazine boasted that the "people of Mississippi are no longer ashamed of Their

University" and the "pulpit has ceased its clamorings against the place it once considered so wicked."

But the clergy's good will and the university's improved reputation were short-lived. Just nine years later, in 1908, the student magazine expressed the hope that "the time is not far off when the parents of the State of Mississippi will no longer regard the University as a place where boys are taught dissipation in all forms, but will feel . . . safe in sending their sons and daughters here." In the first few years of the twentieth century, the conduct of Ole Miss students was a throwback to the 1880s, and widespread reports of misbehavior renewed the criticism that the university was a party school for rich kids. The number of expulsions for gambling and intoxication, along with a lingering controversy over the Greek system, brought a new round of criticism from the university's old enemies.

At the turn of the century, Stark Young remembered several years later, "a good number of our professors were men who had come off penniless from the Civil War [and] were old-school gentlemen, with the education which that term might imply." Most of the university's professors were moralists, men of the nineteenth century, who retained a plantation mentality toward their students. The university's students were coming of age in a bold new century and deeply resented the way the faculty patriarchs and trustees dealt with them. In April 1901, John Robertson, editor of the student magazine, criticized two recently established university regulations banning Sunday travel by the football team and student-sponsored dances during commencement week. "Of all the farcical maneuvers on the part of college authorities, and of all the burlesques on university management," he wrote, "some of the recent legislation on the part of Faculty and Trustees exceed any ever known to man. We had hoped that we were at a University . . . but if we are to judge from some of the by-laws lately passed for our government at the University of Mississippi, we are either cadets at a military academy, or pupils at a second-rate primary school."

The real issue to Robertson and other Ole Miss students was not the ban on dancing and Sunday travel. They felt stymied, confined, and hemmed in by rules and regulations carried over from an earlier time. Students "who come to Oxford expecting the freedom of university life, and feeling that they are men, not infants," he wrote, are shocked "when they discover that they have been literally manacled and shackled." Then he tapped what was to Chancellor Fulton and the faculty a sensitive issue. "Those who will consider," he said, "may with little difficulty find a correct explanation for the constantly diminishing attendance at the University of Mississippi." The previous year enrollment had been 303; the year the article was published it was 257, and the following year enrollment was 247.

Robertson's article outraged the faculty, especially his insinuation that they were responsible for the university's enrollment decline. The angry professors declared the article "subversive of good order and propriety" and expelled Robertson. In a petition (signed by 108 of the 257 students), Ole Miss students conceded the article was severe but asserted their right to criticize the faculty. Robertson's dismissal, the students claimed, was "hasty and should be rescinded," and the faculty should consider the matter closed. The students expected a prompt and courteous reply. Robertson's friend and fellow student M. M. Sullivan appeared before the faculty to assure them that Robertson did not intend the article as a "personal insult" to the faculty. But the article did express, he said, the sentiment of the student body, which only wanted to change unpopular rules and do what was best for the university.

The faculty responded with a statement that current policies, even the unpopular ones, were in the best interests of the university and that "loyal support of its students is confidently expected." The faculty acknowledged the students' right to petition, but "contemptuous public censure, though a disclaimer of intention of ill will or injury be offered, can not be lightly regarded by the faculty." Robertson's dismissal was not hasty and would not be rescinded.

The faculty's reaction to Robertson's criticism is evidence that his complaints were not without merit, and his dismissal drew extensive newspaper coverage across the state. After the faculty rejected the student petition, seventy-five students issued a direct appeal to the people of Mississippi to support their effort to have Robertson's dismissal rescinded. Their petition and their names appeared in newspapers around the state. On May 15, 1901, the faculty announced that the seventy-five students, whose "ardor of friendship" had misled them to support Robertson, would be given until 2:00 P.M. Saturday, May 18, to withdraw their names from a list posted on the university bulletin board. Students who did not would be expelled. Some students withdrew their names; others scratched through theirs but noted that they agreed with the article. Students who did not make an unqualified withdrawal were given until 8:30 P.M. to do so. Most of them did. At the next faculty meeting, M. M. Sullivan appeared personally to state that he would not withdraw his name. The faculty expelled him immediately, and suspended five other students.

At its June meeting, the board of trustees, with only one dissenting vote, sustained the faculty. Louis M. Southworth, an 1887 graduate of the University of Mississippi law school, voted against the motion because he believed that most students had lost confidence in Chancellor Fulton, and that many, especially those who were not in fraternities, held him in "utter contempt." Chancellor Fulton's standing with the student body was damaged by the increasing hostility between the Greeks and non-Greeks. Many independents believed that Chancellor Fulton was partial to the Greeks and questioned his capacity for fairness in disputes between the two sides.

In 1900 the ten fraternities and sororities, with a membership of 169 out of 303 students (56 percent), dominated every aspect of campus life, even the university's athletic program. In the November 1900 issue the *Magazine* blamed the Greek system for dissension on the football team and branded fraternity politics "the most vicious institution that has ever grown up in any college." Independent students criticized the fraternities for disregarding the individual merit and worth of non-Greeks and accused them of promoting their own interests rather than the broader interests of the university.

On January 4, 1902, Lee Russell, an Ole Miss student, appeared before the board of trustees at a called meeting in Jackson and leveled several charges against the secret Greek societies. According to folklore, Lee Russell was a poor country boy from Lafayette County who was blackballed by the Greek societies and he vowed to get even. Other than being ostracized by the Greek system, Russell enjoyed a moderately successful college career; he was a member of the track team and business manager of the *University Magazine.* Three years after his graduation from the law school in 1903, Russell was elected to the state legislature, and in 1919 he was elected governor of Mississippi.

On the basis of Russell's charges and other evidence, the board condemned the Greek system for the "absurd ostracism of non-fraternity students" and threatened to "abolish all such societies" if immediate improvement was not shown. The situation did not improve; it deteriorated. In the spring of 1903 the campus was rife with rumors that the Greeks and the non-Greeks were about to "meet in combat." The combat did not take place, but six months later a joint legislative committee conducted an investigation. The committee found that fraternity members promoted the notion among Ole Miss coeds "that non-fraternity men are rather second class men." The committee majority concluded that the rivalry between Greeks and non-Greeks was "so serious that it was impeding the work of the University." A minority report described the situation even more gravely and recommended "the total abolition of the secret societies once and for all, now and forever." A bill to abolish fraternities was introduced but did not pass, in part because Chancellor Fulton persuaded his supporters in the legislature to vote against it. The fraternity issue, he said, was not as serious as many claimed, and the friction between Greeks and non-Greeks was greatly exaggerated.

A year after Chancellor Fulton reassured his supporters in the legislature that "there was never a better spirit in the student body," the faculty suspended seven seniors for violating fraternity rules. All seven were sons of prominent Mississippi families. In an act of "mercy and clemency," the faculty lifted their suspension and allowed them to graduate. Non-fraternity students resented the faculty's mercy, and the act of clemency angered Duncan H. Chamberlain, a 1905 graduate of the law school who published a "virulent pamphlet . . . attacking the chancellor, the faculty and the board of trustees." In his pamphlet, *The Facts About the Troubles of the University of Mississippi: The Jim Crow Laws Against Whites at the University,* Chamberlain criticized the state press for not reporting the extensive corruption in Fulton's administration and accused the university of catering to "the so-called upper classes." For maximum effect, he published the pamphlet in January 1906 while the legislature was in session.

At Chancellor Fulton's request, a joint legislative committee investigated Chamberlain's charges. When the committee exonerated the chancellor, Chamberlain published a second pamphlet entitled *The Mud Be-*

neath the Whitewash. Like many others, he claimed that the committee had been stacked in Fulton's favor. Senator James Alcorn Glover of Coahoma County, a member of the panel that exonerated Fulton, was so critical of *Mud Beneath the Whitewash* that Chamberlain assaulted him in the lobby of the Edwards House and knocked him over a chair. A popular Jackson hotel, the Edwards House was a favorite rendezvous for legislators, lobbyists, and "ladies of the evening." According to folklore, the Mississippi legislature had three houses—the upper house, the lower house, and the Edwards House.

Several members of the legislative panel that investigated the charges against Chancellor Fulton issued a minority report demanding a full inquiry by the board of trustees. At a called meeting on April 3, 1906, the board of trustees examined the accusations against Fulton, gave him a vote of "entire confidence" and proclaimed him to be "eminently worthy of the exalted position he holds." Unfortunately for Chancellor Fulton, between the called meeting in April and the board's annual meeting in June, Governor James K. Vardaman would make three appointments to the board of trustees. The three new trustees agreed with Governor Vardaman that Fulton should be dismissed. One of Vardaman's new appointees was Judge Robert Powell, whose son was one of the seven seniors suspended in 1905. Powell personally blamed Dean Garvin Shands of the law school for his son's suspension and was determined to "drive" him from the university.

After making his new appointments to the board of trustees, Governor Vardaman let it be known that he intended to dismiss Chancellor Fulton in June. In 1903 dirt farmers and day laborers elected Vardaman on his promise to drive the wealthy elite from their positions of power and privilege. Like the common people he championed, Vardaman considered Ole Miss the last bastion of the old aristocracy, and he was determined to democratize it. The first step in that process would be the removal of Chancellor Fulton. A man of aristocratic bearing and background, Fulton represented all that Vardaman disdained. He had been a fraternity boy as an undergraduate and was known to be partial to the secret Greek societies. It would not be easy for Governor Vardaman to dismiss Chancellor Fulton, who had been at the university for nearly forty years and was the brother-in-law of Congressman John Sharp Williams,

Vardaman's opponent in the upcoming senate race. Vardaman's political enemies could claim that partisan politics prompted Fulton's dismissal. Nevertheless, Vardaman was determined to remove Fulton.

For several weeks before the June board meeting, there was speculation that the board would dismiss Fulton if he did not resign, which he had vowed not to do. But a few days before the meeting, Fulton's friends on the board convinced him that he did not have enough votes to survive, and he tendered his resignation. In a bitter and tense meeting, the board accepted his resignation by a vote of ten to eight. Fulton then declined the board's offer of the chair of astronomy, saying, "I could not serve with self respect even my own alma mater whom I love more than all others" under a board of trustees "swayed by the will of their master, Vardaman."

Chancellor Fulton was not the only casualty of that June 1906 meeting. The board reduced Dean Shands's salary by four hundred dollars in a move calculated to induce his resignation. On August 23, Shands "found it in his interest" to resign and accept a position at the Tulane Law School. The supporters of Chancellor Fulton and many Ole Miss alumni castigated Governor Vardaman, but F. C. Holmes, a member of the class of 1890 and the law class of 1892, and one of the eight trustees who had voted not to accept Fulton's resignation, conceded that many people had lost confidence in Chancellor Fulton. Some Ole Miss alumni believed Fulton had stayed beyond his time, and was so controversial that a change in leadership was necessary.

Following Chancellor Fulton's resignation, the board of trustees "deferred to a future time" the appointment of his successor. The trustees directed Alfred Hume, vice chancellor and professor of mathematics, "to perform the duties" of the office until they named a chancellor. Four months later, the board of trustees offered the position to Andrew Armstrong Kincannon, president of the Industrial Institute and College at Columbus. Although Kincannon received a vote of eleven to one, he declined the appointment "for reasons satisfactory to himself." After Kincannon declined the appointment, the board named Alfred Hume acting chancellor for the 1906–1907 academic year.

At a called meeting on March 2, 1907, the board of trustees elected James B. Aswell chancellor over Alfred Hume by a vote of nine to eight. Aswell's election was "a great surprise," but the student magazine praised the appointment of someone from another state whose "name can not be dragged into State politics." Aswell was state superintendent of education in Louisiana. Shortly after his election, but two months before his appointment took effect, Chancellor-elect and Mrs. Aswell visited the university. During their brief visit, Aswell addressed the student body. The student magazine applauded his "well-chosen remarks" and wrote, "We expect much of him and believe he will fulfill our expectations." Congressman John Sharp Williams was also on the campus during Aswell's visit. At the time of his visit to Ole Miss, Williams was in the midst of a tight and bitter senatorial election with Governor James K. Vardaman. In the 1907 senatorial election 118,344 votes were cast. Williams defeated Vardaman by 648 votes. It is not known if Williams, the brother-in-law of former Chancellor Robert Fulton, influenced Aswell in any way, but a month later Aswell informed the board of trustees that he had decided not to accept the appointment. An indignant board of trustees accepted his resignation on May 18, 1907, but "not with thanks," and announced its intention to consult the nation's leading educators in the selection of a new chancellor, which would occur at the board's meeting in early June.

When the board convened on June 3, a group of Ole Miss alumni appeared before the trustees and asked them to postpone the appointment and conduct a national search for a new chancellor. A motion to postpone the appointment was introduced but not seconded. The trustees, on a motion by John W. T. Falkner, then elected Andrew A. Kincannon by a vote of eleven to zero, with four abstentions. Kincannon accepted the appointment effective July 1, 1907. The trustees assured Kincannon that they would not interfere with the internal governance of the institution, and, at his request, the board increased the chancellor's salary from thirty-two hundred dollars to five thousand dollars. The board of trustees also increased the power and authority of the chancellor. The student newspaper applauded the board of trustees for conferring upon the office of chancellor the "authority and freedom" that would enable him to make the University of Mississippi "one of the foremost institutions in the country." Under the board's new policy, the chancellor had the authority to appoint all university personnel, subject to the approval of the board of trustees, and could dismiss faculty members for "sufficient cause." The chancellor also had authority over the university curriculum, the class schedule, the rules of student discipline, and complete control over university property.

Andrew A. Kincannon was the third former student of the university to serve as chancellor. Kincannon attended the university in the fall of 1877, but economic circumstances forced him to withdraw. In 1883 he received a baccalaureate degree from National Normal University in Lebanon, Ohio, earning a master's degree at the same institution the following year. From 1884 to 1887 he was instructor of English at Mississippi A & M. In 1887 he was appointed superintendent of the Meridian school system, where he remained until his election as state superintendent of education in 1895. At the time of his appointment as chancellor, Kincannon was president of the Industrial Institute and College for Women.

CHAPTER 8

A DEMOCRATIC UNIVERSITY, 1907–1927

The University for many years past has been the plaything of politics.
WALTER CLARK, FEBRUARY 24, 1914

Andrew Armstrong Kincannon was installed as the university's seventh chancellor on September 19, 1907, in an elaborate ceremony attended by collegiate officials, faculty, students, alumni, and public officials. John W. T. Falkner, a local banker, a member of the board of trustees, and the grandfather of William Faulkner, presented Kincannon to the audience. In his inaugural address, Chancellor Kincannon gave his solemn pledge to transform the old aristocratic university into a new democratic institution. "Aristocratic or Democratic, which rule shall we have here at the University. . . . I, for one," he said, "shall ever be the supporter of the latter. I am for popularizing the University." Chancellor Kincannon closed his brief address by asking the university's alumni and friends to join him in "the movement for a Greater University." The phrase "Greater University of Mississippi" became a slogan during the early years of Kincannon's administration. The student newspaper included on its masthead the words "For The Greater University of Mississippi." The campus magazine conceded in February 1908 that a "Greater University" was only a dream now, but predicted it would be "a reality in the future."

Chancellor Kincannon's first initiative to democratize the university was the creation of a student labor fund and a self-help bureau similar to those at Mississippi A & M and the Industrial Institute and College for Women at Columbus. To dispel the myth that the University of Mississippi was a school for rich boys, Kincannon established a student employment system that enabled students from poor families to work their way through school by waiting on tables in the dining hall and working in various campus offices, including the chancellor's office. Chancellor Kincannon was soon boasting that the self-help bureau employed many of the university's 480 students. Supporters of a democratic university also applauded the work-study program. The Jackson *Mississippian* regaled: "It might be astonishing news to the knockers of the University who are of the opinion that this is a 'rich man's school' that nearly one-fourth of the whole student body, including co-eds, . . . are earning some part of their expenses while at the University."

The student magazine was jubilant about the apparent lack of social distinction among the student body. The new Ole Miss spirit was especially evident, according to the magazine, in the men's dining hall, where "Ole Miss men gather for meals" and where "the rich man's son . . . sings along with the poor man's son." Governor James K. Vardaman so appreciated the wonders wrought by Chancellor Kincannon that he sent his own two sons to Ole Miss. There was one student, however, who was not so convinced that all Ole Miss men were equal, and he did not test the issue. Chester Andrew McLarty, a poor man's son from rural Lafayette County who enrolled at the university in 1907, rode his mule from the Tula community to the Oxford square, tied it to a hitching post, and walked the remaining mile to the campus. Just in case some of the rich boys might be looking, he did not want them to see him riding a mule.

Another of Chancellor Kincannon's early initiatives to democratize the university was the establishment of a student honor council. Following several years of animosity between Greeks and non-Greeks, the yearbook cited the honor council as a major step "toward molding order out of chaos," and the student editor praised the chancellor for placing "the government of the student body on a democratic basis." Each class in the college of liberal arts and the professional schools elected a member to the honor council, which had judicial authority over a wide range of disciplinary problems. The honor council was the forerunner of the Associated Student Body, established in 1917. Chancellor Kincannon hoped the honor council would restore "the lost confidence of the people of the state in the morality of the students," and he expected "magnificent results" from it.

With the moral situation at the university in a general state of improvement, at least for the present, Chancellor Kincannon turned his attention to its physical condition. In a classic understatement, Kincannon noted in his first annual report that the "legislature has not lavished its favors here." His 1907 report detailed the university's "deplorable physical condition" and outlined its most pressing needs. The three most immediate needs were a new power plant to replace the one destroyed by fire in 1906, a men's dormitory, and a large dining hall.

Chancellor Kincannon, like his predecessor Robert Fulton, believed the lack of dormitory rooms, not its public image, kept the university's enrollment down. Kincannon's report on the physical needs of the university was persuasive, and the 1908 legislature made the largest appropriation in the university's sixty-year history. With that appropriation, Kincannon built a new power plant, a campus laundry, a student infirmary, and a men's dormitory, which he named in honor of James Gordon, a famous Ole Miss alumnus and a member of the board of trustees. Gordon Hall provided housing for two hundred male students and included "a beautiful dining hall capable of seating four hundred at tables." As the building was nearing completion, the trustees authorized the chancellor to invite alumni back to the campus to celebrate the opening of Gordon Hall. The 1909 homecoming celebration was popular with the alumni and by the mid-1920s homecoming had become an annual event.

A few years after its opening, Chancellor Kincannon cited Gordon Hall as "the monumental error" of his administration. The concentration of two hundred boys in one building produced a noise level that virtually prohibited studying and sleeping and a mischief level that proved to be costly to the university. Boys shot firecrackers in the building's spacious hallways, whooped and hollered half the night, defaced the walls and furnishings, and in general badly abused the university's newest and largest building. After this unfortunate experience, Kincannon recommended that future dormitories be constructed on a smaller scale and house fewer boys.

Though disappointed in Gordon Hall, Kincannon was highly pleased with the addition of Peabody Hall and a new library building. Built by a forty-thousand-dollar grant from the Peabody Fund, Peabody Hall was completed in the fall of 1913 and occupied by the school of education. The building currently houses the department of psychology. By 1905 the university's library holdings had outgrown the existing building, constructed in 1889 during Chancellor Mayes's administration. Chancellor Fulton secured a matching grant from the Carnegie Foundation for a new library building in 1905, but the board of trustees under Governor Vardaman declined the grant. Soon after his appointment, Chancellor Kincannon reopened discussions with the Carnegie Foundation, which renewed the offer. By the time this second offer was made, an entirely new board of trustees had been installed, and the new trustees accepted the Carnegie grant on January 28, 1909.

The sixty-thousand-dollar library building was occupied in the spring of 1911, and Mrs. Elizabeth Murry Hunt, the university librarian (and William Faulkner's aunt), transferred the library's thirty-two thousand volumes to the new building in time for the fall semester of 1911. The university's holdings would have been much larger, but "urgent needs for the expenditure of the funds . . . in other directions," the board of trustees explained, had necessitated "a practical suspension of the purchases of books." Although the holdings did not increase for several years, the library hours did. In response to a student petition to expand the library hours, the board of trustees authorized the university administration, beginning in the fall of 1905, to keep the library open for seven and a half hours daily, except on Sunday.

Although Chancellor Kincannon presided over the construction of several major buildings and established a work-study program and a student honor council, he was unable to increase student enrollment. In addition, his administration was beset by controversy from its beginning. A combination of under funding and poor management created a mounting deficit at the university and left many bills unpaid. University creditors filed several suits against the university and Kincannon personally to collect overdue payments.

During one of the several investigations of university finances under Chancellor Kincannon, a legislative committee discovered that the university had borrowed twenty thousand dollars from the LaBauve Fund and lesser amounts from the Taylor and Odum funds, two other small endowments. The LaBauve Fund was an endowment established in 1889 by the will of Felix LaBauve of DeSoto County. The endowment provided scholarships for orphans from DeSoto County to attend the University of Mississippi. As early as 1892, Chancellor Fulton, with the knowledge and approval of the board of trustees, had begun borrowing from the LaBauve Fund for operating expenses and emergency repairs. Following several legislative investigations that produced no evidence of financial illegalities, a special legislative appropriation in 1920 restored the LaBauve Fund and the two smaller endowments and prohibited the university's borrowing from any existing or future endowments.

On January 20, 1912, the student newspaper reported persistent rumors "from Jackson . . . that Chancellor Kincannon was to be supplanted [and] that there will be a general changing of executive heads of educational institutions." Those rumors coincided with the inauguration of Governor Earl Brewer, the first Ole Miss alumnus elected governor of Mississippi, and the passage of legislation restructuring the board of trustees. The 1912 reorganization was the second shake-up of the board of trustees in two years. The dismissal of Chancellor Robert Fulton in 1906 and the long delay in naming his successor convinced Mississippi's leadership that some way must be found to shield the state's institutions of higher learning from the furies of factional politics. There was also strong public support to moderate the bitter rivalry between the university and the state's other public colleges. In response to this growing consensus, in 1910 the legislature abolished the four boards of trustees that governed the university, Alcorn A & M, Mississippi A & M, and the Industrial Institute and College for Women. In place of those four separate boards, the legislature established one central board of trustees that governed all four institutions. The law creating the central board of trustees prohibited elected officials from serving on the board.

The new consolidated board, composed primarily of businessmen, met for the first time in July 1910 and pledged to meet its responsibility with an "openness of mind." The board announced that it would reorganize the three white institutions into a coordinated state system of higher education. There would be many changes, the board warned, and some of them might appear radical, but the trustees assured the people of Mississippi that they would "make haste slowly." The consolidated board of trustees did not govern the two teachers colleges. Mississippi Normal School, established at Hattiesburg in 1910 (later Mississippi State Teachers College, Mississippi Southern College, and University of Southern Mississippi), and Delta State Teachers College, established at Cleveland in 1924, were governed by separate boards of trustees until the legislature combined the three boards in 1932.

The businessmen who governed the state's institutions of higher learning in 1910 recognized the link between Mississippi's economic progress and its educational system, and that relationship was the subject of the first speech by James Sexton, the consolidated board's first and only president. In a speech at Ole Miss Sexton heralded the creation of the unified board as a "mile post in the educational history of our state" and made an impassioned plea for a coordinated system of public education extending from the elementary level up to the state university. An improved, coordinated system, he asserted, was essential for the development of Mississippi's economic resources. Duplication and rivalry among the state's collegiate institutions had impeded Mississippi's economic development, and Sexton called on college officials to "banish forever the puerile idea" that there is "any sort of rivalry" between the university and other state colleges. "But," he quickly added, "it is preeminently the mission of the University to set the pace for all our educational institutions."

It can only be wondered if Mississippi's new board of trustees could have achieved the great promise that its first efforts foretold. In 1912 the nonpolitical board was superseded by an eight-member board of trustees with the governor as ex officio chairman and the state superintendent of education as an ex officio member. The legislature concluded that the state's schools and colleges should not be left to "designing school men" who were not responsible to the taxpayer or subject to the popular will. That conclusion was predicated on a long-standing tradition, especially among members of the legislature, that the governor was the head of the state's educational system in the same way that he was head of the state militia. A house resolution, for example, authorizing a special visit to various state colleges noted that "Governor Edmund F. Noel, as chairman of the state's educational institutions," would lead the delegation. The senate held the same presumption. The presiding officer of the senate ruled a resolution to abolish coeducation at Ole Miss out of order because "the Governor had not recommended the subject matter."

While the legislature was debating the bill to reorganize the college board in 1912, Senator William Ellis of Carthage introduced a resolution to study the feasibility of consolidating the state university and the agricultural college into one institution located in Jackson. Although Ellis's bill would not consolidate the two schools but would merely create a committee to study that possibility, it did not pass. In its analysis

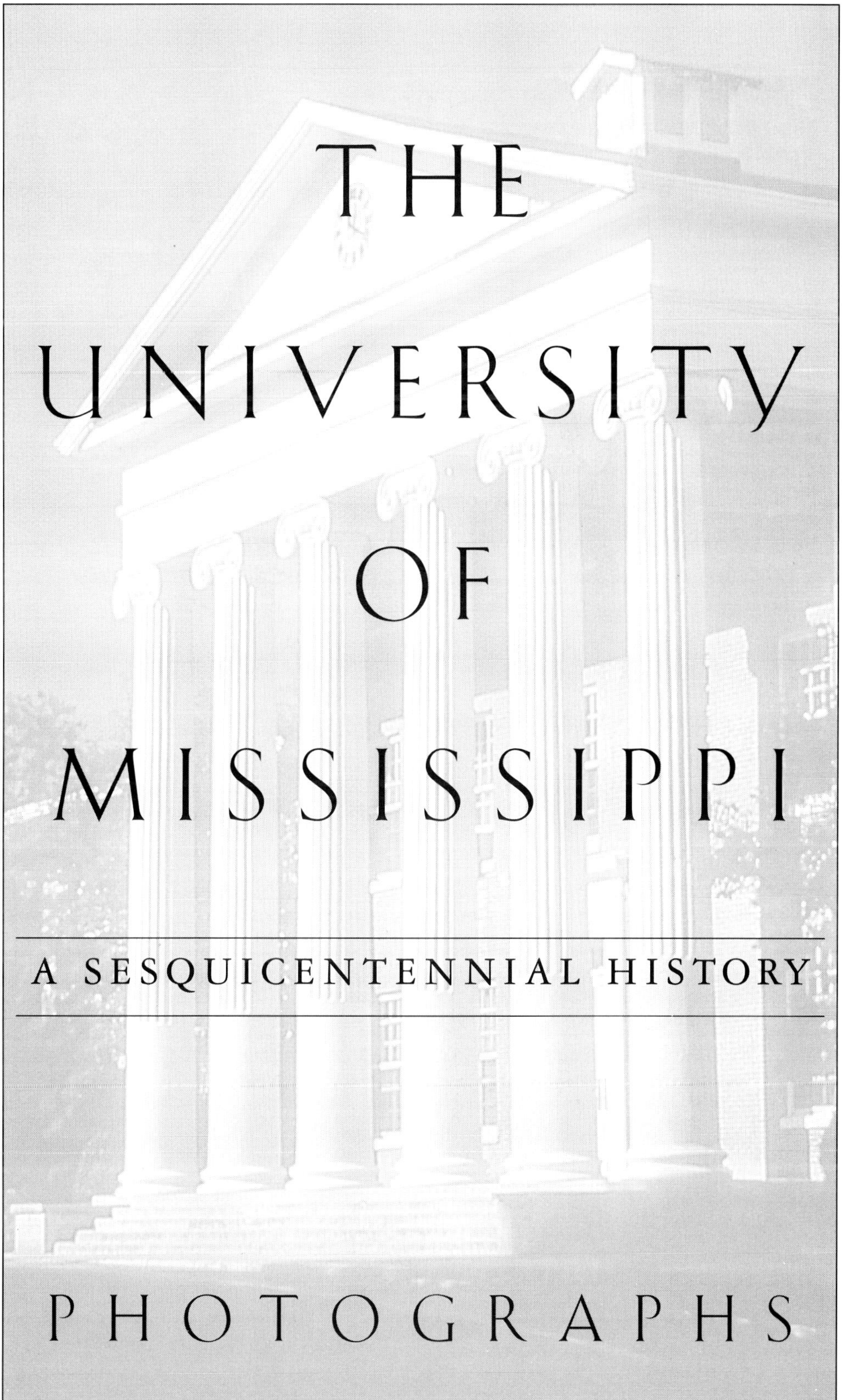

THE UNIVERSITY OF MISSISSIPPI

A SESQUICENTENNIAL HISTORY

PHOTOGRAPHS

CHANCELLORS OF THE

GEORGE FREDERICK HOLMES
1848-1849

AUGUSTUS BALDWIN LONGSTREET
1849-1856

ALEXANDER P. STEWART
1874-1886

EDWARD MAYES
1886-1892

UNIVERSITY OF MISSISSIPPI

FREDERICK A. P.
BARNARD
1856-1861

JOHN NEWTON
WADDEL
1865-1874

ROBERT FULTON
1892-1906

ANDREW ARMSTRONG
KINCANNON
1907-1914

CHANCELLORS OF THE

JOSEPH NEELEY POWERS
1914-1924, 1930-1932

ALFRED HUME
1924-1930, 1932-1935

PORTER LEE FORTUNE
1968-1984

GERALD TURNER
1984-1995

UNIVERSITY OF MISSISSIPPI

ALFRED BENJAMIN BUTTS
1935-1946

JOHN DAVIS WILLIAMS
1946-1968

ROBERT CONRAD KHAYAT
1995-PRESENT

Campus in 1861 Courtesy of Debra Freland

New Steward's Hall, 1857

Lyceum, c. 1861

Boys dormitory with original facade, 1848

Boys dormitory after ornate facade was added in 1870s

Class of 1861 in front of Chapel, 1853

Barnard Observatory, 1857-1859

1894 Football Team

Ricks Hall, 1903

Ventress Hall, 1889

New Science Hall, 1906

Library, 1911, now Bryant Hall

Wier Hall-Student Union, 1939

Bondurant Hall, 1929

Johnson Commons, 1929

World's largest Confederate flag, 1949

University Greys re-enactment, 1948

John Davis Williams Library, 1951

University of Mississippi Medical Center, 1955

Coulter Hall, 1962

Chancellor's Residence

Twin Towers, 1969

U. S. Marshals surround the Lyceum, 1962

Blind Jim Ivy

Ole Miss Union, 1976

Lamar Hall, 1977

Oxford-University Staduim / Swayze Feild, 1988

Jamie L. Whitten National Center for Physical Acoustics, 1989

John Davis Williams Library – 1995 Addition

University of Mississippi Medical Center, 1998

Women's Indoor Sports Facility, 1997

Holman Hall in the Business-Accountancy Complex, 1998

view from University Avenue

Architect's drawing of the Gertrude C. Ford Center for the Performing Arts, 1998

of Ellis's bill, the *Mississippian* agreed that both institutions were not necessary, but predicted that the sense of place, so prominent among Mississippians, would make the relocation of Ole Miss impossible. "Move the University," the student editor said, "and a century will not give the new domicile the things it now possesses. Expend all the skill of the architect and the landscape gardener on some other spot and call it the University of Mississippi; yet it will not be . . . what it now is and has been."

Although rejected in 1912, the notion of consolidating Mississippi's institutions of higher learning remained a lively topic over the next several years and the university's literary societies debated the issue on several occasions. On February 13, 1914, the Phi Sigmas considered "the many advantages of having the University of Mississippi, Mississippi A & M, the Normal College and the Industrial Institute & College united into one Greater University." After a spirited discussion, the issue was decided in the negative. The Phi Sigmas again considered the topic on February 20, 1918, with the same results. The strongest argument against consolidation in 1918 was that Ole Miss would lose its identity. One student raised the specter that Ole Miss might even "be called A and M (think of it)."

One of the contributing factors to the 1912 reorganization of the board of trustees and the reinstatement of the governor as ex officio chairman was the spate of financial controversies besetting the Kincannon administration. Lawmakers argued that the university needed more, not less, legislative oversight. Students and parents also frequently complained that the cost of living at Ole Miss was unnecessarily high—almost double what it was at Mississippi A & M and the women's college at Columbus. Those complaints were laced with implications of financial irregularities. Some students claimed that the dining halls and the campus bookstore overcharged students and that the university did not receive its full share of the proceeds. On one occasion, students placed above Chancellor Kincannon's seat in chapel a sign in large red letters that read: "Here it is! Graft!"

Chancellor Kincannon, D. L. Ross, the university's business manager, and Professor James Warsaw Bell were accused of violating the state's conflict of interest law because they "purchased pigs, fattened them on the swill from the boy's [*sic*] boarding house, and when the animals reached the age of slaughter they were sold to the University boarding department." Professor Bell wrote a long letter that appeared in several state newspapers defending his sale of hogs to the university. A popular professor, an influential member of the faculty athletic committee, and for many years dean of the school of business, Professor Bell made light of the accusations against him. If he was accused of stealing hogs, Bell conceded, he would be in serious trouble, but to be accused of stealing swill was so ridiculous he would not waste the reader's time by responding to the charge.

Chancellor Kincannon and D. L. Ross were also accused of illegally renting rooms in university dormitories to schoolteachers attending summer institutes in Oxford. In March 1912 a legislative committee ruled this action legal "but beneath the dignity of the head of so great an institution." After its on-site investigation, the legislative committee reported that a general "financial embarrassment seems to prevail" at the university, but cleared the chancellor, the business manager, and Professor Bell of any illegal activities. The rumors, charges, and complaints did not end, however; they intensified.

In September 1913 several parents of Ole Miss students filed a broad set of complaints with the state legislature. The complaints included charges that Chancellor Kincannon's salary, which the legislature had reduced from five thousand dollars to thirty-five hundred, was illegally supplemented with fifteen hundred dollars from student fees, and that he overdrew his travel expenses by several hundred dollars. Another complaint was that the university deposited its funds, interest free, in an Oxford bank and actually paid the bank for "handling the funds of the institution," although another bank offered to pay interest on deposits and to act as the university's financial agent free of charge. Chancellor Kincannon was personally criticized for giving self-help jobs to the two sons of now Senator James K. Vardaman, to a nephew of Governor Earl Brewer, to sons of various board members, and to athletes who performed little if any work for their scholarships. The chancellor was also accused of giving LaBauve Scholarships "to the sons of well-to-do people in DeSoto County" rather than to orphans, as Felix LaBauve's will mandated.

Soon after the university parents made their complaints public, John L. Deister filed a civil suit against Chancellor Kincannon and the board of trustees. A former language professor dismissed in June 1913, Deister filed suit to recover a portion of his salary that he did not receive at the time of his dismissal. To bolster his case, Professor Deister published an eighteen-page pamphlet and wrote several letters to newspapers across the state exposing what he believed was corruption at the university and demanding a legislative investigation of Chancellor Kincannon, Governor Brewer, and the board of trustees. Deister claimed he was fired because he opposed the chancellor's decision to allow an ineligible player to participate in several football games and accused Kincannon and Brewer of "converting the University into a bureau of political patronage" where professors were judged "by the political influence [they] can wield rather than by scholarship." Deister also claimed that he and several other professors planned to resign, but, after Chancellor Kincannon and Governor Brewer announced they were going to fire several troublemakers at the end of the school year, most decided not to.

In response to this latest round of charges and accusations, another special legislative committee, chaired by Representative Albert C. Anderson of Ripley, brought several auditors and accountants to Oxford in early October 1913 to examine the university's financial records and to interview several people. After the legislative committee began its work, Professor Deister published a letter in several state papers complaining that the committee would not conduct an honest investigation because Chancellor Kincannon had given the committee chairman's son a self-help job at the university. The 1914 legislative journals do not include a report from this committee, but press accounts of the investigation indicated that the committee found no evidence of any criminal or illegal activities.

While Chancellor Kincannon was responding to the queries of the 1913 legislative investigation, he was also contending with an investigation of the university's athletic program by the Southern Intercollegiate Athletic Association. From its inception in 1893, football has captivated Ole Miss students and alumni, and the faculty has struggled, for the most part successfully, to keep a balance between academics and athletics. During Chancellor Kincannon's administration, eligibility controversies plagued the university's athletic program and eventually caused the dismissal of two coaches and the suspension of Ole Miss by the SIAA. The university also forfeited or canceled several games, including the 1912, 1913, and 1914 games with Mississippi A & M.

The situation that prompted the university's suspension involved several prominent alumni and professors who signed a $288 note in 1911 to pay the fees and other expenses for five football players. Two of the men who signed the note were Professor James Warsaw Bell, a member of the faculty athletic committee, and William Hemingway, a Jackson attorney who later became professor of law and served for many years as chairman of the faculty athletic committee. (The university's Vaught-Hemingway Stadium is named for Professor Hemingway and Coach John Vaught.) The $288 promissory note was to be liquidated from the gate receipts of the Ole Miss-A & M game on Thanksgiving Day in 1911. SIAA rules strictly prohibited such payments to student athletes, and all other forms of "alumni scholarships." In addition to this violation, the university also allowed a player the SIAA declared ineligible to participate in several games during the 1912 and 1913 seasons.

At its annual meeting in New Orleans in December 1913, the SIAA suspended the University of Mississippi and "debarred" the football coach from coaching at any member school. The resolution suspending Ole Miss stated that the faculty athletic committee had declared a player ineligible and had instructed the football coach not to allow him to participate. Under intense pressure from alumni, Chancellor Kincannon dissolved the existing faculty athletic committee and appointed a new committee that ruled the player eligible. The association charged Kincannon with exerting "his influence against the purification of athletics."

For several years following the suspension, there was mounting support for the withdrawal of the university from the SIAA. Eventually, the larger schools of the SIAA withdrew and established the Southern Intercollegiate Conference in 1921. Two years later its name was changed to the Southern Conference. In 1932 the Southern Conference, which included schools from the Atlantic Coast to Texas, was divided into the Southeastern and Southwestern conferences. The original Southeastern Conference included the University of the South (Sewanee), Vanderbilt, University of Tennessee, Georgia Tech, University of Georgia, University of Florida, University of Alabama, Auburn, University of Mississippi, Mississippi A & M, Louisiana State University, Tulane, and University of Kentucky. Sewanee, the first school to leave the Southeastern Conference, withdrew in 1940.

During the gloomy year following the SIAA's suspension, Casey "Dutch" Stengel brought a measure of cheer to the university's athletic program. In the spring of 1914, the legendary Stengel, a Brooklyn Nationals outfielder who hit .316 the previous season, spent several weeks at Oxford coaching the Ole Miss baseball team. The *Mississippian* announced Stengel's association with the university in large front-page headlines and informed Ole Miss coeds that he was an eligible bachelor. After attending a campus dance and seeing his players perform in the ballroom, Casey told the sports editor of the student newspaper that the dance had greatly improved their footwork. On March 4, 1914, the *Mississippian* reported that "Dutch" had joined the Nationals for spring training in Augusta and announced that "everyone regrets the departure of our friend of the blonde hair." Stengel's brief stay with the Red and Blue, according to the campus paper, "was helpful in the formation of our state championship team." The following spring, the student paper regretfully announced that Stengel "can't be with us this year."

The effects of the SIAA suspension in 1914 were evident in the first Ole Miss-A & M game after the university came off probation. The 1915 contest was the first game between the in-state rivals in three years. Played in Tupelo, the game generated enormous interest and excited the creative instincts of Ole Miss students. For the fans who did not make the trip, the game was carried live in Oxford, play-by-play, over the telephone. In a large hall filled with students and Oxford residents, as information was received, the "position and direction of the ball was registered on a large blackboard, drawn off to represent a football field." Ole Miss lost the game 65–0, but by the early 1920s Ole Miss football was again ascendant. The university played its first post season game and the only game outside the United States on New Year's Eve in 1921 against the Havana Athletic Club in Havana, Cuba. The men's basketball team also made the trip and played a Cuban team. Both Ole Miss teams lost.

The university's financial problems and its suspension by the SIAA seriously damaged Chancellor Kincannon's public standing. The report of the legislative committee that investigated the university in the fall of 1913 would probably have further eroded his reputation, but before the committee could file a formal report, Kincannon resigned. If the chancellor was looking for an excuse to resign, and thus avoid further embarrassment, Governor Earl Brewer's intrusion into matters of student discipline provided that opportunity. In early October 1913, the faculty expelled five students for hazing. The students promptly arranged a conference with Governor Brewer, who wrote to Chancellor Kincannon explaining that the five boys, who were in his office, expressed deep contrition and promised never to haze again. Governor Brewer asked the chancellor to reinstate the students, all from "honorable families" who, along with several board members, considered their expulsion for hazing too severe. The student honor council had made a genuine but unsuccessful effort to eradicate this "barbarous practice." The governor's intercession on behalf of students expelled for hazing made the council's goal practically impossible. In his letter to the chancellor, the governor added a postscript. He had learned, apparently from the students in his office, that another boy had also been expelled, for a reason unconnected with the hazing incident. Although he was not familiar with the details of the other expulsion, Governor Brewer thought it would be unfair for him to intercede on behalf of these five boys and allow the expulsion of the sixth student to stand, so he asked Chancellor Kincannon to reinstate that boy along with the other five. Governor Brewer expressed his hope to the chancellor that student discipline would not be "marred" by his intervention on behalf of these students.

On November 1, 1913, Chancellor Kincannon instructed the faculty to reinstate all six students. "I recognize the superior authority... of the trustees," he wrote the faculty, "and see no recourse except to re-admit the young men." He also advised the faculty that their only option was "to take action" not "express opinion." Three months after he wrote this letter to the faculty, Chancellor Kincannon resigned, effective at the end of the 1914 session. At the time of his resignation, which the student paper reported on February 18, 1914, he did not offer a specific reason for doing so. Several years later Kincannon said he resigned because he "was unwilling for the school to become a political chattel."

The resignation of Andrew Kincannon and the political machinations surrounding it prompted another outcry about politics and public education. The *Itta Bena Times* declared: "It is time to quit playing politics in the management of institutions of higher learning. We must get a better faculty, provide them with a sense of security and stability in order that the University may provide the kind of educational instruction necessary." Kincannon's resignation also prompted an angry letter to the editor from Walter Clark of Clarksdale, who complained that the university was a "plaything of politics." On February 24, 1914, he wrote, "None of our chancellors has been in a position to go before the legislature and make a dignified and impartial statement of the needs of the University without incurring the hostility of the political faction which he does not happen to represent." Writing only days after Kincannon resigned, Clark described the kind of chancellor the University of Mississippi should seek. "A successful university president must be a man of big caliber, of university training and ideals," he wrote. The university's new chancellor "must be a commanding figure, . . . a man capable of leading the best thought of the state, . . . a big brained man of immense capacity and national influence. . . . And Mississippi should never be satisfied until she has such a man at Oxford."

Three months after this profile of an ideal university president appeared in the state press, the board of trustees offered the position to Joseph Neely Powers, Mississippi's state superintendent of education and an ex officio member of the board. Powers accepted the offer, and, on June 4, 1914, Governor Earl Brewer cast a single ballot on behalf of the entire board electing Powers chancellor. The board considered no other candidates for the position. A native of Havana, Alabama, Powers attended several colleges and universities, including Louisville Medical College and the University of Chicago. While superintendent of the Grenada city schools, Powers enrolled at the University of Mississippi during the 1901–1902 academic year. In 1907 Governor Vardaman appointed Powers state superintendent of education. He was elected to the position in 1908 and reelected in 1912. His two major accomplishments as state superintendent were the establishment of rural agricultural high schools, which became the state system of two-year community colleges, and the founding of Mississippi Normal College at Hattiesburg, which became the University of Southern Mississippi. The *Mississippi Educational Advance,* the journal of the state teachers association, hailed Chancellor Powers's appointment. Assuring his readers that Chancellor Powers would continue the process of democratizing the university initiated by Andrew Kincannon, the editor wrote, "The University needs popularizing; it needs to be more democratic to the core. College presidents and professors owe much more to the people than to prepare their lectures and meet their classes."

When Joseph Powers assumed the office of chancellor, faculty dissension was the highest and morale the lowest in the university's history. At his first faculty meeting, on September 16, 1914, Chancellor Powers met the issue of faculty dissension and institutional loyalty head-on. "Pardon me for being so candid, perhaps so blunt," he told his colleagues, "as to say with all emphasis, that if any of you feel that you cannot deal with each other in a spirit as to always reflect credit on the administration, than it might be well, if such there be, for them to sever their connection with the University at this time, rather than to bring trouble later." In addition to faculty dissension and political intrusion, Chancellor Powers also had to contend with the proper denominational balance among the faculty. When the southern field director of the YMCA recommended a Presbyterian for sponsor of the university chapter, Powers said he could not appoint another Presbyterian to the faculty or staff, explaining that the last two appointments, in chemistry and engineering, had gone to Presbyterians and there were already five others on the faculty. "I am a Methodist myself," Powers said, but "[I need] a Baptist for this position."

In keeping with his long-standing philosophy of "carrying the school to the people," Chancellor Powers initiated "The University Weekly Letter." A short article prepared by various faculty members on a wide variety of topics, the "Weekly Letter" was mailed each Saturday morning to newspapers throughout the state. Among the many topics covered in these essays were the evils of patent medicines, diseases common to Mississippi livestock, Greek art, Rhodes Scholars, moral training in public schools, and the benefits of manufacturing. This was the chancellor's attempt to make the university relevant to the people whose taxes sustained the institution and to demonstrate that a democratic university could be of practical benefit to the people of Mississippi. The letters also showed that the university's professors were willing to do more than just "prepare their lectures and meet their classes."

In welcoming Chancellor Powers to the university, and in celebration of a record enrollment, the campus newspaper heralded the opening of the 1914 session as the "most auspicious . . . in the history of the institution." Powers did not hold an inaugural ceremony, but Governor

Brewer, the board of trustees, and other dignitaries joined the Ole Miss faculty and students in late November to celebrate the matriculation of Ullen Leavell, the five hundredth student to enroll at the university in 1914. To a jubilant crowd assembled at the Lyric Theater in Oxford, Chancellor Powers predicted the next year's enrollment would be six hundred, and seven hundred the year after that. Powers's prediction came true. Another record enrollment of 641 students matriculated in the fall of 1915. Chancellor Powers welcomed this second successive record-breaking student body and assured them they were entering "a graftless University." He also promised them the new university bookstore would not charge them "one dollar" more than was absolutely necessary for their textbooks and other supplies.

Chancellor Powers's prediction that seven hundred students would enroll in the fall of 1916, however, could not be realized under existing circumstances. In March 1916 a legislative committee reported that the university had reached its growth potential and needed more dormitory space. Some of the 641 students, the committee found, lived in makeshift quarters in the old gymnasium in the basement of the Lyceum. The committee also found that not all of the financial problems of Kincannon's administration had been corrected. Professors were still not paid on time because some of the salary funds were used for operating expenses and permanent improvements. The committee discovered that $897 in salary funds were used to purchase furniture for the chancellor's residence and that Powers had overdrawn his travel allowance. The legislature normally appropriated funds to the university in a lump sum, but the lawmakers began earmarking certain funds to prevent the university administration from diverting them to other purposes. The legislative committee sharply criticized the board of trustees for devoting too much of its time to the university and neglecting other state institutions. The committee also scolded the board for holding some of its meetings in Memphis.

In spite of the university's obvious needs, the 1916 legislature did not provide additional funds for new dormitories or other capital improvements. The university's 1916 appropriation was $5,000 less than the 1914 appropriation, but the situation could have been much worse. The student newspaper gleefully announced that, even with the $5,000 cut, the university's friends and supporters "won a signal victory over the low pressure set in the lower house of the legislature" who wanted to cut the appropriation by $33,000. The university's appropriation bill was the "cause of much wrangling between the low pressure element and those favoring an adequate appropriation for the University." The bill, as finally passed, included $185,000 but no new funds for capital expansion. The low pressure faction in the Mississippi House of Representatives was a powerful coalition of fiscal conservatives dedicated to the proposition of low taxes, retrenchment, and economy in government.

Eighteen months after the 1916 legislative appropriation, and six months before the 1918 appropriation, a large section of a boys' dormitory collapsed, providing a dramatic illustration of the condition of the university's antiquated physical plant. The state architect, who went to Oxford to inspect the university's buildings, made several startling discoveries. Another boys' dormitory was found to be "absolutely dangerous," and its occupants were immediately evacuated. The chapel, the Lyceum and Gordon Hall were "in a bad state of repair [and] were deteriorating rapidly." After closing the two unsafe dormitories, university authorities reopened Taylor Hall, the former steward's hall that was converted into a dormitory in 1905. Some of the students who evacuated the dormitories occupied rooms in the Lyceum, and several classrooms were converted into temporary living quarters. Students who could afford to do so took rooms in Oxford. Even under those dire conditions, and even though the legislature did not appropriate any capital improvement funds, the university's enrollment continued to increase, except for the war years.

After the United States entered World War I on April 6, 1917, many Ole Miss students withdrew during the spring semester and enlisted in the military service. Because so many seniors were in the armed forces, commencement exercises were not held in 1917. During the war the campus briefly took on the appearance of an armed camp. Four military companies were formed among Ole Miss students, and regular army personnel were stationed on the campus to instruct the students in military science. Many Ole Miss coeds enrolled in the Red Cross to support America's war effort. Students received academic credit for military training and for Red Cross activities.

In the first year after the war, enrollment was back up to nearly six hundred, and more than seven hundred students applied for admission in the fall of 1919. Students were jammed three to a room in Gordon

Hall. Ricks Hall was filled to capacity, and some women students were living in the infirmary. Professors took in boarders, and Oxford residents rented every available room to students. Some of the scions of the state's affluent families lived comfortably in Oxford hotels. The final matriculation in the fall of 1919 was six hundred thirty, with perhaps as many as one hundred turned away. In announcing that so many applicants were denied admission, the *Mississippian* complained that the university had been "shamefully and deplorably neglected by the state legislature." In an interview with the student paper, Chancellor Powers said the university needed at least $750,000 in capital construction to put it "firmly on its feet." The most pressing needs were more dormitories and a science building. The chemistry laboratory, which Chancellor Frederick Barnard built for Professor Edward Boynton in 1856, had only 144 desks for the 205 students enrolled in freshman chemistry.

Noting that university officials were in Jackson on their "biennial begging trip," the editor of the *Mississippian* confessed in January 1920 that he did not like to "show the world our dire needs," but said it was necessary to get the legislature's attention. He later wrote an editorial outlining the university's priorities under the caption "The Shame of It." Just prior to a campus visit by a legislative delegation in February 1920, the editor of the *Mississippian* outlined the condition of the university's buildings. According to his assessment, there were six modern structures and twelve "makeshifts" or "excuses" that he would not dignify with the term "building." The Lyceum was seventy-two years old, the chapel was sixty-seven, the physics building (Barnard Observatory) was sixty-four, and Taylor Hall was sixty-seven. As it had been for several years, the university's most pressing need was more dormitory space. There were 614 students enrolled in 1920 and only 226 dormitory rooms.

When fifty-six members of the legislature arrived on the campus in mid-February 1920, a special assembly of faculty and students was convened in the chapel. The primary topic of that special Saturday assembly was a bill pending in the legislature to consolidate Mississippi A & M, the Industrial Institute and College for Women, and the University of Mississippi into one institution to be located at Jackson. George L. Sheldon, the author of the bill, pointed out the obvious advantages of building a new university in Jackson rather than repairing the old dilapidated buildings in Oxford. He also explained the benefits that medical, pharmacy, and law students would enjoy if the University of Mississippi were located in a large and flourishing city like Jackson. Other members of the legislature, and at least one faculty member, spoke in opposition to consolidating or moving the university. On Saturday evening the university and the city of Oxford feted the legislators at a sumptuous banquet that lasted until one in the morning.

Several bills to restructure higher education were introduced in the 1920 session, but the most ambitious and comprehensive was the measure proposed by Sheldon. Under the terms of his bill to consolidate the state's three white colleges into one university at Jackson, the Industrial Institute and College would be continued in Columbus as a junior college for women. Senator Julius C. Zeller of Yazoo County was the bill's floor leader in the senate, and the press usually referred to the consolidation measure as the Sheldon-Zeller Bill. After the bill was introduced, the legislature received petitions from alumni of all three institutions opposing the consolidation plan, but many favored it, including Governor Theodore G. Bilbo, whose first term was just ending. Jackson newspapers reported that the incoming governor, Lee Russell, and house speaker Martin S. Conner also supported consolidation.

Senator Zeller met with a group of Jackson citizens on January 21, 1920, to discuss the advantages of consolidating the three institutions at Jackson. Zeller explained that the university's physical plant was in poor condition and that Ole Miss officials had requested $750,000 for emergency repair and expansion. The other two institutions had also made urgent requests for repair and renovation, and the legislature was considering a special $2,000,000 appropriation. Allocating funds for a new greater university, Zeller said, is preferable to repairing old, worn-out buildings. Zeller quickly added that consolidation should not be based on considerations of brick and mortar alone: "This is the psychological moment for the legislature to realize that if we are ever to have a great university, an institution that will compare favorably with universities in other states, we must build anew, locate the institution at a center of population, broaden the scope of its work, and make it a University in something more than a name."

As convincing as Zeller's argument was, there was no public support for consolidation outside of Jackson, and the Sheldon-Zeller bill was not enacted. After defeating the consolidation measure, the lawmakers considered several other options. Some legislators opposed consolidation but favored relocating the university to Jackson. To get that option before the legislature, Lamar Quintus Cincinnatus Williams of Newton County introduced "An Act to move the University of Mississippi from its present location near the town of Oxford to the city of Jackson." When Williams's bill reached the floor for debate, Representative Buz Walker, Jr., (whose father was the dean of the school of engineering and future president of Mississippi A & M), offered an amendment to abolish the school of engineering at Ole Miss and transfer all engineering courses to Mississippi A & M. Walker's amendment was tabled and the bill to move the university to Jackson lost by a vote of eighty-two to thirty-seven. Ironically, the only change that came from all the maneuvering in 1920 was a name change. During the debate on the Sheldon-Zeller bill, President Henry Whitfield invited the legislature to visit the Industrial Institute and College for Women. Following their visit to Columbus, the lawmakers voted to maintain the institution and changed its name to Mississippi State College for Women.

After the consolidation bill failed, the Mississippi legislature appropriated $750,000 to the university for capital construction and $300,000 in support funds. The university bill passed handily in the house but the senate passed it by only one vote, where it was managed by Senator Zeller. In announcing the university's large appropriation, the *Mississippian* reported that the legislature was beginning to care for its "neglected child." The 1920 appropriation launched a construction program that eventually transformed the appearance of the campus. The new money was used for a chemistry-pharmacy building, four boys' dormitories and one girls' dormitory. The new science hall, now known as the Old Chemistry Building, was a beautiful structure of neoclassical design. The fifty-thousand-square-foot building, which housed the chemistry department and the pharmacy school, was scheduled for use in the fall of 1922, but it was not occupied until the spring of 1923. With the opening of the new science building, the old chemistry laboratory in the Lyceum was converted into four classrooms. Several other major structural changes were made within the Lyceum, and its external appearance was also dramatically altered in 1923 with the addition of columns at the west entrance to replicate the appearance of the main entrance.

Three of the four boys' dormitories—Deupree, LaBauve, and Odum—were built around a quadrangle northwest of the Lyceum "on ground not hitherto included on the campus." The fourth, George Hall, was the first of a similar group of buildings planned, but the other two dormitories were not built. The four small dorms included only thirty rooms and were more easily managed than the much larger Gordon Hall. The 1921 catalog cited these dormitories as the "first [new] buildings entering into the landscape of a greater University." Ward Hall, the new girls' dormitory, was a duplicate of Ricks Hall and built at a right angle to Ricks, with a dining room at the intersection of the two buildings. Ward Hall, which was ready for occupancy in the fall of 1921, increased women's dormitory capacity to 130 rooms. The four new boys' dorms added 120 more rooms.

With this additional dormitory space, enrollment increased in 1922 to over 700 for the first time in the university's history. The following fall, over 850 students applied for admission. Every available room on the campus was in use, and some students lived in makeshift rooms in the chapel. Fifty-five students were placed on a waiting list, but none was admitted because there were no more rooms on the campus. To the university's detriment, state appropriations did not keep pace with the burgeoning enrollment.

Among the university's expanding enrollment during Chancellor Powers's administration were two of America's most unusual students. One was Mrs. Minerva Farmer of Brooksville in Noxubee County. Mrs. Farmer matriculated at the University of Mississippi in the fall of 1915 at the age of seventy-three. Following a thirty-three-year teaching career, Mrs. Farmer returned to college for a degree in home economics. She was a graduate of Iuka Normal Institute, a non-degree-granting teachers college. She had also attended summer teacher institutes at several colleges. Mrs. Farmer received her fifteen minutes of fame, being touted in the national press as the oldest college student in America.

The university's other extraordinary student, a high school dropout who made a D in college English, garnered a much larger share of fame as one of the world's great literary figures. In the fall semester of 1919, Chancellor Powers gave William Faulkner, whose father was the university's business manager, special permission to take classes on an informal basis. In addition to the D in English, Faulkner made an A in

Spanish and an A in French. In the spring semester he took a course in mathematics to improve his thinking skills but withdrew and received no grade. Although Faulkner published several poems, reviews, short stories, and illustrations in various campus publications, a literary society blackballed him for his "arrogance" and for "putting on airs." A fellow student remembered the uneasy relationship between the man who would become the bard of Oxford and his classmates at Ole Miss. Louis Cochran, quoted in Joseph Blotner's biography of Faulkner, explained that "Faulkner was painfully shy; he felt that many students did not like him, and he retaliated by affecting a total indifference he did not totally feel."

Because of his courtly manner and dapper dress, Faulkner was called the "Count" by some of his peers and "Count No 'Count" by others. Faulkner once ran up such a large bill at a Memphis haberdashery that his mother, Maud Butler Faulkner, had to sell a diamond ring to liquidate her oldest son's debt. During his college days, the future Nobel laureate sported "a small neatly trimmed moustache which struck [his friend Ben Wasson] as quite worldly and daring." Wasson often observed Faulkner extracting a handkerchief from his coat sleeve. "The British wear their handkerchiefs in their jacket sleeves," Faulkner explained.

While a sometime student at the university, Faulkner formed a lasting friendship with two students from Greenville, Ben Wasson and Lucy Somerville. Through his association with them, he became a member of The Marionettes, the campus drama club. In 1920 Faulkner hand-lettered and illustrated a one-act play, *The Marionettes.* The play was "too amateurish" even for the university drama club and was never performed. Ben Wasson suggested Faulkner produce several additional copies, which Wasson would sell for five dollars each. Faulkner agreed and produced six copies, one of which he gave to Wasson as a commission for selling the other five. By the early 1990s the value of Faulkner's *Marionettes* had increased 5,000 percent.

William Faulkner's association with the university offers but one example that the state university was a "bureau of political patronage." His grandfather John W. T. Falkner was a member of the board of trustees and a law partner of Governor Lee Russell. His aunt Elizabeth Murry Hunt was university librarian. His father Murry C. Falkner was the university business manager. His uncle John Falkner was a law professor.

William Faulkner, although he did not make the highest score on the civil service exam, was named university postmaster in December 1921 at the tender age of twenty-four. In what must rank as an all-time put-down, William Faulkner, the inattentive, lackadaisical, and often impolite postmaster, was voted "Hardest Worker" by Ole Miss students in the 1923 Who's Who contest.

When complaints of Faulkner's inefficiency and calls for his removal reached Senator Byron "Pat" Harrison, Phil Stone, Faulkner's friend and mentor, pleaded with Harrison not to fire him because he was "going to quit pretty soon anyway." Faulkner did soon resign, under threat of dismissal, on October 31, 1924. As he was leaving the post office for the last time, he told his friend Skeet Kincannon, "I reckon I'll be at the beck and call of folks with money all my life, but thank God I won't ever again be at the beck and call of every son of a bitch who's got two cents to buy a stamp." In the autumn of 1924, William Faulkner left Oxford for New Orleans and Europe. He came back home to stay in 1929, married Estelle Oldham, took a job in the university power plant where he wrote *As I Lay Dying* on the bottom of an upturned wheelbarrow, and in 1930 purchased Rowan Oak, his home for the remainder of his life. Oxford's Nobel laureate died on July 6, 1962.

Although the university's enrollment continued to increase during the 1920s, Mississippi's support for its state university remained the lowest in the nation except for New Mexico. The 1922 appropriation was virtually the same as it had been in the previous biennium. The board reduced Chancellor Powers's salary from six thousand dollars to forty-eight hundred, and faculty salaries, already the lowest in the country except for Florida, New Mexico, and Wyoming, were also cut in 1922. The university's student-teacher ratio was also much higher than allowed by the Southern Association of Colleges. There were, for example, two hundred eighteen students enrolled in history courses but only one history professor. That imbalance would soon draw stinging criticism and incite still another round of controversies.

Some of the controversies during the Kincannon and Powers administrations can be attributed to the lingering animosity between Greeks and non-Greeks, which culminated in a legislative ban on fraternities in 1912. The anti-fraternity students did not trust Chancellor Kincannon, a fraternity man, because he did not enforce the ban. Chancellor

Powers often scolded students for maintaining membership in secret societies, but took no steps to eliminate fraternities. Members of William Faulkner's fraternity, Sigma Alpha Epsilon, met openly in the home of Lemuel Oldham, Faulkner's future father-in-law, and later in the home of John Falkner, his uncle.

After Governor Lee Russell's inauguration in January 1920, the university's policy toward fraternities changed drastically. Since his student days at Ole Miss, and especially while he was in the state senate, Lee Russell tried to restrict the social functions of the state university. Now that he was governor and chairman of the board of trustees, he would strictly enforce the anti-fraternity law, which he authored in 1912. At its meeting on November 3, 1920, the board of trustees, "having before it evidence . . . that there has existed in the last few years sub-rosa Fraternities," announced that they were "joining with the faculty . . . and Officers of the State earnestly and honestly with the view of wholly eradicating these organizations." All records, paraphernalia, and other relics of the secret societies were to be surrendered, all students were required to sign a statement that they were not a member of a Greek society and pledge not to join one while a student at the university. The board decreed that students must file the signed statement with the secretary of the university before "high noon on November 10, 1920."

This proclamation was followed by a series of resolutions on dancing. "It is a matter of current report," the trustees resolved, "that public dances given by students . . . have been accompanied at times with forms of gross evils and have interfered with the progress . . . of instruction." To create a more wholesome environment on the campus and to stamp out the evils of dancing, the board of trustees imposed severe restrictions on all campus social functions but on dances in particular. The new restrictions on fraternities and dances sparked an angry campus demonstration. A "small group of students," according to the *Mississippian,* burned an effigy of Governor Russell near the center of the campus. The student paper downplayed the incident and dismissed the late-night episode as a harmless prank by a handful of college boys. But the faculty considered the incident "a source of humiliation" for the university. Powers convened the student body in a special assembly and asked the guilty parties, as a matter of honor, to "come forward." When none did, he vowed to "seek them out during the whole semester."

Without dissent, the faculty voted to expel the perpetrators if they were identified and pledged its full support for the new rules on fraternities and dances.

When "high noon on November 10" came, thirty students, including William Faulkner, refused to sign the anti-fraternity pledge. Given an extension of time, five of those thirty relented and signed the pledge. The faculty expelled the other twenty-five and announced that any students unwilling to abide by the fraternity regulations should withdraw immediately. The expulsion of the twenty-five students prompted strong and vocal reaction, and sufficient pressure was brought to bear on the trustees that they readmitted the students for the second semester in January 1921.

Their readmission did not, however, end the anti-Russell sentiment among the Ole Miss student body. In December 1922 Frances Birkhead, the governor's former secretary, filed a seduction and breach of promise suit against Governor Russell in federal court in Oxford. A reporter covering the trial for the United Press Services, C. H. McNeill, wanted a sensational story to go along with his report of the trial, so he plied about fifty students with "Mississippi moonshine" and induced them to stage a reenactment of the earlier burning of the effigy of Governor Russell. McNeill's report of the repeat performance drew extensive coverage in the state press and in the Memphis papers. A day or so after this second episode, the *Mississippian* published a resolution adopted at a "mass meeting of all students" expressing their "absolute and indignant astonishment" at McNeill's "framed-up story." The student paper castigated McNeill and the Mississippi press for running the story without exposing McNeill's involvement. The *Mississippian* also thanked the Memphis papers, especially the *Memphis News Scimitar,* for exposing the hoax and for carrying "denials of the story in conspicuous places on the front page." Although the student demonstrations angered Governor Russell, he did not hold Chancellor Powers responsible, and their relationship, which had begun at Ole Miss when they were both students in 1901, was undisturbed. Over the years their personal friendship became a political alliance, and they were almost always on the same side in the state's factional warfare. The strength of that friendship was tested in June of 1921.

In the late spring of 1921, rumors were circulating around the state that charges of immorality would soon be filed against Chancellor Powers. After several newspapers reported the rumors, the board of trustees convened a special meeting to discuss the situation. At that meeting, on June 16, Professor Roswell W. Rogers, acting dean of the school of education, filed formal written charges with the board of trustees alleging that Chancellor Powers was "morally, intellectually, and professionally unfit" for the high office he held. Specifically, Professor Rogers alleged that Chancellor Powers "did go with a red-headed woman alone into a room at the Lawrence Hotel, a second class rooming house in Jackson, Mississippi, then and there for an immoral purpose." He also accused the chancellor of a sexual liaison with a telephone operator at the Chisca Hotel in Memphis. Rogers further claimed that Chancellor Powers had attempted to break up his family by telling Mrs. Rogers that he had frequent affairs with other women. In addition to one other lesser charge, Rogers also accused Chancellor Powers of falsifying his academic credentials by claiming degrees he did not have. The *Jackson Daily News* highlighted in front page headlines the most salacious charge: "Auburn Haired Woman Figures [in] Rogers' Charge, His Specifications Allege University Head Escorts Girl of Titian Hue Upon Indiscreet Occasion."

After Rogers filed his charges, the board of trustees ordered "a full, fearless, thorough and open investigation of the charges against Chancellor Powers." The public hearing, chaired by Governor Lee Russell, opened on Saturday morning June 18 in the house chamber of the state capitol. During the hearing, Chancellor and Mrs. Powers were the guests of Governor Russell in the Governors Mansion. Professor Rogers and Chancellor Powers were both represented by counsel and called more than twenty-five witnesses. As the hearing opened on Saturday morning, Professor Rogers began his testimony by reading several "testamentary letters" clearing him of sexual misconduct charges that had led to his indictment several years earlier when he was a professor at a small Texas college. He explained that he introduced this matter because Mrs. Powers had warned Mrs. Rogers if her husband filed charges against the chancellor "they would bring up the Texas trouble . . . and the troubles he had experienced in the summer school in 1916." Professor Rogers had been implicated in an affair with a schoolteacher during that summer's teacher institute.

Professor Rogers then testified that he had an affidavit from Mrs. H. C. Herren stating that she had arranged a sexual liaison between Chancellor Powers and a "red-haired woman" in the Lawrence Hotel in Jackson. On cross-examination, Professor Rogers would not say whether he had known Mrs. Herren before obtaining the affidavit from her. When asked directly when he had first met Mrs. Herren, he replied, "I refuse to answer." During cross-examination it was also revealed that Professor Rogers had received a letter from Chancellor Powers on March 28, 1921, informing him that Professor A. O. Shaw would be named dean of the school of education and that Rogers would have to step down from that office.

On Saturday afternoon Professor Rogers read into the record a biographical sketch of Chancellor Powers from *Who's Who In America.* The biographical sketch, which Powers had submitted to the publication, indicated that he had an M. A. and an LL.D. from the University of Chicago. Rogers then read a letter from the registrar of that institution stating that Powers did not hold any degrees from the University of Chicago. At the conclusion of the Saturday afternoon session, Professor Rogers's attorney sought to read Mrs. Herren's affidavit into the record. When Governor Russell learned that Mrs. Herren lived in Jackson, he ruled that she must appear in person and adjourned the meeting until Mrs. Herren could be located and brought to the house chamber.

At a Saturday night session Mrs. H. C. Herren, "a red-haired woman," was called as a witness for Professor Rogers. Mrs. Herren explained she was a widow and "took in boarders for a living," but she "refused to give the names of her boarders or say what they paid." Mrs. Herren testified that she had arranged a liaison between Chancellor Powers and a woman in the Lawrence Hotel. Mrs. Herren stated that she occupied an adjoining room and, because the door between the rooms was open, she saw them disrobing just before she closed the door. Mrs. Herren also testified she had never met Professor Rogers before he filed charges against Powers. During cross-examination, Mrs. Herren stated that she had never been at the Lawrence Hotel "at any time in her life" other than the occasion when she accompanied Chancellor Powers.

After being on the stand for two hours and enduring "a grilling cross examination," Mrs. Herren asked for a brief recess. As she walked out of the house chamber into the rotunda, she fainted. Although she was quickly revived, she could not continue the cross-examination, and the hearing recessed until Monday morning. The Sunday *Jackson Daily News* reported Mrs. Herren's testimony under a front page headline: "Red-Haired Woman Testifies Against Powers: Faints."

The Monday morning hearing opened with a startling development. Chancellor Powers's attorney offered into evidence an affidavit signed by Mrs. Herren repudiating the testimony she had given at the Saturday hearing. The attorney informed Governor Russell and the trustees that Mrs. Herren, who faced the prospect of twenty witnesses who would "testify regarding her character," called him late Saturday night and told him "that it was her earnest desire to drop the whole matter." In the affidavit she stated: "I want to make a confession. I was forced to tell what I told on the witness stand. . . . The whole thing is a lie. Do what you want with me. I am through with the whole mess." In the meantime, she had rented a car to take her to Crystal Springs where she caught an Illinois Central train and left the state.

After his attorney introduced Herren's affidavit, Chancellor Powers took the stand for two hours. He attributed the entire controversy to Professor Rogers being passed over as dean of the school of education. The chancellor also "entered positive and peremptory denials" of all charges except the accusation that he had falsified his academic credentials. Powers explained that "his father was a Methodist preacher, and a poor man, and it was necessary for me to go to work for a living at the age of 18." He further explained that he had attended several educational institutions, including the University of Mississippi. In 1907 he was attending a summer institute at the University of Chicago, but dropped out when Governor Vardaman appointed him state superintendent of education. After reviewing his work as state superintendent, Chancellor Powers concluded, "I have one degree of which I am proud, the honorary LL.D. from Mississippi College."

Following the chancellor's testimony, several faculty members were called to the stand. Professor James Warsaw Bell testified that he knew of Rogers's Texas troubles and had heard that Rogers registered with a woman in a Memphis hotel as "Mr. and Mrs. Bookout." Alfred Hume testified that Professor Rogers had a reputation of being "loose with women." Hume also admitted under questioning that many of the faculty were embarrassed, if not incensed, because the chancellor of the university had no earned degrees. On the basis of W. L. Pope's testimony, the owner of the Lawrence Hotel, and others, it was evident that Mrs. Herren, the "red-haired woman," was the mistress of Professor Rogers and had fabricated the story about Chancellor Powers and the woman at the hotel. Pope testified that Professor Rogers and Mrs. Herren had met several times in his hotel. There was also an insinuation that Mrs. Herren operated a house of assignation. After hearing this testimony on late Monday afternoon, the board retired "for a discussion of the matter." At ten-thirty Monday night, a "shout of delight greeted the finding . . . that by unanimous vote Chancellor J. N. Powers . . . had been fully exonerated of the charges preferred by Professor Roswell W. Rogers." Chancellor Powers "was placed in triumph upon the shoulders of sturdy friends and borne aloft from the hall of the house of representatives."

In a lengthy commentary on "The University Scandal," editor Fred Sullens of the *Jackson Daily News* wrote, "The strange whirligig called Mississippi politics has caused many queer frame-ups and acts of blackmailing in recent years, but it has never produced an affair like this one." Even though Professor Rogers accused Chancellor Powers of sexual misconduct and had "used his own mistress to bring about the [chancellor's] downfall," the scandal, Sullens said, was about politics, not sex. Sullens explained that Governor Russell had tried to get Professor Shaw appointed president of Mississippi A & M. When he failed in that, Russell connived with Chancellor Powers to appoint Shaw dean of the school of education, displacing Professor Rogers. Motivated by "a bitter and unreasoning desire for revenge," Rogers filed the salacious charges against Powers. Both men had sullied their reputations and disgraced the university and both should go, Sullens concluded. And they did go—Professor Rogers immediately and Chancellor Powers three years later.

Several months after the "university scandal," a joint legislative committee visited the state institutions of higher learning in the spring of 1922 and found the campuses in varying degrees of ill repair. After expressing concern about the physical condition of the institutions, the committee spoke of politics and inveighed against its effects: "If the Czar of Russia and the Kaiser of Germany could pursue a policy of hands off when it came to their university professors, then surely we can observe this rule. . . . Otherwise, we shall never develop an esprit d'corps for learning and culture in our state." What the czar and the kaiser were able to do, Mississippi governors could not or would not do.

The 1923 governor's race illustrates the link between politics and academics and documents its consequences. When Henry L. Whitfield, the former president of Mississippi State College for Women, ran for governor against Theodore G. Bilbo in 1923, members of the board of trustees made a special effort to keep the colleges out of that election and deluded themselves into thinking that they had. Ambrose B. Schauber, the board secretary, wrote to Governor Russell on July 23, 1923:

> I am glad to advise you . . . that these schools are not in politics. The Board of Trustees adopted a policy some time ago of keeping the schools out of politics and we have requested that everyone connected with these institutions refrain from taking any part in any political campaign. It is their right to vote as they please but we think it serves the best interest of the institutions for them not to get involved in any political campaign and I am glad to be able to report that this policy of the Board of Trustees has been adhered to by everyone connected with these institutions.

Secretary Schauber's statement is incredible, given the fact that from the outset of the 1923 campaign the institutions of higher learning were deeply entangled in the contest. Whitfield sought and secured a public endorsement from President Joseph Cook of the Mississippi State Teachers College at Hattiesburg. His state campaign manager was Harry Bryan, the son-in-law of Vice Chancellor Alfred Hume of the university. Whitfield also had the active support of the MSCW alumnae association. Like Whitfield, Bilbo sought and received the public support of several college officials, including Chancellor Powers.

Henry Whitfield defeated Bilbo in 1923, and his victory meant that the new board of trustees would probably dismiss Chancellor Powers. Whitfield and Powers had been adversaries since the early 1900s when both men had served as the elected state superintendent of education. At the June 1924 board meeting, a motion to reelect Chancellor Powers produced a tie vote. Governor Whitfield's three appointees, along with Willard F. Bond, the superintendent of education and an old ally of

Whitfield, voted no. The four carry-over board members voted yes. Governor Whitfield broke the tie by voting to dismiss Chancellor Powers. A motion to elect Alfred Hume chancellor also produced a tie vote, and Whitfield again broke the tie by voting in favor of Hume, the father-in-law of his state campaign manager. Six years later, when Bilbo gained control of the board of trustees, he removed Hume and reinstated Powers.

His own political entanglements notwithstanding, Whitfield was an enlightened governor whose progressive leadership was cut short by his death in 1927. During the 1923 campaign Whitfield had addressed the problems of rural unemployment and the alarming increase of racial violence. Once in office he embraced a broad legislative program including better mental health care, tax reform, industrial development, expanded vocational training, improvement in the quality of life for Mississippi's black citizens, and major educational reform. Whitfield's moderate position on race received a generally favorable response and even praise from some of the Mississippi press. In commenting on Whitfield's pledge to be the governor of all the people, including blacks, the *Jackson Daily News* admitted: "We all know . . . that we have not given the Negro a square deal, and it is gratifying to know that we have a governor endowed with the courage to speak out and tell the truth about it." The Committee of One Hundred, an organization of leading black citizens, also praised the governor for his courageous stand.

Governor Whitfield's efforts to mollify race relations were only one part of his larger plan to reorder the state's priorities. Whitfield realized that Mississippi's economic development was linked to its educational system, and the system obviously needed fundamental reform. The governor was especially concerned that the state university had not broadened its service role or directed its research efforts toward solving the state's most pressing problems. Governor Whitfield went to Oxford and personally appealed to university officials to form an alliance with the state of Mississippi as the University of Wisconsin had done with the state of Wisconsin. That pragmatic, problem-solving relationship between a state and its state university was known as the "Wisconsin Idea." Governor Whitfield envisioned the same kind of relationship between Mississippi and its public institutions, and soon after his inauguration he took steps to make that goal a reality.

In the fall of 1924 the governor took a delegation of farmers, bankers, businessmen, and educators to Wisconsin to study the Wisconsin Idea. That trip convinced the state's business leaders that a similar program was possible in Mississippi, and they returned with newfound faith in the state's economic future. While the business community, in cooperation with the legislature, designed a strategy for industrial development, Governor Whitfield arranged for a University of Wisconsin consulting team, under the direction of Michael V. O'Shea, to conduct a comprehensive examination of Mississippi's educational system. Professor O'Shea published an extensive report of his findings in 1927.

In a preamble to his report, O'Shea acknowledged that Mississippi was just "emerging from the period of depression and discouragement" following the Civil War, and he applauded the state's leadership for recognizing "that their prosperity individually and as a state depends upon universal education." Unfortunately, Mississippi's institutions of higher learning, O'Shea found, were clinging to the "genteel tradition [that] was in vogue throughout our country fifty years ago." O'Shea wrote that he frequently heard the phrase, "We plan our courses so as to develop character in our young people" but rarely found a curriculum designed to "train young people to develop the agricultural, industrial, economic, and human resources of Mississippi." That assessment was followed by a warning: "If the higher institutions do not modify their program in view of the special needs of Mississippi, it may easily happen that the state will be seriously drained of its superior young men and women, educating them for other states where they stand a chance of finding employment."

Consequently, O'Shea recommended a thorough reorganization of Mississippi's system of higher education. Specifically, he recommended the establishment of a state board of education with authority over public schools and higher education, the appointment of a commissioner of higher education, and the merger of the three white institutions of higher learning into one University of Mississippi. The three separate campuses would be maintained, but each would be assigned and limited to specific degree programs. The two teachers colleges, Mississippi State Teachers College at Hattiesburg and Delta State Teachers College at Cleveland, would also be maintained, but their degree programs would be strictly limited to teacher education. O'Shea spent little time studying Alcorn

A & M, and the report included few recommendations about higher education for blacks.

The O'Shea Study singled out the University of Mississippi for special criticism and several specific recommendations. The O'Shea staff called for more research activity directed toward solving Mississippi's social and economic problems and for a stronger faculty. According to O'Shea, faculty development should be the university's top priority. "The University of Mississippi can render service to the state much more effectively," the report stated, "by building up its faculty than by expanding its physical plant." O'Shea issued his report during the gubernatorial campaign of 1927, and the state's institutions of higher learning were in the thick of the fray.

CHAPTER 9

BILBO AND THE GREATER UNIVERSITY, 1927–1935

I was looking fifty years ahead for Mississippi.

GOVERNOR THEODORE G. BILBO

In the 1927 governor's election Dennis Murphree, the former lieutenant governor who succeeded Governor Henry Whitfield, was seeking a full four-year term. Also running were Representative Albert C. Anderson, Martin S. Conner, and former governor Theodore G. Bilbo. Anderson and Conner were eliminated in the first primary, and Bilbo then defeated Murphree in the run-off election. Bilbo's original platform, which he announced in July 1926, did not include the consolidation of the state's three white colleges or the relocation of the university to Jackson, and it is not known when Bilbo added educational reform to his legislative agenda. He was probably influenced by the O'Shea report, which he studied with some care, his consultations with Professor Austin Phelps of Peabody College, and by the increasing involvement of college officials in the 1927 campaign.

President John C. Fant of Mississippi State College for Women, and former professor of education at Ole Miss, for example, gave Dennis Murphree a glowing introduction at a student assembly and stopped just short of formal endorsement, though he left little doubt how he stood in the governor's race. MSCW alumnae, who made no effort to conceal their support for Murphree, established committees of correspondence to write letters in support of his candidacy. Two members of the college board, Mrs. Daisy McLaurin Stevens and Mrs. Robert Ralston, and the wife of a former board member, Mrs. O. F. Lawrence, all of whom had connections with MSCW, were active members of Murphree's state campaign committee. The opposition to Bilbo among MSCW alumnae stemmed primarily from his support of the Sheldon-Zeller bill in 1920, which would have consolidated the state's white colleges and changed MSCW to a junior college. There was also active opposition to Bilbo at

Mississippi A & M and at the State Teachers College in Hattiesburg. Bilbo's own partisans at those institutions kept him well informed.

The opposition of Ole Miss officials embittered this seasoned veteran of six campaigns more than might have been expected. During the 1927 campaign, Robert Farley, a young law professor, wrote letters to friends and former students urging them to work for Bilbo's defeat. "A vote for Bilbo is a vote against Chancellor Hume," Farley explained in his letters. Farley's presumption was based on rumors that Bilbo, if elected, would reinstate his old friend and former chancellor Joseph Neely Powers, who was fired four years earlier by Governor Whitfield. Powers's public support for Bilbo and his endorsement of Bilbo's populist promise of free textbooks lent credence to Farley's presumption. Bilbo asked Chancellor Hume to reprimand Farley and instruct the professor to quit the campaign against him, but Chancellor Hume told Bilbo that Farley's politics did not come under his jurisdiction and he would not intervene.

Other officials at the university who publicly supported Dennis Murphree included William Hemingway, a former mayor of Jackson and professor of law. Hemingway openly ridiculed Bilbo and his Redneck platform in his classes. Thomas Turner, a student at the university who would later become president of the Board of Trustees of Institutions of Higher Learning, kept records on university faculty and staff who campaigned against Bilbo and passed that information on to him. The opposition of Ole Miss officials to him and his populist platform, Bilbo believed, was evidence that the university was still catering to the sons and daughters of Mississippi's gentry and was contributing little to the solution of the state's economic and social problems. As he began to formulate his plan to reorganize Mississippi's system of higher education in the summer of 1927, Bilbo was now armed with the findings of the O'Shea Study and not merely the accusations of the university's old enemies.

As Bilbo was formulating his plan, bits and pieces of it leaked to the press. One version of the plan called for sweeping changes in the system's leadership, and there was speculation over who would go if Bilbo was elected. Another feature of his plan, which became the subject of increasing conjecture and several resolutions, was the relocation of the university to Jackson. Shortly after Bilbo defeated Murphree in August

1927, the *Clarion-Ledger* reported that a bill would be introduced in January 1928 to move the law school and the medical school from Oxford to Jackson.

That report drew extensive comment from W. A. Lomax, editor of the student newspaper. Lomax endorsed the transfer of the medical school and also favored upgrading the two-year course to a four-year degree program. He was even more emphatic about moving the law school. Lomax cited a 1927 report by H. C. Horack, secretary of the Association of American Law Schools, that said the Ole Miss law school consisted of one classroom, a totally inadequate library, one office for four professors, and a class schedule that "resemble[d] an Egyptian hieroglyphic puzzle." Horack also offered sharp criticism of the faculty. "I do not believe," he wrote Chancellor Alfred Hume on October 15, 1927, "that any of your men are keeping up with modern law school methods or progress. . . . Nor did I find in my visit that the school seemed to be alert or aware of what was being done in legal education elsewhere." Since large expenditures were necessary to upgrade the professional schools, Lomax preferred to move them and build anew in Jackson where students in both schools would have opportunities for laboratory experiences that Oxford did not afford.

As the question of moving the university to Jackson became increasingly the subject of public discourse, the tone of the discourse became increasingly sentimental. In an open letter to the people of Mississippi in December 1927 Chancellor Hume invoked the memory of the Lost Cause in support of keeping the university at Oxford. "The University of Mississippi is rich in memories and memorials and a noble history," the chancellor wrote. "If its children did not come to its defense," he continued, "the very stones of the memorial arches and the Confederate monument would cry out. The memorial window in the old library erected in loving memory of the University Greys, the Confederate monument nearby, and the Confederate soldiers' cemetery a little farther removed are as sacred as any ancient shrine, altar, or temple. Instead of moving the University away that it might be a little easier to reach, ought not the people of Mississippi look upon a visit here as a holy pilgrimage."

The state press reported Chancellor Hume's statement as if Ole Miss students endorsed his appeal not to move the university. The *Mississip-*

pian denied one report in particular that claimed Ole Miss students "bitterly opposed" moving the university. To gauge their opinion, the campus newspaper conducted a student poll. Students were asked to vote for or against the removal of the university and for or against removal of only the medical school and the law school. On the question of removing the entire institution to Jackson 419 students voted for and 219 against. On the question of moving only the law and medical schools, 150 students voted for and 350 against. The students preferred to move all or none of the university.

On January 13, 1928, the day he reported the results of the poll, the student editor asked the legislature, "What Will You Do With Your State University?" Lomax lectured the lawmakers, admonishing them to move it or leave it, "but do something" about the university. If they left it at Oxford, they should "make it a real university." It is not known if Lomax had read the O'Shea report, but his editorial reflected O'Shea's exuberance about Mississippi's future and the role the university should play in its future. Lomax saw the coming decade as a time of "great destiny" and predicted electric power would generate a "New Era" of industrialization in Mississippi. The future of Mississippi was linked to the future of the state university, and he proclaimed, "We advocate a greater University of Mississippi at Jackson for the good of Mississippi." Lomax expected opposition to the "greater University" from those "who wish to see Ole Miss remain in a secondary position," and closed his editorial with one last admonition to the lawmakers: "Gentlemen of the Legislature . . . take a firm stand . . . and give us a University worthy of the name."

Four days after Lomax's editorial, Governor Theodore G. Bilbo delivered his inaugural address. It was a well-crafted statement, and even *Jackson Daily News* editor Fred Sullens, one of Bilbo's bitterest critics, gave grudging due. Sullens wrote that Bilbo's inaugural "[i]n a goodly number of respects" was "the ablest message . . . in the memory of this writer." Many other papers, even some of the opposition press, praised his speech but had reservations about the cost of his agenda, which some estimated at sixty to one hundred million dollars.

The high cost of Bilbo's reforms triggered a conditioned response from the low pressure faction of the Democratic Party. The low pressure coalition was led by a small clique known as the "Big Four," which included

Walter Sillers, Thomas A. Bailey, Joseph W. George, and Lawrence T. Kennedy. These men served at various times as speakers of the house, chairman of the appropriations committee, and chairman of the ways and means committee. Governor Bilbo represented the populist faction of the party, also known as the Redneck faction, which outnumbered the low pressure group. Even so, the populists enjoyed little success because they were outmaneuvered by the crafty conservatives who controlled the house of representatives. The low pressure faction was stunned by the visionary and costly proposals in Governor Bilbo's inaugural, and they, with help from the stock market crash in 1929, eventually defeated Bilbo's legislative program. Bilbo's inaugural address embraced a wide range of populist reforms and other programs he considered essential to Mississippi's social and economic advancement. He reiterated his campaign proposal for free textbooks, a mental hospital, two charity hospitals, a separate correctional facility for young inmates, and a major highway construction program. To these recommendations Bilbo added another costly and controversial proposal.

"If I were called upon," he said, "to name the one thing that would do more to develop Mississippi and bring to her the highest degree of progress and future glory than anything else, I would not hesitate in saying that the moving of the University of Mississippi to the capital city of Jackson and the building and equipment of a twelve or fifteen million dollar institution would be that thing." Anticipating bitter opposition, Bilbo added, "Let me express the hope that every legislator and citizen in passing judgement upon this proposition may be able to rise above any sectionalism or local or selfish interest and decide the question from a patriotic standpoint and from the standpoint of happiness, and glory of her people. From the political standpoint, I owe the city of Jackson little and I owe the citizens of Lafayette County and the sections surrounding the University much, but I owe my state and her people the best there is in me and in recommending the removal of the University I have only one purpose in view. That is the best interest of all the people of the state."

Governor Bilbo cited the O'Shea Study and asserted that "thoughtful men and women throughout the state . . . agree that some radical changes are absolutely necessary [for] Mississippi's higher educational institutions." He added, "We are spending too much money to longer delay this reform. The people demand it, the times require it, and the youth of the state must have it. After much study, observation, and consultation with leaders of educational thought and activities I beg to recommend and urge upon the legislature to undertake this important task." Governor Bilbo then outlined his reorganization plan, which had been the subject of so much speculation during the summer and fall of 1927. In addition to his proposal to relocate the university, Bilbo recommended an eight-member board of education that would appoint the state superintendent of education and a commissioner of higher education. A unified educational administration could assign a role and scope to each of the state's public colleges and correlate course offerings and degree programs with Mississippi's social and economic needs.

The eight members of the board of education would serve eight-year terms, with one member rotating off the board each year, which would preclude future governors from appointing a majority of the board. Bilbo conceded that "[i]t may be charged that the present administration will have the right to appoint the full board, this is true, but after the system is once inaugurated the future will be safe." The scope of Bilbo's proposal, which included other sweeping educational reforms, dazzled Mississippi's political and educational leadership and is reminiscent of the state's response to Chancellor Frederick Barnard's reforms nearly a century earlier. Actually, Governor Bilbo's recommendations were only slight modifications of those made by the O'Shea Study in 1927, and reiterated by the Brookings Institution Study in 1932, the Peabody Study in 1933, the Gibson Study in 1946, the Brewton Study in 1954, the Legislative Study in 1962, the Mortorana Study in 1966, the Booze-Allen Study in 1968, and the Academy Study in 1979.

The day after Bilbo's inauguration, Senator Linton Glover North of Belzoni introduced a resolution to establish a joint legislative committee to "plan the removal of the University of Mississippi to Jackson." The *Jackson Daily News* applauded Senator North's resolution and reassured its readers that he "was not acting in behalf of any selfish interests of Jackson, but for the welfare of the entire state, and with the sole hope of building a bigger and better University" that would in future years attract thousands of students instead of its "present meager enrollment." The Jackson paper identified North as a native of Vicksburg, an alumnus of A & M College and "an upstanding, progressive young man in the upper branch of the lawmaking body." The *Daily News* also reminded its readers that Senator Julius C. Zeller had recommended in 1920 the consolidation of the state's colleges into one university at Jackson. "But the legislature," according to the Jackson paper, "lacked the largeness of vision to see it."

Two former chancellors, Andrew A. Kincannon and Joseph Neely Powers, endorsed this latest effort to relocate the university. Fred Sullens also supported moving the university to Jackson but did not endear himself to the people of Oxford with his remark that "Oxford is, always has been, and always will be, a stupid country town." The Jackson business community tried to restrain its excitement over the prospect of relocating the university and correctly anticipated an accusation that they favored the proposal for economic rather than educational reasons. That accusation was made by many, including Martin Van Buren Miller, a prominent Ole Miss alumnus and later president of the board of trustees. Miller accused the Jackson establishment of being "selfish and greedy."

On January 19, 1928, a delegation from the Jackson Chamber of Commerce met with Governor Bilbo at the Governors Mansion to discuss his proposal for what he called "The Greater University of Mississippi." The committee heartily endorsed the plan to build a modern, state-of-the-art university in their city but had reservations about the ten to fifteen million dollar cost of the institution. T. M. Hederman, editor of the *Clarion-Ledger,* attended the meeting and reported the governor's response to their concerns. "I fully understand," Bilbo told the delegation, "that the proposal suggested in my inaugural address is a big one, but I was looking fifty years ahead for Mississippi. . . . It is my dream to make this the outstanding University in the entire South; one that will attract students from beyond the borders of the Southland. . . . I do not insist upon a fifteen million dollar program to begin with; the start could be made in a smaller way, but the plans must be made for the distant future."

While the populist governor and the Jackson plutocrats were forging what some must have considered an unholy alliance, Chancellor Alfred Hume, Oxford Mayor Taylor McElroy, and local citizens were plotting a strategy to keep the university at Oxford. The city fathers invited members of the legislature to come to Oxford and see for themselves why Ole Miss should remain in that "country town." On February 3,

1928, a large delegation of legislators visited Oxford to tour the city and the Ole Miss campus. In the evening they were feted at a banquet where several speeches were made in opposition to Bilbo's plan to move the university to Jackson. The most stirring speech was made by Chancellor Hume, who appealed to the Southern sense of place and memory. "Gentlemen," he said, "you may move the University of Mississippi. You may move it to Jackson or anywhere else. You may uproot it from the hallowed ground on which it has stood for eighty years. You may take it from these surroundings that have become dear to the thousands who have gone from its doors. But, gentlemen, don't call it Ole Miss."

Chancellor Hume addressed the complaint that Oxford and the university were not accessible to the southern half of the state in his December letter and again in his February speech. He countered that claim with two arguments, or rather one statement of fact and one prediction. First, he correctly pointed out that most state universities were located in remote country towns. He then predicted that Bilbo's proposed system of "modern highways" would soon make the university accessible to every part of the state. Unfortunately, Bilbo's highway system was first thwarted by the low pressure faction and then rendered impossible by the Great Depression. The state university did not become accessible by a four-lane highway until fifty years after Hume's prediction, and then only from the west. The anonymous author of a pamphlet entitled *Some Facts Against the Removal of the University of Mississippi* argued that the university's remoteness was an asset, not a liability. The writer asked, "But why should a university be accessible?" He answered his own query by saying that it should not be, because students were there to study and to contemplate, not to socialize. Students had the Christmas vacation and summer recess "to renew touch with the outside world."

It was inevitable that the Grove would be injected into a discussion about removing the university. The author of *Facts Against the Removal* stated indignantly that less than half of the thousand-acre site for the proposed university in Jackson was tree lined and shaded. He compared that barren landscape to the classic groves of Oxford. In his February speech to the lawmakers, Chancellor Hume also alluded to the beauty of the campus, to the Grove and its classic oaks. He even read them poetry:

Woodman spare that tree,
Touch not a single bough,
In youth it sheltered me,
And I'll protect it now.

When the talking and the feasting were finished, the lawmakers backtracked to Jackson. Chancellor Hume's speech was persuasive, and ten days later Representative F. K. Belk of Holly Springs introduced a resolution to prohibit the removal of the university to Jackson. The house passed the resolution by a vote of 109 to 9. John C. Stennis, then a young representative from Kemper County, a graduate of Mississippi A & M and later a distinguished United States senator, cast one of the nine votes against the resolution.

Two weeks after the house of representatives killed his proposal to move the university to Jackson, Governor Bilbo addressed a joint session of the legislature. He badgered the low pressure conservatives for blocking his reforms, conceded that the university would not be relocated, and invited the lawmakers to cooperate with him in building a great university at Oxford. Bilbo recommended a $5 million appropriation for new buildings at Oxford. Anything less, he said, would be a dereliction of duty. He also recommended the construction of hard surface roads from various points in the state to Oxford to make the university accessible. Bilbo conceded that some "tightwad" might argue that Mississippi could not afford to appropriate such a vast sum for the university and also build highways to Oxford. If the state could build a "bughouse" for $5 million (the sum that had recently been appropriated for a mental hospital), why, he asked, would it not spend as much to educate its young men and women? Bilbo's entreaties went unheeded, but the legislature did appropriate $1,600,000 to the university in 1928, the largest appropriation in its eighty-year history. The governor was not satisfied with that appropriation, but he was even more upset with the board of trustees and Chancellor Hume for not asking for more. In 1927 Hume asked for $165,000 for capital improvements even though he had a $1,000,000 long-range campus improvement plan on the drawing board. In 1928, notwithstanding the university's dire needs, he requested only $265,000.

As concerned as he was about the condition of the university's physical plant, Governor Bilbo was even more concerned about the quality of its academic program, which had come under heavy criticism in recent years. In 1922 the Association of American Law Schools extended conditional accreditation to the law school and recommended several specific improvements. Five years later H. C. Horack, secretary of the American Association of Law Schools, found that those conditions had not been met, and the Ole Miss law school lost its accreditation in 1927. Horack recommended the suspension of the law school because of its inadequate classroom facilities, library space, library holdings, and instructional staff. He found the class schedule and enrollment records in utter disarray. Four different lists of law students existed, no two of which were the same. There were five students whose identity was completely unknown to Dean T. C. Kimbrough. The dean also admitted to Horack that he "could not recall when a student made a failing grade."

The university's medical school was also having problems, though not quite as serious. In 1927 the Association of American Medical Schools placed the two-year medical school on probation and "exerted strong pressure [for] certain improvements." Failure to make those improvements would result in the school's loss of its "A" rating. In addition to making budgetary and staff recommendations, the AAMS recommended that the medical school be relocated to a larger city and expanded to a four-year degree program with a teaching hospital.

In addition to the investigations by the legal and medical associations, the Southern Association of Colleges and Schools also conducted a study of the university's academic program. The 1929 investigation found that the university did not meet several SACS standards. The study, which focused particularly on the university faculty, noted that faculty salaries were "far below the average" of even the association's "weaker members." The SACS report characterized the faculty as "somewhat weak" with a "large proportion" having degrees from the University of Mississippi. The Southern Association did not rescind the university's accreditation but urged Chancellor Hume to eliminate the deficiencies as soon as practicable.

The 1928 special appropriation infused the "neglected child" with new vitality and enabled Chancellor Hume to initiate steps to remedy the most glaring deficiencies in the university's academic program. In 1929 he informed the board of trustees that the AALS had reinstated the law school and announced that a "transformation is being wrought" at the University of Mississippi. Hoping to capitalize on the expansive spirit of that "transformation," a department chairman went to Chancellor Hume with a request to purchase "the back issues of an important professional journal related to the department's field for $125." According to procedures then in place the chancellor personally approved all library purchases. Even though part of the 1928 appropriation was slated for library improvements, Hume declined the department chairman's request. The chancellor told the department chairman that he "found it difficult to persuade the students to read the textbook, much less outside reading assignments [and] saw no reason why $125 should be spent on old periodicals."

Chancellor Hume allotted a portion of the 1928 appropriation for the purchase of modern, steel library shelves. In urging the chancellor to seek an emergency appropriation for additional shelving, Whitman Davis, the university librarian, reported that "thousands of books, periodicals, and newspapers, many of them invaluable, . . . are thrown into the basement, uncatalogued, damaged, and unavailable to students." The announcement that new shelves would soon be installed prompted an editorial on April 6, 1928, by W. A. Lomax, who stated bluntly, "Let's first get a Library." He did not mean a building; he meant books. Lomax ridiculed the library holdings, claiming that most books had either been donated or "bought at auctions." Books on philosophy, science, and mathematics, he wrote, "are jokes, and rather antiquated, most of them written before 1900." Lomax continued, "If a book even hints at disturbing the established political, social, or religious questions of the day, it is not on the University Library shelves." In a thinly veiled reference to the philosophy professor's predestinarian theology (the philosophy professor was a Presbyterian minister), Lomax wrote that "books on free will and the like are not to be found in evidence."

The student editor then issued a stinging indictment of Mississippi's closed society. "This spirit of endeavoring to find out for one's self the essential truth of things," Lomax wrote, "should be given free range, not stifled [as it is at] the University of Mississippi. . . . Original thinking on the part of a student simply can't be done. Kant, Haeckel, Hegel, and the rest are not represented, and even Col. Bob Ingersoll is an Ishmael. In their stead we find some priceless gems such as 'How to get

Pep' or such other soothing syrup philosophic treatises. We maintain that such would not be the case in a great University, the alleged home of free thought."

In 1928 Governor Bilbo realized that Ole Miss was not a great university, that its library was inadequate and its physical plant was in disrepair. He knew that its faculty did not have the academic credentials to staff a modern university. These were not conjectures but the findings of various accrediting agencies. Bilbo was also convinced that Chancellor Hume was "temperamentally unfit" to transform Ole Miss into a great university. In June 1928 Bilbo stated publicly his intention to remove Hume if he could persuade the board of trustees to do so. But the university's board of trustees rejected the governor's recommendation and reelected Hume.

Bilbo was successful, however, in persuading the board of trustees of the State Teachers College at Hattiesburg to remove President Joseph Anderson Cook, the institution's first and only president, having served continuously since his appointment in 1911. President Cook had been under fire for some time, and many former students, alumni, and public school teachers believed that his administrative philosophy was seriously outdated. He routinely locked the gates to the campus at twilight and restricted access to the campus after dark. Many professional and business leaders in Mississippi's rapidly growing coastal region envisioned a broader role and scope for the Hattiesburg institution and were convinced that Cook, who was sixty-five years old, had neither the vision nor the vigor to develop the school's enormous potential. Governor Bilbo agreed, and, in June 1928, he recommended that the board not renew President Cook's contract and appoint a younger, more aggressive administrator. The board accepted his recommendation and elected Claude Bennett, the superintendent of the Biloxi city schools, to replace President Cook.

In 1929 Bilbo became more convinced than ever that Chancellor Alfred Hume was "temperamentally unfit" to be chancellor of a modern state university, and renewed his effort to replace him. The incident that strengthened Bilbo's resolve was Chancellor Hume's dismissal of two student editors and his censorship of student publications. The 1929 yearbook contained sketches of female figures and suggestive puns that

Hume considered "libelous slurs at girlhood and womanhood." The chancellor impounded the annual, expelled the two editors, and established a board of control to censor student publications.

The expulsion of the two editors received extensive press coverage, and Hume was the target of sharp criticism for the arbitrary manner in which he had handled the situation. He also came under intense pressure to reinstate the students. Eventually, Chancellor Hume readmitted one of the students, but denied that he had done so under pressure from the board or anyone else. Hume explained that his reinstatement of the student was an "act of free grace" and that he had meted out "mercy not justice" because the student had come to him as a "penitent child or sinner." Hume proclaimed that he would "never compromise a principle" because he was, in an obvious reference to Bilbo's characterization of him, " 'temperamentally unfit' for that sort of thing."

In his 1929 report to the board of trustees, Chancellor Hume explained the expulsion of the two students and addressed the larger issue of academic freedom at a university. "The average faculty member is a man of self-respect," Hume wrote, and "is entitled to his own view point and has a right to express his own opinions. . . . [But] occasionally freaks are found who prove exceptions to the rule." The chancellor, a Presbyterian of deep persuasion, went on to say that "[p]ernicious doctrines, teachings that are subversive of the best in our Christian civilization, should not be tolerated" and no plea of " 'academic freedom' may shield the man who would use his position to overthrow the principles . . . which constitute the strength and hope of our national life."

Chancellor Hume added that the claim of "academic freedom" can sometimes be "academic nonsense" and gave an example in which a college president could and should dismiss a professor or otherwise restrict his right of expression. Hume's concept of academic freedom is best understood in his own words: "Once more, take another hypothetical case. A professor of history in this section believes that Robert E. Lee was a traitor and teaches men so. Ought not that chair of history to become instantly vacant? Should it avail anything if the professor argues that 'academic freedom' has been invaded and that he conscientiously believes that Lee was guilty of treason. The emphatic answer, coming quick and hot, is 'Sir, . . . you may not trample under foot what we regard as sacred as long as you hold a position in our institution.' " Thirty years later, on the eve of the Meredith crisis, one of the formal written charges against Ole Miss history professor James W. Silver, author of *Mississippi: The Closed Society,* was an accusation that he had criticized the military strategy of Robert E. Lee and other Confederate generals.

As ex officio chairman of the board of trustees, Governor Bilbo received a copy of Chancellor Hume's report, but he was not swayed by it. Shortly before the June 1929 board meeting, Bilbo announced that he would again recommend the dismissal of Chancellor Hume. As before, the board rebuked Bilbo and reelected Hume for another year. After this second setback, Fred Sullens wrote an editorial entitled "Forget It, Theodore," advising Bilbo to give up his effort "to remove Dr. Alfred Hume as Chancellor of the University of Mississippi." Sullens warned Bilbo that Hume's removal would provoke "bitter resentment among hundreds of 'Ole Miss' graduates, many of them prominent in public life." He went on, "It would mean that these men will forthwith commence whetting their knives for your modern highway program, and in retaliation they will throw every possible obstacle in the path of your administration." Governor Bilbo did not need his old adversary to school him in the art of retaliatory politics. The wily governor realized that his direct participation in the reorganization of higher education would subject the plan to the charge of politics, but he would not quit his cause against Hume nor abandon his reorganization plan. To shield his plan from the charge of politics, however, Bilbo asked the legislature to take the lead.

On January 6, 1930, Bilbo addressed a joint session of the legislature and repeated his 1928 recommendation for sweeping reform of the state's educational system. "I want to earnestly urge upon the legislature," he said, "the imperative and pressing need of this reform. To undertake to do this work myself I have been afraid that I would be misunderstood. However, if the legislature is unwilling to assume and make the change . . . it will become my duty and responsibility. I am going to do my best for the educational welfare of Mississippi." Governor Bilbo commended the legislature for its record appropriation in 1928 and recommended an additional million dollar allocation for the university. "Come, let us complete the job," he urged, "and generations yet unborn will bless your memory for your vision and judgement for a greater Mississippi."

Not even incantations and promises of unfaded glory could move the legislature to action, and the lawmakers did not enact any of Bilbo's major reforms.

Time was running out for the governor. He had only two more years on his four-year term, and at that point he had achieved virtually none of his major goals. Consequently, Bilbo decided to act on his own in those areas subject to executive authority. One of those areas was higher education. In his address to the joint session, Bilbo reiterated his intention to appoint younger and more innovative presidents at the state's public colleges. The *Jackson Daily News* reported the governor's speech under the caption "Bilbo promises Clean Sweep of College Presidents," and quoted the governor as saying that "younger men" were needed to lead the state's institutions of higher learning. Over the next few months the subject of age was a central issue in the discussions of the impending "shake-up" at the state colleges. Robert Edward Lee Sutherland, who was rumored to be the next president of MSCW, refused to reveal his age to reporters. "If it is necessary to say anything about my age," he told them, "you might say that I would pass for 48, perhaps younger." Sutherland was fifty-two years old.

Age and energy were not Bilbo's only considerations in his determination to replace the college presidents, especially in Chancellor Hume's case. Bilbo had stated publicly several times that he did not believe Chancellor Hume was "temperamentally fit" to transform Ole Miss into the Greater University of Mississippi that he believed essential to the state's economic and social development. The governor not only favored the removal of Hume; he also wanted to increase the chancellor's salary to twenty-five thousand dollars, which would enable the board to recruit someone of national prominence. In 1930 the salary of the president of the University of Alabama was twelve thousand dollars; at the University of Arkansas the president's salary was ten thousand dollars; the chancellor's salary was forty eight hundred dollars. Governor Bilbo cited the University of Wisconsin, which had recently appointed Glenn Frank, and the University of Chicago, which had recently appointed the thirty-year-old Robert Maynard Hutchins, as examples the University of Mississippi should emulate.

Six months after Bilbo's address to the joint session, the three college boards that governed Mississippi's state-supported institutions of higher learning convened in Jackson on June 13, 1930. For several days the Jackson press reported the machinations that preceded those meetings. The press gave the boards that governed the two teachers colleges minimal attention, because the board of trustees of the State Teachers College at Hattiesburg had already made a change in the presidency. Governor Bilbo asked the Delta State Teachers College board of trustees to dismiss President William Kethley, but his recommendation lost by a tie vote. After this setback, the governor turned his full attention, as did the press, to the board of trustees that governed the University of Mississippi, MSCW, Alcorn A & M, and Mississippi A & M.

Fred Sullens of the *Jackson Daily News* wrote that most members of this board of trustees were not even "acquainted with the spirit and the purpose of the work which they were chosen to direct" and knew "nothing whatsoever about the relative merits of educators." Squandering an opportunity to treat his readers to a reasoned assessment of the relative merits of the board's action, Sullens resorted to a frivolous personal attack on the board members. "In cold truth," he wrote, "there is not a trustee on the Board who possesses a degree from a reputable educational institution. It is gravely to be doubted whether there is a member of the body who, without the assistance of a bright-minded stenographer, could write an ordinary business letter without violating all of the major rules of the English language."

In an article for *The New Republic,* John B. Hudson referred to this board as "the Governor's dummy board of trustees." Both Sullens and Hudson were incorrect in their characterization of the board. Every member of the board of trustees had a college degree, over half of them from Mississippi institutions, and all but one had two degrees. Two trustees had graduate degrees from the University of Chicago. Hudson's claim that the board was a "dummy board" was also at variance with the voting record of two of Governor Bilbo's appointees. The 1930 board of trustees included Willis Walley, D. E. Nabors, Ambrose B. Schauber, A. B. Kelly, Paul Bowdre, A. A. Cohn, Leo Seal, and Oscar Gober. Superintendent of Education Willard Bond and Governor Bilbo were also voting members. These trustees assembled in the governor's office on the morning of June 13, 1930, and reorganized the administrations of the three white colleges. The faculty at Alcorn A & M College was left undisturbed.

At the June 13 board meeting, Dean Nellie Keirn, who had been acting president of MSCW since the death of John C. Fant in 1929, was not nominated for president, though she had some support among the institution's alumnae. R. E. L. Sutherland, who was president of Hinds Junior College and was studying at Yale in 1930, was nominated and unanimously elected president of MSCW. Hansford L. Simmons, a former state senator and political ally of Governor Bilbo, was then elected vice-president and registrar. Simmons is often cited as an example that Bilbo appointed political hacks to high office in the institutions of higher learning. Simmons is not a good example. He was an educator with fourteen years of experience in the public schools of Mississippi, including the superintendency of the Itawamba County Agricultural High School.

The selection of a new administration at MSCW was simple compared to the machinations at the university and at Mississippi A & M. President Buz Walker of Mississippi A & M was a key fund raiser in Bilbo's 1927 campaign and was a well-known Bilbo partisan. Walker was approaching seventy years of age and had been associated with the college for nearly fifty years. On June 5 the *Clarion-Ledger* reported that Walker's position was safe and predicted his easy reelection. On the day before the board meeting, however, Fred Sullens alluded to the probable "retirement" of President Walker and wrote that his "displacement" would be unfortunate "from many points of view." If Walker was dismissed, however, Sullens would favor the appointment of Hugh Critz, "the most popular member of the A & M alumni." After detailing Critz's credentials, which included graduate degrees, professorships, and the presidency of Arkansas A & M, Sullens concluded, "If he is chosen . . . there will be no justification for complaint from any quarter."

There was some speculation that Alfred Benjamin Butts, a professor of political science at the agricultural college, might be elected president of Mississippi A & M or Ole Miss. It was also known that Joseph Neely Powers was Bilbo's first choice for the chancellor's position. Alfred Hume's supporters maneuvered to get Butts elected to the A & M position, because they believed Bilbo did not have the votes to elect Powers chancellor. Their strategy was simple: get the A & M presidency for Butts, and that would save Alfred Hume. They were frustrated, however, because Butts showed so little interest in either position that he was eventually eliminated from both. His elimination guaranteed the A & M presidency to Hugh Critz and sealed the fate of Alfred Hume.

At the June 13 meeting, the board of trustees elected Hugh Critz president of Mississippi A & M. The board then took up the election of the chancellor. Ambrose B. Schauber, a member of the board of trustees when Powers was fired in 1924, nominated the former chancellor. Paul Bowdre, a Bilbo appointee, nominated Alfred Hume. The minutes indicate that the vote was six to four in favor of Powers, but do not reveal how each trustee voted. The *Clarion-Ledger* reported that Bilbo, Schauber, Walley, Gober, Cohn, and Nabors voted for Powers and that Bond, Bowdre (a Bilbo appointee), Kelly, and Seal (Bilbo's most recent appointee) voted for Hume.

Alfred Hume, known fondly as "Little Allie," was probably the most popular and beloved chancellor in the institution's history. This "grand old man" was born in Beech Grove, Tennessee, December 1, 1866. After receiving three degrees from Vanderbilt University, including a Doctor of Science, he joined the university faculty in 1890 as a professor of mathematics. Soon after his appointment as chancellor in 1924, Hume spoke of the singular goal of his administration. "My greatest aspiration for the present administration," he said, "is not that we may put on a big building program, though we certainly need badly a number of new buildings; not that we grow rapidly in enrollment of students and size of faculty, however necessary and desirable both may be; not that we excel in scholarship and athletics, however much I want these too; but when the historian makes record of what this administration stood for pre-eminently, I am hoping that it may be truthfully said that it was characterized by the exalting of character, by putting the emphasis on things moral, by stressing religious and spiritual values.... All our education should be shot through and through with the preeminence of moral force and spiritual power and the clear recognition of God."

Chancellor Hume's administrative policies were an extension of his personal faith, and he cloaked the university in a religious atmosphere. Ole Miss was often called in jest "Hume's Presbyterian University." He did not allow students to smoke, drink, dance, wear shorts on campus, or play tennis on Sunday and required their daily attendance at religious services in the chapel. Michael O'Shea may have aimed his pointed criticism that Mississippi's institutions of higher learning planned their "courses so as to develop character" at the state university. Chancellor Hume embraced "the University's traditional role as the institution devoted primarily to the needs of the upper classes of Mississippi society," and under his leadership Ole Miss became "a lonely outpost amid the quiet splendors of the old regime" and "whispered the last enchantments of an earlier age." Governor Bilbo was determined that the University of Mississippi would not remain an isolated liberal arts academy hidden away in the rolling hills of northeast Mississippi. If he could not relocate the university, he would transform it.

The shake-up of the college presidents would probably have provoked no more than the customary gust of outrage, but at a meeting on June 27, and a subsequent meeting on July 5, the board of trustees reorganized the faculty and staff at Ole Miss, Mississippi A & M and MSCW. The trustees of the State Teachers College had also dismissed several professors at the time they replaced President Cook in 1928. The exact number of faculty members dismissed is difficult to determine. Fred Sullens reported that approximately forty professors were fired. Governor Bilbo informed the Southern Association of Colleges and Schools that forty-five professors were dismissed as follows: ten at MSCW, thirteen at Mississippi A & M, five at State Teachers College, and seventeen at Ole Miss. In a letter dated February 11, 1931, Chancellor Powers informed W. L. Fulton, president of the Washington, D.C., alumni association, that sixteen faculty members were dismissed. Governor Bilbo's reference to seventeen included Chancellor Hume.

At the June 27 meeting, the board of trustees elected Julius C. Zeller vice chancellor and professor of philosophy, replacing Professor Winn David Hedleston. At the time of his appointment to the faculty in 1909, Professor Hedleston was the pastor of the Oxford Presbyterian Church. Professor Hedleston received a bachelor's degree from Ole Miss in 1883 and held an honorary doctor of divinity degree. (Reverend Hedleston performed the wedding ceremony for William and Estelle Faulkner at the College Hill Presbyterian Church.) Bilbo was not insensitive to the plight of aging professors, especially the popular and much-loved Hedleston, who was sixty-eight at the time of his dismissal. Governor Bilbo asked the legislature to provide a pension for senior faculty, but a retirement system was not enacted until many years later.

Vice Chancellor Zeller was a former state senator who listed farming as his occupation in the biographical section of the senate journal. Zeller authored the 1926 statute that repealed the ban on fraternities at the university. Although his appointment is cited as an illustration that Bilbo rewarded his friends and took no accounting of their qualifications, Zeller is the worst possible example. For several years before his appointment, he had been a member of the anti-Bilbo faction, but in 1928 he supported Bilbo's proposal to relocate the university at Jackson, a proposition Zeller had favored nearly a decade earlier. Having failed in their attempt to move the university, they united in an effort to modernize it.

Academically, Zeller was qualified for the position of vice chancellor and professor of philosophy. He had a B.A. and a B.D. from the University of Chicago, an M.A. and B.O. from Grant University in Athens, Tennessee, an M.A. and D.D. from the University of Chattanooga, and a doctor of civil law degree from Illinois Wesleyan University. He had held the chair of philosophy at Illinois Wesleyan University and had served as president of the University of Puget Sound. A year before his appointment, the *Jackson Daily News* wrote that "there is not an abler member in either branch of the lawmaking body than Senator Zeller. He is both a scholar and a statesman."

On July 5, two weeks after Zeller's appointment, Chancellor Powers presented sixty-nine faculty nominations to the board of trustees. The board initially declined to reelect nine of his recommendations. The dismissal of two of those nine was later rescinded, and a third was reappointed when no suitable replacement could be found. Chancellor Powers did not recommend ten members of the current faculty for reappointment. Several of the Ole Miss professors dismissed were in their late sixties and did not have graduate degrees. Some had only a bachelor's degree from the University of Mississippi. Except in the case of Chancellor Powers, the academic credentials of all professors appointed or promoted were equal or superior to those being replaced, and in most cases the credentials of the new faculty were superior.

Among the Ole Miss faculty dismissed were the dean of women, who also taught home economics, the dean of men (whose dismissal will be discussed in connection with the mathematics department), the dean of medicine, and the dean of the school of engineering. The dean of the law school, T. C. Kimbrough, and the graduate dean, Alexander Bondurant, were demoted but retained on the faculty. Bondurant, who did not hold an earned doctorate and had been at Ole Miss for forty years, was demoted because Governor Bilbo insisted that the graduate dean have a Ph.D. Nathaniel Bond, a current member of the faculty and a newly minted Ph.D. in sociology from Tulane, replaced Bondurant.

Dean Kimbrough was demoted, according to Governor Bilbo, because the law school had languished under his leadership. Bilbo said that "any group of men who had let the law school fall into a condition described by Dr. Horack [in 1927] was certainly not a group . . . who could make the school what it should be. . . . Therefore, in good faith, we proceeded with our plan to reorganize the Law School." Stone Deavours, a highly regarded Mississippi jurist who was not identified with any of the state's political factions, replaced Kimbrough. Dean Kimbrough told a representative of a professional association "if he were not Dean there was no man in Mississippi under whom he would rather serve than Judge Deavours."

The dean of women, Edna Lowe Eatman, actually resigned rather than be discharged, but is numbered among the sixteen dismissed faculty members. Bilbo said she was discharged because she had old-fashioned ideas about the role of women in society and because she was not qualified to teach home economics. Eatman had a bachelor's degree in English from Ole Miss. She was succeeded by Louise Duncan, who held a B.A. degree from the University of Alabama.

The dismissal of the dean of medicine, Joseph Crider, and the aging professor of pharmacology, Peter W. Rowland, brought a warning from the medical accrediting agencies that the university would lose its "A" rating if the dean were not reinstated. Dean Crider was initially dismissed, according to Bilbo, because the medical school was placed on probation in 1927 and was already in danger of losing its accreditation. Although Bilbo believed new leadership was essential if the two-year program was to survive, the board of trustees acquiesced to the demands of the medical accrediting agencies and reappointed Dean Crider. Then, to everyone's surprise and to Chancellor Powers's consternation, Crider resigned two days before the opening of the fall semester. After his first two choices declined the appointment, Chancellor Powers named Phillip Mull, a professor of anatomy in the medical school, to the vacancy. The medical accrediting agencies approved Mull's appointment.

Professor Rowland, who was born two months before the firing on Fort Sumter in April 1861, was relieved of his position because of his advanced age. When a suitable replacement for Professor Rowland could not be found, the board reappointed him. For several years after his reinstatement, Professor Rowland continued to serve the university and the medical school as "Librarian Plenipotentiary." During the 1930s, Professor Rowland drove his pickup truck across the state collecting books and donations from Mississippi physicians for the medical school's small library, which the board of trustees named in his honor in 1939. This remarkable man, born just before the start of the Civil War, said on the eve of World War II, "I still have some good years in me."

Bilbo recommended the dismissal of John H. Dorroh, who had been dean of the school of engineering since 1915, because he was not a progressive and energetic leader. Bilbo thought a younger man with new ideas was needed. Dorroh, who had a B.E and a C. E. from Vanderbilt, was succeeded by Thomas E. Gladney, who held a B.E., M.S., and C.E. from the University of Virginia. The circumstances of Professor Dorroh's dismissal are at variance with contemporary press accounts and with Mississippi's historical memory of the Bilbo purge. The anti-Bilbo press erroneously reported that Bilbo handed each college president a black list that contained the names of professors who were to be fired and hired and the new presidents were appointed on the condition that they carry out the purge. Chancellor Powers made a strong appeal to the board of trustees on Dorroh's behalf, and the dean of engineering wrote to Powers on August 8, 1930, expressing his appreciation. More significantly, Professor Dorroh was a known Bilbo partisan who had supported the governor for several years, but the governor, in contravention to Mississippi's historical memory of the purge, recommended his dismissal for academic rather than political reasons.

Chancellor Powers's support for another professor in the school of engineering provides additional evidence that there was no black list at the university. On July 7, 1930, Powers sent a telegram to Alfred Hume informing him that George E. Tomlinson, assistant professor in the school of engineering, and several other faculty members had been dismissed. Two days later Powers wrote Hume telling him that he had made the "strongest fight" possible for Tomlinson, whose three degrees were from Ole Miss. Apparently, Powers persuaded the board to reappoint Tomlinson, because on August 27, 1930, several weeks after Powers's letter to Hume, Tomlinson submitted a letter of resignation. Moreover, Tomlinson does not appear on Powers's list of the sixteen professors dismissed. His late resignation made it difficult to find a replacement. Hugh Worley, a recent graduate of the university's school of engineering, succeeded Tomlinson.

With the board of trustees meeting on the Gulf Coast and the anti-Bilbo press printing the wildest rumors about the number of professors who had been or might be dismissed, the atmosphere on the Oxford campus, naturally, was tense. In the early days of July many senior faculty members huddled with their friends and supporters, anxiously awaiting their fate. On July 8, 1930, Joseph Powers wrote to Alfred Hume, reassuring him that an article in a Memphis newspaper reporting that twenty additional professors would be fired was not true. Powers told Hume, "I have tried faithfully to keep you informed."

The law school, the mathematics department, and the English department experienced the heaviest turnover. In the law school, the dean was demoted, two of the other three professors, Robert Farley and William Hemingway, were dismissed, and the fourth professor, William Roberds, resigned. Hemingway, who was notorious for his easy grading of athletes, held a Ph.B. from Ole Miss but did not have a law degree. Like many other jurists in the early twentieth century, Hemingway had read law and passed the bar exam. Governor Bilbo said that Hemingway and Farley, a future dean of the law school (and the son of a former dean), were fired because of their political involvement in the 1927 election. The board appointed Circuit Judge John Falkner of Oxford to Farley's position and Joseph J. Smith, a Phi Beta Kappa graduate of the University of Alabama and Harvard law school, replaced Hemingway. Richard Payne, a graduate of Yale law school, succeeded Roberds.

The dean of men, Charles Wunder, was also chairman of the mathematics department and a loyal friend of Alfred Hume. Wunder, who had a Ph. D. from the University of Virginia, was discharged because of his extreme criticism of Bilbo and the board for firing Hume. Marce C. Rhodes, who held a Ph.D. from Peabody College, replaced Wunder. The board also dismissed two young mathematics professors. Paul Rees, an assistant professor, was fired because of his bitterness over Wunder's dismissal, and John T. Atkin, an instructor, was discharged because he held only a bachelor's degree. Jay W. McClimmons and T. A. Bickerstaff, both of whom held master's degrees, replaced them. The trustees dismissed another well-known Bilbo partisan, Robert Torrey, an associate professor of mathematics who had only a bachelor's degree from Ole Miss, because they did not consider him a qualified mathematician. Hugh L. Quarles, who had a B.A. and M.A. from the University of Alabama, succeeded Torrey.

Governor Bilbo regarded "the Department of English as the most important division of the University, and felt that the head of this responsible department should hold the degree of Doctor of Philosophy." Although Chancellor Powers nominated Professor David Horace Bishop, the chairman of the English department, and Associate Professor L. D. Wallace, the board did not reappoint them. Professor Bishop, who had only a master's degree, had been on the faculty for almost forty years. Professor Wallace, against whom the students had registered many "bitter complaints," had only a bachelor's degree. The board offered Professor Bishop's position to Arthur Palmer Hudson, who was on a leave of absence, but he declined the appointment and accepted a position at the University of North Carolina. Henry Pochman, a member of the Ole Miss faculty with a Ph.D. from the University of North Carolina, was promoted to Bishop's position. Minor L. Bott, who had a master's degree from Vanderbilt and two years on his Ph.D. from Peabody, replaced Wallace. The board of trustees added a new position in the English department, which went to A. Wigfall Green, a Ph.D. from the University of Virginia.

Other Ole Miss faculty members dismissed or not reappointed were Professor John Swan, chairman of the chemistry department, Assistant Professor Ralph Grim in geology, Professor Lloyd Thatcher in biology, Kenneth P. Vinsel in political science, and Carl H. Pegg in the history department. Chancellor Powers recommended Swan but the board did not reappoint him because he was sixty-eight years old. Guy Woolett, who held a Ph.D. from the University of Minnesota, replaced Swan. Grim, who had only a bachelor's degree, was dismissed "for reasons best known to the Board of Trustees." Hugh Morse, who had a B.A. from the University of Oklahoma, replaced Grim. Thatcher, who had only a bachelor's degree from Ole Miss, was replaced "for sufficient reasons" by Frank Hull, who soon received a Ph.D. from Harvard. Kenneth Vinsel, who had two degrees from Ole Miss, had previously served as a coach, and there was friction between him and the current athletic department. Vinsel was succeeded by Huey B. Howerton, who held a B.S. and M.A. from Ole Miss. Pegg had a one-year appointment while Professor P. L. Rainwater was on leave. When Rainwater returned in 1930, Pegg was recommended for an appointment in political science, but he was not retained.

In addition to the sixteen faculty members, the board of trustees demoted or discharged twelve clerical and staff personnel. Among the staff personnel demoted was the university business manager, Murry C. Falkner, whose family were long-time supporters of the Vardaman-Bilbo-Russell political faction. A brother of John Falkner, the new law professor, Murry Falkner was replaced by William "Chuck" Trotter but was retained as Trotter's assistant. One of the staff members dismissed was J. C. Eskridge, the director of buildings and grounds, who, when informed of his dismissal, fired off a letter to Governor Bilbo. After recounting his long years of loyal support, Eskridge demanded an explanation. "Everyone in Lafayette County knows," he wrote Bilbo, "that I have championed your cause from your entry into Mississippi politics until the present time. So come clean in this matter and let me have the whole truth without reservation. Now if it is something too serious to write, I will see you personally if I have to hitch-hike to Jackson or Gulfport. I know as well as everyone else knows that I have not had a square deal and I want to know why."

Several days later Eskridge received a letter from Governor Bilbo explaining the cause of his dismissal. "The chief cause of complaint," the governor replied, "seems to be that you were lazy or in other words, not as alert on the job as you might have been. You know in this day and time when there is so much unemployment and so many people are waiting for a chance, it behooves us all to be constantly on the job. I am very sorry that it was necessary to dismiss you, but there were others who felt that they could be on the job at any and all times and one of them is being given this chance." The letter was personally signed, "Faithfully yours, Governor Bilbo."

The reaction to the "Bilbo purge" was swift, severe, and subject to the most partisan interpretation. Ole Miss students hoisted up the university flag pole a burning effigy of Bilbo clad in loud pajamas. Newspapers across the country reported the incident, which occurred in December of 1930 after the Southern Association of Colleges suspended the university. When reporters informed Bilbo of the incident, he laughed heartily and said the joke was on the students, because he did not wear pajamas.

One of the first and fiercest condemnations of the purge came from Bilbo's old nemesis Fred Sullens. Because of the "whirligig game we call politics," Sullens wrote, "with each succeeding governor we have seen competent men voted out, able faculties torn to pieces, and new regimes established." It was not just this latest incursion but its epic sweep that shocked Sullens. He reported that the college faculties were not "revised" but "ravished." Editor T. M. Hederman of the Jackson *Clarion-Ledger* accused Bilbo of "criminally, brutally, and deliberately ravishing . . . higher education . . . for his own sordid political advantage, to punish enemies and reward friends." The president of Vanderbilt University, and an old friend of Chancellor Hume, characterized the Bilbo purge as "the most notorious and disgraceful act in the history of American higher education."

Lost amid this outrage was a grudging concession. "The men who succeed [Hume and Walker]," Fred Sullens wrote, "will carry on with more energy and efficiency than the two pale, slender, gray-haired scholars. . . . They are younger and probably more progressive in purpose than the men they are soon to succeed." Also among Sullens's lamentations was a prediction that political intrusion into higher education would continue "until some clever brain devises a plan to remove our colleges wholly beyond the realm of political influence." Sullens took no notice that Bilbo had recently recommended just such a plan to the state legislature.

John Hudson, a Mississippi journalist who had a running feud with Governor Bilbo for many years and was implicated in a recent highway scandal, described the purge in an article for *The New Republic* entitled

"The Spoils System Enters College." Hudson reported that Bilbo had fired 50 professors at Ole Miss and 129 at other colleges, and that 233 more were in jeopardy. His estimate of those fired or in jeopardy totaled 412, although there were only about 300 faculty members in the entire system. Hudson also reported that the "man selected as chancellor... had never earned a college degree and... up to the time of his appointment, had been a small-lot real-estate salesman in Jackson." He identified Hugh Critz as the "director of public relations for the Mississippi Power and Light Company," but did not indicate that both Powers and Critz were previously college presidents. John Hudson's article was the primary source for many of the early accounts of what one writer called the "Mississippi Imbroglio."

The official publication of the state teachers association, the *Mississippi Educational Advance,* reported that fifty Ole Miss professors were dismissed and concluded: "[E]verybody knows that... Bilbo's only motivation [was] to punish enemies and to reward friends." The author of that article was Walter N. Taylor, the executive director of the Mississippi Education Association and a state senator who had opposed Bilbo's free textbook plan. After receiving a letter from Chancellor Powers correcting his figures, Taylor wrote another article a month later apologizing for the inaccuracies in the first one. He had used John Hudson's figures and presumed they were correct. After apologizing to Chancellor Powers, Taylor surmised: "After all, ultimate good will probably come from the evils herein discussed."

Bilbo's reorganization of the college faculties also prompted swift and severe retribution from various accrediting agencies. The American Association of Law Schools suspended the law school, and the two medical associations "reluctantly" placed the medical school on probation but allowed it to keep its accreditation. The director of one medical association wrote Chancellor Powers, "[G]reat good will no doubt come out of the whole mess. The school has had a good jolt which should shake it into life and give it a more wholesome aspect and more activity. Maybe the new dean can and will do what is needed... to build up the school."

The Society of Civil Engineers, the American Association of University Professors, the American Association of University Women, and the Association of American Universities dismissed or expelled the university or placed it on probation. None of those associations, however, conducted on site investigations. The Society of Civil Engineers did not even contact university officials before dismissing the school of engineering, basing its action on media accounts. The two professional associations that conducted on-site investigations did not revoke the university's accreditation. Following its investigation, the American Pharmaceutical Association actually commended Dean Elmer Hammond and authorized the Ole Miss pharmacy school to maintain its "A" rating.

The other association that conducted an investigation and did not censure the university was the American Association of State Universities. President Emeritus W. O. Thompson of Ohio State University, chairman of the association's committee on university control, spent two days at the university in the fall of 1930. In his report to the association, Thompson verified many of the public statements made by Bilbo and Powers in which they justified or explained the basis for the faculty dismissals, and he exonerated the university from "many criticisms levied against it." Thompson also reported that most media accounts—he specifically cited John Hudson's article—distorted the circumstances and exaggerated the number of dismissals at the university and should not be taken at face value. On the basis of Thompson's investigation, the American Association of State Universities at its annual meeting in 1931 expressed its disagreement with the various accrediting agencies that had censured or suspended the University of Mississippi.

The action that most damaged the university's academic standing was the loss of accreditation by the Southern Association of Colleges and Schools. Following an investigation by Chancellor James H. Kirkland of Vanderbilt University, who spent only a few hours on the campus, the Southern Association at its annual meeting in December 1930 suspended the University of Mississippi, Mississippi A & M, MSCW, and State Teachers College at Hattiesburg. Alcorn A & M was not accredited at that time and was not affected by the suspension. The association did not cite the Mississippi institutions for violating any of its standards. Instead, SACS based the suspension on "the tone of an institution" and "the spirit of administration." Perhaps in a move calculated to embarrass Governor Bilbo and the board of trustees, SACS admitted Delta State Teachers College to "full membership," even though it did not meet several of the association's standards.

Governor Bilbo and the board of trustees petitioned SACS to reconsider its suspension. In a letter justifying the dismissal of sixteen Ole Miss professors, Bilbo said the university was more endangered from "dry rot" than from a "temporary upheaval." The board even revoked its longstanding policy that faculty members served "at the pleasure of the Board," but the suspension remained in force. The association would not even acknowledge or respond to communications from Governor Bilbo or from the Mississippi board of trustees. After the association refused to discuss a remedy, the board of trustees considered the establishment of a state accrediting agency. A. A. Cohn boldly declared that "states' rights is not dead yet." Some trustees believed that the Southern Association's action was punitive and not entirely free of political taint. The O'Shea Study, which formed the basis of Governor Bilbo's reorganization plan, questioned the validity of several of the association's standards and asserted that Mississippi's fulfillment of those arbitrary standards was not as important as meeting the more pressing educational needs of its people.

Whatever the motives that caused SACS to suspend Mississippi's institutions of higher learning, Fred Sullens did not like it. He was as critical of the association as he was of Bilbo. Sullens branded the suspension as "cruel, wanton, brutal, unnecessary, and devoid of any semblance of constructive thought." Many Mississippians shared Sullens's anger at both Bilbo and SACS but nevertheless saw in the imbroglio an opportunity to "devise a plan to remove our colleges wholly beyond the realm of political influence." At the time the Southern Association suspended the state's collegiate institutions, Mississippi was in the process of choosing a successor to Governor Bilbo, and the plight of the colleges was a prominent issue in that campaign. During the 1931 campaign, all of the candidates for governor and several legislative candidates promised the people of Mississippi and pledged to the various accrediting agencies that they would end the reign of politics at the state's colleges. For a variety of reasons, the voters found Martin Sennett Conner to be convincing and elected him governor. Conner was a former speaker of the house of representatives, a member of the low pressure faction, and an Ole Miss alumnus.

One of the successful legislative candidates in the 1931 campaign was Joseph Anderson Cook, the former president of State Teachers College Bilbo had fired in 1928. Cook was elected to the state senate from Lowndes County, and, soon after the legislature convened in January 1932, he introduced Senate Bill 59. The bill was a carefully crafted measure designed by a wily old veteran of the school wars to place the institutions of higher learning beyond the reach of politics, and it passed easily in both houses. The 1932 statute consolidated the three boards of trustees into one board with governance over all of the state institutions of higher learning, including the two teachers colleges. Trustees, who could not succeed themselves, served twelve-year staggered terms with one-third of the members rotating off the board every four years. The governor was the only ex officio member of the board.

Following the enactment of this law, Governor Conner appointed a new board of trustees, whose most pressing duty was to regain the accreditation of Mississippi's institutions of higher learning. At its first meeting on March 1, 1932, the board of trustees opened negotiations with SACS and in July the board requested a formal review of the Mississippi situation. The association advised the board of trustees that all restrictions would be lifted if certain conditions were met. The association required, specifically, an increase in faculty salaries and academic support funds. The Great Depression, however, precluded that possibility, and faculty salaries were not raised. Actually, they were reduced by 25 percent, and even then professors went unpaid for several months. On January 9, 1932, the campus newspaper praised the Ole Miss faculty for its patience and long-suffering: "HATS OFF TO OLE MISS PROFESSORS. At midnight tonight it has been exactly ten months and nine days since the professors at Ole Miss have received a salary check." Even though the university's financial circumstances were not improved, SACS and other professional associations restored accreditation to Ole Miss over the next two years.

The Southern Association's primary condition for reaccreditation of Mississippi's collegiate institutions was the reinstatement of the administrators and professors dismissed in 1930. To meet that condition, the new board of trustees dismissed Chancellor Powers, Vice Chancellor Zeller, and several professors on June 2, 1932. The board reinstated Alfred Hume, David Horace Bishop, Robert Farley, William Hemingway, and Robert Torrey. Some of the professors appointed during the

Bilbo purge, most notably A. Wigfall Green, Frank Hull, and Huey B. Howerton, remained at the university and enjoyed long and distinguished careers.

During the three years of his second tenure, Chancellor Alfred Hume handled what could have been an unpleasant situation with grace and dignity, and he left office as the university's revered elder statesman. On January 25, 1935, as he was approaching sixty-nine years of age, Alfred Hume relinquished the office of chancellor and returned to the classroom. Hume continued as chairman of the department and professor of mathematics until his retirement in 1947 at the age of eighty. On the day Hume presented his resignation, the board of trustees elected Alfred Benjamin Butts the university's eleventh chancellor. The chancellorship was something of a consolation prize to Butts. A year earlier he had lost by one vote the position he really wanted, the presidency of his alma mater, Mississippi State College. (Mississippi A & M was renamed Mississippi State College in 1932.)

On April 4, 1935, Chancellor-elect Butts, who was vice-president of Mississippi A & M at the time of his appointment, visited the university and addressed a special convocation of faculty and students. "I am interested and greatly appreciative of the history of the University of Mississippi," the new chancellor said, "but I am frank to say that I am more interested in its present and future than I am in its past. This then, will be my policy: to keep in mind that the University is above all an intellectual institution. . . . Above all, we need fine students and fine teachers. We must have both. . . . We can have a good football team in addition, but the primary purpose of this institution is to educate." Delivered as Mississippi was recovering from the depression and as Ole Miss was emerging from the Bilbo imbroglio, Butts's speech was an affirmation of the university's future. The campus newspaper praised Butts and his speech, which provoked many "outbursts of applause." Although he was a graduate of Mississippi State and had spent most of his academic career at that institution, Butts was accepted with enthusiasm by most Oxford residents and by Ole Miss faculty, staff, students, and most alumni.

Chancellor Butts's eleven-year tenure was interrupted by his three-year military service during World War II. When Butts finally returned to the campus, neither he, nor the faculty, nor the students were prepared for the enormous consequences of the war. In the aftermath of Hiroshima and Nagasaki, the high school class of 1945 that joined the hardened veterans of a global war on the crowded campus that fall had lost an innocence that no generation of young Americans could ever have again.

Chapter 10
A MODERN UNIVERSITY, 1935–1960

White columns, Colonel Rebel, Blind Jim, Confederate flags,
all of these are our Ole Miss.

OLE MISS, 1950

Alfred Benjamin Butts was the University of Mississippi's best educated and most visionary chancellor since Frederick Barnard. The forty-five-year-old North Carolinian moved with his family to Starkville, Mississippi, when he was a small child. He earned his baccalaureate degree at Mississippi State in 1911. After receiving a second degree at Mississippi State in 1913, Butts earned a Ph.D. in political science at Columbia University in 1920 and a law degree from Yale in 1930. Law was his primary academic interest, and, during his tenure at Ole Miss, Chancellor Butts taught a course in constitutional law and published several articles in legal journals. During the summer months of his long and distinguished academic career, Butts also taught at several major universities, including Ohio State, Virginia, Duke, Texas, Yale, University of California at Los Angeles, and Hawaii.

Representatives from forty-eight colleges and universities attended Chancellor Butts's installation during the homecoming weekend of October 19, 1935. His inauguration, and the football game with Florida, drew one of the largest crowds in the university's history. A few days before homecoming, the *Mississippian* wrote that Ole Miss alumni were coming back to "holy ground." Chancellor Butts's inaugural address was a forceful expression of what a modern research university could and should be. He quoted the *Federalist Papers,* Thomas Jefferson, and H. G. Wells, cited at some length Thomas Huxley's address at the opening of Johns Hopkins University, and linked the University of Mississippi to the traditions of "Oxford and Cambridge of old." Butts concluded his speech, "Every University must . . . encourage the freest play of intellectual endeavor. The highest function, I believe, of a university is to seek out those men who are able to advance knowledge a step farther than their predecessors advanced it. . . . The glory of a University should rest upon the character of its teachers and scholars. A University is no nobler than its faculty."

Chancellor Butts's first formal action to modernize the university was the establishment of the "Ph.D. rule." Under that policy, no faculty member who did not hold a Ph.D. would be promoted above the rank of assistant professor, and, in future appointments, preference would be given to applicants with doctorates. The only exceptions were in law and accounting, in which a C.P.A. was acceptable in lieu of a doctorate. Among the twenty-four young Ph.D.s attracted to the university under this rule were Dudley Hutcherson in English, John B. Wolfe in psychology, and James W. Silver in history. A corollary to the Ph.D. rule was Chancellor Butts's pledge that no professor would ever be appointed or dismissed for political reasons.

Chancellor Butts's second step in transforming Ole Miss into a modern university was the expansion and development of the library. At the time of Butts's appointment, the university's general library holdings included 48,834 volumes. The medical library's scant holdings were housed in a separate collection within the general library and were included in the general library count. The law library, which numbered about six thousand volumes, was housed in the law school. The University of Mississippi, in Butts's estimation, could not function as a modern research university with such meager holdings. It was also obvious that the state of Mississippi was neither able nor willing to make the financial commitment necessary to upgrade the university's library. Consequently, Chancellor Butts applied for a library development grant from the General Education Board of the Rockefeller Foundation. Butts based his library development plan on a study of the university library by A. F. Kuhlman, Director of the Joint University Libraries of Nashville, Tennessee. Kuhlman found a significant gap between the new emphasis on research at the university and the library's holdings and staff. Under the new faculty being assembled by Chancellor Butts, library usage increased dramatically. In the 1929 academic year, with an enrollment of just over twelve hundred, approximately eight thousand volumes were checked out of the library. During the 1938 academic year, with about the same enrollment, the number of circulations increased to almost thirty thousand. Kuhlman complimented the recently appointed young Ph.D.s for their use of the library's resources and recommended a larger staff to facilitate that increased usage. In 1938 the University of Mississippi library had four full-time staff members, compared to twenty-four at the University of Tennessee, thirty at the University of North Carolina, and forty at Louisiana State University.

On December 7, 1939, the Rockefeller Foundation awarded the university a twenty-five-thousand-dollar library development grant, with the stipulation that the university match it two for one and that matching funds be obtained by December 31, 1940. Through the efforts of the Friends of the Library (a group established in conjunction with this fund drive), the citizens of Oxford (who raised two thousand dollars), and with help from a variety of other sources, the university raised a total of forty-one thousand dollars. The Carnegie Foundation donated the remaining nine thousand dollars. Chancellor Butts characterized the seventy-five-thousand-dollar library fund, which was used exclusively for the purchase of books and periodicals, as the most significant "boost" to the university's academic program in its ninety-two-year history. By the end of Chancellor Butts's tenure in 1946, the general library had more than doubled its holdings to 101,464 volumes. The law library had also more than doubled its holdings to approximately 15,000 volumes. The medical school had its own separate library in the medical building and each of the three libraries had a full-time director. Whitman Davis was director of the general library, Miss Rebekah E. Dean was the law librarian, and Miss Ross Jeffress was the medical librarian.

Chancellor Butts's emphasis on faculty and library development was an important factor in the university's regaining and maintaining membership in the professional associations, particularly in the American Association of Medical Schools. In December 1931, the AAMS had cited eight areas in which the university's medical school was deficient. Number one on the association's list of needs was "A Medical Library in the Medical Building with an all-time librarian in charge," but a state that could not pay its university professors could hardly buy books for a medical library.

In the spring of 1932, the legislative committee on colleges and universities recommended closing the Ole Miss medical school because Mississippi could not afford to meet the accrediting standards. The accrediting agencies, however, were accommodating to Mississippi. The agencies realized that the poorest state in the union could not afford the capital outlays necessary to meet the standards required of fully accredited medical schools. Consequently, the AAMS placed the university in a status of conditional probation and allowed the medical school to retain its accreditation on a year-to-year basis. When Butts was appointed chancellor in the spring of 1935, the medical school's future was as gloomy and grim as it had been during the darkest days of the Great Depression. Dean Phillip Mull informed the chancellor, "We have about come to the end of our period of grace." The *Mississippian* reported that the medical school was "on the verge of being discontinued." So uncertain was its future, the medical school did not enroll a class in the fall of 1935.

One of Chancellor Butts's most notable achievements was the appointment of Professor Billy Sylvester Guyton dean of the medical school. Initially, Dr. Guyton declined the appointment, but at the urging of Chancellor Butts he agreed to serve one year as acting dean. When he accepted the position in 1935, the medical school crisis was not just a matter of accreditation but of survival. The American Medical Association opposed the continuation of two-year programs and the AAMS had to be convinced on a school-by-school basis that two-year programs were still viable. At a critical meeting in Chicago in February 1936, Dean Guyton won the university a timely reprieve. He persuaded a special joint committee of the AAMS and the AMA to validate the credits earned by the students currently enrolled and those entering in the fall of 1936. That ruling allowed Ole Miss medical students to transfer to four-year institutions.

With the problem of transfer credits resolved, at least temporarily, Dean Guyton and Chancellor Butts persuaded the legislature to find the funds necessary to save the medical school. In the spring of 1936 the legislature made a substantial appropriation, and a freshman class enrolled in the fall. The rejuvenation of the medical school over the next two years was spectacular; it was removed from probationary status and its "A" rating was reinstated without conditions by the AAMS in November 1937 and by the AMA in February 1938.

When the accrediting agencies restored the medical school to full standing in 1938, its faculty and staff numbered thirty-three, which was four times as large as it had been in 1930. The enlarged staff enabled Dean Guyton to expand the curriculum, and new laboratory facilities allowed him to supplement the lecture system with clinical instruction. The medical school's new laboratories were part of the campus development program initiated at Governor Bilbo's urging and made possible by the $1.6 million appropriation in 1928. One of the most important facilities included in that expansion was a student hospital and medical building. Constructed in the early 1930s at a cost of $125,000, the medical building sat idle and empty for several years. In 1937 the building was finally completed and furnished with state-of-the-art laboratory equipment. Miss Jeffress (who came to Ole Miss from the New York City Public Library) also transferred the medical holdings from the university's general library to the new medical building. Through the dedication, determination and the vision of Dean Guyton, Chancellor Butts and Dr. David Pankratz, the dean of medicine when the medical school was transferred to Jackson in 1955, the university's two year medical school survived those gloomy days of depression and eventually became one of America's premier medical institutions.

When Alfred Butts assumed office in 1935, Mississippi was emerging from the depression caused by the crash of 1929, and the university was recovering from the enrollment decline caused by the loss of accreditation. An important element in both recoveries was the financial aid provided by the National Youth Administration, one of President Franklin D. Roosevelt's many New Deal agencies. In the fall of 1935, a thousand college students in Mississippi were receiving fifteen dollars a month from the NYA. There were almost two thousand applications for those one thousand grants. Students on NYA stipends performed a variety of jobs ranging from clerical assistance in libraries to small construction projects. In 1940, of the two hundred thirty-eight NYA student workers at Ole Miss, almost 70 percent declared their family's annual income to be under two thousand dollars. There is a striking contrast between the antebellum period, when many scholarships went unclaimed because families would not admit to their need, and the age of the Great Depression, when some families may even have exaggerated their poverty to qualify for federal aid. The New Deal student aid program anticipated the postwar GI Bill, which stimulated the latent but potent desire for a college education among Mississippi's young women and especially among its African American population.

Chancellor Butts was the first chancellor to assume the role of fund raiser, and he was adept at securing federal dollars. During the first five years of his administration, the university received more than a million dollars in federal funds for capital improvements. In addition to the facilities built with federal funds in the late 1930s, fourteen new buildings were also made possible by the $1.6 million special appropriation in 1928. One of the most imposing of those fourteen new structures was the medical building, named for Dean Guyton in 1961. When Guyton Hall was built on the far western edge of the campus, a large previously unused area was brought into the campus proper. One of the university's six original buildings, the Old Steward's Hall, which was behind or west of the Lyceum, was demolished and a new landscaped mall extended from the Lyceum to Guyton Hall. The first two buildings constructed along that spacious walkway were Bondurant Hall, a classroom building named for Professor Alexander Bondurant (known to several generations of Ole Miss students as the Graduate Building), and the cafeteria now known as Johnson Commons. The other eleven buildings constructed with the 1928 appropriation included a gymnasium, an athletic field house, a women's dormitory, six men's dormitories, a new law school, and University High School, which the school of education had recently established as a demonstration school. To make it more accessible to Oxford students, University High was built east of the Illinois Central Railroad. In the late 1920s a rickety, two-lane wooden bridge spanned the deep railroad cut that ran along the eastern perimeter of the campus.

Even with this major building program, the university was still cramped for space, especially for classrooms and living quarters. After a fire destroyed Gordon Hall in the summer of 1934, the lack of dormitory space reached crisis proportions. The loss of Gordon Hall, which accounted for one-fourth of all dormitory rooms for male students, was a great disappointment to university officials because it had just been renovated. Over the next two years, medical students lived in temporary quarters in Guyton Hall, athletes were living in the gymnasium and the field house, and some students were quartered in University High

School. More than two hundred students were turned away in the fall of 1936 because there was no place to house them.

When Chancellor Butts was unable to persuade the legislature to replace Gordon Hall, he turned with success to the various recovery agencies of the federal government, and during the next five years the number of buildings more than doubled. In 1939 a reporter for the Oxford *Eagle* counted fifty-five building projects on the campus. The addition to the campus that most enhanced a visitor's first impression of the university was the new four-lane bridge across the Hilgard Cut. Completed in the summer of 1940, the concrete bridge replaced the wooden structure used for many years. The Hilgard Cut, the deepest cut on the Illinois Central Railroad between Chicago and New Orleans, was named for Professor Eugene Hilgard, who had studied its steep banks when he was the state geologist in the 1850s and discovered several geological formations that were not known to exist in north Mississippi.

The most urgently needed of the facilities built with federal funds were the six new dormitories, four for men and two for women. Although these buildings provided accommodations for approximately five hundred students, the university still needed more student housing, and Chancellor Butts persuaded the board of trustees to allow fraternities and sororities to build chapter houses on the campus. By the fall of 1940, nineteen of the twenty-two Greek societies had built houses along Sorority Row and Fraternity Row. Those new facilities, valued at one hundred thousand dollars, were added at no cost to the university or to the state.

As the Public Works Administration was being phased out in 1938, the university received a grant for a physics building and an astronomical observatory. The grant stipulated that construction on the project must begin before New Year's Day of 1939. To complete the paperwork, advertise and accept bids, and begin construction would take so long it was unlikely that the university could meet the deadline. While the paperwork was being prepared in Jackson and Washington, Andrew Hargis, the university engineer and superintendent of buildings and grounds, selected on his own a vacant lot between the chemistry building and the gymnasium, surveyed and staked off a construction site, dug footings with a pick and shovel, poured concrete, and took pictures of the site. He mailed them to Washington and convinced PWA officials that the university had met the deadline. Thus did the university acquire the physics building named for Arthur B. Lewis, dean of the college of liberal arts, and the observatory named in honor of physics professor Wilson L. Kennon.

The most popular and frequently used building added to the campus in the late 1930s was the student union, named Wier Hall in honor of Rush C. Wier of Vaiden, whose large donation made its completion possible. Housing the bookstore and post office, a grill, game room, barbershop, clothing store, and several meeting rooms, Wier Hall became the "real center of campus life." In addition to the construction of academic and housing facilities, including twenty-two faculty cottages and a faculty apartment building, funds from New Deal agencies were also used for improvements in the university's athletic facilities. The baseball field was graded and enhanced and a new grandstand was added. The golf course was also enlarged and reconstructed, with new grass greens replacing the sand greens. The entire student body greeted with great excitement the Olympic-sized swimming pool that was completed in July 1936.

The most prominent addition to the university's athletic facilities was the eighteen-thousand-seat Hemingway Stadium. Begun in 1937 and completed in 1941 at a cost of ninety-six thousand dollars, the construction of Hemingway Stadium came at an opportune time for the university's athletic program. In the late 1930s Ole Miss was emerging as a national football power. On New Year's Day in 1936, Ole Miss played Catholic University of Washington, D.C., in the Orange Bowl at Miami, the first of its many postseason bowl games. Ole Miss was coming off a 9–2 season climaxed by a thrilling but costly victory over Mississippi State. Ole Miss won the 1935 Egg Bowl, the name of the annual Ole Miss-State game that was inaugurated in 1927, but lost the team's star running back, Clarence "Big-Un" Hapes, to a knee injury. Although Ole Miss lost to Catholic University 20–19, the 1936 Orange Bowl appearance, together with the appointment of Coach Harry Mehre in 1938, launched the University of Mississippi into big-time football. The 1942 *M-Book* praised Coach Mehre, who had not lost more than two games in any season, for bringing to Ole Miss that "long-coveted recognition as a football power among football powers." The 1947 yearbook referred to Coach Mehre's first four years, 1938 to 1941, as the "Golden Era of Ole Miss Football."

In the spring of 1936, following the university's first bowl appearance, the campus newspaper thought it was time for Ole Miss to choose a new name for its athletic teams, a name that would "symbolize the spirit, traditions and ideals of Ole Miss." On May 5, 1936, the *Mississippian* announced a contest to select a new name, the second such contest in less than ten years. In the 1920s, as consumer products were increasingly identified by brand names and collegiate football was becoming a national obsession, Ole Miss and other colleges across America also identified their athletic teams with names and mascots that inspired loyalty and stirred enthusiasm among their fans. On November 2, 1929, the *Mississippian* asked students to submit names for the university's athletic teams. Some students objected to the contest, claiming that the University of Mississippi was already known as Ole Miss and that another name would detract or confuse rather than inspire the public. Though some students did not favor a new name, the contest proceeded, and from the eight hundred entries a committee selected "Mississippi Flood," a name submitted by Ole Miss student Dick McCool. Apparently, the lingering memory of the great Mississippi River flood of 1927 influenced the selection. Unlike the Crimson Tide of Alabama and the Green Wave of Tulane, the Mississippi Flood never caught on, and Ole Miss teams continued to be called the Red and Blue, a name that had been used for several years. After an unimaginative sportswriter referred to the Ole Miss football team as the "Mudcats," the student newspaper decided it was time for another contest and a new name.

In the 1936 contest, a committee of sportswriters selected the name Rebels, which was submitted by Ben Guider of Vicksburg. The name was a natural and quickly captured the imagination of Ole Miss students, fans, friends, alumni, and sportswriters. In 1937, Colonel Rebel made his first appearance on the cover of the yearbook, and two years later Ole Miss students began electing a Colonel Rebel to reign with Miss Ole Miss as the students who best represented the traditions and ideals of the University of Mississippi. The Confederate flag did not appear on the campus until the university's centennial celebration in 1948.

As fate would have it, in their first game the newly named Ole Miss Rebels played Union College. The *Mississippian*'s lead-in to its report of that game read: "The Johnny Rebs re-enacted the Battle of Bull Run [Manassas] when they downed Union 45–0." The 1936 season was not a particularly good year—Ole Miss went 5–5–2—but the university's football program won national recognition with the selection of Frank "Bruiser" Kinard as the university's first All-American, an accomplishment he repeated in 1937. Kinard's repeat as an All-American was even more remarkable because he played on a team with a losing record. Ole Miss was 4–5–1 in 1937. The university's football program gained additional national exposure in 1937 with its night game against eastern power Temple University in Philadelphia, which it played to a 0–0 tie game. The Ole Miss football team's trip to Philadelphia also made history, as America's first collegiate team to travel by air.

In 1938 this small university tucked away in the rolling hills of north Mississippi produced two All-Americans in two different sports and one Rhodes Scholar. The All-Americans were Bonnie "Country" Graham, who held thirty-six Southeastern Conference basketball records when he completed his career at Ole Miss, and Parker "Bullet" Hall, one of Ole Miss's greatest running backs. With the selection of J. Hector Currie in 1938, Ole Miss Rhodes Scholars outnumbered Ole Miss All-Americans fourteen to four. As the nation was beginning to take notice of the University of Mississippi, Cary Middlecoff, an Ole Miss golfer during the 1940 and 1941 seasons, added luster to Ole Miss's growing reputation as an athletic power. Middlecoff, and most other Ole Miss athletes, did not return to Oxford for the 1942 season because the board of trustees suspended the university's athletic program during World War II.

On the day after the Japanese attack of Pearl Harbor on December 7, 1941, Ole Miss students and faculty assembled in Fulton Chapel to hear President Franklin Roosevelt call the nation to arms. Within six months, Chancellor Butts and thousands of Ole Miss students and alumni were in the nation's military forces. Butts served in the judge advocate general's office, developing the new code of military justice eventually adopted by the war department.

Like other colleges across the country, the University of Mississippi contributed to America's war effort in many different ways. The university offered an accelerated academic program that allowed students to complete a four-year college course in two and a half years and provided a variety of training courses to more than two thousand military personnel. As male enrollment declined during the war years, Ole Miss coeds assumed leadership roles in many campus activities. In the spring of 1943, Maralyn Howell Bullion, a junior from Oxford and a member of the Ole Miss Hall of Fame, became the first woman student elected president of the Associated Student Body. Miriam Horne was the first woman editor of the *Mississippian* (1944–1945) and Lorane Lowry was the first woman editor of the *Ole Miss* (1944). Huldah Cousins Merchant edited the campus paper in 1946 and Frances Moore was the yearbook editor in 1945.

In September 1942, the United States army established the nation's first Army Administration School at the university and stationed 160 officers at Oxford. After the army transferred the AAS to a military base in Maryland in August 1943, a unit of the Army Specialized Training Program was established at Ole Miss to provide a thirty-six-week basic course in engineering to army personnel. Students in the ASTP participated in the extracurricular activities along with the university's regular students, and university professors under the direction of Victor A. Coulter provided their academic instruction. The army also located a Specialized Training and Re-Assignment unit at the university. The function of the STAR unit was to screen and classify military personnel for admission to the army's various college programs all across America. When the STAR unit closed in March 1944, there were 564 military personnel enrolled in various army and navy programs on the campus. The 58 military personnel enrolled in the medical school kept the university's two-year program open during the war and were vital to its survival.

An important development that occurred during the war years, though it had nothing to do with the war itself, was the establishment of a constitutional board of trustees. The consolidated board of trustees established in 1932 in the wake of the Bilbo imbroglio failed to end the reign of politics in the state's public colleges. Following the 1935 governor's campaign, Governor Hugh White accused several college officials of campaigning for his opponents, and some collegiate officials were ousted, including John L. Gainey, the university's financial secretary. After the 1939 campaign, Governor Paul Johnson, Sr., dismissed several officials at State Teachers College in Hattiesburg. The Southern

Association of Colleges immediately placed the school on probation and threatened to withdraw accreditation from the state's other institutions.

The Southern Association's threat rallied a small dedicated group of men who were determined to find some way of shielding the institutions of higher learning from continued political intrusion. They met with Governor Johnson to discuss the possibility that Mississippi's institutions of higher learning might again lose their accreditation, and explained to him the long-term damage that would cause. They proposed a constitutional amendment creating a politically independent board of trustees as an alternative to the existing statutory board. The advantage of a constitutional board would be that any change in its organization or modification of its authority would require an amendment to the state constitution, a longer and more complicated process than statutory revision. A constitutional board had been under consideration for several years but not adopted because no one wanted any governor to have the power to appoint an entire board; it was increasingly evident, however, that if Mississippi's institutions were ever to be free of politics that risk would have to be taken.

In the first few days of the 1942 legislative session, a constitutional amendment creating a new board of trustees was introduced. With Governor Johnson's support the measure passed both houses in early March and the Mississippi electorate ratified the amendment during the general election in 1943. In the next session the legislature passed a bill implementing the amendment and created the new constitutional board of trustees, which met for the first time on May 18, 1944. It is ironic, given the great effort that went into the establishment of a politically independent board, that the *Jackson Daily News* heralded the new board's first meeting with the caption FOOTBALL IS ASSURED FOR STATE COLLEGES. At its first meeting the board reinstated intercollegiate athletics, which had been cancelled because of the war. Mississippi's new college board was preparing the state's colleges for the return of peace, the veterans, and the predicted surge in enrollment.

Set off by rising expectations and sustained by the GI Bill, the postwar enrollment explosion changed the American collegiate system. Following the Civil War, American colleges were secularized. After World War II, American colleges were democratized. Students "took charge of change" and by their sheer numbers remodeled the American college and university. In 1870 only 1.7 percent of college-age Americans were in college; in 1948 the number had risen to 20 percent. A collegiate system designed for an elite 2 percent of the population could hardly meet the demands of America's burgeoning middle class, and, as enrollment expanded, so did the curriculum, each reacting to the other. Higher education in Mississippi experienced similar enrollment patterns. In 1900, collegiate enrollment in the state was about 2 percent of the college-age population; by 1950, it was nearly 15 percent. Like college enrollment nationally, Mississippi's growth was gradual until the postwar college boom, and then it soared—from ten thousand in 1940 to twenty thousand in 1950, to thirty-five thousand in 1960, fifty-five thousand in 1965, and seventy thousand in 1970.

As Mississippi entered the postwar college boom, the board of trustees realized that it must act quickly if expansion was to be orderly, controlled, and directed. To provide a data base for some quick and difficult decisions, the board retained Joseph E. Gibson to conduct a general study of higher education in Mississippi. This year-long study was the first comprehensive survey of higher education in Mississippi since the O'Shea Study, and Gibson chastised the board for not having implemented more of O'Shea's recommendations. Gibson conceded that consolidation of the state's white colleges into one university at Jackson was not a popular idea and was not going to happen, but his study group "felt compelled" to recommend this "excellent way of achieving most of the things the Board and the people of Mississippi so earnestly desire." Gibson asked, "What greater monument could the first constitutional board bequeath its state than this greater University of Mississippi?" After acknowledging that the state's public colleges would not be consolidated, Gibson stated bluntly that the board of trustees must design a role and scope for each institution and keep them within the parameters of that design.

While Gibson was conducting his study, the new board of trustees were governing Mississippi's institutions of higher learning under difficult circumstances. Several college presidents were embroiled in public controversies, and agitated alumni groups were calling for new leadership. The board of trustees realized that the rapidly changing role of higher education in postwar America required a new philosophy of management, and, in spite of its promise not to make wholesale changes, the board replaced four of the seven college presidents during its first two years. One of those four was Chancellor Butts.

The dismissal of Chancellor Butts on January 25, 1946, was precipitated by his firing of head football coach Harry Mehre. Butts would say years later that he lost his job because he fired a "drunk coach," but the situation was more complicated than that. Following three losing seasons, Ole Miss alumni, including Martin Van Buren Miller, president of the board of trustees, were clamoring for a coaching change, but many Ole Miss students supported Coach Mehre, especially after the upset of Mississippi State at Starkville on November 25, 1945. Chancellor Butts and Coach Mehre had not been on good terms for some time, and after charges surfaced that Mehre was inebriated and could not coach during the Florida game at Jacksonville on September 29, Chancellor Butts decided to fire his head coach. As the pressure for a coaching change mounted, Coach Mehre resigned under threat of dismissal on December 5, 1945. His resignation sparked a "student uprising." According to press reports, a group of students who were dissatisfied with both the coach and the chancellor burned an effigy of Butts and Mehre. Students planned a counter demonstration that same evening in support of Mehre but cancelled it at his request. The *Mississippian* complained that the state press exaggerated the episode and characterized the "uprising" as nothing more than a milling crowd of rowdy students.

Many Ole Miss students were dissatisfied with the university's food service, the outdated regulations governing women students and the limited bathing hours in the dormitories. Eventually, the president of the ASB and other student leaders asked the board of trustees to conduct an investigation, which the board did in early January 1946. Following its investigation, the board of trustees voted on January 25, 1946, not to reelect Chancellor Butts because they "felt it was best for the University that a change be made." After his tenure ended in the summer of 1946, Butts moved to Washington to serve as director of the educational training program in the war department.

On June 14, 1946, following a nationwide search and a review of more than two hundred applications, the board of trustees appointed John Davis Williams the twelfth chancellor of the University of Mississippi. A forty-five-year-old Kentuckian, Williams received his bachelor's and master's degrees from the University of Kentucky in 1926 and

1930. After teaching for several years in public schools, he earned a D.Ed. in 1940 at Columbia University. In 1942 Williams was appointed president of Marshall College in Huntington, West Virginia.

During his first interview with the board of trustees, a board member asked J. D. Williams how he felt about athletics. Williams said if he were president of a college without an athletic program he would not establish one, but if he were president of an institution that had intercollegiate athletics, he would want to win. That answer did not lose him any votes, and it is ironic that his first major appointments as chancellor were in the department of intercollegiate athletics. Before Chancellor Butts left office, he appointed Harold "Red" Drew head football coach. Among Drew's assistant coaches was John Howard Vaught. When Drew resigned in 1947 to become head coach at the University of Alabama, Williams promoted Vaught to head coach and appointed C. M. "Tad" Smith athletic director. With those appointments, Chancellor Williams ushered in the second "Golden Era of Ole Miss Football."

During John Vaught's twenty-five years as head coach (1947–1970, 1973), Ole Miss compiled a 190–61–12 record, including three national championships, six SEC titles, eighteen bowl games, and twenty-seven All-Americans. Coach Vaught retired in 1970, but returned in 1973 after the head football coach was dismissed early in the season. Perhaps the most remarkable statistic of John Vaught's career is that all but two of the full-time assistant coaches who joined him in 1947 were still on his staff when he retired in 1970. The 1959 Ole Miss Rebels were the SEC team of the decade and the third best all-time collegiate football team in America. To many Ole Miss alumni the Autumn Heroes of the second golden era—Charlie Conerly, Barney Poole, Kayo Dottley, Charlie Flowers, Glynn Griffing, Kenny Dill, Jake Gibbs, Stan Hindman, Archie Manning—can still be seen on the playing fields of their memory.

One of the leading candidates for the office of chancellor in 1946 was Robert Farley, who had recently been appointed dean of the law school following the death of T. C. Kimbrough. The board selected Williams over Farley largely because he was an outsider, with no connections to any of Mississippi's political factions, and the new constitutional board of trustees assured him there would be no political interference in the internal affairs of the university. Chancellor Williams had hardly learned his way around the campus before he realized that the trustees, no matter how much they believed or hoped they could insulate the university from politics, were unable to do so. Soon after his appointment, Williams received a telephone call from Governor Fielding L. Wright, who left word with the chancellor's secretary instructing him to appoint a certain person manager of the university laundry. The next day, rather than returning his call, Williams drove to Jackson to meet with the governor. The chancellor told the governor he had been assured by the board of trustees there would be no political intervention in the affairs of the university. Governor Wright explained that an influential state senator was sitting in his office when he made the call and advised Williams to do what he thought was best about the appointment. Governor Wright said, "You have your row to hoe, and I have mine."

Chancellor Williams learned to hoe his political row quite well during his years in Mississippi, and before his Ole Miss career was over he was being prominently mentioned as a gubernatorial candidate. In 1948, as Chancellor Williams was becoming acquainted with the contours of Mississippi's political landscape, eleven Ole Miss students were elected to the state legislature. Every Monday morning when the legislature was in session, Chancellor Williams had breakfast with them before they left for Jackson. The student lawmakers supported Williams's policies, and he remembered years later that the University of Mississippi never again had such strong support in the legislature.

Another experience with the campus laundry convinced Chancellor Williams that the university's management system required a thorough reorganization. While he was coping with an enrollment that nearly overwhelmed the university, a restless student body, an impatient faculty complaining of overcrowded classrooms and lack of office space, and disgruntled alumni demanding a winning football team, Chancellor Williams met with the business manager. The university's chief financial officer brought with him to the chancellor's office the current price list for the university laundry. In view of postwar conditions the business manager thought the price list should be modified and wanted Williams to review the list with him to decide how much the university should charge for laundering a shirt and other items. To his dismay, J. D. Williams soon discovered that twenty-six administrators, deans, and department heads reported directly to the chancellor. An unfortunate legacy of his predecessors, Hume and Butts, this highly centralized and personalized management system was outdated, and Williams began the arduous task of reorganizing the university.

As he was implementing his plan to modernize the university's infrastructure, Chancellor Williams also launched a massive building program dictated by the postwar enrollment explosion. In 1946, on a campus designed for 1,500 students, the university enrolled 3,213, almost 1,000 more than the year before, and there was no relief in sight. The next year's enrollment exceeded 3,500, and more than 1,000 applicants were denied admission because there was no place to feed and house them. The university's capital improvement needs extended across the spectrum. Four and five professors shared an office, the forty-year-old library building had no room for new books, the cafeteria was overcrowded, and there were not enough classrooms for the scheduled courses. To meet the long-range needs of the university, Chancellor Williams retained the Olmstead Brothers of Brookline, Massachusetts, in September 1947 to draft a twenty-five-year campus development plan. The Olmstead plan recommended the continued use of all existing structures and the addition of several new buildings. The new facilities, which would be consistent in form and style to existing structures and built on sites within the campus proper, were to be completed in time for the "baby boomers" who would arrive on the campus in the early 1960s.

To alleviate the immediate crisis, university authorities secured several army surplus buildings from Camp Shelby at Hattiesburg and a POW camp in Coldwater. Some of these buildings, which provided temporary classroom space for journalism, political science, home economics, psychology, ROTC, and English, remained in use until the late 1950s. The opening of four hundred apartments in Vet Village, constructed from war surplus buildings in 1947, relieved the housing shortage for married veterans. Several faculty apartments in a converted war surplus building also became available in the fall of 1947. The opening of a new women's dormitory and four men's dormitories in 1948 temporarily relieved the problem of student housing. Although the enrollment of veterans peaked during the 1951–52 academic year, the university's enrollment continued to increase, and two additional women's dormitories and one for men opened in 1959.

In the 1950s and early 1960s, several new academic facilities relieved the critical shortage of classroom space. In 1954 an engineering building was constructed with funds donated by Robert and Lenore Carrier and named in their honor. Carrier, who was also a major contributor to the university's athletic program, made an additional five-hundred-thousand-dollar grant to the university in 1955 to establish the Carrier Scholarships, which are awarded solely on the basis of academic merit. Carrier expressed the hope to Chancellor Williams that his gift would attract outstanding students to Ole Miss, the kind who would challenge and inspire their professors. The first Carrier Scholar was Mary Ann Mobley who was also, in 1959, the first of Ole Miss's three Miss Americas. The university's other two Miss Americas were Lynda Lee Mead in 1960 and Susan Akin in 1986.

Other academic buildings constructed in the 1950s and 1960s included the school of education, built adjacent to University High School. Although University High closed in 1960, the expanding school of education made full use of those facilities. A biology building, named in honor of former board member William M. Shoemaker, was completed in 1960, and a new center for the university's business school, named for former governor Martin S. Conner, was built a year later. With the construction of Meek Hall in 1960, the university's music department finally found a permanent home. Established in 1930, the department had been housed in Taylor Hall, the former steward's hall built in 1857, and was later moved to Brady Hall, the old infirmary. The Ole Miss band, officially established in 1924, met in the armory until 1950 when a new band hall was built. The armory was the dining room in the middle wing of Gordon Hall, which had not been destroyed during in the 1934 fire.

In 1947 the University of Mississippi alumni association initiated a movement to build an alumni center on the campus as a gift to the university in honor of its centennial. The alumni house, which originally included thirty-four motel rooms and several small conference rooms, opened in 1951. Three years later a center for continuing studies was built adjacent to the alumni house. Named in honor of E. F. Yerby, the center housed the university's extension work (which began in 1917) and the correspondence department (established in 1926). In 1997 the University of Mississippi alumni center was refurbished and named in honor of Dr. and Mrs. R. Faser Triplett, whose contribution made the renovation possible.

The centerpiece of Chancellor Williams's building program was the library that now bears his name. He personally selected the site so students would have to go by, through, or around the library on their way to the student union. The first centrally air-conditioned building at a state-supported institution of higher learning, the university's new library had a seating capacity of 1,250 and was designed to house 450,000 volumes. When the library was built in 1951, the university's combined holdings were under 200,000, including 11,000 volumes in the medical library and 30,000 in the law library. After the new library opened the staff converted the holdings from the Dewey decimal system to the Library of Congress system in 1952, in part by a grant from the Rockefeller Foundation. The former library building became the center for the fine arts, housing the departments of art, speech, and theater. The fine arts building was later named for Alton Bryant, a former vice chancellor.

Library development was only part of Chancellor Williams's larger plan to transform Ole Miss into a modern comprehensive university. In 1948 the graduate school reestablished its doctoral program, offering a Ph.D. in the medical sciences, and within a few years added doctoral programs in education (1951), English and chemistry (1957), and history (1959). With these new doctoral programs and the addition of many master's degree programs, graduate enrollment increased dramatically in the late fifties. From 1955 to 1960 graduate enrollment was up 70 percent. The university's emphasis on research and graduate education led to the founding of the first endowed chair in September 1958, when the Mississippi Bankers Association established the chair of banking.

The hallmark of Chancellor J. D. Williams's endeavor to modernize the university was the expansion of the two year medical course into a four year degree program and the establishment of the University of Mississippi Medical Center in Jackson, which now includes schools of medicine, dentistry, nursing, and health related professions, graduate programs in the medical sciences, and the University Hospital. The original eight story building located on a 164 acre site is the nucleus of a complex that has more than quadrupled in size since the Medical Center opened on July 1, 1955. Major additions to the Medical Center's original campus include the James W. Hardy Clinical Sciences Building, named in honor of one its original professors and one of its great teachers; the Verner S. Holmes Learning Resource Center, named for a long-time member of the board of trustees; the Arthur C. Guyton Laboratory Research Building, named in honor of Dr. Arthur C. Guyton, the world renowned professor emeritus of physiology and biophysics; and the Mississippi Children's Cancer Clinic.

During its fifty-three year history, the Medical Center has been a major factor in the improvement of health care and the quality of life in Mississippi and has achieved national and international acclaim for its teaching and research in the medical sciences. Through its first half century the Medical Center's chief administrative officers were David Pankratz (1955–1961), Robert Marston (1961–1967), John A. Gronvall (1967–1968), Robert Carter (1968–1971), Robert E. Blount (1971–1973), Norman C. Nelson (1973–1994), and Wallace Conerly, who was appointed vice chancellor for health affairs in 1994.

As the university was modernizing and expanding its curriculum in the early postwar years, similar developments were occurring at the state's other public institutions of higher learning. As early as 1949, Chancellor Williams observed that a "pattern of higher education in Mississippi has emerged and taken shape since the close of the war" that undermined the role of the university "as the capstone of public education in the state." As other institutions expanded into academic areas that had long been the exclusive domain of the University of Mississippi, Chancellor Williams cautioned the board of trustees that the "dispersal or duplication of those special functions" would lead to a "general mediocrity which is the inevitable consequence of an over-extended operation." As the board of trustees, the legislature, and the general public attached increasing importance to enrollment figures, university officials found themselves arguing that "the size of the on-campus student body is by no means an adequate basis for judging the expense of operating an institution of higher learning." The original missions and the traditional roles of institutions of higher learning, according to Chancellor Williams, "are the most reliable standards" for the allocation of state funds.

The "question of whether Mississippi is to have a great University in addition to its system of junior and senior colleges," Chancellor Williams conceded in 1951, would not be decided by the Ole Miss faculty and administration. That question, he said, would ultimately be decided by the people of the state, the legislature, the building commission, and the college board. In the aftermath of World War II, the faculty, friends, and alumni of the state's other public institutions, Mississippi

State and Southern Mississippi in particular, decided that it was not the university's prerogative to be "the capstone of public education in Mississippi." While the university waited for others to decide its fate, Mississippi State and Southern Mississippi outstripped the university in enrollment, broadened their course offerings, upgraded their academic programs, and established themselves as peers, not rivals, of the state university. In October 1959, Chancellor Williams stripped the academic folderol from the issue of role and scope and asked the board of trustees: "Shall Mississippi develop one great university recognized nationally and regionally?" Or shall there be two or three universities "of lesser stature?" He went on, "I do not recommend combining any of the present institutions. My proposal is to allocate further appropriations for highly specialized doctoral programs to one specific place." Stating the obvious, the chancellor concluded, "It is too expensive and impractical for the state to permit duplication by institutions in these areas."

However obvious or wise Chancellor Williams's proposal was, it came too late. Mississippi State College had already achieved university status. The legislature had expanded the mission of Southern Mississippi, and it, too, would become a university within a decade. In 1955 the legislature changed the name of Delta State Teachers College to Delta State College and authorized the expansion its curriculum, course offerings, and degree programs. In the 1950s Mississippi State College for Women abandoned school uniforms and expanded its curriculum. In one year alone, MSCW added fifty-five new courses, most of which were in liberal arts and business. In 1956 the legislature renamed Jackson College for Negro Teachers to Jackson State College, and its graduate and undergraduate divisions were enlarged. Two decades later Mississippi would be supporting not one, or two, or three, but eight public universities.

Although university officials and other Mississippi collegiate authorities might have preferred to devote their attention to academic matters, the United States Supreme Court's *Brown vs. the Board of Education* decision in 1954 signaled a return of race and politics to their deliberations. Shortly after the *Brown* decision, the state legislature directed all public officials and state agencies to "prohibit, by any lawful, peaceful, and constitutional means, the implementation or the compliance with the Integration Decisions of the United States Supreme Court" and created the Mississippi State Sovereignty Commission to carry out that mandate. The board of trustees was subject to the legislative directive prohibiting integration and hoped to respond to the *Brown* decision in a peaceful, unpublicized way, but board members were bound by history and heritage to resist it. The trustees were emotionally and psychologically unprepared for the changes that would soon engulf them, and most college presidents were too timid to tell them that they must accept those changes.

To say that the trustees were emotionally and intellectually unprepared for the impending civil rights revolution is not to say they had no warning of what was to come. On July 11, 1939, Chancellor Butts wrote to the chairman of the board of trustees advising him that blacks were seeking admission to professional schools in other Southern states and that Mississippi could soon expect the same. The board's response to that warning was an expression of public policy and an intimation of the measures a closed society might take to keep itself intact. Calvin Wells, the chairman of the board of trustees, told Chancellor Butts that the board would "litigate until the cows come home before we permit any such thing as that [integration]. I sincerely trust that no effort will by made by any negroes to enter [our] institutions. I believe they have too much sense to do so. . . . I would feel sorry about what would happen to them in 24 hours after they got there. However, we will not anticipate any trouble along that line until we meet it." The trouble would start sooner than Wells anticipated.

To African Americans in postwar Mississippi, higher education was the avenue of upward mobility, the "yellow brick road" to the American dream, and few white Mississippians understood the hold that dream had on blacks and how determined they were to reach it. One of the few whites who did was Hodding Carter, the Pulitzer Prize-winning editor of the Greenville *Delta Democrat-Times.* In 1948 Carter delivered the commencement address at Alcorn College. When asked by the *Atlanta Journal* to summarize his speech, Carter said, "I felt that what I said to them was not needed, for I had advised them not to be content with the manifold inequalities experienced by their race." He continued, "I know that they are identical in their aspirations and their good citizenship with college graduates anywhere" and "there can be no good reason for fearing or longer subjugating any American who dreams our common, sturdy dream of a fair chance and a place, our place, in the sun." Carter concluded,"That's all those Alcorn graduates want, and it's the least that they deserve."

Hodding Carter's commencement address at Alcorn in 1948 coincided with the University of Mississippi's centennial celebration, which coincided with the rise of massive resistance to President Harry Truman's initiatives on civil rights. When the Democratic Party adopted a strong civil rights platform and renominated Truman at its Philadelphia convention in July 1948, Southern delegates bolted the party, reconvened in Birmingham, formed the States' Rights Democratic Party (the Dixiecrats), and nominated South Carolina Senator J. Strom Thurmond for president and Mississippi Governor Fielding L. Wright for vice-president. As the Dixiecrats were gathering in Birmingham, an eleven-car caravan carrying fifty-five Ole Miss students left Oxford on July 16 for the Birmingham convention.

Press accounts describing a grand entrance of Ole Miss students into the convention hall carrying a large Confederate flag and wearing Confederate-style hats are not accurate. In a statement to the *Mississippian,* an Ole Miss student-delegate explained, "It is true that we had Confederate flags, but we left them in our rooms at the request of [the] chairman of the conference." While they were in Birmingham, the Ole Miss students did, however, meet with Governor Wright and posed for pictures "with the Ole Miss and state flags." A picture of several Ole Miss delegates, wearing Confederate-style hats and standing in front of a large Confederate battle flag, appeared on the front page of the campus newspaper and in several other state papers.

The flag identified in press reports as the "Ole Miss flag" was a replica of the colors of the University Greys. During the university's centennial celebration in 1948, the Ole Miss ROTC unit procured Confederate uniforms and other accouterments, including a replica of the colors, and reenacted the enlistment of the University Greys. For many campus events during the year-long celebration, the ROTC unit donned its Confederate regalia, and, in the mind's eye, the storied Greys who won imperishable glory at First Manassas and suffered 100 percent casualties at Gettysburg, reappeared on the campus they had abandoned for war in 1861.

During the centennial celebration, the Rebel flag became the focus of the Confederate imagery that would soon cloak the Ole Miss campus. In 1948 the Ole Miss band introduced a wildly popular halftime routine during which it marched onto the field unfurling the world's largest Confederate flag to the stirring strains of *Dixie.* The 1948 *M-Book* explained to new students that the giant Rebel flag did not mean that Ole Miss was not in the United States. It meant they did not want anyone telling them what to do. By the late 1940s students had also settled on "Hotty Totty" as the school cheer that represented the Ole Miss spirit. "Janie Reb," a weekly column in the 1948 *Mississippian* written by Lib Blanchard, signed off her column, "Hotty Totty." University of Mississippi students of that generation believed there was something very special about Ole Miss and about them. "There's magic in the words Ole Miss . . . they cast a spell wherever one hears them" and Ole Miss students are "the cream of Mississippi youth, the flower of Mississippi families," wrote the *Mississippian.*

By the early 1950s the symbols of the Lost Cause were woven into the fabric of student life at Ole Miss. On November 27, 1950, Ole Miss students inaugurated Dixie Week, a seven-day celebration of their Southern heritage during which Colonel Rebel and Miss Ole Miss reigned. The opening ceremony of Dixie Week was the reading of the Ordinance of Secession, usually by the president of the student body, from the balcony of the student union or from the courthouse on the square. Enlistment of the University Greys, ceremonial consumption of mint juleps, speeches in praise of Robert E. Lee, beard-growing contests, and mule races were the rituals of Dixie Week. One of the most popular events was the auctioning of cheerleaders who served as slaves for the week to their buyers.

In the fall of 1950 the guest of honor for the first Dixie Week, which coincided with the Ole Miss-Mississippi State football game, was ninety-eight-year-old "General" James A. Moore, one of six living Confederate veterans. General Moore, the Commanding General of the Confederate States of Ole Miss, was conveyed to the Ole Miss-State game in a horse-drawn carriage and saluted at halftime while "aircraft, forming a Confederate flag, [flew] over the campus." After the game General Moore was the lead-out at the Confederate ball, which featured twenty Ole Miss belles escorted "by Rebels in Confederate uniforms."

In the fall of the first Dixie Week, the world's attention was focused on Oxford, and Ole Miss basked in the reflected glory of its onetime student, William Faulkner, who was now Mississippi's Nobel laureate. The announcement that Faulkner won the Nobel Prize occurred three weeks after the Oxford world premier of *Intruder in the Dust,* the movie version of Faulkner's novel about race in a small Southern town. Race, in fact and in fiction, was a major story at Oxford and Ole Miss that fall.

On October 20, 1950, the *Mississippian* reported in a front page article that "Negroes may [soon] apply for admission to the Ole Miss law school." The paper quoted Ole Miss officials who said "the application of a Negro to enter Ole Miss must be turned over to the Mississippi Board of Trustees of Institutions of Higher Learning, according to a ruling of the Board." A week after this article appeared, Albin Krebs, editor of the *Mississippian,* wrote an editorial stating that "qualified Negro applicants should be allowed to enter" the law school. Krebs also predicted that Mississippi "will in the end have to admit Negroes to not only Ole Miss, but Mississippi State and other state-supported schools." Krebs's editorial precipitated a torrent of comment and criticism. He printed many letters to the editor, a surprising number of which supported integration of the university. During the furor over his editorial, a cross was burned on the lawn in front of Sam Hall, the boys' dormitory where Krebs lived. In subsequent editorials Krebs objected to the excessive coverage and criticized Mississippi newspapers for reporting that two thousand students had burned a cross on the campus when only about two hundred had participated in the demonstration. Krebs was also genuinely sorry for the negative publicity his editorial had brought to Ole Miss.

While some students were gathering materials for a cross burning, other Ole Miss students were quietly sharing their art supplies with M. B. Mayfield, an African American artist who worked as a janitor in the fine arts building. Professor Stuart R. Purser, chair of the Ole Miss art department, discovered Mayfield and arranged for him to move to Oxford in the fall of 1950. Professor Purser would leave the door to his classroom open, and Mayfield would sit in his broom closet listening and taking notes during the lectures. Many of the art students knew of the arrangement and, Mayfield remembers fondly, shared their supplies with him. Mayfield is now one of Mississippi's acclaimed artists whose work was exhibited on the Ole Miss campus at the Center for the Study of Southern Culture in the summer of 1986 and at Southside

Gallery in Oxford in early 1998. Although the cross burning in front of Krebs's dormitory received wide coverage, Mayfield's instruction was carried on quietly and without incident.

The public dialogue Krebs's editorial prompted was unsettling to some state officials. There was already an "undercurrent of nervous apprehension," as there had been after the Civil War, that blacks might soon seek admission to one of the state's professional schools, the medical school in particular. A year before Krebs published his editorial Walter Sillers, speaker of the house of representatives, wrote to Governor Fielding L. Wright expressing his concern that Mississippi might soon face that issue. Sillers considered the admission of blacks to the medical school "unthinkable" and vowed to close it if necessary to avoid "the tragic consequences" of integration. Eventually, the board of trustees armed the presidents of Mississippi's collegiate institutions with what they thought was the power to avoid those "tragic consequences." In August 1950 the board gave college presidents the authority to "accept or reject any applicants according to the best interest of everyone."

Three years after the board of trustees authorized college presidents to act in "the best interest of everyone," and a year before the *Brown* decision, Chancellor Williams and Dean Robert Farley recommended the admission of Charles Dubra, a black minister from Gulfport, to the Ole Miss law school. Dubra had an undergraduate degree from Claflin College in Orangeburg, South Carolina, and a master's degree from Boston University. Dubra explained to Dean Farley that he did not want any publicity connected with his admission. He said he was not an activist, all he wanted was a law degree, and he would live quietly off campus in Oxford's black community. The board of trustees discussed the chancellor's recommendation intensely. The president of the board, H. M. Ivy, favored Dubra's admission, but others strongly opposed it. Dean Farley remembered that one trustee "got almost violent over the idea." The board rejected Dubra's application on the grounds that Claflin College was unaccredited, though his graduate work at Boston University would have made him eligible for admission. Dubra did not challenge the board's decision and his acquiescence seemed to confirm the board's belief that the "unthinkable" would never happen in Mississippi.

In early January 1954, six months after Dubra's rejection and five months before the *Brown* decision, Medgar Evers, a graduate of Alcorn

A & M College, applied for admission to the Ole Miss law school. The board also rejected his application, which was forwarded to the board office in Jackson, because Evers did not include two letters from alumni recommending his admission. In 1954 admission to state-supported colleges required two letters from alumni in the applicant's home county attesting to his or her good moral character. Evers was advised that he must submit the two letters before his application could be processed. A short time later Evers submitted two letters from Ole Miss alumni in Newton County (his home county) recommending his admission.

Somewhat surprised that Evers had obtained the letters of recommendation, the board reinterpreted the requirement and advised Evers that those letters did not satisfy the admission standards. E. R. Jobe, executive secretary of the board of trustees, told Evers that he must have two letters from alumni in the county where he was then living, not his home county. At the time of his application Evers worked for the NAACP in Bolivar County. While Evers was securing those letters, the board increased the required number of letters from two to five. In the midst of the increasingly complicated application process, Evers was offered the position of state field secretary of the NAACP, and, rather than pursue his admission to Ole Miss, he accepted that appointment. Medgar Evers's decision not to pursue his application, coming so soon after the acquiescence of Charles Dubra, reinforced the belief that the state's power structure could, by delay and duplicity, prevent integration in Mississippi. To hold such a belief in the postwar world, William Faulkner said, was "like living in Alaska and being against snow." Yet, fidelity to another lost cause again skewed the world view of white Mississippians, and they closed their society in the 1950s as their forebears had in the 1850s.

The white power structure's determination to cordon off Mississippi's college campuses from the outside world was manifested at Ole Miss in the fall of 1955 when Will Campbell, director of religious life at the university, invited the Reverend Alvin Kershaw to participate in the annual religious emphasis week. Kershaw's invitation was part of Campbell's larger plan to engage the issue of racial injustice in Mississippi. Reverend Kershaw won a large sum of money on a popular television show and announced that he would contribute part of his winnings to the NAACP. The announcement that the university invited a speaker for religious emphasis week who praised and financed the work of the NAACP prompted, as Campbell anticipated, a stormy debate and a demand that the university withdraw the invitation.

Several members of the faculty, the student newspaper, the student senate, and, according to a student poll, three-fourths of the students opposed the cancellation of Kershaw's invitation. As the debate intensified, however, both the student newspaper and the student senate sided with Chancellor Williams, who, under great public pressure, withdrew Kershaw's invitation because his presence would disrupt the educational process. Professor Morton King, chairman of the sociology department, resigned in protest of Chancellor Williams's action. After Kershaw's invitation was withdrawn, all of the other invited ministers canceled their appearances. Local ministers also declined invitations to participate. Consequently, in lieu of the traditional religious emphasis week, students, faculty, and Oxford residents assembled in Fulton Chapel each day for an hour of silence and meditation. The Kershaw affair, along with the appearance of the renowned pacifist Reverend Henry Hitt Crane, who told students at Southern Mississippi that they could as a matter of conscience refuse to go to war, and an Aaron Henry (state president of the NAACP) speech at Ole Miss prompted the board to establish a speaker ban policy. As the civil rights revolution became increasingly volatile, Ole Miss and other state colleges had to obtain the specific approval of the board of trustees before an individual could be invited to speak on campus.

While a three judge panel of the fifth circuit was reviewing these new speaker regulations, an Ole Miss student organization invited Earl Reynolds, a Quaker pacifist, to lecture at the university. On the day that Reynolds was scheduled to speak, M. M. Roberts, president of the college board, petitioned Judge J. P. Coleman of the fifth circuit for a temporary restraining order preventing the speech, which Coleman granted. On March 14, 1969, a federal marshal entered a classroom at the University of Mississippi and served Reynolds with the restraining order prohibiting his speech. The intrusion of the federal marshal startled Reynolds and the class, but Reynolds honored the injunction and ended his lecture. The Ole Miss chapter of the American Association of University Professors condemned the interruption of Reynolds's speech as an intolerable breech of academic freedom that would severely and permanently damage the reputation of the university.

During the Kershaw controversy in the fall of 1955, a classic example of what Walker Percy called the "terrible complexities" of race occurred at the University of Mississippi when Ole Miss students paused to mourn the passing of Blind Jim Ivy. On the eve of homecoming 1955, James Ivy died at his son's home in Chicago at the age of eighty-two. The legendary African American "dean of the freshman class," Ivy lost his sight in 1892 when creosote was accidentally splattered in his eyes while he was working on a bridge across the Tallahatchie River. To support his family, Blind Jim conducted a one-man vending operation on the campus.

In the spring of 1896, Blind Jim was selling candy and peanuts at a baseball game between the University of Mississippi and the University of Texas. When he was told that Mississippi was losing, he began cheering for the home team. The students heard his loud booming voice and invited him to sit with them in the stands. With Blind Jim leading the cheers, the baseball team rallied to beat Texas, and from that point on Blind Jim Ivy was a part of Ole Miss. By the 1920s a freshman tradition required new students to assemble on the Lyceum steps on Thursday night of the first week of the fall semester to receive a special greeting and words of advice from their dean.

In 1931 a contract between the university and a food service company that operated the cafeteria excluded private vendors from the campus. When the students learned that Ivy was being forced off the campus, they asked the administration to exempt him from the terms of the contract. Blind Jim "does not ask for charity," the editor of the campus newspaper wrote, but "prefers to make a living by honest toil" and should be allowed to do so. In a called meeting the student senate passed a resolution asking that he be permitted to remain on campus. The senate asserted that "during the whole time Jim has been on the campus he has never begged, but has made his living honestly as a vendor." Through those and other student appeals, the university allowed Blind Jim to maintain his refreshment stand in the corridor of the Lyceum, though in later years he moved it to the foyer of the cafeteria.

As Ole Miss entered a second golden era of football in the 1950s, Blind Jim became a celebrity. At football games, including the 1953 Sugar Bowl, he was often interviewed by journalists and broadcasters. Although he had attended hundreds of athletic contests during his nearly sixty years on the campus, Blind Jim boasted, "I've never seen an Ole Miss team lose." Jim Ivy's happy countenance and dignity endeared him to Ole Miss students. There was honest affection for him, and he loved the students and the institution that provided him "a place in the sun." One student editor wrote that he "is loved with the same love that students have for... the Lyceum. Blind Jim is part of Ole Miss." Blind Jim may have been the model for Colonel Rebel who first appeared on the cover of the yearbook in 1937.

The relationship between Ole Miss students and Blind Jim Ivy was genteel racism in its purest form and it broke none of the codices of white supremacy, but their fondness for him was genuine. When he died on October 20, 1955, Ole Miss students and alumni raised more than a thousand dollars to endow a scholarship in his honor. The Blind Jim Scholarships would enable "Mississippi Negro youngsters to attend Negro institutions of higher learning." Because of the terrible complexities of race, the young African Americans who would benefit from the affection Ole Miss students had for Blind Jim could not attend the school he loved and had been a part of for so long.

The militant phase of the civil rights movement began in Mississippi, as it did elsewhere, on the college campus in the springtime. In March 1957 a group of Alcorn A & M students boycotted the classes of Professor Clennon King, who had recently come to Alcorn College from Georgia. King was also a minister and had been an organizer for the NAACP, but, after a disagreement with its leadership, he disassociated himself from that organization. While teaching at Alcorn, King wrote several articles criticizing the NAACP and endorsing segregation, and he became something of a celebrity among whites. But there was more to the Alcorn students' protest than King's criticism of the NAACP; they also accused Professor King of demeaning women in his classes, and they were dissatisfied with the administration's response to their complaints. The boycott soon spread to other classes.

A special board committee went to Alcorn to investigate the situation. In a fashion reminiscent of the plantation tradition, committee members scolded the students and threatened to close the school if they did not return to class immediately. The board committee was startled when an Alcorn student replied, "We don't give a damn if you burn it down." That declaration marked the dawning of a new era in race relations in Mississippi. Following that angry student's declaration, the board committee removed the president, closed the college, and fired Professor King. After the new president, J. D. Boyd, took office, the situation began to ease, and the board announced that students who wished to return to Alcorn would be reinstated without penalty if they signed a statement that they would not continue the boycott or support it in any way. When the trustees dismissed Professor King in April 1958, they presumed their troubles with him were at last resolved, but it was not so.

In May 1958, Clennon King called E. R. Jobe, the executive secretary of the board of trustees, and told him that he wanted to pursue a Ph.D. in history at Ole Miss. Jobe advised King to write for an application, provide all the documents required, and submit his application to the registrar at the university. King did not want to seek admission under the normal procedure, however, because he believed university officials would find some technicality on which to deny his admission. He told Jobe that he was going to Oxford and would make a personal application for admission. Jobe informed Governor J. P. Coleman and the Mississippi Highway Patrol that King would apply for admission in person at the university on June 5.

Governor Coleman, who was determined to prevent any violence that might result from King's attempt to register, went to Batesville, a town about twenty miles west of Oxford, to coordinate the highway patrol's response if violence did occur and to consult with university officials. Coleman did not go to Oxford because he thought his presence at the university would attract attention, especially from the press. When King arrived at the Lyceum, he was taken to a room where he was left alone for quite some time. Fearing he was in physical danger, King began shouting for help and pleading for someone to save him. When he was informed that King was shouting, "Help! Help! They are going to kill me!" loudly enough for the press in front of the Lyceum to hear him, Governor Coleman told the highway patrol to "go in there and get him . . . and take him off the campus" and release him. After King vowed to come back to the campus, Governor Coleman told the patrolmen to "take him down to Jackson and have two doctors examine him" and then commit him to Whitfield, the state mental institution.

While Clennon King was serving his short stay in Whitfield, a current and former member of the legislature filed a broad set of charges against Chancellor Williams and several university professors accusing them of subverting the Mississippi way of life. On November 18, 1958, one of the accusers presented a thirty-six-page document to the board office. He explained that he had been accumulating this information since 1952, when he first learned that several university professors were attempting to subvert "our civilization here in Mississippi." The other accuser presented a similar though shorter document. After explaining in some detail how serious he thought the situation at Ole Miss was, he added, "Since my name is not for publication, I would like to name some of the pinkos on the faculty." He then listed several faculty members whom he considered subversive.

Among the specific charges filed with the board of trustees were the following: religious counselor Will Campbell was accused of playing Ping-Pong with a Negro in the YMCA building; law professor William Murphy was accused of trying to secure legal counsel for Clennon King; Robert Farley was accused of stating publicly that Mississippi must obey the United States Supreme Court; and Roscoe Boyer, a faculty member in the school of education, was accused of poking fun at the Southern drawl and bragging that he had been born in the North.

James Wesley Silver, who was in his twenty-second year at the university and was chair of the history department, was singled out for special attention. One of the charges against Professor Silver was that he criticized the military strategy of Robert E. Lee and other Confederate generals. To substantiate that accusation, Silver's accusers cited a master's thesis, written by an Ole Miss student, that was critical of several Confederate generals. Silver's accusers declared that "this thesis could well be the fruit of Dr. Silver's lectures." At the time those accusations were made, Professor Silver was a visiting professor at Harvard University, teaching courses in the Civil War and Southern history.

Perhaps the most sensational charges were leveled against philosophy professor Quinter M. Lyon, who was accused of apostasy. Lyon's detractors condemned his popular and widely used college textbook, *The Great Religions,* because it did not declare Christianity as the only true religion and all others as false. Professor Lyon was an ordained minister and an eminent scholar with two earned doctorates. An Oxford newspaper referred to Professor and Mrs. Lyon as "active members of the Methodist church." At the time of these accusations, Lyon was preparing a series of lectures to be delivered, in Spanish, at the University of Panama where he was a Fulbright Scholar in 1960.

In addition to these and many other charges against specific individuals, the two men who filed the charges also claimed there was a communist cell and, possibly, an NAACP chapter at the university. Stanley Dearman, editor of the *Mississippian,* blasted the accusers and warned his readers that these "self-righteous do-gooders," would "eradicate . . . academic freedom" if left unchallenged. The real threat to academic freedom, he said, "comes not from the North . . . but from within our own state."

After the two men submitted their formal allegations, the board directed university personnel to respond in writing to the charges against them. The board's Special Committee on Charges of Apostasy at the University of Mississippi studied those written responses. Following a year-long investigation, the committee filed a report at a called meeting in August 1959. At that meeting, according to the *Jackson Daily News,* the board asked Chancellor Williams to sign an oath stating that he believed in one omnipotent God, in the literal truth of the Bible and the Tenth Amendment, that Mississippi was a sovereign state, that the Supreme Court was not above the constitution, and that racial integration often leads to intermarriage. The minutes of that board meeting, however, do not include any discussion of what took place and do not indicate if Chancellor Williams was asked to sign such an oath. The minutes state only that the board adopted the committee's report, cleared Chancellor Williams and all faculty members of the charges against them, and considered the case of apostasy and subversion at the university closed. A board statement released to the press after the meeting expressed unanimous and unreserved confidence in Chancellor Williams and his administration. The statement also disclosed that, after an intense investigation, the committee had found neither a communist cell nor a NAACP chapter at the university.

As the furor over apostasy and subversion at Ole Miss was winding down, an even more volatile situation was developing in Hattiesburg, where Clyde Kennard announced that he would soon file an application for admission to Mississippi Southern College. An unnamed organization told President William D. McCain that it would place "twenty thousand people around this campus to prevent" its integration. After a meeting with Governor Coleman and President McCain, Kennard agreed to postpone his application until after the 1959 governor's race between Ross Barnett and Carroll Gartin. The conventional wisdom was that a racial flare-up at Mississippi Southern would work to the benefit of Barnett rather than Gartin, who, like Coleman, belonged to the more moderate wing of the Democratic Party.

After the election, Kennard filed his application at Mississippi Southern. Kennard was a decorated veteran of the Korean War, a former student at the University of Chicago, and a small poultry farmer in Forrest County. Eventually, after he refused under great pressure to withdraw his application, local authorities arrested Kennard and charged him with buying twenty-five dollars' worth of stolen chicken feed. In a miscarriage of justice excessive even by Mississippi standards during that period of racial oppression, an all-white jury convicted Kennard and a white judge sentenced him to seven years in the State Penitentiary at Parchman. The only witness against Kennard was the young black man accused of stealing the goods, who was given clemency for his testimony against Kennard. After his incarceration Kennard became gravely ill with intestinal cancer. Under the best of circumstances his chances for survival were not good, and under prison conditions he deteriorated rapidly. When civil rights activists accused prison officials of denying Kennard proper medical care, the governor gave him an early release. Kennard weighed less than a hundred pounds when he was taken to Chicago for emergency treatment, but he was beyond recovery and died shortly after his release.

In November 1959, in his third try, Ross Barnett was elected governor of Mississippi. It was the fulfillment of his lifelong dream of living in the Governors Mansion, "that big white house on Capitol Street." His friends were elated and the power structure emboldened by his victory, confidant that he could keep his campaign promise to maintain Mississippi's way of life. While Governor Barnett was assuring the white people of Mississippi that he would maintain segregation "now and forever," a young African American sergeant in the United States air force, "with a mission and a nervous stomach," was planning his assault on Mississippi's closed society. Their lives would intersect on the serene and quiet campus of Ole Miss.

CHAPTER 11

CONFLICT, CHANGE, AND CONTINUITY, 1960–1968

The quiet, peaceful way of life we had known was shattered. But still in our minds are memories of those wonderful days given only to college students at Ole Miss.

OLE MISS, 1963

In a speech at Greenwood in early July 1962, Chancellor J. D. Williams asked Ole Miss alumni to help him preserve academic freedom at the university. Six months later he was asking them to help him save the university itself. Ten days before his Greenwood speech, the fifth circuit court of appeals had ordered the admission of James Howard Meredith, an air force veteran from Kosciusko who was then enrolled at Jackson State College. Chancellor Williams and other university officials accepted the verdict of the court and began preparations for Meredith's admission in the fall of 1962.

Important though it was, breaking the color barrier at Ole Miss was only a part of Meredith's larger plan. He came back to Mississippi, he wrote, "to accomplish my divine mission." Meredith's mission was to change the system, to open the closed society that had shut him and other blacks out for so long. He began his assault on the closed society in September 1960 when he enrolled at Jackson State College. The election of President John Kennedy triggered his resolve, and, on January 21, 1961, the day after Kennedy was inaugurated, Meredith wrote to the University of Mississippi requesting a catalog and application forms. A week later he received a letter from registrar Robert B. Ellis saying, "We are very pleased to know of your interest in becoming a member of our student body. . . . If we can be of further help to you in making your enrollment plans, please let us know."

Before returning his application, Meredith wrote the NAACP Legal Defense Fund requesting legal assistance in the event a costly court case was necessary to gain admission. Without waiting for a reply, Meredith returned his application and added a historic postscript: "I sincerely hope that your attitude toward me as a potential member of your student body... will not change upon learning that I am not a white applicant. I am an American-Mississippi-Negro citizen." James Meredith genuinely hoped his admission could be achieved without violence and turmoil. In a letter along with his application, he wrote, "With all of the [changes] taking place in our country in the new age, I feel certain that this application does not come as a surprise to you. I certainly hope that this matter will be handled in a manner... complimentary to the University and the state of Mississippi.... I am very hopeful that the complications will be as few as possible."

Meredith informed the registrar that he had not complied with the requirement of five letters of recommendation from Ole Miss alumni because the university's alumni in his home county were white and he did not know any of them personally. Since 1954 in-state applicants to Mississippi institutions of higher learning were required to furnish five letters of recommendation from alumni of the institution to which they were applying. In lieu of those letters, Meredith included five letters of recommendation from black citizens in his community. In the meantime, he asked the colleges he attended while in the air force to send his transcripts to the University of Mississippi.

Meredith's application triggered a mechanism that had been in place since the late 1940s. In accordance with an unwritten policy, the university sent copies of his application and other correspondence to the board office and six copies to the state attorney general's office. The board of trustees and state officials, in consort with the university, implemented a strategy to dissuade Meredith from his bid to break the color barrier at Ole Miss. Based on the surmise that Meredith would go away if they did not admit him, as Charles Dubra and Medgar Evers had, the strategy was set in motion with a February 4, 1961, telegram to Meredith from the registrar:

> FOR YOUR INFORMATION AND GUIDANCE IT HAS BEEN FOUND NECESSARY TO DISCONTINUE CONSIDERATION OF ALL APPLICATIONS FOR ADMISSION... RECEIVED AFTER JANUARY 25, 1962. YOUR APPLICATION WAS RECEIVED SUBSEQUENT TO SUCH DATE AND THUS WE MUST ADVISE YOU NOT TO APPEAR FOR REGISTRATION.

After receiving this initial rejection, Meredith wrote the justice department to inform the civil rights division that Ole Miss had denied his application. The opening sentences of that letter illustrate Meredith's frustration with the indignities that he and "his people" experienced: "It is with much regret that I present this information to you concerning myself. Whenever I attempt to reason logically about this matter, it grieves me keenly to realize that an individual, especially an American, the citizen of a free democratic nation, has to clamor with such procedures in order to try to gain just a small amount of his civil and human rights."

On the day Meredith wrote to the justice department, he received a letter from Thurgood Marshall, director of the NAACP defense fund (and future justice of the United States Supreme Court). Marshall asked Meredith for a copy of his transcripts and a university catalog, and said in closing, "I think it should go without saying that we are vitally interested in what you propose." Neither Meredith nor Marshall had any way of knowing that the admission requirements listed in the catalog Marshall requested were being revised on that very day.

At a called meeting on February 7, 1961, the board of trustees designed a new set of entrance requirements that would make it more difficult for Meredith to gain admission to Ole Miss. The new admissions policy stated that a student could not transfer from one state institution to another unless "the student's work is acceptable to the receiving institution and to the Board of Trustees." The new policy also stated that "applications which present . . . questionable or uncertain data . . . shall be rejected or referred to the Board of Trustees." The trustees seriously misjudged Meredith's determination to negotiate those minor hurdles. Even more so, they miscalculated the effectiveness and constitutionality of the measures.

After Marshall examined Meredith's transcript and other credentials, the NAACP offered him legal assistance and assigned Constance Baker Motley to the case. On February 16, 1961, Meredith received a letter from Motley advising him to make certain that all his transcripts and other papers were in order and to apply for the summer term beginning June 8. As he was preparing his application for the summer term, he received a letter dated February 21 from the registrar that read: "Since we are unable to accept your application for admission, I am returning your . . . room deposit." Meredith immediately returned the deposit with an application for the June 8 summer term. After he received no response concerning his summer application, he asked about its status in a letter on March 18. In the meantime Meredith maintained an active correspondence with Constance Motley. After almost two weeks without hearing from the registrar, Meredith again wrote and inquired about the status of his application. He closed this letter, "However, realizing that I am not a usual applicant to the University of Mississippi, and that some timely items might need to be considered, I certainly hope that the entire matter will be handled in a manner complimentary to the University of Mississippi."

When Meredith heard nothing from the university for almost two more weeks, he wrote the dean of the college of liberal arts, asking him to evaluate his transcript, review the application, and advise him if he had met all admission requirements. On May 9 Meredith finally received a letter from the registrar informing him that the university would accept only forty-eight of the ninety hours he had earned. The university would not accept the credits from Jackson State College, which was not accredited by the Southern Association of Colleges. The presumption, or perhaps the hope, was that Meredith would be so discouraged by the loss of almost half of his college credits that he would abandon his effort to gain admission to the university. The registrar emphasized that the evaluation of Meredith's transcript did not in any way indicate approval or disapproval of his application, and wrote in closing, "In view of the foregoing [the loss of 42 hours of credit] please advise if you desire your application to be treated as a pending application." After conferring with Constance Motley, Meredith informed the university that he would accept the evaluation of his transcript and wanted his application to be considered for the summer term. He also applied for married-student housing for the summer.

On May 15, the day Meredith advised the registrar that he wanted to keep his application active, a campus committee revised the university's entrance requirements to conform to the board's new admission policy. The new policy stated that Ole Miss would not accept transfer students from unaccredited colleges or students who withdrew from their institutions "in the midst of a quarter, or tri-semester." These two new provisions were adopted to preclude Meredith's admission. Jackson State

College, where Meredith was currently enrolled, was not accredited by the Southern Association of Colleges and was on the quarter system. Meredith could not transfer to Ole Miss without withdrawing "in the midst of a quarter," which would make him ineligible to enter Ole Miss. The new standards also included a statement that the university would reject applications "containing false, contradictory, questionable, or uncertain data." These requirements first appeared in the 1962 catalog. Also appearing in that catalog was a notation of astonishing candor: "Changes or revisions [in admission requirements] are sometimes made without prior notice in order to cope with changing conditions."

In a letter dated May 25, 1962, ten days after the adoption of these new admission standards, the university registrar formally rejected Meredith's application. The registrar informed Meredith that he rejected his application because the university did not admit transfer students from unaccredited institutions and because he did not present five letters of recommendation. The letter concluded: "I see no need for mentioning any other deficiencies. Your application file has been closed."

After this formal written rejection, James Meredith filed a law suit on May 31, 1961, in the federal district court. Constance Motley favored appealing directly to the board rather than filing suit. Meredith, however, preferred a suit, because he believed the courts would decide the issue quickly. Judge Sidney J. Mize set a hearing on Meredith's suit for June 12 at Biloxi. After much legal wrangling the district court rescheduled the hearing and transferred it to Jackson. Finally, on December 12, 1961, six months after the hearing on the preliminary injunction began, the district court ruled in favor of the university. Judge Mize held that Meredith had not shown that he was denied admission solely on the basis of race. The ruling was based on the registrar's testimony that "he gave no consideration whatsoever to the race or the color of the plaintiff." Judge Mize further ruled that the admission policies adopted by the board of trustees, even those enacted after Meredith filed his application, were not designed "in any attempt direct or indirect, to discriminate against anyone solely on the grounds of race and color.... The testimony shows, and I find as a fact, that there was no discrimination against any student... solely because of his race or color."

Two days after Judge Mize's ruling, Meredith asked the fifth circuit to grant his request for a preliminary injunction so he could enroll for the spring semester beginning February 8, 1962. A three-judge panel consisting of Elbert Tuttle, Richard T. Rives, and John Minor Wisdom denied Meredith's request. In unusually pointed language, however, the panel reversed Judge Mize on several points and admonished him for his conduct of the hearing. Judge Wisdom was baffled by the record of the hearing, which he said was argued "in the eerie atmosphere of never-never land." Judge Wisdom also took judicial notice that Mississippi "maintains a policy of segregation" and that is "a plain fact known to everyone." The panel struck down the requirement of five letters of recommendation because that requirement was "a denial of equal protection of the laws in its application to Negro candidates."

The fifth circuit's response was favorable to Meredith, but the court ruled that he had not conclusively proven that he was denied admission because of race. Judge Wisdom, therefore, sent the case back to the lower court and ordered a full trial on the merits of the case. That trial opened on January 16, 1962, only to be delayed another week due to the illness of an assistant attorney general. The trial finally began in the last week of January 1962. University officials testified that they handled Meredith's application in the same way as all other applications. Constance Motley asked the registrar to explain specifically why he rejected Meredith's application. The registrar responded, "It struck me . . . that he was trying . . . to make trouble at the University." The registrar also testified that there was "questionable or uncertain data" on Meredith's application. Meredith, for example, claimed to be a resident of Mississippi, but the registrar considered him an out-of-state student.

Members of the board of trustees testified that they had never held any "formal" discussions regarding Meredith's application, and that he had not been treated any differently from other applicants. After this testimony, Motley attempted to introduce into evidence several newspaper articles that referred to James Meredith's effort to enroll at the "all white University" and "to break the color barrier" in Mississippi. After Judge Mize did not allow Motley to admit the news stories, the plaintiff rested.

When court resumed on Friday morning, January 26, the registrar was the final witness called by the state. After a lengthy discussion of

Meredith's moral character and his mission in life, the state's attorney asked the registrar:

> Q. What did the race or color of James Meredith have to do with any action you have ever taken . . . with regard to his application?
>
> A. Meredith's race or color has had no influence on the decisions which I have taken.

In its closing argument on Saturday morning, January 27, the state asserted that James Meredith was a troublemaker who was lacking in good moral character, and it was for that reason, rather than race, that the university denied him admission. Judge Mize took the case under advisement and announced that he would issue a ruling before February 8, the start of the spring semester. On February 3, he found that Meredith was not denied admission on the basis of race. In his ruling, Judge Mize stated:

> [T]he Board of Trustees . . . testified unequivocally [that] all policies and regulations were adopted without regard to race . . . and that at no time was the application of James Meredith . . . discussed by any members of the Board of Trustees.
>
> The registrar . . . testified . . . that the question of race of the Plaintiff was not discussed or considered in any way whatsoever when his application for admission to the University was being considered. All of the other officials of the University testified to substantially the same thing.
>
> The proof shows . . . and I find as a fact that there is no custom or policy now, nor was there any at the time Plaintiff's application was rejected, which excluded qualified Negroes from entering the University. The proof shows, and I find as a fact, that the University is not a racially segregated institution.

A week after Judge Mize's ruling, the *Mississippian* ran a front-page story entitled "Meredith—the Man." Written by editor James Robertson, a future member of the Mississippi supreme court, the article reported that Meredith was from Kosciusko, that his parents owned land in Attala County, and that the Merediths were "good, solid, substantial citizens." The article concluded, "A history major, [Meredith] plans to enroll—if admitted—in the College of Liberal Arts." The article was a straight news story without a hint of advocacy, yet it provoked an angry response because Robertson had referred to Meredith as a history major, not a troublemaker, as a transfer student, not an outside agitator, and as a man, not a Negro. The *Rebel Underground,* an anonymous and irregular mimeographed ledger, countered the article with one of its own, "Meredith — the darkie," and accused Robertson of degrading "the great trust and faith given him by his fellow students." A resolution to reprimand Robertson was introduced in the student senate but was defeated in favor of a "watered down" statement that the student lawmakers were "not in complete agreement" with his editorial policies.

That was the second time in two months that Robertson's editorial policies had landed him in trouble with lawmakers. In a January editorial, Robertson criticized the State Sovereignty Commission for its surveillance of Pulitzer Prize-winning editor Hazel Brannon Smith of the Lexington *Advertiser.* The day after that editorial appeared, a seventy-four-year-old unreconstructed representative from Copiah County took to the floor of the house of representatives to inform his colleagues that someone named Robertson "up at Ole Miss" had criticized the Sovereignty Commission for spying on Hazel Smith. "We will run that school as it ought to be run," he said, "or I am for closing it down even if it is the principal school in the state." The *Clarion-Ledger* also scolded the student editor for harping on civil rights rather than states' rights and for criticizing the Sovereignty Commission while ignoring Meredith's suit for the "right" to attend "our University," which was the "real danger" confronting Mississippi.

At a called meeting on Saturday, February 10, 1962, the board of trustees discussed the "real danger" confronting Mississippi and unanimously adopted a statement entitled "Findings of Fact . . . As to the Application of James Meredith." The "Findings of Fact" reiterated the board's assertion that Meredith was denied admission for several valid, nonracial reasons and directed Chancellor Williams not to admit Meredith. Symbolic of those topsy-turvy times, the page containing the "Findings of Fact" was inserted upside-down in the bound volume of the board minutes.

On February 12, 1962, James Meredith appealed Judge Mize's ruling and asked the fifth circuit to order his immediate admission, but a three-judge panel did not grant the order. Elbert P. Tuttle, a member of the panel, urged his fellow judges not to wait but to act immediately to grant the injunction while the appeal was pending. Judge Tuttle argued that the probability of the court's final verdict in favor of Meredith was so overwhelming that any further postponement would be unfair to him. More importantly, he said, a long delay would encourage the "rise of massive resistance." The judges of the fifth circuit, correctly called "unlikely heroes" by writer Jack Bass, may have missed an opportunity to prevent the violence that occurred in the fall by not admitting Meredith in the spring.

On June 25, the fifth circuit reversed the district court's decision and directed Judge Mize to order Meredith's admission for the fall semester. Judge Wisdom's sharply worded opinion criticized the procedural and legal delays and pointed out numerous errors in Judge Mize's conduct of the trial. "A full review of the record," Judge Wisdom wrote, "leads the court inescapably to the conclusion that from the moment the defendants discovered that Meredith was a Negro they engaged in a carefully calculated campaign of delay, harassment, and masterful inactivity. It was a defense designed to discourage and defeat by evasive tactics which would have been a credit to Quintus Fabius Maximus." At Tuttle's insistence the court order stated that anyone acting to thwart, obstruct, or otherwise prevent the admission of Meredith would be in contempt of the fifth circuit. James Howard Meredith had finally won his case in court. "In every other state but Mississippi that would have solved the matter," wrote Russell Barrett, a professor of political science at the university who advocated Meredith's admission, and author of *Integration at Ole Miss.* "Instead," he wrote, "it soon became clear that he had reached but one more detour of the many that remained."

At a called meeting in early September, the board of trustees divested Chancellor Williams and other university officials of the authority to act on James Meredith's application. According to the board's directive all "authority... relating to action on the application of James Howard Meredith is withdrawn from every official of the University of Mississippi... and the same is hereby expressly reserved exclusively unto this Board of Trustees of Institutions of Higher Learning, effective immediately." The board directed the executive secretary to obtain Meredith's application file and "keep the same in his possession until the Board makes final disposition of this matter."

A week after the board divested the university of its authority to act on Meredith's application, Supreme Court Justice Hugo Black vacated all legal stays and objections and ordered the admission of James Meredith. On September 13, 1962, three days after Justice Black's decree, Judge Mize directed the university to admit Meredith. On the evening of Judge Mize's order, Governor Ross Barnett, on a statewide television network, informed the people of Mississippi that they had only two choices: "We must either submit to the unlawful dictates of the federal government, or stand like men and tell them NEVER!" In a veiled threat to close the university, Barnett promised the people who had elected him that no school would be integrated as long as he was governor. Under a 1960 constitutional amendment Governor Barnett had the authority to close a public school to prevent its integration, and his oblique reference to that authority startled many Ole Miss alumni, who feared Barnett's counselors might induce him to close the university. A few days after Barnett's speech a group of prominent alumni organized a secret committee. The committee's singular purpose was to keep the university open, even if it meant admitting Meredith.

The day after Governor Barnett's televised address, the board of trustees met at Jackson to review the court orders pending against them and university officials. There were two significant features of those orders. First, the trustees and university officials were specifically named in the fifth circuit's injunction and would be in contempt if the order was not carried out. Second, the injunction would apply to their successors should the existing board of trustees resign or be impeached. After the board reviewed the various injunctions, Attorney General Joe Patterson and special counsel Charles Clark met with the board and discussed their options. It was evident early in the discussion that the board's only choices were defiance or compliance. Patterson and Clark advised the board that the state had reached its legal limits of resistance, they were under direct orders to admit Meredith, and the failure to do so would likely result in contempt citations. Following Patterson's dismal assessment, Governor Barnett's executive assistant assured the trustees that the governor was formulating a new legal strategy and asked them to take no formal action until they heard from him. The board did not adjourn on that Friday but recessed until Monday and invited Barnett to meet with them and explain his new strategy. Over that weekend Governor Barnett began a series of secret telephone conversations with Attorney General Robert Kennedy and other officials in the justice department.

On Monday, September 17, the trustees reassembled at Jackson for a meeting with Governor Barnett, Attorney General Patterson, and Charles Clark. Barnett briefly outlined his options in the continuing legal battle with James Meredith. A special session of the legislature, which had been called several weeks earlier, would convene the next day, and the governor anticipated legislation that would give him new options for dealing with the crisis. Barnett also told the trustees that Hinds County authorities had charged Meredith with false voter registration, and that it might be possible to arrest and incarcerate him on those charges. When Meredith enrolled at Jackson State in 1960, he registered to vote in Hinds County. State officials claimed he was a legal resident of Attala County, where he owned property, and filed the charges against him. Governor Barnett raised two other options that startled some of the trustees. First, he mentioned the possibility of closing the university. Second, he asked the trustees if they would be willing to accept contempt citations and go to jail.

After Governor Barnett left the meeting the trustees had a lively discussion about contempt of court. Registration was the next week, and, if the university did not admit Meredith university officials and the trustees would be in contempt. Several members of the board stated bluntly that they were not going to be in contempt, which prompted M. M. Roberts, a lawyer and Barnett's most stalwart supporter on the board, to argue that "contempt of court means nothing" and that the federal courts would not cite the trustees. After that haggle, the board reluctantly agreed to give Governor Barnett more time to find a legal means of keeping Meredith out of the university.

As the meeting adjourned, a Jackson reporter asked Verner S. Holmes, vice-president of the board of trustees, if he was willing to go to jail to prevent the integration of his alma mater. Holmes responded, "I have always said that I am willing to go the last mile to preserve the integrity of the University of Mississippi . . . but . . . I am not willing to go to jail . . . and . . . I will not vote to close the University." Holmes's statement angered Barnett's supporters but encouraged Ole Miss students who wanted to keep the university open at almost any cost. Jackson newspapers had already complained that students were more concerned about keeping Ole Miss open than keeping Meredith out.

The day after Holmes stated he would not vote to close the university, Chancellor Williams announced that James Meredith would come to the campus to register on September 20 and he would be treated like any other student. The chancellor's statement was a severe blow to the popular notion that Governor Barnett had the unanimous support of university officials. As it became increasingly apparent that the university would admit James Meredith, the legislature passed Senate Bill 1501, which prohibited the admission of any person to an institution of higher learning who was convicted of a certain class of offenses that included, specifically, false voter registration. The plan, which required the complicity of a large number of public officials, was to convict Meredith on this charge. His conviction would then trigger the provisions of Senate Bill 1501, referred to on the day of its passage as the "Meredith law."

As the legislature was crafting the Meredith law, a Jackson television station challenged the trustees to do their duty. "These men are to be envied by all," an official spokesman said, "for the heroic opportunity that comes to a man only once in his lifetime, whereby he can, if necessary sacrifice his life for his State and, in turn save his country. . . . Their decision is one of not just preventing a negro from entering the University. It will be one to set the precedent that Mississippi is a State of integrity." On the day this editorial aired, Ira Harkey wrote, "In a madhouse's din, Mississippi waits. God help Mississippi." Harkey was the Pulitzer Prize-wining editor of the Pascagoula *Chronicle* and one of the few editors who criticized Governor Barnett's policy of defiance.

On Thursday morning, September 20, the board of trustees convened for its regular monthly meeting in Jackson. The president of the board announced that Meredith would be on the campus later that day to register. A motion directing the chancellor to register Meredith failed by one vote. Then, on a motion by M. M. Roberts, the board of trustees appointed Governor Barnett registrar of the university "with the . . . authority, right, and discretion of this Board to act upon all matters pertaining to . . . James H. Meredith at the University of Mississippi." As the board debated Roberts's motion, Governor Barnett was on his way to Oxford. The governor was armed with an injunction issued earlier that morning by a Hinds County justice of the peace prohibiting the admission of James Meredith to the University of Mississippi. The injunction read in part: "It is against the public policy of the state of Mississippi as well as its laws for a colored person to be admitted as a student at said institution and his enrollment and entry therein would be in violation of the laws of the state of Mississippi." The injunction ordered the board of trustees to carry out a public policy they had sworn under oath did not exist. But it no longer mattered, because by mid-afternoon on September 20, 1962, the board of trustees had relinquished its governance over the University of Mississippi.

At approximately four-thirty, Meredith and a small escort of federal officials arrived on the campus and walked through a boisterous but not unruly crowd to a small auditorium in the Yerby Center where Governor Barnett was seated at a table. As they approached him, the governor asked, "Which of you is Mr. Meredith?" When Meredith identified himself, he was invited to sit at the table. Governor Barnett then read a statement interposing his authority as governor between the United States Supreme Court and the sovereign state of Mississippi and officially denied James Meredith admission to the university. Following a brief but polite exchange, Meredith and his escort returned to Memphis.

After Meredith's departure, Governor Barnett and a few "insiders" celebrated at the alumni center. Many years later, Thomas Turner, one of the celebrants, remembered the conviviality of that occasion. As he and the governor were enjoying the triumph of the moment, he asked, "Ross, how far are you going to go with this thing?" The governor asked Turner how far he would go, and Turner responded, "I'd make them point a gun at me and tell me to move over. Then I'd move over and say come on in." To peals of laughter, the governor said, "That's exactly how far I'm going." Though he spoke in jest in an unguarded moment, Governor Barnett unwittingly scripted the scenario he would later suggest in seriousness as a resolution to the deepening crisis.

Because the university had now officially denied Meredith's admission, Chancellor Williams and other university officials were in contempt and the fifth circuit ordered them to appear in federal court the next day. While the chancellor and several lawyers were preparing his defense in a downtown Jackson office the next morning, Governor Barnett appeared. The governor asked the chancellor to stand firm and go to jail if necessary. Barnett promised to double his salary, but Chancellor Williams refused even to discuss any further resistance, and the matter was dropped. Later that afternoon Judge Mize dismissed the contempt charges against all university officials, because the board of trustees had divested them of the authority to act on Meredith's application. Still later in the day, a three-judge panel issued contempt citations against the board of trustees and ordered the trustees to appear in New Orleans on Monday, September 24, to show cause why they should not be cited.

In the fifth circuit courtroom at New Orleans on Monday morning, the board of trustees heard the plain and simple facts of the case against them. If the trustees did not direct the University of Mississippi to enroll James Meredith, they would be removed from office, fined, imprisoned, and replaced by court-appointed trustees who would order Meredith's admission. After informing the trustees of those facts, the court took a fifteen-minute recess to allow them to confer among themselves and with their counsel. After the recess, the board announced to the court that all trustees present had voted to register James Howard Meredith at two o'clock in Jackson the next day. The one absent member was polled by telephone, and he also agreed.

The board's unanimous vote stunned Governor Barnett. "That's really shocking," he told Attorney General Robert Kennedy when Kennedy called him on Monday night to arrange for Meredith's registration the next day. "I heard it a little while ago," he told Kennedy, "I'm surprised at that, really. They were so firm about it two days ago. They changed their minds mighty quick." Barnett was so shaken he could not carry on a coherent conversation and frequently interrupted his telephone conversation with Kennedy to confer with his advisors. Meredith's safety was uppermost in Kennedy's mind, and he pressed Barnett for assurance that state authorities would maintain peace and order. The governor finally ended the conversation, "I am in a big hurry here now. I appreciate your calling. I will let you know tomorrow whether or not I can advise you of our proceeding and," Kennedy interrupted, "And work out his protection?" Barnett answered, "I will let you know what our proceedings will be." Kennedy said, "Thank you, Governor."

Robert Kennedy's fabled skills for problem solving failed him in the Meredith crisis. Both President Kennedy and the attorney general were extremely reluctant to use federal troops to force Meredith's admission.

"As smart as they were," Governor J. P. Coleman observed, "they let Ross Barnett finally drive them . . . into a corner where they finally had to [use troops] anyway." Robert Kennedy basically agreed with Coleman's assessment, though he used a different metaphor. "What I was trying to avoid," he wrote several years later, "was having to send troops and trying to avoid having a federal presence in Mississippi. In my judgement, what [Barnett] was trying to accomplish was the avoidance of integration at the University of Mississippi, number one. And if he couldn't do that, to be forced to do it by our heavy hand; and his preference was with troops. . . . He had people pulling and pushing him from so many different directions that I think he just got himself into a bigger and bigger box. He eventually pulled me in with him." If there had been any way to avoid the use of troops, and if Kennedy could have done anything to prevent Barnett from pulling him into that box, it had to happen on Tuesday, September 25, because, after that, the drama would play itself out.

When the board of trustees convened in Jackson on Tuesday, September 25, they found their offices in the Woolfolk state office building overrun with legislators, Barnett's counselors, highway patrolmen, and the media. When E. R. Jobe finally got to his office, he found Barnett sitting at his desk talking on the telephone. It was shortly after one o'-clock and the governor was talking to Robert Kennedy, who told the governor that Meredith would be at the Woolfolk building within an hour. Barnett was evasive and ambiguous about what might happen when he arrived, which made Kennedy uneasy. He would not put Meredith at risk.

Shortly after that conversation, Burke Marshall of the justice department called Thomas Tubb, the president of the board of trustees. Tubb told Marshall that Robert Ellis, the university registrar, was testifying before a legislative committee that "would use police if necessary to prevent him from leaving the room where he was being questioned." Charles Clark, who was in the board office when Marshall called Tubb, advised the justice department that the board of trustees would "stick to the letter of the court's order," which required that Meredith appear at the board office by two o'clock to register. If Meredith was not there by two o'clock, Clark said he would have to "be registered . . . at Oxford at some time in the future." Burke Marshall telephoned Judge Tuttle and asked him to extend the time during which Meredith's registration could take place. Tuttle did so, but Robert Kennedy was still concerned for Meredith's safety. At four o'clock Kennedy called Barnett and again pressed for an assurance that Meredith would be protected, and that state police would maintain order. Governor Barnett assured him that everything was under control.

At about four-thirty, John Doar of the justice department and Chief U.S. Marshal James McShane arrived at the Woolfolk building and escorted Meredith through a large crowd to the board office. As they arrived, a Barnett aide rapped sharply on the closed door. The governor appeared and asked, as he had at their meeting on the campus, and now for the bank of television cameras, "Which of you gentlemen is Mr. Meredith?" The governor then read a proclamation denying Meredith admission to the university, adding "I do so politely." The federal officials, mocking the governor, agreed to leave politely. As they walked down the corridor, Governor Barnett called out in a practiced afterward, "Y'all come see me at the mansion." He turned back into the crowded office amid cheers, Rebel yells, shouts of "Yea, Ross," "You told 'em, Ross," and the popular strains of his theme song, "Roll with Ross."

Most people in that restive crowd of two thousand milling around the Woolfolk building were caught up in the emotion of the moment. Some had come to berate the board of trustees, others to support another lost cause. A few had come to stand, quietly across the street, in the eye of history. As Meredith and his federal escort were leaving the Woolfolk building, their car stopped at a traffic light. "Just as the light was about to change," Meredith remembered, "Marshal McShane asked me if those were some of my friends, indicating a group of six or seven Negroes standing on the corner. I suppose they had been waving at us, but I hadn't seen them. I waved at them as we pulled away from the light. They were all common folk, my people, maids still in uniform and common laborers, but the enthusiasm, the friendliness, and above all the pride they displayed [was] overwhelming. This is what I was fighting for, and I had my reward in the brief seconds that I saw my unknown friends on that corner."

Early the next morning, Wednesday, September 26, Burke Marshall called Tom Watkins, one of Governor Barnett's most trusted advisors. Watkins agreed that the "matter had gone too far" and told Marshall that "if there is to be any school integration in Mississippi it would have to be done forcibly." Watkins suggested that on the "next effort to escort Meredith into the University" federal officials "should 'gently' attempt to push the Governor aside [but] should use the mildest kind of force." Watkins explained, "This would make the Governor's point, and give him an out because the federal government would have forcibly brought about desegregation." Marshall passed that information on to McShane and Doar, who put the thesis to a quick test.

When Meredith and his escort arrived at the university later that morning, Lieutenant Governor Paul Johnson and a phalanx of highway patrol blocked the entrance. Barnett remained in Jackson in case Meredith tried to register at the board office. Doar and McShane were instructed to "gently" muscle their way through the line. Not privy to the plan, Johnson jostled McShane and Doar as they tried to break through, and "a ridiculous pantomime" rippled up and down the line. The *Mississippian* was bemused by the "comic elbowing and shoving." James Meredith enjoyed the scene, admitting, "I could not pass up this golden opportunity to get in a little elbowing." He elbowed a representative of the Citizens' Council. After a few minutes McShane doubled up his fist, shook it in the face of the lieutenant governor and said, or perhaps he was asking, "You understand that we have got to break through." Apparently Johnson did not understand or, more likely, he did not want to be remembered as the "one who stepped aside." "The Little General," as Meredith called him, balled up his fist and shook it at McShane. When all the fist shaking and shoving was over, Doar, McShane, and Meredith left Oxford and returned to Memphis. And the telephones started ringing.

On the morning of this "ridiculous pantomime" the *Mississippian* printed the following telegram:

> Dick Wilson, President
> Student Body
> University of Mississippi
>
> Students at Mississippi State University have watched with concern your grave situation. On behalf of our student body we send our concern and hope that the students and the University will not be seriously injured. Sincerely,
>
> Robert L. Taylor, President
> Student Association
> Mississippi State University

After Paul Johnson blocked Meredith from the campus, Burke Marshall called Watkins and asked him what had gone wrong. Watkins explained that the federal authorities "had not used enough force." How much force is enough, Marshall asked. Watkins suggested that the next escort should include "marshals with sidearms." Marshall agreed to send Meredith back to the campus the next day, Thursday, September 27, with an escort of twenty-five armed marshals "if it were clearly understood that the resistance to this amount of force would be token." Watkins told Marshall that he would talk to the governor and get back with him.

Over the next several hours Barnett and justice department officials discussed a most bizarre arrangement. They first agreed that the lead marshal would draw his gun, but Governor Barnett later decided that a single gun was not enough show of force. They then agreed that the lead marshal would draw his gun and the other marshals would slap their holsters as if ready to draw. That was acceptable, at first, until Governor Barnett had second thoughts and said to Robert Kennedy, "I was under the impression that they were all going to draw their guns. This could be very embarrassing. We got a big crowd here and if one pulls his gun and we all turn it would be very embarrassing. Isn't it possible to have them all pull their guns? . . . They must all pull their guns. Then they should point their guns at us and then we could step aside." As this haggling continued, Robert Kennedy pressed the governor for a guarantee that he would keep the peace and protect Meredith and the marshals. When Barnett wavered, Kennedy called the whole deal off and directed McShane and Doar not to take Meredith to the campus Thursday afternoon. He told Governor Barnett they would try again next week, maybe Monday or Tuesday.

After this impasse developed, President John Kennedy called Governor Barnett on Saturday morning, September 29, to join the search for a peaceful resolution of the Meredith crisis. The affable young president from Massachusetts and the wily old governor of Mississippi had a pleasant talk. President Kennedy assured the governor, however, that he would use all the resources of his office to carry out the court order. The governor explained to the president that Tom Watkins was at that moment trying to work out a plan to resolve the situation. Within less than an hour the president and the governor were back on the telephone.

The president called Barnett to discuss a proposal Tom Watkins had just made to the attorney general. President Kennedy put Robert Kennedy on the line to explain the plan. Watkins suggested a "hidden ball trick." The plan was for federal authorities to announce that Meredith would go to Oxford on Monday, October 1. On the basis of that information, Governor Barnett and Lieutenant Governor Johnson would both be at Oxford to block his admission. In the meantime Meredith would actually go to Jackson where he would be registered in the board office. Governor Barnett could claim the Kennedys had misled him. President Kennedy even agreed to let Barnett scold him in the sternest language if that would serve his political interest in Mississippi. With Meredith registered, Barnett would then declare that the battle was lost and would allow Meredith to attend the university. Governor Barnett was enthusiastic about the proposal and saw it as a solution to the impasse.

To President Kennedy the one remaining but most important consideration was Meredith's safety, and he was relieved when Governor Barnett called him at five o'clock Saturday afternoon. Barnett assured the president that the diversion plan was the best possible solution and he would see to it that the highway patrol maintained order. Governor Barnett spent the rest of the afternoon trying to persuade his counselors to accept the agreement he made with the president. By half time of the Ole Miss-Kentucky football game that night, the governor, known fondly as Ole Ross, had lost his own resolve to honor the agreement. As the Ole Miss band unfurled the world's largest Confederate flag on the playing field and the stands were awash in a sea of Rebel flags, Governor Barnett stood at the fifty yard line. One of Mississippi's last great stump speakers, Ole Ross, in his raspy voice, his right fist clinched, circling in rhythm with his words, proclaimed:

> I love Mississippi . . .
> I love her people . . .
> I love her customs . . .

The words ricocheted through Mississippi Memorial Stadium as forty thousand fans erupted in thunderous ovation and hailed their leader and lofted their Rebel flags into a night sky.

After the game, Governor Barnett called a justice department official, who forwarded the call to the attorney general at his home. Governor Barnett told Kennedy he wanted to call off the deal. That unexpected turn of events angered Kennedy and he accused the governor of breaking his word to the president. The two men ended the conversation amicably with Barnett agreeing to keep working on the situation. Governor Barnett also promised to call Kennedy early Sunday morning to let him know if the situation changed during the night. Robert Kennedy called the president at the White House and told him the deal was off. The president reluctantly signed the documents federalizing the Mississippi National Guard and authorized the secretary of the army to send troops to Oxford if it became necessary. It did become necessary, and, over the next few weeks, several thousand troops went to Oxford to enforce the court order admitting James Meredith to the University of Mississippi.

On Sunday morning, September 30, 1962, Governor Barnett called Attorney General Kennedy. That disjointed conversation dragged on for thirty minutes, with the governor making one last desperate effort to postpone the whole affair. Failing at postponement, Barnett and Tom Watkins proposed another mock confrontation between federal and state authorities.

> Governor: We will have about 175 or 180 highway patrolmen in there—unarmed; no guns, no sticks of any kind. We will have quite a number of sheriffs unarmed—probably 75 or 100 deputy sheriffs.... Then they will form this second line. The highway patrolmen will form the first line; the sheriffs the next. The sheriffs will have probably 200 or 300 soldiers behind them. No one will be armed. I will be in the front line and when Meredith presents himself, I'll do like I did before. I will read a proclamation denying him entrance. I will tell the people of Mississippi now that I want peace and we must have no violence, no bloodshed. When you draw the guns, I will then tell the people. In other words, we will step aside and you can walk in.
>
> Kennedy: I think it is silly going through this whole facade of your standing there; our people drawing guns; your stepping aside; to me it is dangerous and I think this has gone beyond the stage of politics, and you have a responsibility to the people of that State and to the people of the United States.
>
> Governor: I have said so many times—we couldn't have integration and I have got to do something. I can't just walk back.

This latest suggestion was fraught with such calamitous potential that Robert Kennedy finally rejected it and threatened to expose the governor's secret deal with the president:

> Kennedy: The president is going on TV tonight [Sunday]. He is going through the statement he had with you last night. He will have to say he called up the National Guard; that you had an agreement to permit Meredith to go to Jackson to register, and your lawyer, Mr. Watkins, said this was satisfactory. . . .
>
> Governor: That won't do at all.
>
> Kennedy: You broke your word to him.
>
> Governor: You don't mean the president is going to say that tonight?
>
> Kennedy: Of course he is; you broke your word; now you suggest we send in troops, fighting their way through a barricade.
>
> Governor: Don't say that. Please don't mention it.
>
> Kennedy: The president has to say that. You said we would fly him to Jackson and register him while you had everyone in Oxford. . . .
>
> Governor: Why don't you fly in this afternoon—please let us treat what we say as confidential?
>
> Kennedy: You talk to Watkins and call me back this afternoon. I have discussed this with you before; I want to know specifically the plan you have and how it is going to work. I want to maintain law and order.

Governor Barnett was startled to learn that his conversation with federal authorities had been taped, and that President Kennedy might reveal those negotiations on national television. Bobby Kennedy realized that he had finally gotten through to the governor, and he took advantage of Barnett's fear of exposure. Tom Watkins and Burke Marshall quickly worked out a plan to bring Meredith to the campus later that afternoon.

Since university officials were not expecting Meredith to return to the campus until Monday or Tuesday, Tom Watkins asked Burke Marshall to call Chancellor Williams and tell him that Meredith was coming in that afternoon. Anxious to get one more assurance that state authorities would maintain order, Marshall replied, "We are not going to put Meredith in until the situation is physically stabilized." Watkins told Marshall that the highway patrol had already been sent to Oxford, and he assumed the situation was stable. Marshall then agreed to call Williams.

A few minutes after three o'clock on Sunday afternoon, Hugh Clegg, Chancellor Williams's administrative assistant, answered the downstairs telephone in the chancellor's residence. It was Burke Marshall. Chancellor Williams, L. L. Love (the dean of students), and Clegg were making preparations for Meredith's arrival, which they thought would be on Monday or Tuesday. The three men were stunned when Marshall told them that federal marshals would bring Meredith to the campus within the hour. Clegg told Marshall that the university could not get ready for Meredith's arrival on such short notice and pleaded for a delay, but Marshall replied, "They are coming this afternoon." A short time later Marshall called back and said, "Mr. Clegg, the highway patrolmen have just admitted the U.S. marshals on to your campus." After a brief discussion with Chancellor Williams, Clegg went to his office in the Lyceum. Unaware of the deal between Barnett and Kennedy, Clegg called the governor to tell him that federal marshals were already on the campus and that Meredith was on his way. A secretary in the governor's office told Clegg that Governor Barnett had gone fishing and would not be back until Monday.

Through the late afternoon and into the early evening, a milling crowd of students gathered in front of the Lyceum building, which was surrounded by marshals and other federal officials. Meredith would register in the Lyceum the next morning. The crowd, having been gradually augmented by "outsiders," was by nightfall much larger and more rowdy. At seven-thirty Governor Barnett announced on a statewide radio and television network that Meredith was on the campus. He explained that he had been forced to yield to the "armed forces and oppressive power" of the United States and that he was allowing Meredith's admission to avoid violence and bloodshed.

After the governor's speech, federal officials became increasingly uneasy about the potential for a large-scale riot. The crowd was no longer hurling epithets; they were throwing brickbats, lead pipes, and Molotov cocktails. A bulldozer was driven toward the line of marshals around the Lyceum. Tires on army trucks were slashed and canvas truck tops were set afire. Gunfire could be heard sporadically and rumors circulated through the mob that a coed and a highway patrolman had been killed. At about eight o'clock, just moments before President Kennedy went on national television to announce that Meredith was safely on the campus and would register the next morning, the crowd surged toward the marshals and the order to fire tear gas was given. As the marshals fired the gas into the surging mob, several people, including some highway patrolmen, were hit by the canisters and suffered fractures and broken bones. The pep rally atmosphere was gone, and most of the college students, who had come to see what was happening, went with it. Only the real resisters, the true believers, remained to fight what Willie Morris has called an "echo of the Civil War's last battle."

"We all [sat] on the Chancellor's porch," Hugh Clegg wrote of that long dark night, "watching the sickening scene from a hundred yards away. Automobiles were afire. We feared the Lyceum Building would be burned." One of the men on the chancellor's porch said, "There goes the University." "Just when things seemed the gloomiest," the first contingent of soldiers moved onto the campus. "We almost shouted with joy," Hugh Clegg remembered. The situation stabilized gradually and at six-fifteen in the morning General Charles Billingsly reported that the campus was secure. During the riot Meredith was under guard in his dormitory room in Baxter Hall.

One of the most remarkable aspects of the Sunday night riot, in which two people were killed, was the debate over who started it. In the immediate aftermath, most of the Mississippi press, the highway patrol, and some university officials blamed the riot on the "trigger happy" federal marshals who "jumped the gun" and prematurely fired tear gas into the crowd in front of the Lyceum. To counter those charges, sixty-five Ole Miss faculty and staff issued a signed, public statement. The document, which took no little courage to sign, especially for the untenured, exonerated the marshals and blamed the rioters. At the request of university officials, Senator James Eastland, chairman of the judiciary committee, was putting together a subcommittee chaired by Senator Sam Ervin of North Carolina to investigate the riot when Governor Barnett's emissaries asked Eastland to quash the federal inquiry. Barnett and other public officials preferred an investigation by the state legislature or by a Lafayette County grand jury. Both entities conducted investigations, and both blamed the riot on the marshals and the justice department.

Just before eight o'clock Monday morning, October 1, 1962, James Meredith, in the company of federal marshals, entered the Lyceum. Meredith completed a registration form, paid his fees, broke the color barrier in Mississippi, and hurried off to an eight o'clock American history class taught by Professor Clare Marquette. As Meredith left the Lyceum, he was asked if he was now happy to be a student at the University of Mississippi. Meredith looked around at the battle-scarred campus and said, "This is not a happy day."

Sidna Brower, editor of the *Mississippian,* now published daily, also found little to be happy about. On September 21 she complimented Ole Miss students for their good behavior, especially those who prevented a small group of students from taking down the American flag and raising the colors of the Confederacy. On October 1, however, Brower was disappointed in the "students who started out yesterday by shouting slogans of pride in Mississippi and ended up with nothing to be proud of."

As Brower expressed her disappointment in the behavior of Ole Miss students, William H. Mounger, an Ole Miss alumnus and president of Lamar Life Insurance Company, communicated the same sentiment to a much larger audience. Early that morning, Mounger appeared on a Jackson television station owned by Lamar Life and made an impassioned plea for law and order and for public support of the university. The next day Mounger and 127 other business leaders met in Jackson and issued a statement urging all Mississippians to accept a "sane [and] sensible" approach to the social and racial changes taking place. The peaceful acceptance of those changes was absolutely necessary, they said, if Mississippi was to "march forward with honor, dignity and respect." Though it might seem mild from the perspective of nearly forty years later, it was a bold and significant statement for that time and place. The import of the statement was that Governor Barnett could no longer count on the business community's support in his defiance of the United States Supreme Court. It was also a public pronouncement that the University of Mississippi should and would remain open, even if integrated.

While Chancellor Williams was surveying the extensive damage early Monday morning, campus security informed him that only one professor was unable to get to the campus. The army had cordoned off the campus and severely restricted access. Williams was also relieved to learn that about 60 percent of the students were in class, though some classes were cancelled because of the tear gas. By week's end most of the students who had been called home by their parents were back on campus, and the predicted exodus did not occur. The spring enrollment of 4,280 was down less than 500 from the 4,770 fall enrollment.

In the weeks following Meredith's enrollment, Chancellor Williams's greatest challenge was to keep the university open. In the early fall, history professor James Silver wrote his daughter that the "chief desire now of the extremists is not to *get* Meredith but to provoke an incident [that] Barnett would use to close the school. Closing the school is now their aim." The homecoming football game with the University of Houston on October 6 was an opportunity for just such an incident. Early in the week Robert Kennedy called Coach John Vaught and asked him to do what he could "to keep the situation calm." Vaught recalled in his memoirs, "I said I would, but by Tuesday our Homecoming game with Houston had become a pawn between state and federal forces. . . . It took a tremendous fight to keep the game . . . from being canceled. I felt it essential that the game be played, that it might be the key to getting the campus to settle down." Through the early part of the week it was uncertain if, when, and where the game would be played; the only thing for sure was that it would not be played in Oxford, a decision Vaught said was "made in Washington." By mid-week the game had been moved to Houston, and Vaught told his players to be ready to fly to Houston on Friday. However, after "much maneuvering by Chancellor Williams and Tad Smith, the Justice Department and the Army agreed to let the Homecoming game be played in Jackson" on Saturday afternoon.

Vaught kept his pregame pep talk before the Houston game brief and simple. He said, "It is very important that we play this game, boys, and we have to win it." Ole Miss did win, and, according to Relman Morin, the Pulitzer Prize-winning associated press sportswriter, Ole Miss's 40–0 victory over Houston "temporarily dulled the anguish of racial strife." The Houston victory was the second win of a ten-win perfect season, but on that cool autumn afternoon in Jackson's Memorial Stadium, the only other game Ole Miss fans cared about was the Michigan-Army game. Ole Miss fans greeted the announcement that Michigan defeated Army with thunderous applause.

The Houston victory was crucial, according to Coach Vaught, for the 1962 season and for the university. "Boys became men that [day]," he wrote, "and I think then and there they sensed that no one would be able to stop them, and that a university rode on their shoulder pads." Coach Vaught may have overstated the importance of football when he titled the chapter in his memoirs on the Meredith crisis "Football Saves a School," but maybe not. The 1962 team was the only undefeated and untied team in the university's history, and produced two All-Americans, lineman Jim Dunaway and quarterback Glynn Griffing. The 1962 team won the Southeastern Conference championship and defeated Arkansas in the Sugar Bowl. That level of success created an enormous interest and pride in the Ole Miss football program and generated strong public support for keeping the university open.

As Coach Vaught and his assistants were preparing for the Mississippi State game, Chancellor Williams and other university officials were preparing for the annual meeting of the Southern Association of Colleges and Schools in Dallas. On the agenda of that meeting was the accreditation of Mississippi's institutions of higher learning. This was the third time in thirty years that the issue was before the association, and there was strong support for the expulsion of Ole Miss. Even though the board of trustees had transferred its authority to admit or reject James Meredith to the state's political establishment, the Southern Association did not expel the university. Instead, it placed Ole Miss on "extraordinary status" and warned Mississippi officials that the institution would remain under "close observation" until the 1963 annual meeting, at which time its status would be reviewed.

At the association's next annual meeting in December 1963, Chancellor Williams reported that the university's academic integrity was not compromised during the last year and that a second African American student had enrolled at Ole Miss without incident. The College Delegate Assembly accepted Williams's report and returned the University of Mississippi to full and unqualified membership. Following that action, the chancellor reported to the board of trustees that the university survived the Meredith crisis and retained its accreditation. He also assured the board that good order and student discipline were being restored on the campus.

During the Sunday night riot, federal authorities apprehended approximately 160 rioters, 25 of whom were Ole Miss students. An additional 25 students from other southern colleges were also taken into custody. Of the 25 Ole Miss students, 8 appeared before the student judicial council and were subjected to varying degrees of disciplinary action, though Russell Barrett wrote that "outside pressure prevented any expulsions." When it became known that several Ole Miss students were taken into custody, Governor Barnett appointed "a nine member Legal Committee to protect the rights of the students at the University to practice freedom of speech and freedom of assembly." The Jackson press warned university officials that the legislature and the governor would "watch with a jaundiced eye any attempt to apply punitive action against [student] patriots."

Although there was tremendous off-campus pressure not to discipline Ole Miss students, the administration was severely criticized for not taking stronger action against students who harassed Meredith and the white students who befriended him. One of the administration's severest critics was Sidna Brower, editor of the *Mississippian.* Although nominated for a Pulitzer Prize and praised by the faculty, who said her courageous editorials "significantly contributed to the University's integrity," Brower was formally reprimanded by the campus senate for her criticism of student behavior.

Sidna Brower was also one of the strongest defenders of Raymond Kerciu, an Ole Miss professor of art who became entangled in a legal dispute. In several of his paintings depicting the riot, Professor Kerciu used the Confederate flag as a backdrop; across it were scribbled racial epithets he had heard during the riot, one being "Kennedy's Koon Keepers." A law student charged Kerciu with violating the state's desecration statute, a law that makes it illegal to deface the Confederate flag. The university defended Professor Kerciu's right of free speech and offered to provide him with legal counsel, but the charges were eventually dropped.

A student demonstration in late October finally prompted university officials to adopt a "get tough" policy regarding student discipline. On Monday night, October 29, 1962, students bombarded Baxter Hall with cherry bombs for about an hour and threw eggs and bottles at Meredith and his escort as they left the building. Two days after this incident, Chancellor Williams assembled the male students and announced the new policy. The chancellor told the students if they could not support "peaceful and orderly conditions, be advised that I am prepared to see us part company." Chancellor Williams's announcement was followed by the arrest of seven of the Monday night demonstrators and the expulsion of four of them. Students, faculty, and even the general public, which was weary of the continuous reports of disorder at the university, welcomed the new restrictions on student behavior. In a Jackson speech defending the policy, Vice Chancellor Alton Bryant accused "faceless and nameless . . . adult agitators" of being "moral and physical cowards" who used students as "pawns" to further their aim of closing the university. Bryant called on "responsible citizens" to offset the influence of such people and to support "order and sanity" in Mississippi.

The "get tough" policy announced in November 1962 was followed in January 1963 by the "gag rule," which prohibited inflammatory statements or speeches by university students, faculty, and staff. Sidna Brower saw good results from the new disciplinary policy and reported in early January 1963 that things were almost back to normal. As the campus was returning to normal and Ole Miss students were celebrating the 1963 Sugar Bowl win over Arkansas, James Meredith made an announcement that "stunned most of his friends and delighted his enemies."

At a Baxter Hall press conference on January 7, 1963, Meredith announced, "I have decided not to register for classes during the second semester . . . unless very definite and positive changes are made to make my situation more conducive to learning. . . . As to what I will do, I am not prepared to say at this time." Meredith's announcement, and the increased harassment that immediately followed it, brought renewed pressure on the university from the justice department and others to make Meredith's "situation more conducive to learning," which may have been the intent of his announcement. Meredith's supporters on the campus (especially James Silver and Russell Barrett), President Kennedy, and the attorney general all urged Meredith to remain at Ole Miss and complete the requirements for graduation.

At a press conference in Jackson on January 30, Meredith announced that "the Negro" was not returning to Ole Miss. After a brief pause, he said, but "I, J. H. Meredith, will register for the second semester." Meredith concluded that Ole Miss students were "basically good people" and that there were indications that he could remain at the university "under adequate, if not ideal, conditions." During the spring and summer sessions, conditions improved significantly, and, by the late spring, most of the troops were gone. In the summer Meredith's family visited him, and he gave them a guided tour of the campus. When they dined with him in the cafeteria, there was none of the "table banging" that had often greeted Meredith when he entered the cafeteria during the fall semester. The admission of Cleve McDowell in the summer of 1963 was also accomplished without incident. McDowell, the university's second

African American student, was admitted to the law school under court order, though the law school had already notified him that he would be accepted. Meredith and McDowell roomed together that summer in Baxter Hall. McDowell's first semester at Ole Miss was Meredith's last.

In early August, Meredith took his final exams and completed the requirements for a bachelor of arts degree in political science. On the last day of final examinations, he wore a lapel pin that was popular during the weeks before his admission. On the pin, against a black background, was the word NEVER printed in white. Meredith wore the pin upside down. Even though Meredith had met the requirements for graduation, he had one last hurdle to overcome. Several members of the board of trustees accused Meredith of violating the chancellor's "gag rule" against inflammatory statements. They cited his speech following the assassination of Medgar Evers and moved to deny him his diploma. A few days after Evers's murder on June 11, 1963, Meredith had condemned "Southern governors . . . blind courts and prejudiced juries" for creating a climate of hate that produced the murder of his good friend. The motion to deny Meredith his diploma lost by a six-to-five vote.

On August 18, 1963, James Meredith and other candidates for graduation wound their way from the Lyceum through the tree-shaded campus to the Grove where approximately fifty of his friends and family took their places among the hundreds of other friends and families of the graduates. Among Meredith's guests were Mrs. Medgar Evers, Aaron Henry, state president of the NAACP, and R. Jess Brown, one of Meredith's Mississippi lawyers. The "carefully planned ceremony went off with deceptive simplicity." The thought occurred to Russell Barrett, "how easy it all could be."

Nearly a month before Meredith's graduation, the few remaining federal troops moved off the campus, and by July 24 they had left Oxford. After Meredith's graduation, the marshals were also gone, which made Cleve McDowell uneasy. When he returned for the fall semester in September 1963, he brought a small handgun to the campus, a violation of university policy. On September 23, McDowell was returning from a meeting with the United States attorney in Oxford, where he had gone to ask for protection, and was running late for class. As he hurried into the Lamar Building, he dropped his sunglasses. When he leaned over to pick them up, the gun fell out of his pocket. Two students who witnessed the incident called the Lafayette County sheriff, who arrested McDowell after class. The student judicial council eventually expelled McDowell. University officials regretted his expulsion, because, after going through so much travail, the university was again "an all white school," a condition that delighted a Jackson newspaper, which hailed McDowell's expulsion because it erased the "ONLY MIXING BLOT IN STATE."

If the board of trustees had its way, Ole Miss would have remained an all-white school. In late February 1964, Cleveland Donald, a seventeen-year-old honor student from Tougaloo, applied for admission to the university. In May the university informed Donald that his application was in order and mailed him a certificate of enrollment for the summer session. When the trustees learned of Donald's application, they filed a motion in federal court to deny his admission because of the "exploding tensions" associated with Mississippi's impending "Long Hot Summer." The federal court denied the board's motion and ordered Donald's admission. Cleveland Donald was admitted and received his undergraduate degree from Ole Miss with a major in history. He later earned a Ph.D. at Cornell University. In 1979 Professor Donald returned to his alma mater to become the first director of the university's African American Studies Program.

In the fall of 1964, Irwin Walker became the first African American student admitted to Ole Miss without a court order. Following his enrollment, the number of black students increased gradually, and by the spring semester of 1966 fourteen African Americans were enrolled at the university. Among them were Reuben V. Anderson, the law school's first black graduate and the first black justice of the state supreme court, and four coeds, Joyce Jones, Verna Bailey, Billie Joyce Ware, and Patricia Anderson, a law student. In a candid discussion with Marshall Frady in the spring of 1966, several African American students talked about their collegiate experience. The conversation inevitably turned to symbols. Irwin Walker asked Frady to imagine what it was like to go to a football game with all those white folks singing *Dixie* and waving Rebel flags. Earnest Watson said he wished Ole Miss had a song he could sing and a spirit symbol he could wave at football games, but he just could not sing *Dixie* and wave the Rebel flag. In a moment of comic relief, Walker said, "Next year, you watch, I'm gonna have me a Rebel flag to wave and I'm gonna stand up for *Dixie.*" Verna Bailey added, seriously, that it would "be 20 years before things are normal" for black students at Ole Miss. In the summer session following this interview, black enrollment more than doubled, from fourteen to thirty. The *Mississippian* noted that the registration of those thirty African American students attracted "no attention."

The lack of attention given to those thirty students was in striking contrast to the interest generated by Robert Kennedy's visit to Ole Miss earlier that spring. The law school speakers' bureau invited Kennedy, who was then a senator from New York, to address Ole Miss students and faculty on March 18, 1966. His appearance created so much interest that his speech was moved from a small auditorium in the law school to the coliseum. As Senator and Mrs. Kennedy entered the coliseum, more than five thousand people greeted them with a standing ovation. Mary Cain, the fiery lady editor of the *Summit Sun,* cited this ovation as positive proof that the University of Mississippi was a "hotbed of liberalism." In his introduction of Senator Kennedy, Ed Ellington, chairman of the speakers' bureau, cited Kennedy's appearance as proof that the University of Mississippi was a place where all views and opinions are freely expressed. "After this day," he said, "never again let it be uttered that this is a closed society."

Like Mark Twain's comment that the reports of his death were greatly exaggerated, Ellington's remark was a bit premature. Aaron Henry's lecture to an Ole Miss law class in November 1966 prompted the board of trustees to adopt a policy requiring board approval before any person could be invited to speak on campus. When Professor William Dellinger announced that Henry would speak to his class, a white student informed the professor that he would not sit in the same room with Henry, but he would like to hear what Henry had to say. The professor agreed to leave the classroom door open and allow the student to sit in the hallway to listen to Henry's lecture. The same terrible complexities of race that kept the artist M. B. Mayfield inside the broom closet kept this law student outside that classroom.

William Dellinger, Michael Horowitz, George Strickler, and Michael Trister were among a group of Yale-trained law professors Dean Joshua Morse brought to Ole Miss in the late 1960s. Their "liberal leanings" and their participation in the Legal Services program, especially after they filed a school desegregation suit in Holly Springs, provoked the wrath of several legislators, who introduced several resolutions to move the law school to Jackson. Three law professors — Stickler, Trister, and Luther McDougall — became casualties of the closed society after they refused to discontinue their association with Legal Services. They were not actually dismissed but were "removed from the payroll."

Other casualties of the closed society were Robert Farley, William P. Murphy, Russell Barrett, and James Silver. When Dean Farley reached the mandatory retirement age for administrators, the university did not offer him the customary opportunity to remain on the teaching faculty. "Gentleman that he was," James Silver said, "Farley left quietly" in 1962. Law professor William P. Murphy was denied tenure and left that same year. After the *Brown* decision in 1954, Farley and Murphy stated publicly that Mississippi must obey the orders of the United States Supreme Court based on the Fourteenth Amendment. The Sovereignty Commission and the Citizens' Council accused the two professors of teaching legal heresy and demanded their dismissal. Nearly a century earlier, another University of Mississippi law professor, Thomas Walton, had been excoriated for saying the same thing. Professor Russell Barrett remained at the university until his retirement, though he did not receive the salary increments a full professor would have normally received.

The most celebrated casualty of the closed society was James Silver, the Ole Miss history professor who coined the phrase. In the fall of 1963 Professor Silver was president of the Southern Historical Association. His presidential address, which he expanded and published as a book titled *Mississippi: The Closed Society,* created a firestorm. The state's power structure was in nearly unanimous agreement that Silver was a threat to "our way of life" and that he should be dismissed from the university. Following his presidential address, the board of trustees appointed a special committee, chaired by M. M. Roberts, to gather evidence of "contumacious conduct" necessary to dismiss Silver from his tenured position as professor of history, which he had held since 1936. To gather information that might be useful in their case against him, the board of trustees hired private detectives to spy on Professor Silver and to follow him to speaking engagements around the country.

While the board of trustees was conducting its investigation, the Mississippi legislature also took up the Silver issue. On March 25, 1964, a state representative demanded Silver's dismissal and pledged himself to any course of action short of violence to oust the professor. A state senator introduced a bill to restrict Silver from speaking on certain topics, but as he warmed to the idea, he decided Silver should be fired. The senator conceded that Silver's dismissal would enhance his reputation in the North, but that should not be a consideration because "it is better," he said, "that he get national fame than for us to receive social death." The senator concluded that if the university would not fire Silver, the legislature should. As the board of trustees was investigating and the legislature was fulminating, Professor Silver took a year's leave of absence to serve as a visiting professor at Notre Dame University. Following that year, Silver did not return to Ole Miss, although he wanted to very much. University officials indicated to him that it would be best if he did not return to Oxford, his home for the last thirty years. Gentleman that he was, James Silver did not return.

Although the University of Mississippi suffered, still suffers, from the Meredith crisis, Ole Miss has endured and flourished because of the change that conflict engendered. The admission of African Americans enlarged, enhanced, and enriched the university. In time James Meredith would call himself a loyal son of Ole Miss and his alma mater now houses his personal papers, along with those of James Eastland, J. D. Williams, Verner Holmes, James Silver and Russell Barrett. Future generations of students and scholars who study the contours of American race relations will come to Ole Miss and consult these papers. If the history of the University of Mississippi were to be written in one word, it would be continuity.

Chapter 12

ON THE EVE OF A NEW MILLENNIUM, 1968–1995

Ole Miss is for Civil Rights.

John Ates, ASB President, 1989

In the aftermath of the Meredith crisis Chancellor J. D. Williams conceded that "riot and lawlessness" is America's image of Ole Miss. "I will not try to brighten that picture," he said, "but . . . that is not the whole picture." The public perception of the University of Mississippi, shaped during a long night of racial violence and reinforced by three decades of controversy over the Rebel flag, is not inaccurate, but it is incomplete; it is a truthful image, but it is only part of the truth. Some students did riot on the eve of Meredith's admission, but the elected editor of the campus newspaper condemned their actions. Many students did harass James Meredith, but others befriended him. Mississippi was an authoritarian state but student editors Albin Krebs, Stanley Dearman, James Robertson, Sidna Brower, and many of their professors defied the keepers of the closed society. More than sixty Ole Miss faculty and staff put their livelihoods at risk when they defended the federal marshals against the charge that they caused the riot. When black students were arrested after a demonstration in Fulton Chapel in 1970, the faculty senate took up their cause, recommended that charges against them be dropped, and called on the university to address their "legitimate grievances." When a racist group held a demonstration on the campus in 1989, John Ates, the Ole Miss student body president, organized a counter demonstration. One of the placards that greeted the racists read: "Ole Miss is for Civil Rights." Even though the controversy over the Rebel flag continues, and the national press spotlights every new flap, the student senate, the faculty senate, the administration, the alumni association, and the athletic department have publicly and officially disassociated the university from the Confederate flag.

During the three decades between Chancellor Williams's retirement in January 1968 and the national town hall meeting conducted by the President's Initiative on Race in Fulton Chapel in March 1998, another image of Ole Miss has emerged. John Hope Franklin, chairman of the President's Initiative on Race who visited the university in the 1960s, found upon his return visit for the town hall meeting a "complete revolution" in race relations at Ole Miss. So encouraged by what he saw at the University of Mississippi, Franklin said maybe "we don't have quite as far to go as we thought we did."

When Chancellor Williams ended his twenty-two year administration, the longest in the institution's history, Porter L. Fortune, Jr., was appointed the thirteenth chancellor of the University of Mississippi. After serving in the South Pacific during World War II and earning a Ph.D. in history from the University of North Carolina in 1949, Fortune began his academic career at the University of Southern Mississippi. During his twelve-year tenure at Southern Mississippi, Fortune served as professor of history, dean of the basic college, and dean of the graduate school. At the time of his appointment in February 1968 Fortune was executive secretary of the National Exchange Club.

One of the legacies of Chancellor Fortune's sixteen-year tenure was an extensive construction program that changed the physical appearance of the Ole Miss campus, though its beauty, green spaces, and ancient oaks remained. The process began in 1971 when the chancellor's family moved from the residence in Barnard Observatory to the Carrier House on west Fraternity Row. The chancellor's new residence was a gift to the university from Mr. and Mrs. Robert Carrier. After the chancellor vacated the observatory, the building was eventually restored to the period of its construction. This classic antebellum structure, which is listed on the National Register of Historic Places, is now the home of the Center for the Study of Southern Culture.

Perhaps the two buildings that most dramatically altered the appearance of the campus were the Ole Miss Union, completed in 1976, and Lamar Hall, finished the following year. The Ole Miss Union houses the university bookstore, post office, cafeteria, student government offices, and game rooms. Lamar Hall houses the law school, the James O. Eastland Law Library, and the *Law Journal.* These two large structures are not consistent in style or design with other campus buildings and both were controversial at the time of their construction. Two other new facilities also altered the appearance of the campus. A chemistry building, named for Victor A. Coulter, a professor of chemistry from 1926 to 1960 and dean of the college of liberal arts from 1936 to 1957, was completed in 1978. The other facility, which is one of the most popular and frequently used buildings on the campus, is the Health, Physical Education, and Recreation Center named in honor of Thomas N. Turner, a Bilbo informant, a Barnett confidant, and a member of the college board. At the time of its completion in 1983, the Turner Center was the most expensive facility ever built at a Mississippi institution of higher learning.

Another major addition to the university's physical plant, and to its intellectual landscape, was the first phase of the Cultural Center, a collection of several buildings devoted to the visual and performing arts and to the preservation of the university's literary heritage. The initial phase of this long term endeavor began in 1972 with the acquisition and restoration of Rowan Oak, William Faulkner's home; the purchase of the Walton-Young House in 1974; the acquisition of the Skipwith estate, which included the Mary Buie Museum; and the construction in 1977 of the Kate Skipwith Teaching Museum. The Skipwith Museum contains the only major collection of the dream and vision paintings of Oxford's Theora Hamblett, a primitive artist in the tradition of Grandma Moses. Hamblett's work is featured in several major museums and a number of private collections. The Walton-Young House, constructed in 1880 by Horace Walton, is now a unit within the university museum complex that features the decorative arts of the late nineteenth century. During his years at the university, as a student and professor, Stark Young lived in the Walton house. A poet, novelist, and literary critic, and a contributor to *I'll Take My Stand,* published in 1930, Young was a leading figure in the Agrarian Movement that was prominent in mid-twentieth century American literature.

The restoration of Rowan Oak and the inauguration of the annual Faulkner conference in 1974, along with the appointment of Willie Morris as writer in residence, spawned a literary renewal in Oxford and Ole Miss. Chancellor Fortune often said that of the appointments made during his administration, Morris's was one of those that gave him the greatest pleasure. As a prominent author and former editor of *Harper's* magazine, Morris was a friend to many of America's contemporary writers, and through his visiting writers program he brought many of them, including William Styron, to Ole Miss during the 1980s.

While Morris was promoting a literary culture on the campus, the city of Oxford was also undergoing major changes. The election of Mayor John Leslie and the legalization of beer signaled the beginning of a new era in Oxford's history. The opening of the Gin, the Warehouse Restaurant and Richard Howorth's Square Books (whose owner was the 1998 president of the American Booksellers Association and a winner of several national awards for excellence among privately owned bookstores), the establishment of Ron Shapiro's Hoka Theater and Coffee House, the late night discussions at Morris's home on Faculty Row and the founding of the Center for the Study of Southern Culture created a new intellectual atmosphere that turned Oxford into an artists' and writers' town.

Recently cited by *USA Today* as one of the top six college towns in America, Oxford numbers among its current and recent residents Willie Morris, Theora Hamblett, Dean Faulkner Wells, Greg Iles, Donna Tartt, Jere Allen, Glennray Tutor, Lawrence Wells, Evans Harrington, Tom Rankin, Charles Eagles, Bill Beckwith, James C. Cobb, Jane Rule Burdine, Barry Hannah, Larry Brown, Ellen Douglas, Evelyn Crockett, Richard Ford, John Grisham, Joan Williams, Winthrop Jordan, Bill Ferris, John Pilkington, Charles Reagan Wilson, Obie Clark, Jason Bouldin, Jack Bass, Nathalie Dupree, Keith Stewart, Connie Flake, Samir Husni, Ron Bartlett, Jennifer Pace, James J. Cooke, Jere Hoar, Wylene Dunbar, Cynthia Shearer, David Galef, Howard Bahr, and Seymour Lawrence (a New York publisher who made substantial donations to the Williams Library and the university museum). The city of Oxford, Square Books, and Ole Miss jointly sponsor the Oxford Conference for the Book, an annual festival that brings the nation's premier literary figures and promising writers to Oxford each spring to celebrate the written word. The *Oxford American,* a monthly literary magazine underwritten by John Grisham, is also published in Oxford.

The visiting writers series, which waned after Morris left the university, was revived and expanded in 1993 by law school alumnus John Grisham, one of America's most widely read novelists, and his wife, Renee. Among the writers who visited the university in the early years of the Grisham endowment are Robert Stone, Madison Smartt Bell, Mary Hood, Doris Bell, Usef Komunyakaa, Charles Simic, and Robert Hass. The Grishams also established the Southern Writer in Residence program, which brings a Southern writer to Ole Miss each year to teach and to write.

One of the most significant influences on the university's changing intellectual landscape was the establishment of the Center for the Study of Southern Culture, which was conceived in 1975 by history professor Robert Haws and philosophy professor Michael Harrington. Haws and Harrington drafted a proposal to establish an interdisciplinary program in the humanities that would focus on Southern history and culture. Chancellor Fortune and Vice Chancellor Arthur DeRosier approved the proposal, and after a feasibility study conducted under a grant from the National Endowment for the Humanities, the Center was formally established in 1977. William R. Ferris, a Vicksburg native and Yale professor, was appointed director of the Center in 1979 and served in that position until 1997.

The Center offers undergraduate and graduate courses in the college of liberal arts and a wide range of specialized courses developed under a curriculum grant from NEH. The Center also promotes lectures, symposia, and exhibitions related to Southern history, art, and culture. The first of these programs was the 1977 Eudora Welty Symposium. In addition to a visiting lecture series and a scholars in residence program funded by the Ford Foundation (1986–1989), the Center also jointly sponsors the Faulkner and Yoknapatawpha Conference, the Porter L. Fortune History Symposium, and the Oxford Conference for the Book. The Center has also sponsored international conferences in Paris and Moscow.

In addition to the widely acclaimed *Encyclopedia of Southern Culture,* edited by William Ferris and Charles Reagan Wilson, professor of history and Southern studies, the Center has published a four volume anthology of Mississippi literature and has richly documented Southern history and culture through tape recordings, photography and films. The Center for the Study of Southern Culture has brought widespread acclaim and national and international recognition to the university. The 1997 appointment of William Ferris as chairman of the National Endowment for the Humanities, and his unanimous confirmation by the United States Senate, is a measure of the nation's high regard for him and for the Center. Professor Wilson was named the second director of the Center in July 1998.

Two years after the creation of the Center for the Study of Southern Culture, the university also established a new professional school. Ole Miss accountancy professor Joseph Cerny envisioned a school of accountancy as early as 1948, and its eventual establishment reflected a growing consensus among professional accountants that traditional business schools could not meet "the needs of the accounting profession." After overcoming strong resistence within the school of business, the university's newest professional school opened under the leadership of Dean Edward Milam on July 1, 1979. In announcing the establishment of the Ole Miss school of accountancy the *Chronicle of Higher Education* cited it as one of the first and most independent accountancy schools in the country. Eighteen years after its founding the school of accountancy was named for E. H. "Pat" Patterson, a 1955 Ole Miss graduate and former vice-president of the Donald W. Reynolds Foundation. In 1997 the Reynolds Foundation donated $16.5 million to the University of Mississippi in honor of Pat Patterson, of which $6 million was specifically allocated to the school of accountancy. A portion of the Reynolds gift was used to renovate Conner Hall, which now houses the E. H. Patterson School of Accountancy.

Building on the university's long tradition of teaching excellence, Chancellor Fortune and Vice Chancellor DeRosier elevated the standards for faculty tenure and promotion and, in essence, reestablished the "Ph.D. rule" initiated by Chancellor Alfred Butts in the 1930s. University professors were no longer tenured or promoted merely on the basis of years of service. The new criteria for tenure and promotion included presentation of papers at learned societies, articles in refereed journals, books and other publications, quality teaching, and service to the academic community. Doctoral degrees are required in many departments for entry level positions.

Along with this commitment to academic excellence, Chancellor Fortune and Vice Chancellor DeRosier established a special recognition for the university's premier faculty. Since 1966 the university has recognized a "Teacher of the Year," who receives a substantial monetary award and has his or her name permanently engraved on a plaque in the office of the chancellor. In addition to this recognition Chancellor Fortune established in 1977 the University of Mississippi Distinguished Professor. The designation was permanent and carried with it additional financial benefits. The first two Distinguished Professors were John Pilkington, of the English department, and Chalmers Butler, in electrical engineering. Chancellor Fortune's successor, Gerald Turner, increased the number of distinguished professors and awarded them the title of Frederick A. P. Barnard Professors. Barnard Professors receive additional financial and research support for a five-year period and retain the title as long as they remain at the university.

By the early 1970s the postwar enrollment boom had run its course, and Mississippi's collegiate institutions were under a mandate from the board of trustees and the legislature to curtail the duplication of course offerings and degree programs. Despite its own mandate, however, the legislature upgraded the state's five senior colleges, Alcorn State, Mississippi State College for Women, Jackson State, Delta State and Mississippi Valley State, to university status. This new designation further exacerbated the funding inequities that had for many years limited the growth and expansion of the state's traditionally black colleges.

As each of the eight public universities vied for its share of Mississippi's limited resources, Jake Ayers filed a class action lawsuit on January 28, 1975, on behalf of black students who claimed that the development of traditionally black colleges had been stymied by the state's intentional and unfair funding practices. The *Ayers* suit, which seeks a sweeping redress of the results of those funding inequities, has been in litigation for twenty-three years. Federal district Judge Neal B. Biggers, a man of learning and wit who has issued two lengthy rulings in the case, compared the *Ayers* suit to the Jarndyce case in Charles Dickens's novel *Bleak House.* The Jarndyce case, which dealt with the probation of a will, droned on for so many years that all the principles died, no one remembered why the case was originally filed, and when it was finally settled there was only enough money left in the estate to pay the lawyers. The long-term effect of the *Ayers* case on higher education in Mississippi is yet to be determined.

During the early years of the *Ayers* litigation, the university and other state institutions of higher learning experienced a series of severe budget cuts. Sharp reductions in the university's state appropriation necessitated cutbacks in several academic programs and the elimination of others. In the fall of 1982, the centennial anniversary of the admission of women, the university announced that the home economics department might be eliminated. That decision was extremely unpopular and "angry home ec majors . . . protested vehemently." Paraphrasing the university's popular cheer, Hotty Totty, they carried signs around the campus and chanted "Hell yes! Damn Right: Home Ec will Fight!" After serious consideration, the university administration did not eliminate the home economics department.

While home economics majors were marching to save their degree program, some students were sitting down to save the grand old oaks in the Grove, and others were complaining that John Hawkins, the university's first black cheerleader, would not wave the Rebel flag. In early September 1982 the *Clarion-Ledger* reported the first rumblings of a coming campus upheaval. "As traditionalists at Ole Miss boiled over the refusal of a black cheerleader to carry the Rebel flag," the Jackson paper wrote, drivers pulling into the Grove had to dodge "the protesters [sitting on] strategically laid blankets." Like home economics, the classic oaks endured and parking is no longer allowed in the Grove, a policy that even the traditionalists now applaud. John Hawkins's refusal to wave the Rebel flag, however, was another matter.

When Chancellor Fortune was appointed in 1968 approximately one hundred African American students were enrolled at Ole Miss. Among them were Robert Walker and Edgar Lee Caples. Walker, a doctoral student who taught two classes in American history, was the first African American to teach at the Oxford campus, though he was not the first African American professor at the University of Mississippi. In 1965 Marion Richards Myles was appointed assistant professor of pharmacology at the University of Mississippi Medical Center in Jackson. When asked several years later if he had any problems in his classes, Walker said, "No, I didn't have any problems. I was the teacher. I graded the papers." An outstanding student, Walker was elected president of the graduate student body and in 1971 was listed in Who's Who in American Colleges and Universities. After completing his studies at Ole Miss, Walker served in state government and as adjunct professor of history at Jackson State University. Walker is now in his second term as mayor of Vicksburg.

Edgar Lee Caples was the first African American graduate of the university's school of engineering. After advanced studies at Massachusetts Institute of Technology, Caples joined Rockwell International. In 1989, Caples was named from among his 19,000 colleagues Rockwell International's Engineer of the Year. Robert Walker and Edgar Lee Caples are highlights of the other Ole Miss and they brighten the picture, but the university's emerging image can not be captured in snapshots. The whole picture of Ole Miss is a motion picture, a developing image.

During Chancellor Fortune's first year, black students asked the new chancellor for permission to organize a Black Student Union and to celebrate Black History Week. Fortune agreed to their request and the BSU was organized in late March 1969. With the establishment of the BSU, African American students now had a voice to give expression to their aims and goals. Following a December 1969 speech by M. M. Roberts, the president of the board of trustees, in which he admitted that he was a racist and for which he offered "no apologies," BSU president Jessie Dent, in a frank interview with the *Mississippian,* said he was dismayed by Roberts's speech and discouraged by the lack of communication between black students and the administration. The Ole Miss chapter of Omicron Delta Kappa, a student honor society, was also incensed by Roberts's speech and demanded his resignation. Dent told the student newspaper he would soon announce a set of demands on behalf of the black student population.

Within a month, the BSU formulated a set of demands and a group of forty students presented them to Chancellor Fortune on the night of February 25, 1970. While those demands were being presented to the chancellor, another group of black students burned a Rebel flag and danced on tables in the cafeteria to the music of B. B. King. The next night almost half of the university's black students participated in a peaceful demonstration in Fulton Chapel at a concert featuring Up With People, an integrated touring musical group. The disruption of the concert was the culmination of two years of increasing frustration among Ole Miss's black students. During and immediately after the demonstration security personnel arrested and incarcerated approximately ninety black students. Several of those arrested were not involved in the Fulton Chapel demonstration but deliberately placed themselves in a position to be arrested in a display of unity with those who were. After the Oxford jail reached capacity, law enforcement officials transported several students to the state penitentiary at Parchman. The students were released the next day.

At a called faculty meeting on March 2, Chancellor Fortune announced that criminal charges were filed against some of the students and he would severely punish any student found guilty of subverting "the orderly process of the University." Before there was any discussion of the matter, the faculty adopted a resolution commending the chancellor and pledging the faculty's "complete cooperation." At a called meeting of the faculty senate later that evening, however, law professor John Robin Bradley introduced a resolution recommending that criminal charges against the students be dropped. The faculty senate adopted Bradley's resolution and also recognized that black students had "urgent, legitimate grievances," which the university should address "immediately." Following an investigation of the Fulton Chapel incident, the student judiciary council suspended eight students until January 1971 and placed forty-five on probation.

The peaceful demonstration at Ole Miss in March was followed two months later by a deadly riot at Jackson State University. During a twenty-eight second fusillade directed toward a women's dormitory, Mississippi law enforcement officers killed two students and wounded twelve others. The Jackson State riot sent shock waves throughout the state, and most white Mississippians finally realized that continued resistence to change was a greater danger than the changes they were resisting. That realization was reinforced by the integration of the public school system in the spring of 1970, which was achieved more peacefully than anyone believed possible.

The Fulton Chapel demonstration was a watershed event in race relations at the University of Mississippi and was followed by several important developments in 1970. Constance Slaughter-Harvey became the first African American woman to graduate from the Ole Miss law school. Jeannette Jennings, the first full-time African American member of the faculty, was appointed assistant professor of social work. History professor Harry Owens, who had taught black history courses since 1965, initiated a black studies program. English professor John Crews chaired a faculty and staff committee to study and improve race relations at the university, and the Reverend Wayne Johnson, of Oxford, served as campus minister to the university's African American students.

One of the most important events in the fall of 1970 was the enrollment of Coolidge Ball of Indianola, the university's first black student athlete, who received a basketball scholarship. In his first year on the varsity squad Ball led the team in scoring, averaging 16.8 points a game. Ball also earned membership in the exclusive 1,000 point club, scoring 1,072 points during his career at Ole Miss. In 1972 and 1973 he was named to several All-SEC teams. Two years after Coolidge Ball's enrollment, James Reed and Ben Williams became Ole Miss's first black football players. Reed played on the freshman squad in 1972, while Williams was one of the few freshman who made the varsity team. An All-American in 1975, Ben Williams was an active and popular student. Named to the student Hall of Fame, Who's Who in American Colleges and Universities, "Gentle Ben" Williams was elected Colonel Rebel in 1975.

As black enrollment gradually increased in the 1970s, college life for black students became more collegial and enjoyable, especially after the establishment of Omega Psi Phi in 1973 (an African American fraternity) and the founding of an Ole Miss chapter of Alpha Kappa Alpha in 1974 (an African American sorority). By the mid-1970s Kenneth Wooten, director of admissions, was actively recruiting black students. Wooten established a precollege orientation and recruitment program that identified leading African American high school students and invited them to the campus for weekend conferences with other African American students at Ole Miss.

Rose Jackson of Clarksdale was among the students attracted to Ole Miss under Wooten's program. By the end of her undergraduate years at Ole Miss, Jackson had won many of the university's highest student honors. She was elected president of the Associated Women Students, named to the student Hall of Fame, Who's Who in American Colleges and Universities, and the homecoming court. In 1979 *Glamour* magazine selected Rose Jackson as one of the top ten women college students in the United States.

In the year *Glamour* magazine featured Rose Jackson, Ole Miss was embroiled in a controversy over a horse named Traveller. The senior class donated to the university a stallion named for General Robert E. Lee's famous steed. At the urging, if not the insistence, of Athletic Director Warner Alford, Chancellor Fortune declined to accept the gift and returned the horse. Ole Miss traditionalists were angered by the university's decision not to accept Traveller. They believed their ancestry was somehow denigrated because Colonel Rebel would not be permitted to ride Traveller into Vaught-Hemingway Stadium to the sounds of Rebel yells and the stirring strains of *Dixie.* One student complained that if some people had their way Ole Miss would be named the "University of Medgar Evers." The controversy over Traveller was but a prelude to the coming battle over the Rebel flag.

In the spring of 1982 the Ole Miss student body elected John Hawkins cheerleader. Although he was disappointed that his tryout partner, Clara Bibb, was not chosen, Hawkins was happy to be the first black cheerleader at Ole Miss. He was enthusiastic and optimistic about his election, saying it would "help recruitment" and that it "would be very encouraging to black athletes to have a representative who is a cheerleader." He also thanked the white students who voted for him. In 1982 there were 715 black students at Ole Miss, and Hawkins received 1,241 votes. "I am sure there will be some sarcasm because some people won't accept a black cheerleader," Hawkins said, "but this is a new age and the time has passed for prejudice." During an interview with Jay Harris of Gannett News Service later that summer, Hawkins said that "he would not wave a Confederate flag" at football games that fall. His statement sparked a "firestorm of protest" from Ole Miss traditionalists. After the controversy broke, Hawkins and university officials first considered replacing the Rebel flag with the state flag, but eventually agreed that only one cheerleader would carry a flag.

As the 1982 football season approached, rumors surfaced that the university would phase out the Rebel flag as an Ole Miss spirit symbol. Many alumni and students were bitter and angry because they thought the Fortune administration had a secret scheme to outlaw the flag. In response to the rumors, and in an effort to calm the situation, student body president William Ray issued a statement saying that the administration could not phase out the flag even if it wanted to, because white students and black students "will do what they want to about the flag."

He also said the flag controversy was aggravated by people "from outside the university community" and overplayed by both the state and national press. "I am pleased but I am also dismayed," he said, "that it's the young people who are behaving with so much more maturity than their elders." As it had in the past, the University of Mississippi suffered more from those who claimed to be its friends than from its enemies. Ray also stated that he would not carry a flag to football games because the raging, relentless controversy was detrimental to the university.

At a press conference shortly before the first football game in the fall of 1982 Hawkins tried to explain to the students who elected him why he could not carry a Rebel flag. "I am an Ole Miss cheerleader," he said, "[which] makes me a representative of the whole student body—blacks and whites—but I am a black man and the same way whites have been taught to wave the flag I have been taught to have nothing to do with it." Hawkins apologized to his partner, Laura Smith, who "has had to suffer because of the enormous amount of publicity I have gotten." Smith expressed a similar feeling, "We aren't having any problems as partners, . . . but the press keeps harassing us trying to stir up their own fabricated problems we supposedly have. We are now having to find secret places for the squad to practice in order to get anything done."

Head football coach Steve Sloan intensified the controversy when he suggested the addition of the letters "UM" or "Ole Miss" to the Confederate flag. About half of the Ole Miss football team was black, and the flag controversy made it difficult to recruit black athletes. The addition of those markings, Coach Sloan said, would distinguish the Ole Miss flag from the Confederate emblem and the historical connotations that made the flag offensive to black students.

Long before the flag issue erupted in the fall of 1982, university officials were planning a convocation marking the twentieth anniversary of James Meredith's admission. Although university officials agreed that the anniversary could not go unnoticed, there was little agreement about what form the observance should take. Associate Vice Chancellor Charles Noyes suggested that an appropriate ceremony would give the university an opportunity to showcase the "progress that has occurred in our state and Ole Miss during the past twenty years." Assistant Vice Chancellor Lucius Williams, the university's first high level black administrator, who was appointed in 1975, planned and coordinated a twentieth anniversary convocation in Fulton Chapel on September 30.

Among the speakers were James Meredith, Governor William F. Winter, and Dr. Robert Harrison, the president of the board of trustees and the first African American to serve on the college board. Margaret Walker Alexander, poet, novelist and professor of English at Jackson State University, was the keynote speaker, but James Meredith was the center of attention. During his speech, in which he commended the university for the racial progress it had made during the previous twenty years, Meredith stated categorically that the university should eliminate the Rebel flag and the Confederate imagery that cloaked the campus.

Following the convocation, many students, black and white, gathered in the lobby of the Ole Miss Union for a lengthy and candid dialogue on a wide range of campus issues. Vice Chancellor Williams remarked later that the frank and free discussion of race relations during and after the convocation, which was covered by most major news organizations, presented an image of Ole Miss in 1982 that was far different from the picture sent from Oxford in 1962. That September impression was soon tarnished, however, first by a Klan rally later that fall and then by a near riot in the spring of 1983.

At the height of the flag controversy, the Ku Klux Klan held a rally in Oxford in support of the Confederate flag and its continued identification with the University of Mississippi. The rally took place on Saturday, October 23 when the football team was playing LSU in Baton Rouge. The twenty-five hooded, robed Klansmen who assembled on the Oxford Square drew few supporters. Many of the estimated 450 spectators heckled the Grand Dragon when he proclaimed that the "Rebel flag . . . is more sacred than anything else in the South." A few applauded, however, when he said that "blacks should go back to Africa."

In the early spring following this Klan rally, the campus newspaper reported that Chancellor Fortune would issue an official statement about the Rebel flag in May 1983. Many students and alumni believed Fortune would formally disassociate the University of Mississippi from the Confederate flag. In anticipation of that announcement, a group of students organized a "Save the Flag" movement and began a drive to collect 6,000 signatures, which they would deliver to the chancellor. While the student senate was drafting a resolution asking Chancellor Fortune to keep the flag as an Ole Miss spirit symbol, some students were driving around the campus, honking their horns, waving Rebel flags and taunting black students.

An already tense climate was further strained by the arrival of the 1983 Ole Miss yearbook, which provoked an angry response from black students. In the front pages of the annual, which featured the major events of the school year, were several pictures of the October Klan rally, including one full page picture and several smaller shots of Klansmen waving Rebel flags. John Hall, the yearbook editor who had toured with the integrated musical group Up With People, was surprised by the reaction to the annual. After black students bitterly complained about the pictures, Hall met with the Black Student Union and explained that he used the pictures to illustrate the connection between the Klan and the Rebel flag. He was deeply disappointed that the pictures had offended black students. Lydia Spragin, BSU president, conceded that Hall's "heart may have been in the right place, but his eyes weren't. He didn't take into consideration the inflammatory thing he was printing."

Notwithstanding the indignities they endured from time to time, most black students were in their own way proud to be students at the University of Mississippi and they were furious that the first thing their parents and grandparents would see when they opened the Ole Miss yearbook were pictures of hooded Klansmen and Confederate flags. In the early stages of their anger, black students considered a ritual book burning on the steps of the Lyceum, but they eventually decided against it. Instead, they refused to accept their annuals and demanded a refund of their student activity fees allocated to the yearbook.

On Monday night April 18, 1983, the night the rumored book burning was to take place, about 1,500 flag waving white students gathered at the Lyceum. Student body officers and fraternity leaders told the angry students that the rumors were not true and pleaded with them to go back to their dormitories and fraternity houses. After the larger crowd disbursed, about 600 students marched to the Phi Beta Sigma house, John Hawkins's fraternity, lofted their Rebel flags into the night sky, and shouted racial slurs and threats. University security, with the assistance of the Oxford police department, eventually disbursed the crowd.

Assistant Vice Chancellor Lucius Williams and Ardessa Minor, director of minority affairs, later reported that black and white students alike were unnerved by the Monday night demonstration at the Phi Beta Sigma house. That rowdy crowd of college students was only a few angry words away from becoming a mob. On the morning after the demonstration a leader of the "Save the Flag" movement came to the Lyceum to say he would no longer support the effort to save the flag. He had always thought of the flag as a symbol of school spirit, he said, but at the Phi Beta Sigma house the night before he saw it as a symbol of hate.

Chancellor Fortune, who was at a meeting of the Southern Association of Colleges in Texas on the night of the demonstration, hurriedly returned to the campus. At the urging of the faculty senate and other advisors, Fortune decided to make the flag announcement immediately instead of waiting until May. At a press conference on April 20, 1983, covered by most of the major news organizations in the country, Chancellor Fortune announced that the University of Mississippi was officially and formally disassociating itself from the Confederate flag and that no unit or organization officially associated with the university, including cheerleaders, would display the flag. That decision was one of the most unpleasant and difficult decisions of Chancellor Fortune's sixteen-year tenure. He was reviled by some of his long standing friends and received several death threats. Others criticized Fortune for not disavowing *Dixie* and Colonel Rebel.

In the tumultuous fall of 1982, in the midst of Klan marches, press conferences, and controversies, Damon Moore, a young African American freshman from Coldwater, Mississippi, enrolled at Ole Miss and quietly went about his studies. He noticed but was not distracted by the controversy over black and white cheerleaders and Confederate flags. Moore had come to the university, like James Meredith twenty years earlier, with "a mission." Moore's mission was "to do well." He was a brilliant student and in 1987, after winning many of the university's highest academic honors, Damon Moore was named Ole Miss's twenty-fifth Rhodes Scholar. Although Damon Moore was a pacesetter, he was a member of a declining black student enrollment. Among black Mississippians the flag controversy and the rowdy crowd of whites shouting racial slurs in front of John Hawkins's fraternity house revived the 1962 image of Ole Miss as a place of riot and lawlessness. That darker picture of the university hurt the recruitment of African American students, and black enrollment declined from 715 in 1982 to 656 in 1983 and to 536 in 1984.

After a sixteen year tenure, the second longest in the university's history, Chancellor Fortune decided to retire in 1984. He remained at the university as Chancellor Emeritus and Distinguished Professor of History until his death in 1989. After Fortune announced his retirement, the board of trustees initiated a nationwide search for his successor. While this search was taking place, a petition was circulating among the university faculty on the Oxford campus. The overwhelming majority of the tenured faculty endorsed the appointment of Governor William F. Winter, whose four year term was about to end. The trustees were persuaded by this remarkable display of unity and offered the appointment to Governor Winter, who was out of the state when the offer was made. Governor Winter initially accepted the offer, but after he returned to Mississippi and considered the matter, he declined the appointment. The board of trustees then elected R. Gerald Turner, the candidate they favored before receiving the faculty's petition for Governor Winter.

Gerald Turner, a native Texan who had never been in the state of Mississippi before he interviewed for the position, was vice-president for executive affairs at the University of Oklahoma at the time of his appointment in 1984. At thirty-seven years of age, Turner was the second youngest chancellor in the university's history. He received a Ph.D. in psychology from the University of Texas in 1975 and taught at several institutions, including Prairie View A & M and Pepperdine University, before his appointment as professor of psychology at Oklahoma. The board of trustees appointed Turner with the understanding that his three primary goals would be to enlarge the university's endowment, to reverse the enrollment decline, and to repair the university's public image.

Following extensive preparations initiated during the last years of Porter Fortune's administration, Chancellor Turner launched the Campaign for Ole Miss six months after his appointment. Over the next two and a half years Chancellor Turner made hundreds of speeches to civic clubs, business organizations, chambers of commerce, churches and schools. He enlisted friends and alumni of Ole Miss who had never before been asked to contribute to the university. The Campaign for Ole Miss was more successful than anticipated and raised $61.7 million in cash gifts and deferred pledges during the official period of the campaign. Donations continued to come in long after the campaign officially ended.

In September 1986, following the successful Campaign for Ole Miss, Chancellor Turner initiated a Drive for Athletics, which raised $11.6 million for new and expanded athletic facilities. Among the new facilities added through this drive were the Oxford-University Baseball Stadium, Starnes Athletic Training Center, and the Palmer-Salloum Tennis facility. Archie Manning, one of the university's most heralded and admired graduates, chaired the drive for athletics. Manning had completed his professional football career and was living in New Orleans in 1986. He was the ideal person to lead the campaign for athletics. During the nearly three decades since his graduation in 1971, Manning has been an ambassador at large for the University of Mississippi. His exploits on the gridiron earned him All-American honors, and his record setting performance in the 1969 Ole Miss-Alabama game, which the university lost 33–32, was the highlight of the first prime time telecast of a college football game. In 1970, a year when college football was rich with quarterbacks, *Sports Illustrated* featured Manning in an article entitled "And the Best of Them All is . . . Archie." Manning led Ole Miss to some of its most famous victories including come from behind wins against LSU in 1968 and 1969, the 38–0 defeat of Tennessee in 1969, and the Sugar Bowl win over Arkansas in 1970. Archie Manning has brought great acclaim to the university, and is one of Ole Miss's enduring symbols, in Chancellor Robert Khayat's words, as much for the mark he made after graduation as for his accomplishments on the playing field.

Because state appropriations for higher education declined significantly in the 1980s, private gifts and federal funds were essential to the university's continued growth and expansion. Through the support of Mississippi's powerful congressional delegation, especially Congressman Jamie Whitten, chairman of the house appropriations committee, several research centers were established or expanded at the university in the 1980s and 1990s. Among the expanded facilities are the Center for Computational Hydroscience and Engineering, which has gained international recognition for its use of computer models to simulate water and sediment flow in the prevention of erosion; the Center for Wetlands Resources, which provides one of the best sites in the world for experimental aquatic research on large scale systems; and the Center for Wireless Communications, which offers educational, research, and service programs to support the development of a new generation of information professionals. The department of electrical engineering, recognized as one of the nation's top five research groups in electromagnetic fields and waves, has recently acquired one of the few vector network analyzers located at an engineering school in the United States. Congress created the Jamie Whitten National Center for Physical Acoustics in 1986 to provide basic and applied research in physical acoustics and to develop designs, techniques, and marketable products to improve the economy of the region. The Whitten Center is housed in an $11.5 million state-of-the-art facility that opened in 1989.

Established under the provisions of the Child Nutrition and WIC Re-authorization Act of 1989, the National Food Service Management Institute is administered through a grant agreement with the United States Department of Agriculture. The Ole Miss Food Management Institute, operated jointly by the University of Mississippi and University of Southern Mississippi, is the national clearinghouse for the development of child nutrition programs, cost-effective methods for delivering nutritional meals to students, training programs for food service personnel, and for the dissemination of this information to school personnel throughout the nation. Construction was begun in 1998 for a $6 million facility, financed by state and federal funds, to house the Ole Miss division of the program.

The school of pharmacy has formed a partnership with the United States Department of Agriculture to establish the National Center for the Development of Natural Products. This center is the nation's only research facility devoted to the discovery and development of new pharmaceutical and agrochemicals derived from natural products. In cooperation with Ole Miss scientists the Natural Products Center builds on the pharmacy school's thirty-year tradition of natural products research and development. The Ole Miss school of pharmacy also operates the nation's only legal marijuana farm, which is funded by the federal government. Scientists in the pharmacy school process and distribute the marijuana to qualified research organizations throughout the country.

To meet the second of his three major goals, the reversal of the university's enrollment decline, Chancellor Turner initiated an expensive and aggressive student recruitment program. Advertising and public relations experts prepared glossy, colorful recruitment brochures that were distributed throughout the nation, and recruiters fanned out across Mississippi and the South touting the special advantages of Ole Miss. The university's new recruitment program was highly successful, and enrollment rose from 8,715 in 1984 to 11,033 in 1992. Much of that growth was from out-of-state students.

An important aspect of the new recruiting program was the targeting of African American students. In less than a decade, the number of black students at the university nearly doubled from 536 in 1984 to approximately 1,000 in 1992. The increase in full-time black graduate students was even more dramatic. That number rose from 22 in 1984 to 305 in 1990. Chancellor Turner was committed not only to increasing black enrollment, he also wanted to make Ole Miss "psychologically accessible" to African American students.

One of his first initiatives in that effort was the appointment of African Americans to high level and highly visible positions at the university. Among his earliest appointments were Donald Cole, associate dean of the graduate school and associate professor of mathematics, and Mary Thompson, a senior staff member in the financial aid office. Cole had been one of the eight students suspended after the Fulton Chapel demonstration in 1970. At the time of his suspension he was a junior mathematics major. After completing his undergraduate degree at Tougaloo College in Jackson, Mississippi, and earning graduate degrees at the University of Michigan and the State University of New York in Buffalo, Cole returned to Ole Miss, earned a Ph.D. in mathematics, and was appointed to the faculty. Mary Thompson was also one of the ninety Ole Miss students arrested after the Fulton Chapel incident, though she was not suspended. She stayed in school, completed her bachelor's degree, earned a master's degree, and accepted an administrative position at the university. Among other African Americans appointed to administrative positions were Don Peters, vice chancellor for student life, Thomas Wallace, associate vice chancellor for student life, Ken Gibson, track coach, Michael Edmonds, assistant dean of students, Rob Evans, head basketball coach, and the late Louis Westerfield, dean of the law school.

In addition to making Ole Miss psychologically accessible to black students, Chancellor Turner also wanted to associate the University of

Mississippi with Mississippi's African American community. To establish this connection Michael Edmonds recommended an awards program to honor the heroes of Mississippi's civil rights movement and also recognize Mississippi's new generation of black leaders. Turner accepted Edmonds's proposal and in 1987 the university established the Awards of Distinction, an annual ceremony that gives special recognition to a select group of black Mississippians.

The first Awards of Distinction were presented to Reuben V. Anderson, the first black graduate of the law school and the first black justice of the state supreme court; William Raspberry, an Okolona native and nationally syndicated columnist; Aaron Henry of Clarksdale, president of the state NAACP; R. L. T. Smith of Jackson, a pioneer in Mississippi's struggle for justice and equality; Beverly Hogan of Jackson, the executive director of the governor's office for federal and state relations; and Richard Wright, a native Mississippian and one of the world's leading black writers. Julia Wright came from Paris to Oxford to accept the award on behalf of her father who died in 1960.

The third of Turner's major goals, the enhancement of the university's public image, was the most difficult to achieve, and he would soon learn as his predecessors had that the image of Ole Miss, like beauty, is in the eye of the beholder. While Chancellor Turner was trying to limit if not eliminate the public display of the Confederate flag at university sporting events, the editor of the campus newspaper wrote that "heaven . . . is full of Rebel flags." The recurring controversy over the flag, however, was only part of the university's public image problem. The university's image was damaged by the spectacle of inebriated fraternity pledges mudwrestling in a rain storm on bid day in 1978 and was blemished in the 1980s by reports of "fights between football players and fraternities, hazing, an alcohol related death, alleged rape and sexual assault, arson and other incidents" along fraternity row. Beer trucks were routinely parked and visible behind fraternity houses on party nights

The most evident and potentially the most dangerous display of youthful excess was the annual Shrimp and Beer festival held at nearby Sardis Lake as the culmination of Dixie Week. The festival began in the late 1970s as an informal gathering of Ole Miss students but soon began to attract large crowds, some of which were estimated at 9,000. When

Shrimp and Beer became an organized annual spring ritual, beer distributors provided free kegs of beer and mounds of boiled shrimp. Although only one student had been seriously injured during the festival, the 1983 event was fraught with such potential danger that Thomas "Sparky" Reardon, who was then director of student programing, told Captain Charles Wood of the University Police Department, "Charlie, this is the last one. There is no way we can control it." The decision to discontinue the festival, while consistent with Turner's overall plan for the university and in keeping with national trends in risk management on college campuses, was made before his appointment. When he approved the decision and the festival was cancelled, students reacted angrily, lodged formal protests, and accused Turner of denigrating Ole Miss "traditions." That particular tradition was less than ten years old. Frank Moak, professor emeritus of higher education and Southern studies, has said that the only thing necessary for the establishment of a college tradition is for something to happen once.

Early in his administration Chancellor Turner made it clear to the division of student affairs "that he expected to have a student body who would bring credit and not shame to the university." Turner was convinced, by two incidents in particular, that the fraternity system was a prime source of embarrassment and that stern measures were necessary to bring the system under control. The first of the two incidents was the burning of the Phi Beta Sigma house. In August 1988 the Phi Beta Sigma fraternity was scheduled to move to fraternity row. The Sigmas would be the first black fraternity to have a house on Ole Miss's famous fraternity row. Sparky Reardon, along with Thomas Wallace, the chapter advisor and later the associate vice chancellor for student life, and Stuart Brunson, president of the Interfraternity Council, had been planning the move for several months. As the Sigmas were making preparations for the move to Fraternity Row, their house was burned. Chancellor Turner, shocked, angry and more determined than ever to integrate Fraternity Row, told an alumni group in Memphis the next day that arsonists would "not defeat us" and announced that an alumnus had already agreed to lend the Sigmas $100,000 to rebuild or purchase another house. With the cooperation of Brunson, the Interfraternity Council, and other fraternities the Sigmas purchased and remodeled another house and the Ole Miss chapter of Phi Beta Sigma moved on to fraternity row in October. Two years later Alpha Kappa Alpha, a black sorority, moved to Sorority Row.

The second incident that convinced Turner of the need for tighter controls on the fraternity system involved the Beta Theta Pi chapter and Rust College. On September 18, 1989, several Beta pledges "kidnapped" an active member in retaliation for his hazing of pledges. During the course of the evening the retribution against the upperclassman took an ugly turn and late that night the pledges stripped the active, along with a pledge, painted their bodies with racial slurs, and dumped them on the campus of Rust College, a predominantly black college in nearby Holly Springs. With about fifty Rust College students looking on in both anger and amusement, the two Betas were taken into custody by security guards as they tried to sneak off the campus. University police were dispatched to Holly Springs and brought the two students, draped in towels provided by Rust College security personnel, back to Oxford. The Beta incident tarred the Ole Miss Greeks with a general charge of racism.

When Chancellor Turner learned of the incident he immediately called the president of Rust College and apologized. Turner also dispatched the president of the Interfraternity Council to apologize to Rust College on behalf of the Ole Miss fraternity system. The chancellor then appointed a committee to recommend suitable punishment for the fraternity and another panel to recommend disciplinary action against the individuals involved. On the basis of the first panel's recommendation, Turner banned the fraternity for three years and ordered the chapter to close its house. Following the second panel's review, the university expelled one student, suspended four, and placed nine on probation.

The burning of the Phi Beta Sigma house and the Beta incident were reflections of Ole Miss, but they were not the whole picture of either the university or the Greek system. There are many positive aspects to the Ole Miss Greek system, and many of the state's business and professional leaders are products of that system. Fraternities and sororities require their members to maintain acceptable academic standards as a condition for initiation. Ole Miss Greek societies conduct charitable and goodwill projects and support many worthy causes such as the prevention of child abuse, summer camps for children with cancer, the Oxford Pantry, and many others. From 1984 to 1988 Ole Miss Greek societies contributed more than $100,000 to the Bessie S. Speed Wellness Center for alcohol and drug education. In the spring of 1987 the University of Mississippi, and indeed the state and the nation, were deeply saddened by the tragic deaths of five Ole Miss Chi Omegas who were participating in their sorority's annual goodwill project. On March 26, 1987, Hess Worsham, Robin Simmons, Margaret Gardner, Mary Pat Langford, and Elizabeth Gage Roberson were killed on a state highway just west of Oxford during the Chi Omega's charity walk-a-thon. Elizabeth Gage Roberson was the great, great, great niece of Jeremiah Gage, of the University Greys, who was killed at Gettysburg.

The publicity surrounding the destruction of the Phi Beta Sigma house in August 1988 overshadowed the integration of the Ole Miss fraternity system and the election of the first African American to a student body office. In December 1988 Kappa Alpha Psi, a black fraternity, inducted two white students, and Carl Lee Powell was elected ASB treasurer the following spring. The Beta incident in 1989 also obscured the results of the 1990 student election in which an African American coed, Kimsey O'Neal, was elected Miss Ole Miss. A pharmacy major and an academic All-American in basketball, O'Neal's election as the woman student who best represents "the traditions and ideals" of the university was an important piece in the emerging image of the other Ole Miss.

The students who elected Kimsey O'Neal also elected Roy Lee "Chucky" Mullins Colonel Rebel, the second black student to receive that honor. During the Ole Miss-Vanderbilt football game on October 28, 1989, Mullins, a defensive back, suffered a severe spinal injury. Ole Miss fans and friends raised more than a million dollars to help him fight the debilitating paralysis that eventually took his life on May 6, 1991. After his death the Phi Beta Sigmas established the Chucky Mullins Courage Award, which is given each year to a senior defensive back who displays the courage and heart that characterized the life of Chucky Mullins. The recipient of the award also wears Chucky's jersey number, 38. Phi Beta Sigma and Alpha Tau Omega, a white fraternity, jointly sponsor the annual Chucky Mullins Banquet at which the winner of the award is announced. In 1990 two other African American students were also named to prestigious campus offices. Katrina Howard became the first black editor of the yearbook and Lee Eric Smith was the first African American to edit the student newspaper. Also, one of the 1990 Awards of Distinction went to Chancery Court Judge Patricia Wise, one of the students arrested in the Fulton Chapel incident twenty years earlier.

The Phi Beta Sigma and Beta incidents occurred during one of the periodic debates over the Rebel flag. At the beginning of the 1989 football season, the senior class introduced the Battle M flag as an alternative to the Rebel flag. The new flag was similar in color and appearance to the Confederate flag except that the blue saltier (the diagonal cross) was replaced with a blue M. Ole Miss traditionalists spurned the Battle M flag, and the emblem of the Lost Cause remained popular among many Ole Miss students and alumni. As the flag controversy continued unabated into the 1990s, the University of Mississippi alumni association issued an official statement concerning the Confederate flag.

At a meeting in Oxford on April 27, 1991, the sixty-member board of directors of the alumni association unanimously adopted a resolution asking "fans and alumni not to bring the Confederate flag to Ole Miss athletic events." George Hewes, president of the alumni association, said the board of directors made the recommendation because the Confederate flag projects a negative "national image for the University." President-elect Raymond Brown, a former Ole Miss football star, also endorsed the resolution because the controversy, he said, makes it difficult for the university to recruit "scholars, faculty, and athletes." As expected, some students and alumni bitterly opposed the resolution. One irate member of the class 1931 said, "If I want to wave the flag, I'll wave it. I paid $22 for a seat and I'll do what I want to." His remarks bring to mind the 1948 *M-Book* explanation that the giant Rebel flag was a symbol that said, "We do not want anyone telling us what to do."

In an interview with the student newspaper Dondi Flemister, a black freshman basketball player, said the flag was more of a problem for his parents than for him, but he said it "definitely affects recruiting." Linebacker Shawn Cobb, a black star on the 1990 football team that went

9–3 and played in the Gator Bowl, agreed with Flemister that the people who are most adversely affected by the flag are "the people who aren't here." Once he got to Ole Miss, Cobb said, he did not necessarily like it, but "the flag did not bother him."

Head basketball Coach Ed Murphy (1986–1992) found that to be a common sentiment among his black players. "It is hard to get black athletes to Ole Miss," he said, "but once they get here they don't want to leave." When they did leave Ole Miss, many African American athletes, especially Coach Murphy's basketball players, left with their degrees in hand. In recent years the University of Mississippi's rate of graduation among its student athletes has been second only to Vanderbilt in the Southeastern Conference. In the late 1980s and early 1990s the university's graduation rate of all athletes was 58 percent compared to 49 percent of the general student population. That high rate of graduation resulted in large measure from Billy Brewer's emphasis on academics during his eleven year tenure as head football coach (1983–1994) and to Warner Alford's commitment to the graduation of student athletes. During his long and distinguished career as athletic direc-tor (1978–1994), Alford provided financial support to many athletes after their eligibility had expired. Ole Miss student athletes knew if they really wanted to graduate, Alford would find a way to help them do so.

The alumni association's resolution asking Ole Miss fans not to bring Rebel flags to sporting events was followed a year later by the appointment of Rob Evans, the first black head coach of a major sport at Ole Miss. Coach Evans's success in raising the university's basketball program to national prominence, and the appointment of Rod Barnes of Satartia to succeed him in 1998, has had a major positive impact on the public image of Ole Miss. Barnes was one of Evans's assistant coaches and an All-SEC guard during his playing career at Ole Miss (1985–1988). Even the appointment of African American coaches, however, could not still the controversy over the university's Confederate symbols. In 1993 Tim Jones, a black member of the pep band that is so much a part of the excitement of Ole Miss basketball in Tad Smith Coliseum, refused to play *Dixie* and prompted yet another debate about the university's image. People in other parts of the country who read press accounts that a black member of the Ole Miss band refused to play *Dixie* at basketball games must have been confused when they read that the head basketball coach and most of the players were also African Americans.

The recycled controversy over symbols obscured, but did not diminish, the substantive achievements of African Americans at Ole Miss or the university's embrace of racial and ethnic diversity. Since the 1960s the university has welcomed, recruited and offered scholarships to foreign students. Displayed in the Ole Miss Union are the national colors of more than sixty countries whose students attend the university. In the year of the university's sesquicentennial the editor of the *Daily Mississippian* is Natashia Gregoire, a citizen of Dominica. With the enormous potential of the Croft Institute for International Studies, in the twenty-first century Ole Miss could become a beacon in the global village.

No collegiate institution in America has been more open and honest about its racial problems or as earnest in its efforts to resolve them as the University of Mississippi. Despite the discourse and distractions over symbols, and the burden of its history, Ole Miss has made remarkable progress. In 1993, the year Tim Jones refused to play *Dixie,* Jesse Holland, an African American, was editor of the *Daily Mississippian.* A year later Louis Westerfield, the Mississippi son of black sharecroppers, was named dean of the oldest law school in the Deep South. In 1995 a group of white students launched a drive for funds to build a memorial to the civil rights movement on the Ole Miss campus. In 1996, as the most intense and bitter dispute over the Rebel flag since 1982 was heating up, black enrollment reached a record high of 1,156 (11.1 percent of the student body), and Debbie McCain was the first African American to win the coveted title of Most Beautiful. The next year Carissa Alana Wells was the first African American to be named Miss University, and in 1998 Ansu Sesay was the second black Ole Miss basketball player in the 1990s—along with Gerald Glass in 1990—to win All-American honors.

While white students were raising funds for a civil rights memorial in 1995, the New York based Burson-Marsteller public relations firm was studying the public's perception of the university's academic standing, and a marketing firm was designing a strategy to enhance the university's image. When it became known that public relations and marketing firms were conducting an image assessment, fringe elements "from outside the university community" hijacked the discussion and, for their own purposes, turned it into another debate over Confederate symbols. For months during the summer and fall of 1997 Mississippi newspapers were bombarded with letters, articles and editorials about the Rebel flag, *Dixie,* and Colonel Rebel. As the controversy was being played out in the state and national press, Chancellor Robert Khayat, who had succeeded Gerald Turner in June 1995, was asked if the university anticipated any formal action concerning the flag and other Confederate symbols. Chancellor Khayat stated that the Ole Miss faculty and administration had officially disassociated the university from the Rebel flag in 1983 and that the alumni association had taken similar action in 1991. Ole Miss students, Chancellor Khayat said, would ultimately resolved the flag issue.

Head football Coach Tommy Tuberville intensified the controversy on September 25, 1997, two days before the homecoming game with Vanderbilt, when he asked Ole Miss students and fans "to discontinue waving the Confederate flag at home sporting events." One irate student responded to Tuberville's statement, "I've never waved a flag before, but I am now because he told me not to." Jenny Dodson, editor of the *Mississippian,* and most Ole Miss students, supported Coach Tuberville. Dodson published several editorials and articles about the flag's history and its identification with the university in an effort to convince Ole Miss students that the recurring controversy damaged the university.

On October 21, 1997, after a candid and intelligent discussion of the controversy's effect on the university's image, the Ole Miss student senate adopted a resolution asking students to "do what will be most beneficial for the advancement of the University of Mississippi and refrain from waving the Confederate flag at Ole Miss athletic events." Introduced by Matt Lott, John Joseph, Stephen Harrell, and MiMi Montagnet, the resolution was adopted by a vote of 97 to 17. The student senate took this action one week before Ole Miss (ranked 25th in the country) played the University of Arkansas on ESPN, a sports television network. Reaction to the student senate's resolution was positive and few Rebel flags were visible on the night Ole Miss defeated Arkansas 19–9 on national television. The Ole Miss students, the university faculty and administration, the alumni association, and the athletic department have officially separated the University of Mississippi from the negative connotations of the Confederate flag. The issue is settled at Ole Miss. The controversy, however, may not be over because there will always be those who "rally round the flag."

In the mid-1990s, after several years of stringent budgets, disputes over the funding policies of the University Foundation, and athletic probation, Chancellor Turner's administration was embroiled in controversy. Although it was standard practice at most public universities, the chancellor and the University Foundation were criticized by the faculty senate for supplementing the salaries of high level administrators while faculty salaries were below other regional institutions, and, in some cases, even other state schools. In addition to those controversies, some students and alumni considered Turner anti-Greek, accused him of denigrating Ole Miss traditions and the symbols of the Lost Cause, and of de-emphasizing athletics. After he dismissed the head football coach just before the beginning of the 1994 season, one alumnus accused Chancellor Turner of promoting "academics at the expense of athletics" and predicted that "by doing so he will destroy Ole Miss." These problems and controversies notwithstanding, Chancellor Turner met and exceeded his major goals and his eleven-year administration was highly successful by any standard of measure. In the spring of 1995 Chancellor Turner, who was then only forty-eight years old, accepted the presidency of Southern Methodist University in Dallas, Texas. Chancellor Turner was succeeded by Robert Khayat, the fifth of Turner's former top level administrators who became college presidents. The other four were Morris Marks, Thomas Meredith, Ray Hoops and Leslie Wyatt.

Epilogue

A GREAT PUBLIC UNIVERSITY, 1995–1998

The enduring symbols of Ole Miss are the lives of its graduates and the mark they make in the world.

Chancellor Robert Khayat, 1997

As the board of trustees was initiating a traditional search for a new chancellor in the spring of 1995, Robert Conrad Khayat emerged as a consensus candidate. As soon as Khayat's name surfaced, he received nearly unanimous support from the state's political establishment, including Mississippi's two United States Senators Thad Cochran and Trent Lott, both of whom are Ole Miss alumni and Khayat's former classmates, the general public, the legal profession, the business community, the alumni association, the board of trustees, the student body, and, most significantly, from his colleagues on the university faculty. Khayat's appointment in June 1995 was universally applauded.

Chancellor Khayat is the scion of a well-known and highly regarded Gulf Coast family. He is married to the former Margaret Denton, the first Ole Miss alumna to serve as first lady of the university. Chancellor Khayat came to Ole Miss on an athletic scholarship in 1956. During his undergraduate days he was All-SEC in baseball and football, a 1959 Academic All-American in football, and he twice led the nation in scoring as a place kicker. In 1993, when the university celebrated its football centennial, Khayat was named the place kicker on Ole Miss's "Team of the Century."

Following a three-year career in the National Football League, Khayat returned to the Ole Miss law school. After graduating third in the class of 1966 and practicing law for several years, Khayat joined the law faculty. In 1980 Professor Khayat received a Sterling Fellowship to take an advanced degree in law at Yale University, and in 1988 he was cited by the National Football League as "one of the NFL's best examples of a successful scholar athlete." After serving three years as president of the NCAA Foundation, Khayat returned to Ole Miss in 1992 as vice chancellor for university affairs, a position to which he had been appointed in 1984. He was later named executive director of the sesquicentennial commemoration.

While he held these two positions, Khayat also retained his professorship in the law school, where he was an admired and popular teacher. Law students named him Professor of the Year in 1994. During his thirty-two year association with the university's law school, Khayat went to school with or taught most of the practicing attorneys in Mississippi, and many of them have maintained a close personal relationship with him. The sentiments of his former students were expressed by John Grisham who spoke at Chancellor Khayat's inauguration. Grisham reminisced warmly and fondly about his association with Khayat, lavishing praise on him as a mentor and friend of long standing.

In Khayat's first formal interview with the board of trustees, he was asked to articulate his vision for the university. He responded by saying that he wanted the University of Mississippi "to be, and be perceived as, a great public university." In expanding on that goal he explained that, as a Mississippian and a graduate of the university, he wanted the state's flagship institution to provide the quality of education that would enable young Mississippians to develop their fullest potential here at home. He wanted the state's brightest high school seniors to know that they did not have to leave Mississippi to get a first-rate education. Recalling what Chancellor Frederick Barnard had said to the board of trustees more than a century earlier, Robert Khayat explained to the college board in 1995 that he wanted to place the University of Mississippi "in the front ranks of American collegiate institutions."

On the eve of a new millennium, the University of Mississippi is a complex, multipurpose institution that serves many constituencies. The university is an academic institution where teachers and students study the old truths and search for new ones. All that is necessary for learning to flourish are teachers, students, libraries and laboratories, and someone to pay the light bill. Ole Miss is also a social and cultural institution where fun and games and growing up parallel and sometimes overwhelm the learning process. To fulfill its social functions, the university requires an infrastructure, an alumni association, a football stadium, a band, a choir, a coliseum, a track, a baseball park, a rifle range, dormitories, parking lots, food services, a bookstore, student groups and clubs, student publications, a school mascot, a spirit symbol, fraternities and sororities, and a police department. Since the 1880s, when the classical curriculum was abandoned and extracurricular activities were introduced, there has been a contradiction between the academic and the social functions of American colleges.

As Chancellor Khayat was implementing his plans to make Ole Miss a great public university, he was also taking steps to reconcile the contradictions between its academic and social functions. Following his appointment Khayat discontinued the allocation of state appropriated funds for intercollegiate athletics, he privatized the university's food services and the campus bookstore, initiated a plan to increase the efficiency of the university's infrastructure, rescheduled fraternity and sorority rush, opened the library twenty-four hours a day and doubled its acquisitions budget, upgraded the university's teaching laboratories, lengthened the school week by scheduling more Friday afternoon classes, approved the restructuring of the university curriculum, applied for a Phi Beta Kappa chapter, established an honors college, and secured major funding for faculty salary increases in the college of liberal arts.

Chancellor Khayat's decision to move rush from the first week of school to the second month of the fall semester is considered by some university officials as one of the most important developments at the university in recent years. This change, which sends the message that arranging membership in Greek societies is no longer the first order of business at Ole Miss, allows new students to meet their classes for a month or so, learn their way around the campus, and adjust to college life before they are distracted by the pressure and anxiety that are often associated with rush.

Keeping the library open twenty-four hours a day, a policy recommended by the dean of university libraries, John Meador, Jr., also signals to Ole Miss students that the university's central educational facility is available to them at all times. Through a reallocation of internal resources and several private gifts, in particular the donation from the Joseph G. Bancroft Charitable and Educational Fund, the general library's acquisitions budget more than doubled between 1995 and 1998. The recent addition to the John Davis Williams Memorial Library, which was dedicated in April 1997, also doubled the building's square footage. An $8 million contribution from the Donald W. Reynolds Foundation has significantly increased the library's expanding endowment.

In addition to his commitment to library development, Chancellor Khayat has also placed a high priority on the improvement of the university's teaching laboratories. Through private funding, major improvements are being made in the chemistry and biology laboratories. The chemistry department is adding a new computer laboratory and refurbishing the premedical lecture center. The cell and molecular laboratory is also undergoing significant upgrades, and the freshman biology computer laboratory is purchasing state-of-the-art equipment. Additions and current renovations to the physiology laboratory will make it one of the best collegiate facilities in the region.

At the time of Chancellor Khayat's inauguration, the university's class schedule, which had evolved over time in response to student demands, allowed some Ole Miss students to begin their weekend on Thursday. Scheduling more Friday afternoon classes and lengthening the school week might not cause the students to engage in intellectual exercises, Khayat said, but it would at least keep them on the campus. Like the class schedule, the university's curriculum also bears the imprint of student demand. During the fifty years since World War II, the collegiate curriculum has been shaped, molded and modeled according to the whims of the times and by what the market, that is, the student population, would bear. Soon after his appointment, Chancellor Khayat endorsed the work of a task force appointed to examine the university's academic program and to formulate a core curriculum that will be required of all lower division students. While the establishment of a basic curriculum does not signal a return to the old classical tradition, the new requirements will provide a solid and balanced academic preparation for upper division courses.

One of the primary elements of Chancellor Khayat's goal to make Ole Miss a great public university is his commitment to secure a Phi Beta Kappa chapter. Established in 1776 at the College of William and Mary, Phi Beta Kappa is a collegiate honor society that promotes scholarship in the liberal arts and sciences. Even though the society has denied the university's previous applications, Chancellor Khayat and the University of Mississippi are committed to meeting the high standards required for membership. Khayat feels an obligation to give Ole Miss students in the college of liberal arts the opportunity to belong to this prestigious society and to secure for the university the recognition of excellence that accompanies membership in Phi Beta Kappa. Chancellor Khayat's ultimate objective is to make Ole Miss a great public university, and, even if the effort to secure a chapter of Phi Beta Kappa is unsuccessful, the commitment to that goal will have kept the university focused on the enhancement of its academic program. For many years the University of Mississippi has had a chapter of Phi Kappa Phi, an honor society for students in the various schools and colleges found in traditional American universities. Although it lacks the antiquity and prestige of Phi Beta Kappa, the standards for membership in Phi Kappa Phi are approximately the same.

When his friends and former classmates James and Sally McDonnell Barksdale asked Chancellor Khayat what they could do that would have the greatest and most immediate impact on the university's effort to secure a Phi Beta Kappa chapter, he said, without hesitation, the founding of an honors college. A well-endowed honors college, Khayat explained, would enable the university to attract Mississippi's best and brightest students, who would infuse the university with intellectual energy and excitement and would inspire the faculty. Consequently, in 1996 James Barksdale, the CEO of Netscape, and his wife Sally contributed $5.4 million to establish the McDonnell-Barksdale Honors College. During its first year in operation, the honors college admitted 125 of the 325 applicants. The average ACT of the first class was 31.8. Eighty percent of the McDonnell-Barksdale scholars were graduates of Mississippi high schools, six were African American, and two were Asian American. Professor Elizabeth Payne was appointed director of the McDonnell-Barksdale Honors College in 1997.

At the first faculty meeting in the fall of 1998, Chancellor Khayat announced that Richard and Diane Scruggs had pledged $25 million over a twenty-five year period to the university for faculty salaries in the college of liberal arts. A political science major at Ole Miss and a graduate of the law school, Scruggs is a Pascagoula attorney and long-time friend of Chancellor Khayat. In expressing the university's appreciation for their gift, Chancellor Khayat said that Richard and Diane Scruggs "made this extraordinaty commitment to Ole Miss because they fully understand the crucial role of the College of Liberal Arts and the importance of faculty salaries in retaining and attracting the very best professors available."

Chancellor Khayat's effort to place the university in the front ranks of American collegiate institutions has already been successful in several ways. The University of Mississippi is featured in both *The Student Guide to America's 100 Best College Buys: 1999* and *The Student Guide to America's Best College Scholarships: 1998–99*. The *Guide to America's 100 Best College Buys* highlights institutions that have an entering freshman grade-point average and SAT score above the national average, but with tuition costs below the national norm. For the second consecutive year publisher John Culler & Son has selected Ole Miss as one of the 100 best college buys in America.

The *Guide to America's Best Scholarships* rates colleges and universities on scholarships that are awarded exclusively on merit and are not need-based or restricted in any way. After surveying 1,658 four-year institutions and examining a large number of merit scholarships that it considers "the best America offers," the *Guide to America's Best Scholarships* rated the University of Mississippi as one of the 93 best colleges and universities in America. According to Lewis T. Lindsey, Jr., senior editor of the guide, "At a time when parents are borrowing more money than ever to send their children to college, these schools offer real hope to parents whose child has applied himself or herself in high school and who should focus on the best opportunities available." The University of Mississippi's merit-based scholarships are awarded to high school seniors of superior scholarship who also demonstrate outstanding citizenship.

In reacting to the university's inclusion on these two prestigious lists, Chancellor Khayat said, "The Ole Miss faculty, administration and staff are steadfast in their commitment to provide an academic environment that is among the best in the nation, and our alumni and friends continue to generously support the University with resources for scholarships and academic programs." In the first three years of Chancellor Khayat's administration the university has added an impressive array of new scholarships. Among the recently established merit-based scholarships at Ole Miss is the $32,000 Fenley Scholarship, the largest undergraduate award in Mississippi. The newly established Croft Institute for International Studies is offering ten $28,000 scholarships. Four McDonnell-Barksdale Honors College Scholarships at $24,000 each and four $24,000 Pichitino Scholarships are also now available. These new awards augment a large number of existing scholarships, including the prestigious $26,000 Newman Scholarships and the $24,000 Carrier Scholarships.

The online magazine *Yahoo! Internet Life* has also placed the university in a select category, citing Ole Miss as number thirty-six among "the nation's 100 most wired colleges." The magazine based the ranking, which includes some of America's most prestigious institutions, on the university's computer hardware and Internet access. Every student has an e-mail account, and all dormitory rooms and married students apartments are linked to the university's mainframe computer. Students can register for classes, check on grades, communicate with their professors and other students by e-mail. Through the university's mainframe Ole Miss students also have access to the Internet and the World Wide Web. Faculty and students who live off campus also have access to the university's mainframe computer. All laboratories, classrooms, conference rooms, and faculty offices have computer network connections. The online magazine also cited the *Daily Mississippian* as "one of the finest examples of online university newspapers." A heavily used Helpdesk is also an integral part of the university's information technology team.

Not only is every building on the campus connected to the university's mainframe, there is a computer on every professor's desk. Donations to the University Foundation through the Chancellor's Partners and Ole Miss Associates gift program have made it possible to provide every professor a desk-top computer. The computer program was one of the projects initiated by Chancellor Khayat when he was director of the sesquicentennial and implemented by Professor Gloria Kellum, who succeeded Khayat as director. With financial support from the office of Provost Gerald Walton, Professors T. J. Ray, Lee Bolen, and Mark Tew established a Faculty Technology Development Center to provide instruction and technical support for the faculty to maximize the use of their computers.

By the beginning of the new millennium not only will every building on the Oxford campus be wired to the World Wide Web, but almost every building will be either new or recently renovated. Many of the university's grand old buildings, including the Lyceum, Ventress Hall, Johnson Commons, Bondurant Hall, the Old Gym, Guyton Hall, the George M. Street University House (the faculty house south of the library), the Kate Skipwith Teaching Museum, the Walton-Young House, the education building, and Conner Hall, will have been refurbished and some will have been renamed.

Among the new buildings constructed during the first three years of Chancellor Khayat's administration are the Women's Athletic Center, which includes three indoor tennis courts, basketball and volleyball courts, and adjacent softball and soccer fields; Holman Hall, the new home of the school of business administration made possible by a lead gift from the Holman family; the Natural Products Center; and an animal research laboratory. The value of the current renovation and construction projects on the Oxford campus is estimated at more than $100 million. Construction in progress at the University Medical Center in Jackson is valued at more than $200 million.

The Old Chapel, also known as the Y-Building and the second oldest structure on the campus, will undergo a $3.25 million restoration and will house the Croft Institute for International Studies. The Croft Institute was established by an equivalent endowment equal to $60 million set up by the Joseph G. Bancroft Charitable and Educational Fund. The Institute will provide ten $28,000 scholarships and offer courses leading to a baccalaureate degree in international studies, focusing primarily on Asia, Latin America, and Europe, which are Mississippi's strongest trading partners. Peter Frost, William R. Harris Professor of International Studies and former chair of the department of Asian studies at Williams College, served as interim director of the Croft Institute from July 1997 to July 1998. Professor Michael F. Metcalf was named director of the Croft Institute in July 1998.

Now in the early planning stage is the Gertrude Castellow Ford Center for the Performing Arts, which is being funded by a $20 million gift from the Gertrude Ford Foundation. The first building on the campus designed specifically for the performing arts, the Ford Center for the Performing Arts will include a 1,200 seat theater, dressing rooms, a scene shop, rehearsal area, storage space, special lighting and other features that will make it one of the finest performance centers in the region. To be located on University Avenue opposite the present school of education building, the Gertrude Ford building will be the centerpiece of the Ole Miss Cultural Center, a concept developed by the late Chancellor Porter L. Fortune. Existing components of the Cultural Center are the University Museums, the Walton-Young House, and Rowan Oak. Future plans include the construction of a department of theater arts building (east of the performing arts center) and the relocation of the department of music to the present school of education building.

The large gifts from the Reynolds, Bancroft, and Gertrude Ford foundations are examples of Chancellor Khayat's enormous success in securing private support for the university. Private contributions to Ole Miss increased from $17.7 million during 1995 to $25.3 million the following year and to $39.9 million in 1997. The university's endowment rose from $114.3 million in 1995 to $202 million by March 31, 1998, an increase of 76.7 percent. In 1997 the University of Mississippi was one of only seventy-eight institutions, and the only public research university, to receive a Circle of Excellence in Education Award from the Council of Advancement and Support of Education. The Council presented this prestigious award to the University of Mississippi in recognition of its outstanding fund raising initiative and success under the leadership of Chancellor Khayat and Don L. Fruge, president of the University of Mississippi Foundation.

As impressive as these numbers are, they are only part of the story. In 1997 the University of Mississippi led the nation with a 200 percent increase in the number of donors who contributed $5,000 or more. During that year approximately 18,000 of the university's 80,000 identified alumni, almost one in every four, contributed to their alma mater. In expressing his appreciation to the thousands of alumni who made financial contributions to Ole Miss, Chancellor Khayat said in the spring of 1998, "We are truly grateful to those who are a part of the Ole Miss family for supporting the University's mission of becoming a great public university. Because of your vision and support, the University of Mississippi is now receiving national recognition as one of the premier institutions of higher learning in America." For many years, Chancellor Khayat continued, the public's perception of Ole Miss has been influenced by "negative events in our past." The university must be free of those negative perceptions, he added, if it is to fulfill its "mission and destiny."

In the thirty years between Chancellor Williams's retirement in January 1968 and Chancellor Khayat's statement to the alumni in the spring of 1998, the public perception of the University of Mississippi has changed dramatically. The university John Hope Franklin perceived and described at the Oxford town hall meeting in 1998 bears little resemblance to the university in the aftermath of the Meredith riot. And the University of Mississippi's academic standing is held in higher esteem in 1998 than in any other period during its 150 year history. Through years of dedication and service by its faculty, staff, students and alumni, the University of Mississippi is at last free of those negative perceptions and is poised to fulfill its mission and destiny as it enters the new millennium.

Notes and Sources

Abbreviations

BM	Board of Trustees Minutes
FM	Faculty Minutes
HEQ	*History of Education Quarterly*
JMH	*Journal of Mississippi History*
JDWML	John Davis Williams Memorial Library, University of Mississippi
JNPP	Chancellor Joseph Neeley Powers Papers, JDWML
PMHS	Publications of the Mississippi Historical Society
UMSF	University of Mississippi Subject File, Mississippi Department of Archives and History

Conventional documentation of the University of Mississippi's first one hundred and fifty years would greatly increase the length and cost of this volume. Consequently, in place of the traditional method of citations, I provide for each chapter a discussion of the sources used in that chapter's preparation, which includes references for direct quotes unless they are identified in the text. The dedication of this book is a paraphrase of Daniel Webster's famous statement, "It is a small college, but there are those who love it," which he made before the United States Supreme Court in a case defending his alma mater Dartmouth College.

The most useful sources consulted for this sesquicentennial history are the minutes from the meetings of the various boards of trustees that have governed the University of Mississippi, the minutes from faculty meetings, student publications, official reports, catalogs, and other university publications. If the dates and locations of board minutes and faculty minutes, house and senate journals, laws of Mississippi, letters, interviews, newspapers, journals, magazines, catalogs, etc., are indicated in the text, those sources will not be cited in the notes for that chapter. A bibliographical entry, including the author, title, and date of publication, will be cited at the first appearance of a source. Subsequent citations include the author's last name and a shortened title.

The most useful secondary sources are *Historical Catalogue of the University of Mississippi 1849–1909* (1910); Edward Mayes, *History of Edu-*

cation in Mississippi (1899) and *The State University: A Reply by Professor Edward Mayes to Senator James Z. George* (1887); William H. Weathersby, *History of Educational Legislation in Mississippi From 1798–1860* (1921); Grover C. Hooker, "The Origin and Development of the University of Mississippi with Special Reference to Its Legislative Control" (Ph.D. dissertation, Stanford University, 1932); Allen Cabaniss, *The University of Mississippi: Its First Hundred Years* (1949); James B. Lloyd, *The University of Mississippi: The Formative Years* (1979); Kevin Pierce Thornton, "Symbolism at Ole Miss and the Crisis of Southern Identity" (master's thesis, University of Virginia, 1981); Franklin E. Moak, *A History of the Alumni Association of the University of Mississippi 1852–1986* (1986) and "A History of Ole Miss," in *The Heritage of Lafayette County, Mississippi (1986), 76–141*; Sanford Charles Gladden, *A History of the Department of Physics and Astronomy at the University of Mississippi, 1848–1932* (1933); Department of Physics and Astronomy, *A History of the Department of Physics and Astronomy at the University of Mississippi, 1933–1996* (1997); John Vaught, *Rebel Coach* (1971); Lawrence Wells, *Ole Miss Football* (1979); Larry Wells, ed., *A Century of Heroes* (1993); W. G. Barner, *Mississippi Mayhem: Ole Miss vs. Miss. State* (1982); Mike Butler, "Confederate Flags, Class Conflict, a Golden Egg, and Castrated Bulls: A Historical Examination of the Ole Miss-Mississippi State Football Rivalry," *JMH* 59 (1997), 123–41. Dale L. Flesher, *Accountancy at Ole Miss: A Sesquicentennial Salute* (1997); and Nadine Cohodas, *The Band Played Dixie: Race and the Liberal Tradition at Ole Miss* (1997). I have used and quoted extensively from Cohodas's thoughtful and perceptive account of race relations at Ole Miss since the Meredith crisis. Franklin Edwin Moak's unpublished manuscript "150 Years of Leadership: The University of Mississippi, 1844–1994" was also a useful secondary source and was made available by Professor Moak.

General histories of higher education in America that provided historical context include Charles F. Thwing, *A History of Higher Education in America* (1906); Richard Hofstadter and C. DeWitt Hardy, *The Development and Scope of Higher Education in the United States* (1952); George P. Schmidt, *The Liberal Arts College: A Chapter in American Cultural History* (1957); Frederick Rudolph, *The American College and University: A History* (1962); John Brubacher and Willis Rudy, *Higher Education in Transition: A History of American Colleges and Universities, 1636–*

1976 (1976); Christopher J. Lucas, *American Higher Education: A History* (1994); and Alma Pauline Foerster, "The State University in the Old South" (Ph.D. dissertation, Duke University, 1939). Histories of southern universities that were especially helpful were Thomas G. Dyer, *The University of Georgia: A Bicentennial History, 1785–1985* (1985); William D. Snider, *Light on the Hill: A History of the University of North Carolina at Chapel Hill* (1992); James Riley Montgomery, Stanley J. Folmsbee, and Lee Seifert Greene, *To Foster Knowledge: A History of the University of Tennessee 1794–1970* (1984); and Paul K. Conkin, *Gone with the Ivy: A Biography of Vanderbilt University* (1985). Histories of other Mississippi universities consulted were John K. Bettersworth, *People's University: The Centennial History of Mississippi State* (1980); Lelia Gaston Rhodes, *Jackson State University: The First Hundred Years, 1877–1977* (1979); Bridget Smith Pieschel and Stephen Robert Pieschel, *Loyal Daughters: One Hundred Years at Mississippi University for Women* (1984); Chester Morgan, *Dearly Bought, Deeply Treasured: The University of Southern Mississippi 1912–1987* (1987). A general history of higher education in the state is David G. Sansing, *Making Haste Slowly: The Troubled History of Higher Education in Mississippi* (1990). This volume has an extensive bibliography of sources on higher education in Mississippi, including many that bear on the history of the University of Mississippi.

Chapter One Founding the University, 1802–1844

For details on the life of Thomas Dudley Isom, see various references in *The Heritage of Lafayette County, Mississippi* published by the Skipwith Historical and Genealogical Society in 1986. Robert J. Walker's quotation is in John K. Bettersworth, *Your Mississippi* (1975), 138. The "flush times" in Mississippi are described by a contemporary, Joseph Glover Baldwin, in *Flush Times in Mississippi and Alabama: A Series of Sketches* (1853). The impact of the land boom on Oxford and Lafayette County is described in *Heritage of Lafayette County.*

Governor Claiborne's educational and political philosophy is discussed in Joseph Hatfield, *William Claiborne: Jeffersonian Centurion in the American Southwest* (1976), and his letters to the territorial assembly are in Dunbar Rowland, *Official Letter Books of William Charles Coles Claiborne, 1801–1816,* 6 vols. (1917), 6:100–101.

See the first two chapters in David G. Sansing, *Making Haste Slowly, the Troubled History of Higher Education in Mississippi* (1990) for details on the early history of higher education in Mississippi. For histories of Mississippi College and Oakland see Richard A. and Nannie Pitts McLemore, *A History of Mississippi College* (1979) and Melvin K. Bruse, "History of Oakland College" (master's thesis, Louisiana State University, 1965). The legislative history of the effort to found the university and the continuing controversy over the seminary fund can be traced through the journals of the state senate and house of representatives. The inaugural addresses are found in Robert E. McArthur, ed., *Inaugural Addresses of Governors of Mississippi* (1980, 1981).

Governor McNutt's circular letter, the responses he received, and his special message to the legislature were printed in various state newspapers in December 1839, and in *Senate Journal 1840,* 33–35, 289–324. For Pray's plan for a statewide system of education, see P. Rutilius R. Pray, *Revised Statutes of the State of Mississippi* (1836), 264–83. This rare document is in the state law library in the Carroll Gartin Building, Jackson, Mississippi.

The southern clergy's opposition to state universities is discussed in John D. Wade, *Augustus Baldwin Longstreet: A Study in the Development of Culture in the South* (1924).

The encounter between the lady abolitionist and the Southern gentleman is reported in the *Vicksburg Sentinel & Expositor,* January 31, 1837. The quotation "process by which a culture transmits itself" is in Bernard Bailyn, *Education in the Forming of American Society* (1960), 14.

Chapter Two Oxford and the University, 1844–1848

A discussion of the role Ventress played in the legislative process leading to the founding of the university and the selection of Oxford is found in Linda Lasswell Crist, Chapter 5, "A Gentleman of Scholarly Attainments," 191–236, "Useful in His Day: James Alexander Ventress (1805–1867)" (Ph.D. dissertation, University of Tennessee, 1980). The sites nominated, the commissioners' report on each location, and the votes on the sites are found in *Senate Journal 1840,* 842–47; *Laws of Mississippi 1840,* 92–95; *House Journal 1841,* 266–71, 311–12.

The sources for the early history of Oxford and travel conditions in antebellum Mississippi are John Sobotka, *A History of Lafayette County, Mississippi* (1976); *Heritage of Lafayette County (1986)*; *Besancon's Annual Register, 1838*; John Cooper Hathorn, *Early Settlers of Lafayette County, Mississippi* (1980 reprint of a 1938 master's thesis); W. J. Hill, "History of Overland Travel in Mississippi Before Railroads" (master's thesis, University of Mississippi, 1930); Thomas D. Clark, *A Pioneer Southern Railroad from New Orleans to Cairo* (1936); David L. Smiley, "William Carey Crane, Professor of Old Mississippi," *JMH* 12 (April 1950), 98–104; *Phi Sigma Magazine,* February 1857 and *Mississippi University Magazine,* May 1857; the Faulkner reference is found in *Requiem for a Nun* (Vintage Books, 1975), 25. Mrs. Wailes's boast is in Charles Sydnor, *A Gentleman of the Old Natchez Region: Benjamin L. C. Wailes* (1938), 264.

The 1844 description of Oxford appeared in the Oxford *Observer,* May 18, 1844, and the "Cumberland Girl" article appeared in the Oxford *Democratic Flag* April 14, 1852. The Oxford *Intelligencer* quotations appear in various issues in the summer and early fall of 1860. For the newspaper quotations concerning the location of the university see *Vicksburg Daily Whig,* February 1, 1841, Holly Springs *Conservative and Banner,* February 19, 1841, and Ripley *Advertiser,* May 15, 1845.

For a brief history of the seminary fund see Edward Mayes, *The State University: A Reply by Professor Edward Mayes to Senator James Z. George (1887).* Delay's criticism of the Planters' Bank is in the Oxford *Observer,* June 22, 1844.

The charter of the university is in *Mississippi Laws 1844,* chapter 56. Biographical information on the members of the board of trustees may be found in individual folders in the university archives. The board's attempt to reconcile the discrepancies concerning the amount of the seminary fund is recorded in the minutes of the board of trustees. The manuscript minutes of the board of trustees have been transcribed by Florence E. Campbell, *Journal of the Minutes of the Board of Trustees of the University of Mississippi, 1845–1860.* This typescript copy of the minutes is available in the university archives.

The influence of sectionalism in antebellum Mississippi, including an analysis of the debate over relocating the university in 1846, is discussed in Samuel T. Lyles, "Conditions Relating to Sectionalism in

Mississippi From 1838 to 1852" (master's thesis, University of Mississippi, 1932).

The issue of the Oxford *Observer* that detailed the cornerstone ceremony is not extant. Fortunately, the *Holly Springs Guard* reprinted the article from the Oxford paper on August 14, 1846. A published copy of Stearns's oration is in the university archives.

Chapter Three The Formative Years, 1848–1856

The most valuable source for this chapter is Campbell, *Journal of the Minutes of the Board of Trustees.* The board of trustees, which met only twice a year, allowed its executive committee great discretion in acting on its behalf between regular meetings. Although historians might wish that the trustees had included more details of their discussions and more information about the decisions they made, the minutes are still the best source available and they have been used extensively for the university's early history. In most cases the actions of the board cited in this chapter are identified by date and can be easily located in Campbell's journal. They are, therefore, not cited in these notes.

John Newton Waddel, *Memorials of Academic Life* (1891) and *Historical Discourse Delivered at the Quarter-Centennial Anniversary of the University of Mississippi* (1873) provide insight as well as information about the early board of trustees, the early faculty, student behavior, and the relationship between the Protestant clergy and the state university. The *Historical Catalogue, 1848–1909* includes some information about almost every antebellum student, the early faculty, academic departments, and statistical information for the formative years. Almost as important is Edward Mayes, *History of Education in Mississippi,* which includes brief histories of Mississippi's old-time colleges and a lengthy account of the early history of the University of Mississippi. Mattie Pegues Wood, *The History of My Father's Family* and *Diaries and Letters of Rebecca Ann Evans Pegues* are rich sources for biographical information on Alexander Pegues, including his relationship to L. Q. C. Lamar, for information on original members of the board of trustees and early faculty, and for general information about this period of the university's history. Copies of these two volumes, which were provided to the author by Richard Stanley, a Pegues descendent, are in the university archives.

An especially useful secondary source for this period is James B. Lloyd, *The University of Mississippi: The Formative Years (1979).* This volume includes many of the photographs taken by Professor Edward C. Boynton in the 1850s.

The biographical information on the early faculty members compiled for this study is available in the university archives.

For a study of the life and career of George Frederick Holmes, see Neal C. Gillespie, *The Collapse of Orthodoxy: The Intellectual Ordeal of George Frederick Holmes* (1972) and George Blake Holmes, "The Life and Contributions of George Frederick Holmes, Scholar, Teacher, and Writer" (master's thesis, Virginia Polytechnic Institute, 1957). The Holmes thesis and other biographical information on President Holmes was graciously provided to the author by Professor and Mrs. Ralph J. Stoudt of the University of Virginia. Mrs. Stoudt is a descendent of George Frederick Holmes.

For a study of Bledsoe, see Willard Murrell Hays, "Polemics and Philosophy: A Biography of Albert Taylor Bledsoe" (Ph.D. dissertation, University of Tennessee, 1971). Samuel Willard's comment about Bledsoe being presidential material is in Hays, "Bledsoe," 144. Sophia Bledsoe Herrick cites Charles O'Conner's statement about Bledsoe saving Jefferson Davis's life in her preface to the 1915 edition of her father's book, which she retitled *Is Davis a Traitor, or Was Secession a Constitutional Right.*

For the life and career of Professor Waddel see Waddel, *Memorials of Academic Life.*

George Frederick Holmes's sketch of Millington is in *William and Mary Quarterly* 3 (1923), 23–35, and the Lafayette County farmer's comment about Millington's knowledge of soil chemistry is in Oxford *Organizer,* May 5, 1849.

Alexander H. Stephens's description of commencement in the Old South is in Wade, *Augustus Baldwin Longstreet,* 261. A copy of Bledsoe's commencement address is in the university archives. The Jackson *Mississippian*'s challenge to the press and the people of Mississippi to support the university is quoted in the Oxford *Organizer,* August 18, 1849. The attack on the university by the sectarians is discussed in the Oxford *Organizer,* April 3, 28, May 12, 26, June 7, 14, August 18, 1849.

Wade's biography of Longstreet, Bishop O. P. Fitzgerald, *Judge Longstreet: A Life Sketch* (1891), and Kimball King, *Augustus Baldwin Longstreet* (1984) are the best sources on Longstreet. The reference by the university alumnus to Longstreet's timely appointment appears in the *Mississippi University Magazine,* April 1859.

During its third session, the university began publishing *Laws and Regulations of the University of Mississippi* and in its fifth session began publishing an annual catalog; these two publications were used extensively in preparing this chapter. Minutes of the meetings of the two literary societies are in the university archives. The names and dates of antebellum fraternities at the university are found in Franklin E. Moak, "A History of Ole Miss," *Heritage of Lafayette County,* 76–141.

Mayes's description of Lamar's debate with Foote is in Edward Mayes, *Lucius Q. C. Lamar: His Life, Times, and Speeches* (1896), 51–55.

The troubles and trials of the agricultural and geological survey are recounted in Eugene W. Hilgard, "A Historical Outline of the Geological and Agricultural Survey of the State of Mississippi," PMHS 3 (1900), 207–35. John Waddel describes Professor Boynton as a profane swearer in *Memorials of Academic Life,* 307.

Jacob Thompson's request for a law school was included in the board's annual report to the legislature in 1854 and is found in Campbell, *Journal of the Minutes of the Board of Trustees,* 201ff.

For a discussion of President Longstreet's political entanglements with Winans and others, see Ray Holder, *William Winans: Methodist Leader in Antebellum Mississippi (1977)*; Cecil S. H. Ross, "Dying Hard, Dying Fast: The Know-Nothing Experience in Mississippi" (Ph.D. dissertation, Notre Dame University, 1982) and David Nathaniel Young, "The Mississippi Whigs 1834–1860" (Ph.D. dissertation, University of Alabama, 1968).

Chapter Four Universitas Scientiarum, 1856–1861

The most important sources for this chapter are John Fulton, *Memoirs of Frederick A. P. Barnard* (1896); William J. Chute, *Damn Yankee! The First Career of Frederick A. P. Barnard* (1978); John Wesley Johnson, "Sketches of Judge A. B. Longstreet and Dr. F. A. P. Barnard," PMHS 12 (1912), 122–48; Frederick A. P. Barnard, "Autobiographical Sketch of Dr. F. A. P. Barnard," PMHS 12 (1912) 107–21; a typescript autobiography of Chancellor Barnard in the university archives; Frederick A. P. Barnard, *Letter to the Honorable The Board of Trustees of the University of Mississippi* (1858); and Barnard's correspondence with Hilgard and others. The Barnard letters quoted here, unless otherwise noted, are in the Barnard Collection in the University of Mississippi archives. Of particular importance for this chapter are the various university publications, especially the annual catalog, because they reflect Chancellor Barnard's new system of student discipline, changes in the academic program, and the restructuring of university governance. The minutes of the board of trustees are also important sources concerning Barnard's career at the University of Mississippi because they chronicle the varying degrees of support for his reforms among the trustees and the progress of those reforms.

On the changing character of American higher education during the 1850s, see Chapter 11, "Crisis of the 1850s," 221–41, in Frederick Rudolph, *The American College and University: A History* (1962).

The descriptions and characterizations of the university's scientific apparatus are in the 1857 catalog; *DeBow's Review,* 28 (September 1859), 356; and Chute, *Damn Yankee*; see also Sanford C. Gladden, *A History of the Department of Physics and Astronomy at the University of Mississippi* (1932). Barnard's diagram of the chemistry lecture room is in an April 30, 1856, letter to Hilgard.

The Pontotoc *Examiner's* discussion of the removal of the university to Jackson is quoted in the Okolona *Prairie News,* March 24, 1859. The praise for Chancellor Barnard and the university cited by Bishop Green is in Jackson *Mississippian,* January 5, 19, 1858; February 29, March 8, April 12, May 31, June 14, 1859; and March 13, 16, 1860. In some of these articles the *Mississippian* quotes favorable comments from the *True Southron.*

Details of the "Branham affair" are found in *Record of the Testimony and Proceedings, in the Matter of the Investigation by the Trustees of the University of Mississippi, On the 1st and 2nd of March, 1860, of the Charges Made by H. R. Branham, Against the Chancellor of the University* (1860). For press coverage of this affair, see the *Memphis Daily Appeal,* March 15, 21, April 13, 1860. The description of Jefferson Davis's public display is in Fulton, *Memoirs,* 259. James Gordon's letter to Barnard, dated March 3, 1860, is in the Barnard Collection at Columbia University.

The excitement leading up to Mississippi's secession, including the straw poll at the university and the formation of the University Greys, is covered extensively in the Oxford *Intelligencer* during the summer of 1860 and the spring of 1861. Barnard's conversation with DeBow is in the typescript autobiography of Barnard in the university archives. Barnard's correspondence with his northern friends is in Chute, *Damn Yankee,* 182–83. Chancellor Barnard's study of southern military schools was published as *Report on the Organization of Military School* (1861). A copy is in the university archives.

Chapter Five Students and Soldiers, 1861–1870

Howard Bahr's quotation is in Oxford *Eagle,* March 6, 1991. Bahr, who teaches English at Motlow State Community College in Tullahoma, Tennessee, is a former English instructor at the University of Mississippi and curator of Rowan Oak (William Faulkner's home). He is the author of a brilliant Civil War novel, *Black Flower,* published in 1997 by the Nautical and Aviation Publishing Company of America. The Jefferson Davis quotation on sending young boys to war is in Barnard, "Autobiographical Sketch," PMHS 12 (1912), 115.

Much of the information on the University Greys and the 11th Mississippi was provided to the author by Stark Miller, author of the forthcoming *Imperishable Glory, A History of the University Greys,* and Steven Stubbs, author of the forthcoming *Duty, Honor, Valor: The Story of the Eleventh Mississippi Infantry Regiment.* For additional information on the Greys and the 11th Mississippi see Steve Davis, "Ole Miss's spirited Greys left their quiet University campus for the war's worst battlefields," *America's Civil War Magazine* (March 1992), 11–12, 70–72, and "'. . . Like leaves in an autumn wind': The 11th Mississippi Infantry in the Army of Northern Virginia," *Civil War Regiments, A Journal of the American Civil War* (vol. 11, No. 4, 1992), 269–312; Terrence J. Winschel, "Heavy Was their Loss: Joe Davis's Brigade at Gettysburg," *Gettysburg: Historic Articles of Lasting Interest* (Issues 2 and 3, 1990); Steven Stubbs, *For My Children* (1993); and Billy Ellis, *Tithes of Blood, A Confederate Soldier's Story,* (1997). See also Shelby Foote, *The Civil War, A Narrative* (3 vols., 1958, 1963, 1974).

Colonel Evander Law made the statement "like leaves in an autumn wind" in describing the losses the 11th Mississippi sustained in a charge at Gaines Mill (June 27, 1862). It is also an appropriate description for the losses the 11th Mississippi suffered during the charge at Gettysburg, and I use it to describe that situation. See Lloyd, *Formative Years,* 34–35, 38–39 for the full text of Gage's letter and a reproduction of the stained glass window in Ventress Hall. Gage's original letter was given to the University of Mississippi by Mrs. Franklin Amos McLendon (the great niece of Jeremiah Gage) and her daughter, Gage McLendon Black (Gage's great, great niece).

For Keyes's quotation, see Frank Keyes, *An Address Delivered to the Alumni Association of the University of Mississippi, on the Fifth Day of July, 1859.* A copy of this address is in the university archives.

For the correspondence between T. W. Caskey, James M. Howry, and Governor John J. Pettus, see Willie D. Halsell, "The Oxford Hospital in 1862," *JMH* 8 (January 1940), 36–44; see also Jemmey G. Johnson, "The University Hospital," PMHS 12 (1912), 94–106, and B. F. Manire, ed., *Caskey's Last Book* (1896). Johnson relates the story of the grounds crew removing the markers in the cemetery.

See Rebecca Pegues's diary, June 20, 1862, for a reference to the first exodus from Oxford. For a brief account of Grant's occupation of Oxford, see Jack Case Wilson, *Faulkner, Fortunes, and Flames* (n.d.), 2–6. William T. Sherman's letter to Barnard, dated July 28, 1863, is in the Barnard collection at Columbia University. See also John F. Marszalek, *Sherman: A Soldier's Passion for Order* (1993) for information about Sherman's presidency of Louisiana Seminary and his military campaigns in Mississippi.

A discussion of the "Jewish order" is found in P. C. Headley, *The Life and Campaigns of Lieutenant General U. S. Grant* (1866), 199, and William McFeely, *Grant: A Biography* (1982), 123–24.

For Mrs. Grant's visit to Oxford and Jesse Grant's recollection, see W. E. Woodward, *Meet General Grant* (1928), 282; Major General U. S. Grant III, *U. S. Grant: Warrior and Statesman* (1969), 173; and John Y. Simon, ed., *The Personal Memoirs of Julia Dent Grant* (1975), 83, 105, 107, 108, 110, 117n.

See J. G. Deupree, "Capture of Holly Springs, December 20, 1862," PMHS 4 (1901), 49–63, for his account of the Van Dorn raid; for Colonel

John S. Griffith's recollection, see Victor M. Rose, *Ross' Texas Brigade* (1881), 81ff. For a study of how Americans make use of historical memory see Carol Reardon, *Pickett's Charge in History and Memory* (1997).

See U. S. Grant, *Personal Memoirs of U. S. Grant* (Da Capo Paperback, 1982), 226–27 for the lesson he learned at Oxford about living off the land. For Grant's order to burn Oxford, see J. V. Frederick, "An Illinois Soldier in North Mississippi: Diary of John Wilson February 16–December 30, 1862," *JMH* 1 (1939), 182–94.

Waddel, *Memorials of Academic Life,* 445–49, discusses the reopening of the university and the appointment of the postwar faculty. The circumstances of Johnson's appointment are found in John Lipscomb Johnson, *Autobiographical Notes* (1958), 204–8. Bishop Green's concern for the university was expressed in a letter to Barnard dated February 20, 1866, and is in the Barnard Collection in Columbia University. Barnard's letter to Hilgard is in the Barnard Collection at the university archives.

The published memoirs of Chancellor Waddel and the Oxford *Falcon* are the best sources of information on the university during the first few years after the war. The "worthy young aspirants" quotation is in Waddel, *Memorials of Academic Life,* 449. For the board's defense of its admission policy, see the Oxford *Eagle,* March 15, 1866. The charges made by the *Jackson Daily News* are quoted in Faculty Minutes, February 21, 1866.

The 1866 commencement is described in Allen Cabaniss, *The University of Mississippi: Its First Hundred Years* (1949), 85. The dispatch given to Waddel is quoted in Waddel, *Memorials of Academic Life,* 425.

For his 1867 commencement address, see T. D. Witherspoon, *The Appeal of the South to Its Educated Men* (1867); a published copy is in the university archives.

For the history of Reconstruction in Mississippi, see William C. Harris, *Presidential Reconstruction in Mississippi* (1967) and *Day of the Carpetbagger* (1978), and David G. Sansing, "The Role of the Scalawag in Mississippi Reconstruction" (Ph.D. dissertation, University of Southern Mississippi, 1969). For Henderson's letter see David G. Sansing, *Mississippi, Its People and Culture* (1981), 208.

Governor Alcorn's enjoinder to purge the university's halls of political factions is in Harris, *Day of the Carpetbagger,* 345, and the "nervous apprehension" quotation is in Mayes, *Education in Mississippi,* 164. The

Robert Hudson correspondence is discussed in Waddel *Memorials of Academic Life,* 465ff., and Flournoy's attempt to integrate the university is discussed in James Garner, *Reconstruction in Mississippi* (1901), 369.

The *anno domini* of higher education in America is discussed in Laurence Veysey, *The Emergence of the American University* (1965). The "militate the condition of man" quotation is by Robert H. Finley, an antebellum president of the University of Georgia, who believed that the purpose of college education was to direct the student's "heart to heaven." His quotation is cited in Sansing, *Making Haste Slowly,* 5.

Chapter Six A Republic of Letters, 1870–1887

Chancellor Waddel's "republic of letters" quotation is in Hooker, "Origin and Development of the University," 109. For a discussion of his northern tour and his reorganization plan, see Waddel, *Memorials of Academic Life,* 477ff. His report can also be found in the 1870–74 published minutes of the board of trustees; Hilgard's report on the school of agriculture is in those minutes as well. Additional information on the agricultural school may be found in Mayes, *Education in Mississippi,* 170ff. Chancellor Waddel explains the circumstances of his resignation in *Memorials of Academic Life,* 494ff. For his twenty–fifth anniversary speech, see Waddel, *Historical Discourse.*

For the Jackson *Clarion* quotation about radicalizing the university and Lamar as a martyr see Harris, *Day of the Carpetbagger,* 345–47. For the Lamar episode in the federal courtroom, see Sansing, *Making Haste Slowly,* 58; see also Mayes, *Lamar: His Life, Times, and Speeches, 131–134.* For a more recent biography of Lamar see James L. Murphy, *L. Q. C. Lamar: Pragmatic Patriot* (1973).

The Crystal Springs *Monitor* is quoted in the Jackson *Clarion,* July 24, 1874. For a brief discussion of Jonathan Tarbell's activities and his quotation, see Harris, *Day of the Carpetbagger,* 345–47. Quinche's letter to Johnson is quoted in Johnson, *Autobiographical Notes,* 206–7. Mayes's reference to Governor Ames is in Mayes, *Education in Mississippi,* 162. For Waddel's quotation about Governor Alcorn and Professor Shoup's resignation, see Waddel, *Memorials of Academic Life,* 472–74.

For biographical information on Stewart see Marshall Wingfield, *General A. P. Stewart, His Life and Letters* (1954) and Timothy Brian Smith,

"Old Straight: The Civil War Career of Alexander Peter Stewart" (master's thesis, University of Mississippi, 1997). See Wingfield, *General Stewart,* 40–41 for Wingfield's statement that Stewart was an "ardent opponent of slavery" and that he voted against the secession of Tennessee. Johnson, *Autobiographical Notes,* 248, is the source for Judge Robert Hill's influence on Stewart's acceptance of the chancellor's office. For the defense of Chancellor Stewart and the university against its religious critics, see *Mississippi University Magazine,* January 1876.

See Mayes, *Education in Mississippi,* 144ff, for a discussion of the law school in the postwar period. Barksdale's statement in support of the university is in Jackson *Clarion,* August 2, 1876.

See FM, June 23, 1880, thanking Hampton Sullivan for his successful effort in persuading the legislature to establish a seminary fund endowment. The quotation from the memorial to the legislature is in Cabaniss, *The University of Mississippi,* 89.

See FM, June 27, 1884, for the appointment of Julia Wilcox as librarian. (It is possible that W. D. Hedleston (1882–83) and John H. Shumaker (1883–84) were full-time librarians, but the records are not clear. Mahalia Savalle in her manuscript history of the library lists Julia Wilcox as the first librarian.) See FM, November 6, 1883, for the faculty's request for funds to classify the library's holdings and the June 26, 1884, BM for the board's dissatisfaction with Chancellor Stewart that the classification had not been done. The dual role of postmistress and librarian is noted in FM, January 4, 1887.

Chancellor Waddel's assessment of coeducation is in *Memorials of Academic Life,* 480. For a brief discussion of the Mississippi career of Sally Eola Reneau and of Annie Coleman Peyton's support for a public women's college, see Bridget Smith Pieschel and Stephen Robert Pieschel, *Loyal Daughters: One Hundred Years at Mississippi University for Women, 1884–1984* (1984). On the role of Sullivan and Clayton in the adoption of coeducation, see BM, June 26, June 28, 1882, and see Mayes, *Education in Mississippi,* 178, for a brief account of the early years of coeducation at the university. The letter justifying coeducation at the university and the Mississippi Industrial College and Institute is in Jackson *Clarion,* June 9, 1886. Hampton Sullivan's letter to Barnard is quoted in Moak, *A History of the Alumni Association,* 42. Sarah Isom's career at the University of Mississippi is recounted briefly in Lloyd, *The Formative Years,* 58.

See FM, March 20, 1875, for the election of the faculty as honorary members of the baseball team and March 3, 1883, for the approval of the team's trip to Water Valley. See BM, June 25, 1874, for the allocation of funds for a music program and FM, January 29, March 15, and March 22, 1881, for the board's decision not to revive the music program.

The "old learning . . . in decline" statement is in Cabaniss, *University of Mississippi,* 95. Chalmers's letter to Barnard is in the Barnard Collection at Columbia University. For Chalmers's recommendations to the board, see BM, June 26, 1884, and the August 5, 1884, minutes for the board's response. Kilpatrick's letters to McInnis are in the L. L. McInnis Collection in the university archives.

The issue of the *Mississippi University Magazine* that published the criticism of Professor Johnson is not extant, but the article was discussed at length during several faculty meetings. For the Meharg episode, see FM, January 15, February 5, May 13, 21, 28, 29, June 12, 18, 1878. On the adoption of a new grading scale, see FM, November 11, 1884. See Johnson, *Autobiographical Notes,* 208–9, for his being called before the board and his altercation with E. DeS. Juny, the son of Professor F. A. Juny, and pages 210, 247, and 248 for his conversation with Professor Sears and his assessment of Stewart, Sears, and Wheat.

Departmental diplomas and certificates are described in various university catalogs.

See BM, April 18, 1870, and FM, May 25, 1886, for the faculty's recommendation to abolish the dormitory system. The few details available on the "lewd woman" are in Frances R. Huff, "The Relationship of Oxford and the University of Mississippi 1848–1947" (master's thesis, University of Mississippi, 1947), 31, and FM, June 10, 14, 1881. See FM, January 30, 1881, for the adoption of weekly inspection, and for Professor Johnson's opposition to the military style discipline, see Johnson, *Autobiographical Notes,* 240. For Judge Campbell's appeal on behalf of his son, see FM, March 11, 15, 1881. See BM, June 29, 1881, for the board's agreement not to hear student appeals.

Clayton's letter to Barnard, dated July 6, 1886, is in the Barnard Collection at Columbia University. The letter praising Mississippi A & M is in Jackson *Clarion,* July 21, 1886. The reference to the faculty as "old landmarks" is in a letter to the editor in the Jackson *Clarion,* July 7, 1886. The "old fossils" quotation is in Jackson *Clarion,* July 11, 1886.

On his maneuvering to keep his position, see Johnson, *Autobiographical Notes,* 249.

Chapter Seven Ole Miss, Football, Pretty Women, and Rhodes Scholars, 1887–1907

For the board's commendation of the faculty, see BM, June 28, 1889. See minutes of June 29 on requiring professors to sign the statement. For the faculty's reelection of Mayes, see FM, July 1, 1887. See the June 1889 issue of the student magazine for its commendation of the faculty and its recommendation of Mayes for chancellor.

On the Mayes-George debate, see Edward Mayes, *The State University: A Reply by Professor Edward Mayes to Senator James Z. George* (1887). For a biographical sketch of Senator George, see Dunbar Rowland, *Courts, Judges and Lawyers of Mississippi 1798–1935* (1935), 99–103. The legislative committee's reference to the university as the pre-eminent state institution is in *Senate Journal 1886,* 504.

For a discussion of the faculty dismissals, see Johnson, *Autobiographical Notes,* 266–70, 273–74 and Oxford *Globe,* June 27, July 11, 1889. See Oxford *Eagle* August 22, 1889, for a report on the suicide of Professor Quinche. For its editor's comment about too many bosses, see *Globe,* September 12, 1889.

For a biographical sketch of Edward Mayes, see David G. Sansing, "Edward Mayes," in James B. Lloyd, ed., *Lives of Mississippi Authors, 1817–1967* (1981), 327–30.

The cost of the library building is cited in BM, June 23, 1890. On the memorial window to the University Greys, see Moak, *Alumni Association,* 45–46; Lloyd, *Formative Years,* 36–39; *Memphis Avalanche,* May 23, 1889; *Booneville Banner,* December 4, 18, 1893.

For the political speculation about Mayes, see Oxford *Globe,* April 2, 16, 23, 1891. On Mayes's unexpected departure, see *Globe,* December 24, 1891.

The student magazine's references to the "preps" are in the November 1890, November 1893, and November 1894 issues.

The 1894 land grant is discussed in *Historical Catalog, 1849–1909,* 1–5.

On the extension of the campus to the railroad, see Fulton's annual reports in BM, June 4, 1894, and June 9, 1897. For the bicycle regulations, see FM, March 29, 1889, March 31, 1898, and June 7, 1899. The expansion and modernization of the campus and the construction of new buildings are noted and described in student publications, university catalogs, and various numbers of the *Official and Statistical Register of the State of Mississippi* published every four years by the secretary of state.

The establishment and evolution of the professional schools is discussed in the *Historical Catalog, 1848–1909*. For a history of the medical school, see Lucie Robertson Bridgforth, *Medical Education in Mississippi: A History of the School of Medicine* (1984).

The reference to intellectuals and aggressive Christians is in Veysey, *The Emergence of the American University*, 137. The reference to research as a threat to Southern values is in Joseph Stetar, "In Search of Direction: Southern Higher Education After the Civil War," *HEQ* 25 (Fall 1985), 358. See Chancellor Fulton's 1893 annual report in BM, June 13, 1893, for his introduction of professorial rank. The careers of the professors mentioned may be traced through the *Historical Catalog 1848–1909*.

For Frederick Rudolph's quotation, see *The American College and University*, 430. For Robert Maynard Hutchins's quotation, see *The Higher Learning in America* (1936), 112–14.

See FM, February 13, 14, 15, 1906, for the investigation of the German Club's ball.

Sarah Isom's complaint is in the June 1905 issue of the *Magazine*.

On the university's first Rhodes Scholar, see the January and December 1904 issues of the student magazine; Ford's letter to Fulton is in the January 1906 issue. See the current university catalog for the establishment of the Taylor Medals.

Details on the early history of the university's football program are in "Ole Miss's First Team," a typescript article written by Professor Bondurant that was provided to the author by the late Vice Chancellor Alton Bryant; see also Alexander Bondurant, "The Significance of College Athletics," in the May 1904 issue of the *Magazine*; "History of the University Football Team," in the June 1903 issue of the *Magazine*; and Lawrence Wells, *Ole Miss Football* (1979). Other sources were faculty minutes, various issues of the *University Record, Varsity Voice, Ole Miss,* Oxford newspapers, and Langston Rogers, ed., *Ole Miss 1997 Football Media Guide*. The poem to the pretty girl was printed in Oxford *Eagle,*

November 23, 1893. On the establishment of the SIAA and its rules, see FM, October 29, 1895, September 29, 1896, May 9, 1899; the June 1903 *Magazine*; the 1906 *Ole Miss*; and the 1906 university catalog. The ode to autumn's hero is in the November 1906 *Magazine.*

Stark Young's reminiscence is in Lloyd, *Formative Years,* 91. For the faculty's reaction to Robertson's article, see FM, May 2, 8, 9, 14, 15, 18, 28, 1901. The Jackson *Clarion-Ledger* article is attached to the faculty minutes.

For the report of the 1904 legislative committee's report, see *House Journal 1904,* 346–49, 406–8; see also William F. Holmes, *The White Chief: James Kimble Vardaman* (1970), 168–76. See Holmes, *White Chief,* 172, for the altercation between Glover and Chamberlain and 176 for F. C. Holmes's assessment of Fulton.

See BM, June 8, 1906, for Kincannon's decline of the chancellorship. The announcement of Aswell's election was reported in the March 1907 issue of the student magazine. The 1907 catalog and *Ole Miss* list Aswell as "Chancellor-elect." Details on Aswell's and Williams's visits are in the May 1907 issue of the student magazine. The board's enhancement of the chancellor's authority is in BM, May 18, 1907, and was discussed in *Varsity Voice,* June 1, 1907.

Chapter Eight A Democratic University, 1907–1927

Chancellor Kincannon's inaugural address is quoted extensively in *Varsity Voice,* September 19, 1907. See Jackson *Mississippian,* January 27, 1912, for its praise of the work-study program. The story of Chester Andrew McLarty was told to the author by his son, John Milton (Jack) McLarty. Minutes of the organizational meeting of the honor council are in the university archives. A copy of Chancellor Kincannon's 1907 annual report is in Hooker, Appendix H, "Origin and Development of the University." Kincannon's reference to Gordon Hall is cited in the campus newspaper now called the *Mississippian,* February 13, 1913.

Reports on the grant from the Peabody Fund and the opening of the library are in the *Mississippian,* October 21, November 11, 1911, June 12, 1912. See various university catalogs for library holdings. The student petition to expand the hours is noted in FM, October 29, 1903, and the board's approval of additional hours is in BM, June 4, 1905.

Regarding the borrowing from the LaBauve Fund, see BM, June 4, 1907; Memphis *Commercial Appeal,* September 30, 1913; Hooker, "Origin and Development of the University," 209–11; and *Mississippi Laws 1920,* 244

For details on the reorganization of the board of trustees, Sexton's speech, and the consolidation of Ole Miss and Mississippi A & M, see Sansing, *Making Haste Slowly,* 81–85. For the Phi Sigma debates on consolidating or moving the university see *Mississippian,* February 14, 1914, and February 20, 1918.

For information about the financial controversies during Chancellor Kincannon's administration and the various legislative investigations, see *Senate Journal 1912,* 746–47; *House Journal 1912,* 1149, 1153–54; *Mississippian,* February 17, 1912; John L. Deister, *Chancellor A. A. Kincannon and the University of Mississippi* (January 1914), and Hooker, "Origin and Development of the University," 199.

The athletic eligibility controversies of 1911–13 are discussed in FM, May 15, 16, 18, 20, 24, September 20, October 28, 1912 (attached to these faculty minutes are documents and affidavits relating to the promissory note); newspaper clippings in UMSF; Deister, *Kincannon and the University;* a letter from Alexander Bondurant to Mr. Pate, dated June 8, 1913; Alexander Bondurant, "A Narrative Account of the Athletic Troubles at the University of Mississippi with special reference to their effect upon me." In his letter to Pate, Bondurant seeks help in keeping his position at the university, which was jeopardized by his opposition to Kincannon's decision to allow an ineligible player to participate. The "Narrative," a twelve-page typescript account of the events leading to the university's suspension, is dated July 23–29, 1913. These documents were given to the author several years ago by the late Alton Bryant. For a justification of awarding self-help jobs to athletes, see *Mississippian,* October 27, 1915. Concerning the university's withdrawal from the SIAA, see *Mississippian,* November 25, 1914, March 31, 1915; regarding the formation of the Southeastern Conference, see Chick Hosch, ed., *The Official Southeastern Conference Football Record Book for 1949,* (1949), 4. The university's game in Cuba is reported in the *Mississippian,* December 16, 1921, January 13, 1922. Casey Stengel's brief association with the university's baseball team is reported in *Mississippian,* February 18, 25, March 4, 1914, February 24, 1915.

Information on the faculty dismissal of the students for hazing, Governor Brewer's letter to Chancellor Kincannon, and Kincannon's letter directing the faculty to readmit the five students are in FM, October 14, 31, November 1, 3, 1913. See also Hooker, "Origin and Development of the University," 213–14.

For the quotation by the *Educational Advance* praising the appointment of Powers and the need to popularize the university, and for Powers's request for a Baptist as YMCA sponsor, see Moak, "Ole Miss," *Heritage of Lafayette County,* 110–11. Copies of various issues of the "University Weekly Letter" are in the university archives.

The celebration of Leavell's enrollment is reported in *Mississippian,* October 21, November 25, 1914. Powers's reference to a "graftless University" is cited in the Oxford *Independent,* September 24, 1915.

For the 1916 legislative committee's report, see Hooker, "Origin and Development of the University," 229ff. The reference to the low pressure faction is in *Mississippian,* April 5, 12, 1916. See *Mississippian,* January 30, 1918, for a report on the collapse of the dormitory and the findings of the state architect. For information on the legislature's neglect of the university and the deterioration of its aging physical plant, see *Mississippian,* February 20, 1918, September 24, December 13, 1919, January 7, 28, February 18, 1920.

For a discussion of the Sheldon-Zeller Bill, Williams's bill to move the university, and Walker's amendments see Sansing, *Making Haste Slowly,* 85–86. See student newspapers and university catalogs in the early 1920s for descriptions of the new dormitories and their locations on the university's expanding campus.

Mrs. Farmer is profiled in the *Mississippian,* October 6, December 1, 1915. For a discussion of Faulkner as a university student, see Joseph Blotner, *Faulkner: A Biography* (1991), 75–110, 748–49; Moak, "Ole Miss," *Heritage of Lafayette County,* 116; and various campus publications. A copy of Faulkner's transcript was provided to the author by Provost Gerald W. Walton.

The comparison of the university's support funds and faculty salaries with other institutions in the 1920s is in Hooker, "Origin and Development of the University," 243–44.

For information on the fraternity controversy see Moak, "Ole Miss," *Heritage of Lafayette County,* 109. A copy of the board's resolutions on fraternities and dances is in Hooker, Appendix J, "Origin and Development of the University." Accounts of the burning of the effigy of Governor Russell in 1920 and 1922 are in *Mississippian,* November 3, 19, 1920, December 15, 1922; FM, October 27, 1920, January 10, 1921; Memphis *Press Scimitar,* December 18, 1922.

See UMSF for many newspaper clippings detailing Professor Rogers's charges against Powers, the board's hearing on those charges, and Fred Sullens's commentary on the scandal.

The reference to the Russian czar and the German kaiser is in *Senate Journal 1922,* 541–42. Schauber's letter to Russell is in BM, July 13, 1923. For a discussion of the 1923 governor's campaign and the administration of Governor Whitfield, see Bill Baker, *Catch the Vision: The Life of Henry L. Whitfield* (1974). For a report of the first formal study of higher education in Mississippi, see Michael V. O'Shea, *Public Education in Mississippi* (1927).

Chapter Nine Bilbo and the Greater University, 1927–1935

For Bilbo's original platform, see Larry T. Balsamo, "Theodore G. Bilbo and Mississippi Politics, 1877–1932" (Ph.D. dissertation, University of Missouri, 1967), 156–57. The political activities of Fant and MSCW alumnae are reported in *Jackson Daily News,* May 27, 1927, and *Clarion-Ledger,* August 19, 1927. For Farley's activities, see interview with Robert Farley at Oxford, May 15, 1979, in Verner S. Holmes Papers, JDWML, and Hardy Poindexter Graham, "Bilbo and the University of Mississippi, 1928–1931" (master's thesis, University of Mississippi, 1965), 49–50. See also Thomas Turner Interview, Oral History Collection, University of Southern Mississippi.

See *Mississippian,* October 15, 1927, for Lomax's comments about moving the university. Horack's letter to Hume is in JNPP, Box 42. Hume's statement about the university as a shrine is quoted in Cabaniss, *University of Mississippi,* 142.

For Sullens's praise of Bilbo's inaugural address, see *Jackson Daily News,* January 18, 1928. The address is reprinted in McArthur, *Inaugural Addresses,* 146–47. See Graham, "Bilbo and the University," 9, for Sullens's reference to Oxford as a country town and Miller's accusation of Jackson's greedy businessmen. Hederman's report on the meeting with Bilbo is in *Clarion-Ledger,* January 19, 20, 1928. Hume's February speech is in Myra Hume Jones, "Tenets and Attitudes of an Old-Time Teacher (Alfred Hume)" (master's thesis, University of Mississippi, 1949). For the vote on Belk's resolution, see *House Journal 1928,* 294, 306, 308. Bilbo's address to the legislature asking for a $5 million appropriation is cited in Oxford *Eagle,* March 28, 1928.

See Horack's letter to Hume on the problems at the law school. Regarding the inspection of the medical school, see *Jackson Daily News,* November 3, 1927, and February 1, 1928. For the SACS report, see W. D. Hooper to Alfred Hume, December 17, 1929, in JNPP, Box 24. The department chairman's request is cited in Graham, "Bilbo and the University," 37–38.

On the removal of Joseph Anderson Cook, see Sansing, *Making Haste Slowly,* 99–100.

Hume's statement on readmitting the student editor is in *Mississippian,* September 28, 1929. For Hume's concept of academic freedom, see University of Mississippi, *Biennial Report 1927–1929,* 14, 17. Sullens's advice to Bilbo is in *Jackson Daily News,* June 20, 1929. For Bilbo's January 6, 1930, address to the legislature, see *Senate Journal 1930,* 8–9. Sutherland's comment about age is in *Clarion-Ledger,* June 5, 11, 1930.

Regarding Bilbo's interest in securing a national figure for chancellor and for salaries of college presidents, see Sansing, *Making Haste Slowly,* 102, 261.

For Sullens's and Hudson's characterization of the board of trustees see *Jackson Daily News,* June 15, 1930, and John B. Hudson, "The Spoils System Enters College," *New Republic* 64 (September 17, 1930), 123–24. See Sansing, *Making Haste Slowly,* 103, concerning the appointment of Sutherland and Simmons.

Chancellor Hume's statement of the goal of his administration is in University of Mississippi, *Biennial Report 1925–1927,* 3. Hume's embrace of the traditional role of the university is in Graham, "Bilbo and the University," 32. For a study of Hume's long and distinguished career, see Francis Egger Watson, "Dr. Alfred Hume: His Leadership as Vice Chancellor, Acting Chancellor, and Chancellor of the University of Mississippi (1905–1945)" (Ph.D. dissertation, University of Mississippi, 1987).

The reference to the University of Mississippi as a "lonely outpost" is in Clarence Cason, "The Mississippi Imbroglio," *Virginia Quarterly Review* 7 (April 1931), 229–40. See also David G. Sansing, "The Ole Miss Mystique," *Mississippi Magazine* (published by the University of Mississippi Department of Journalism, 1982).

Sullens's estimate of the number of faculty members dismissed is in *Jackson Daily News,* December 7, 1930; Bilbo's figure is in a letter to SACS dated November 18, 1930; and Powers's number is in his letter to Fulton. The Bilbo and Powers letters are in JNPP, Box 24.

The names, ages, credentials, and politics of Ole Miss faculty and staff, and the bases for their dismissals, demotions, appointments, or promotions, were compiled from university catalogs, student publications, payrolls, board of trustees minutes, contemporary press accounts, biographical sketches of Ole Miss faculty in Moak, *Alumni Association,* Moak, "Ole Miss," *Heritage of Lafayette County,* and documents in the Joseph Neely Powers Papers. The most useful document was "Information Regarding Faculty of University of Mississippi," a report prepared by Powers at the request of the board of trustees that lists the credentials of the faculty who were dismissed and the credentials of those appointed in their places. A document prepared by Governor Bilbo explaining the reasons for the dismissal of certain faculty members, entitled "Changes at the University of Mississippi," was also useful. These two documents are in JNPP, Box 24. Powers's telegram and his July 8, 1930, letter to Hume are in JNPP, Box 18. George E. Tomlinson's letter of resignation and Dorroh's letter to Powers are in JNPP, Box 42. Governor Bilbo's reference to the English department is in the document "Changes at the University of Mississippi."

J. C. Eskridge's letter to Bilbo and Bilbo's reply are in the Theodore G. Bilbo Papers, William D. McCain Library, University of Southern Mississippi, Hattiesburg, Mississippi. When the author first used the Bilbo Papers they were not catalogued, and these letters were found in a folder marked "Higher Education."

For Sullens's and Hederman's assessment of the purge, see *Jackson Daily News,* June 15, December 7, 1930, and *Clarion-Ledger,* December 7, 1930. Taylor's two articles are in *Mississippi Educational Advance* (October and November, 1930). See Graham, "Bilbo and the University," regarding the actions of various accrediting agencies. President Thompson's report is in JNPP, Box 24. For the action taken by SACS, see *Proceedings of the Thirty-fifth Annual Meeting of the Association of Colleges and Secondary Schools of the Southern States* (1930), 35–37, 57–62.

A. A. Cohn's letter dated February 11, 1931, to other board members suggesting a state accrediting agency is in JNPP, Box 24. For Sullens's criticism of SACS, see *Jackson Daily News,* December 7, 1930.

For the statute reorganizing the board of trustees, see *Laws 1932,* 383–88, and for details on the reaccreditation of Mississippi institutions, see Sansing, *Making Haste Slowly,* 113–14.

Chapter Ten A Modern University, 1935–1960

Biographical information on Chancellor Butts, details of his inauguration, and his speech are in Moak, "150 Years of Leadership." Additional information on Chancellor Butts and his administration was provided to the author by Mrs. Barbara Butts Dunn. Mrs. Dunn is the daughter of Chancellor Butts and the wife of Read P. Dunn, Jr.

The Ph.D. rule is discussed in Cabaniss, *University of Mississippi,* 154–55. For statistics and other information about the university library, see A. F. Kuhlman, "Report of A Survey of the University of Mississippi Library," various catalogs, and University of Mississippi *Alumni News* issues of December–January, 1939–40, January 1941, and March 1941.

On the medical school's problems, see David G. Sansing, "Dr. Billy Sylvester Guyton: His Life and Legacy," a lecture presented at the University of Mississippi Medical Center on August 24, 1995. A copy of this lecture is in the university archives.

For information on the National Youth Administration grants and the university's building program during the depression see Davis Douglas Buchanan, "A Million Dollars in Concrete and Steel: Federal Aid to the University of Mississippi in the New Deal Era" (master's thesis, University of Mississippi, 1997); see also various catalogs for descriptions of the new buildings.

For a brief history of the Ole Miss-Mississippi State football rivalry see, Mike Butler, "Confederate Flags, Class Conflict, a Golden Egg, and Castrated Bulls: A Historical Examination of the Ole Miss-Mississippi

State Footbal Rivalry," *JMH* 59 (1997), 123–41. See also, W. G. Barner, *Mississippi Mayhem: Ole Miss vs. Miss. State* (1982). For the university's football schedule from 1893 to the present, a list of bowl games, and the names of the university's All-Americans, see Rogers, ed., *Ole Miss 1997 Rebel Media Guide,* 160 and 128. For the names of Ole Miss Rhodes Scholars, see Moak, *Alumni Association,* 244.

Wartime conditions at the university are described in *The Ole Miss Alumni Review* (March, 1944) and other campus publications.

For the establishment of the constitutional board of trustees and the enrollment boom, see Sansing, *Making Haste Slowly,* 111–24 and 125–39. See Joseph E. Gibson, *Mississippi Study of Higher Education 1945* (1945) for details of the Gibson study.

Details of the student uprising and the dismissal of Butts and Mehre are in Moak, *Alumni Association*; 121–22 and Moak, "Ole Miss," *Heritage of Lafayette County,* 126; *Clarion-Ledger,* December 5, 9, 10, 15, 1945, January 26, 1946; *Mississippian,* December 14, 1945, January 18, 1946; additional information was obtained in various conversations with Oxford residents and Ole Miss alumni Billy Ross Brown and Will Lewis, Jr.

For biographical information on Chancellor Williams and the details of his appointment, see James Cook Read, "The Williams Chancellorship at the University of Mississippi, 1946–1968" (Ph.D. dissertation, University of Mississippi, 1978), 9–27. For Williams's conversation with Wright and his meeting with the business manager and the student legislators, see Read, "Williams Chancellorship," 158, 34, 60; and 54–65 for Williams's building program.

See Bridgforth, *A History of the School of Medicine,* for details on the founding and development of the University of Mississippi Medical Center.

Williams's observations of a "pattern of higher education" are in University of Mississippi *Biennial Report* 1947–1949, 10 and *Biennial Report 1950–51,* 18. His recommendation to concentrate doctoral programs is cited in *Mississippian,* October 6, 1959.

A copy of Butts's letter to Wells, and his letter in response, were provided the author by Provost Gerald W. Walton. See Sansing, *Making Haste Slowly,* 140–41, for details of Carter's address at Alcorn, and Nadine Cohodas, *Strom Thurmond and the Politics of Southern Change* (1993) for the rise of the Dixiecrats. For a picture of Ole Miss delegates and a description of their participation in the Birmingham convention, see *Mississippian,* July 22, 1948, and for a picture of the "Newly Formed University Greys," see *Mississippian,* October 18, 1948.

The words to Hotty Totty are: Hotty, Totty, Gosh A'mighty/Who in the hell are we?/Hey, flim flam, bim bam!,/Ole Miss by damn! For a typical "Janie Reb" column, see *Mississippian,* March 23, 1948. For the "magic . . . spell" and "cream" quotes, see *Mississippian,* October 1, 1948, September 30, 1949, and February 8, 1930.

On the inauguration of Dixie Week and General Moore's participation, see *Mississippian,* November 10, December 1, 1950; for pictures, details, and descriptions of various Dixie Weeks, see the 1955, 1957, and 1959 yearbooks. Pictures of the giant Confederate flag appear in the 1949 and 1956 yearbooks and the 1958 and 1962 *M-Books.*

The details of M. B. Mayfield's relationship with Professor Purser and Ole Miss art students were obtained in a telephone interview with Mayfield on February 14, 1998. See also M. B. Mayfield, "The Baby Who Crawled Sdrawkcab (Backwards): An Autobiography," a twenty-nine-page unpublished manuscript provided to the author (with the permission of Mayfield) by Professor James Payne, director of African American Studies and associate professor of history.

Sillers's letter to Wright is quoted in Bridgforth, *A History of the School of Medicine,* 130. For details on Charles Dubra's application, see interview with Robert J. Farley, Oxford, Mississippi, May 15, 1979, in Verner S. Smith Holmes Papers, JDWML. For a biographical sketch of Evers, see George Alexander Sewell and Margaret L. Dwight, *Mississippi Black History Makers,* 117–122; for a full account of Evers's life, see Mrs. Medgar Evers and William Peters, *For Us the Living* (1967); on his application to Ole Miss see *Mississippian,* January 19, 1954, and Sansing, *Making Haste Slowly,* 142–46. Faulkner's quotation is in Russell Barrett, *Integration at Ole Miss* (1965), 31.

For the Kershaw controversy, see Sansing, *Making Haste Slowly,* 203. See also Will Campbell, *Brother to a Dragonfly* (1977), 112–21 and James W. Silver, *Mississippi: The Closed Society* (1966), 108–10. For the establishment and implementation of the speaker ban policy, see Lucie Robertson Bridgforth, "'Bomb the Ban': A Study of the Legal Controversy

Surrounding Off-Campus Speakers at Mississippi Institutions of Higher Learning" (master's thesis, University of Mississippi, 1979.) See Sansing, *Making Haste Slowly, 204–05,* for the Reynolds episode.

Biographical information on Blind Jim Ivy was compiled from articles in *Mississippian,* January 22, 1919, May 5, 1920, March 9, June 7, 1923, March 7, April 4, 1931, October 28, November 4, 1955, October 2, 1964; *1954–1955 M-Book*; and from conversations with Ole Miss alumni Jack McLarty, Will Lewis, Jr., John Leslie and Oxford resident Miss Susie Marshall, a member of the Oxford Second Baptist Church and long-time friend of Ivy. There are many other articles on Blind Jim in campus publications that are not cited. The late Frank Everett is the source for Blind Jim as the model for Colonel Rebel. For a discussion of the relationship between Blind Jim and Ole Miss students, see Anthony James, "Paternalism's Demise: Blind Jim Ivy and Ole Miss, 1896–1955" *Mississippi Folklife* 27 (Spring 1995), 17–24.

For the details of the Clennon King episode, including Coleman's quotations, see Sansing, *Making Haste Slowly,* 144–46.

The charges against Williams and Ole Miss professors are listed, along with their written responses, in Hugh Clegg, "Someone Jumped the Gun," an unpublished manuscript made available to the author by George Street, a former administrator at the University of Mississippi. See also James Silver, *Running Scared: Silver in Mississippi* (1984), 66–68. The Clyde Kennard case is discussed in Sansing, *Making Haste Slowly,* 148–54.

Chapter Eleven Conflict, Change and Continuity, 1960–1968

For a chronology of events leading to Meredith's admission, see Barrett, *Integration at Ole Miss,* 247–51. For other general works on Meredith and the University of Mississippi, see James Meredith, *Three Years in Mississippi* (1966); James Silver, *Mississippi: The Closed Society* (1966) and *Running Scared: Silver in Mississippi* (1984); Walter Lord, *The Past That Would Not Die* (1966); Cohodas, *The Band Played Dixie*; see also Read, Chapter 6 "Academic Freedom and Integration," 152–206, "The Williams Chancellorship." A comprehensive study of the influence of race and politics at the university from World War II to the enrollment of James Meredith, by University of Mississippi history professor

Charles Eagles, is nearing completion and should be in print within the next two or three years.

Meredith's quotation on his mission, as well as subsequent quotations and correspondence with the university, and the rulings by Judge Mize and Judge Wisdom are in Meredith, *Three Years in Mississippi,* 20–22, 54–55, 57–58, 59, 61, 143ff. For the trial testimony, see "Meredith v. Fair, et. al., Transcript of Record," vol. 11. A copy of this transcript is in the chancellor's office. See also Jack Bass, Chapter 9 "Crisis in Mississippi," 172–200, *Unlikely Heroes* (1981).

See *Mississippian,* February 9, 13, 15, 21, 1962, for Robertson's article and the *Rebel Underground*'s response. See *Clarion-Ledger,* January 23, 24, 1962, for the legislator's criticism of Robertson and the "real danger" quotation.

Judge Tuttle's quotation on the "rise of massive resistance" is in Bass, *Unlikely Heroes,* 180–81, and Judge Wisdom's ruling is in Meredith, *Three Years in Mississippi,* 143ff.

For a complete transcript of Barnett's speech, see *Clarion-Ledger,* September 14, 1962. For the board's discussion of contempt and its meetings with Barnett, see Sansing, *Making Haste,* 170–71. For Holmes's quotation about not closing the university, see *Jackson Daily News,* September 18, 1962. A copy of the WLBT television editorial was provided by William H. Mounger, an Ole Miss alumnus and former president of the Lamar Life Insurance Company. For Harkey's quotation and other editorials see Ira Harkey, *Dedicated to the Proposition* (1963) and *The Smell of Burning Crosses* (1967).

For Barnett's various attempts to block Meredith's admission, see Sansing, *Making Haste,* 176–94, and for Turner's quotation, see Thomas Turner Interview, Oral History Collection, University of Southern Mississippi.

Transcripts of the telephone conversations between Barnett and federal authorities were provided to the author by Marcia Synnott, professor of history at the University of South Carolina; copies of the transcripts and some tape recordings of the conversations are in the university archives. For Coleman's and Kennedy's quotations on the use of troops, see Verner S. Holmes and J. P. Coleman Interview, June 16–17, 1979, at Oxford, Mississippi, in the Holmes Papers, and Bass, *Unlikely Heroes,* 193. On the use of troops at Oxford, see Paul J. Scheips, "The Role of the Army in the Oxford, Mississippi, Incident 1962–1963," a typescript in the university archives.

For Meredith's quotation about his unknown friends, see Meredith, *Three Years in Mississippi,* 196, and for the Barnett-Meredith confrontation at the Woolfolk building, see *Jackson Daily News,* September 26, 1962, and *Times-Picayune,* September 26, 1962. The elbowing episode is in Meredith, *Three Years in Mississippi,* 202–3.

Governor Barnett's halftime speech is reported in *Jackson Daily News,* September 30, 1962. For details of the riot and Eastland's move for an investigation see Barrett, *Integration at Ole Miss,* 123–61 and 253 for the names of those who signed the document exonerating the marshals.

See Silver, *Closed Society,* 177, for his letter to his daughter. Vaught's and Morin's quotations are in John Vaught, *Rebel Coach* (1971), 113–25. For additional information see Rex W. Baker, "Ole Miss Football the John Vaught Era: 1947–1970" (master's thesis, University of Mississippi, 1989).

For the action of the Southern Association, see Read, "Williams Chancellorship," 223–32; for the struggle to keep the university open, 231–41; for the university's discipline problems, 241–55. See also Barrett, *Integration at Ole Miss,* 163–226 and for Bryant's speech, see 197.

On his decision to return to Ole Miss, see Meredith, *Three Years in Mississippi,* 243ff. For details on Cleve McDowell's admission and expulsion, see Barrett, *Integration at Ole Miss,* 219–24, 226, 236, 238, 242, and for Meredith's wearing the NEVER pin and his graduation, see 221–22.

On the enrollment of Donald, Walker, Bailey, and other black students see Cohodas, *The Band Played Dixie,* 112–16, 134, 168, 209, 124–25, 228–31.

The Frady interview is in *Mademoiselle* (August 1966), 333, 229–32, 236. For similar interviews and several pictures of black student life at Ole Miss see *Ebony* (May 1966), 29–32, 34–36. The *Ebony* article was provided to the author by Joyce Jones Watson, one of the students interviewed.

See *Clarion-Ledger,* March 19, 1966, and *Mississippian,* March 22, 1966, for Kennedy's appearance and Ellington's quotation. For Mary Cain's quote, see Lisa Kay Speer, " 'Contrary Mary': The Life of Mary Dawson

Cain" (Ph.D. dissertation, University of Mississippi, 1998), 14. For details on Murphy, Farley, and Silver leaving Ole Miss, see Silver, *Running Scared,* 67–102, and Sansing, *Making Haste,* 200–02.

Chapter Twelve On the Eve of a New Millennium, 1968–1995

Chancellor Williams's quotation on the whole picture is in *Commercial Appeal,* November 1, 1962. On John Ates's organizing a counter demonstration, see Cohodas, *The Band Played Dixie,* 239, 245. An account of the Oxford town hall meeting and John Hope Franklin's quotation are in *Mississippian,* March 18, 1998, and Oxford *Eagle,* March 18, 1998.

For biographical information on Fortune, see Moak, "150 Years of Leadership"; for the construction of new facilities during his administration, see various catalogs.

Chancellor Fortune's plans for a cultural center are discussed in Moak, "150 Years of Leadership." Information about the university's museum complex and the Walton-Young House was obtained in several conversations with museum director Bonnie Krause. For studies of Stark Young. see John Pilkington, *Stark Young: A Life in the Arts* (1975) and *Stark Young* (1985).

For the establishment of the Southern Writer in Residence program by John and Renee Grisham, see *Foundation News* (Spring, 1996), 7.

For the founding and the history of the school of accountancy see Dale L. Flesher, *Accountancy at Ole Miss: A Sesquicentennial Salute* (n.p., 1997), and *Foundation News* (Fall 1997), 1, 4, for the Reynolds gift.

Information on the Ayers litigation was obtained from published cases. Judge Biggers's original decision appears at *Ayers vs. Allain,* 674 F. Supp. 1523, 43 Ed. Law Rep. 972 (N.D. Miss. 1987). On appeal, a three judge panel of the fifth circuit court of appeals reversed Judge Biggers. *Ayers vs. Allain,* 893 F.2d 732, 58 Ed. Law. Rep. 48 (5th Cir. 1990). The fifth circuit then heard the case *in banc,* which means the entire membership of the appellate court decided the outcome. The *in banc* court affirmed Judge Biggers. *Ayers vs. Allain,* 914 F.2d 676, 62 Ed. Law Rep. 910 (5th Cir. 1990). The United States Supreme Court vacated the decision of the fifth circuit and remanded for further proceedings. *United States vs. Fordice,* 505 U.S. 717, 112 S. Ct. 2727, 120 L. Ed. 2d 575, 75 Ed.

Law. Rep. 81 (1992). On remand from the Supreme Court, the fifth circuit vacated the original decision of Judge Biggers and remanded the case to him for further proceedings consistent with the Supreme Court's opinion. *Ayers vs. Allain,* 970 F.2d 1378, 76 Ed. Law Rep. 724 (5th Cir. 1992).

Judge Biggers's second decision is found at *Ayers vs. Fordice,* 879 F. Supp. 1419, 99 Ed. Law Rep. 279 (N.D. Miss. 1995). The fifth circuit affirmed in part and reversed in part Judge Biggers's decision. *Ayers vs. Fordice,* 111 F.3d 1183, 117 Ed. Law Rep. 840 (5th Cir. 1997). The Supreme Court denied certiorari, which means the court declined to review the case. *Ayers vs. Fordice,* 118 S. Ct. 871, 139 L. Ed. 2d 768 (1998). Judge Biggers continues to have judicial supervision of the *Ayers* litigation.

For the protests by home economics majors and by students against parking in the Grove, and the *Clarion-Ledger* quotation on Ole Miss traditionalists, see the 1983 college yearbook.

Information on Robert Walker's Ole Miss career is found in Anthony Dunbar, *Delta Time: A Journey Through Mississippi* (1990), 224–226; the Walker quote was made to the author in a telephone interview on March 6, 1998. Information on Edgar Lee Caples was provided to the author by Frank Anderson, professor emeritus of engineering, Bonita Terry-Malone, a staff member in the office of alumni affairs, and Tina Hahn and Barbara Lago of the university's office of public relations.

On the establishment of the Black Student Union and the African American Studies Program, see "Twenty Five Years at the University of Mississippi, The African-American Studies Program 1970–1995," an unpublished manuscript provided the author by Professor James Payne.

The Fulton Chapel demonstration is covered extensively in Cohodas, *The Band Played Dixie,* 146–154. For a brief account of the Jackson State riot, see Sansing, *Making Haste Slowly,* 209–211; for a fuller account, see Tim Spofford, *LYNCH STREET, The May 1970 Slayings at Jackson State College* (Kent, Ohio, 1988).

Coolidge Ball's Ole Miss athletic career is detailed in the historical and team records section of Lamar Chance, ed., *Ole Miss Basketball 1997–98 Media Guide.* For details on James Reed and Ben Williams, see the historical and team records section in Rogers, ed., *Ole Miss 1997 Rebel Media Guide.*

For Rose Jackson's student days at Ole Miss and the Traveller controversy, see Cohodas, *The Band Played Dixie,* 189–196, 209, 229, 245–246; 194–195.

Details on John Hawkins and the Confederate flag controversy are in *Mississippian,* April 23, September 1, 10, 30, October 1, 25, 1982 and *Clarion-Ledger,* September 1, 1982 and *Philadelphia Inquirer,* September 5, 1982. For William Ray's quotation, see *Mississippian,* September 2, 1982.

Accounts of James Meredith's return to Ole Miss are in *New York Times,* October 3, 1982 and *Chronicle of Higher Education,* October 6, 1982.

See Cohodas, *The Band Played Dixie,* 211–215, for black student reaction to John Hall's yearbook. On the buildup to Fortune's statement about the flag, see *Mississippian,* March 6, 7, 9, 11, 12, 19, 20, 1983; *Clarion-Ledger,* February 2, 1983, and *New York Times,* May 5, 1983.

On Damon Moore, see Cohodas, *The Band Played Dixie,* 225–227, 235.

A copy of the resolution recommending Governor Winter for chancellor, with faculty signatures, is in the university archives.

The details of Gerald Turner's administration are derived from an article in Oxford *Eagle,* March 25, 1994, commemorating the tenth anniversary of his tenure and a similar article in *Clarion-Ledger,* April 11, 1994; a telephone interview with Turner on March 24, 1998; various catalogs and other university publications; from notes provided to the author by Dean of Students Sparky Reardon and former Associate Vice Chancellor and Professor of English Charles E. Noyes; and Cohodas, *The Band Played Dixie.* See *Mississippian,* August 23, 1987, for editor Frank Hurdle's comment that "heaven . . . is full of Rebel flags."

See the current catalog for details on the national centers and other research centers at the university.

Much of the information on student life, including the discontinuation of the Shrimp and Beer festival, the destruction of the Phi Beta Sigma house and the Beta incident was provided by Sparky Reardon; see also Cohodas, *The Band Played Dixie,* for extensive coverage of these events.

On the life of Chucky Mullins, see Larry Woody, *A Dixie Farewell: The Life and Death of Chucky Mullins* (1993).

Details on the alumni association's resolution on the Rebel flag were provided by Herbert E. Dewees, Jr., executive director of alumni affairs, and Brenda West, associate director of alumni affairs, who also made available her clipping file on the flag controversy. For press coverage of the alumni's action see Oxford *Eagle,* April 30, 1991, Meridian *Star,* May 1, 1991, *Clarion-Ledger,* May 1, 1991, *Commercial Appeal,* May 1, 1991, *Mississippian,* May 1, 1991; for student reaction to the resolution see Oxford *Eagle,* May 1, 1991.

Coach Murphy's comment was made to the author, and the rate of graduation of Ole Miss athletes is based on information provided by Associate Athletic Director David K. Wells.

For an account of Louis Westerfield's appointment, see Kevin Chappell, "Black Law Dean Ushers in A New Day at Ole Miss," *Ebony* (August 1995), 128–132.

For details of the 1997 flag controversy see *Mississippian,* February 27, March 6, April 24, September 25, and October 22, 1997; *Clarion-Ledger,* March 3, October 23, 1997; *New York Times,* March 11, 1997; and *Commercial Appeal,* October 23, 1997.

Epilogue A Great Public University, 1995–1998

Information on Chancellor Khayat's administration was obtained in a March 20, 1998, interview with the chancellor; from the chancellor's annual reports; various issues of *Foundation News*; from information provided by Edwin E. Meek, Tina Hahn, and Barbara Lago of the university office of public relations; and from notes provided by, or interviews and conversations with Charles E. Noyes, Franklin E. Moak, Leone King, John Meador, Jr., Robert Haws, Charles Eagles, James F. Payne, John Robin Bradley, H. Dale Abadie, Gerald W. Walton, Bonnie Krause, Nadine Cohodas, Ronald F. Borne, Ann J. Abadie, John Crews, James W. Davis, Sparky Reardon, Thomas Wallace, Gary Miller, Charles Hussey, Herbert E. Dewees, Jr., Bonita Terry-Malone, Brenda West, Gloria Kellum, Sandra Guest, and Don L. Fruge.

Index